BENCHCLEARING

Baseball's Greatest Fights and Riots

Spike Vrusho

THE LYONS PRESS
Guilford. Connecticut
An imprint of the Globe Pequot Press

The Lyons Press is an imprint of The Globe Pequot Press.

Designed by Sheryl P. Kober

Library of Congress Cataloging-in-Publication Data is available on file.

ISBN 978-1-59921-052-0

Printed in the United States of America

10 9 8 7 6 5 4 3 2 1

CONTENTS

To my dad, Neil, for always moving from the bleachers to the backstop whenever I was up.

INTRODUCTION: *Fightin' Words*

Sitting solo in the loge at Shea Stadium, the coast appeared to be clear. The occasion was a Mets-Pirates tilt, and I innocently expected another game-ending collapse by the Buccos via a Kevin Polcovich throwing error or Brad Clontz wild pitch. But before the ghost of Randy Tomlin could save my team, I was joined by a fellow lonely-guy fan, only he was dressed like a soft drink executive. Which he was.

The information came fast and furious. His company was sponsoring a season-long promotion in Shea's orphaned left-field bleacher section, and he was on a cakewalk assignment to attend the games and make sure "everything goes down the way it should." He was too young to have a whiskey laugh, but he let a long one go as he put his hands together to pantomime a pillow next to his cheek, staring intently in my direction.

Noticing my Pirates cap, he laughed—a familiar reaction in Queens, or anywhere else, for that matter. Then he started to tell me about his buddy. "He cleaned your boy Leyland's clock," the Chess King necktie said.

"Wha??" was my response.

Mr. Six-figure carbonated salary then went on to detail how Dan Miceli pinned Leyland against the clubhouse wall in a fit of rage. Maybe smoke got in his eyes? Who knows? Apparently, the incident led to Miceli's departure from the Pirates to the baker's dozen more franchises he would eventually work for before ending up in that Hillsborough County purgatory known as the Tampa Bay Devil Rays. Somewhere along the way, Miceli tangled with Marlins skipper John Boles and his own brother, but otherwise, his dance card appeared to have many vacancies.

Managerial clock cleanings by well-traveled and amped-up relievers are common for the uniformed citizens of Baseballville. Which brings along this particular volume. There seems to be a permanent high tide of baseball books by guys in stained shirts making up new stats for everything from body temperature of switch hitters with RISP, to how robots should replace managers, and general managers should rely on slide rules instead of "guts." Apparently, this lot became bored with Dungeons and Dragons and moved into a statistical baseball analysis retribution domain where nine-sided dice still carry varied powers.

There are also plenty of intellectuals out there justifying time spent watching games on TV by comparing athletes to hunters, warriors, and tricksters of ancient lore when they are interviewed by beardy literary journals. Really? If this much effort was put into getting me my next beer during a pitching change, then all would be right with the world.

So it was decided, then, that it was time to drop the gloves, or glove, in this sport's case. Grab a handful of Rayon jersey, do some tussling and maybe spike the guy on the bottom of the pile. Hopefully, he's not a team-mate. A note of explanation: this is not a reference book or another "list" book—the fights are grouped thematically and are subject to the warped interpretations of the author. There were far too many to include them all, though most of them follow a human behavior template now available in software form at most office supply stores.

Onward, then, up the dugout steps, and through the bullpen gate for a break in the action, so to speak, where numbers don't mean much and knuckle sandwiches are occasionally served.

Chapter 1:
ROUNDHOUSE

"I went to a boxing match the other night and a hockey game broke out." Much like the origin of baseball, the creator of that oft-used one-liner is hard to trace in precise fashion, especially among the hordes of sticky-fingered comedy writers. Countless columnists have dissected it and desperate beat reporters have coined it. A Toronto newspaper attributed it to Rodney Dangerfield, so with respect to the hoser media types—the late necktie-tugging comedian gets the credit and should be considered a sports visionary.

For the purposes of this volume, Rodney's one-liner marries the two sports and epitomizes raw competition where fighting is allowed and encouraged. In hockey, fights are an old friend, a show business staple known as a crowd-pleaser, with a select group of players chosen to do battle. The fights are surrounded by mysterious terminology such as "pier sixer," which Mets fans came to know via announcer Bob Murphy, who may or may not have borrowed it from Rocky Marciano's television show.

Boxing is just that—two humans beating each other in a confined space for entertainment and gambling purposes. Fight fans who go the pay-per-view route also get a certain titular—if not grubby—thrill associated with the transaction as they fill their dens with iniquity and flickering images of Don King. The sport's legacy carries a warped veneer of romance, encouraged by Hollywood depictions of Marciano's era, smoky arenas bobbing with fedoras and swell dames and bare lightbulbs and Joe Pesci frothing at the mouth as the blood spatters the reporters craning their necks upward to see through the ropes. Large flashbulbs were apparently always used to capture gruesome images for the bulldog edition of a gritty tabloid, to be perused later in the evening while cajoling the waiter to hurry up with that relish tray before the lights go down for the floor show at the Stork Club.

Well, smoking bans and the Fila tracksuit have certainly killed all that, and it is widely known the Marquis of Queensbury could not hit the curveball. A fight during a baseball game atomizes the fringe aroma of danger, dispersing charged ions into the pricey air of the stadium—a place with rules of conduct posted at the turnstiles, in the programs, announced over the PA system, and printed on the back of the ticket. When competitors break the rules during the course of action, the spectators briefly bask in the anarchy, while the press is required to make disapproving clucking sounds, all the while hyping up the adrenaline rush to the standard game storyline. Order restored, both the crowd and media retreat to their safety zones, the fan back to his or her overpriced stale pretzel, the sportswriter back to the plate of cut-rate chicken cordon bleu dolloped from the press box spread.

For the modern fan in attendance, the cable television sports highlight show will replay the events in a violent nutshell ad nauseum when they get home and again when they wake up in the morning. Most onsite spectators also experience sports brawls in hyperspace by using their cell phones to describe the conflict as it unfolds to disbelieving parties on the other end. These dispatches from the front grant them eyewitness status that might carry some weight at the local bar, or years down the road on the proverbial hunting trip with pals. Being able to say "I was at that game" with a ticket stub as an in-hand voucher spawns the game's living history, to be retold and exaggerated time after time. Jaded and cynical sportswriters, of course, sigh at this notion, because they are at *every* game and are paid to be there, despite their whining about the job. Despising the well-paid athletes on the field, many in the press box hope the usual shirt-grabbing baseball donnybrook will escalate into a scene from a Hieronymus Bosch painting, replete with disemboweled umpires and impaled middle relievers hoisted and flanking the foul lines turned red with flowing blood. At Fenway Park in Boston, they wish Stephen King would get out of his expensive seat and file their game stories for them. They long for Oil Can Boyd antics, or a return orbit from Bill "Spaceman" Lee. Instead, the majority of the time, they get the usual vanilla quotes and laughable cliches outlined for official player usage in the movie *Bull*

Durham. Covering pro baseball is a "same old same old" with bumper sticker dialogue and boilerplate commentary from the manager. It is only when something strange happens during a game that broadcasters remind viewers they thought they'd seen everything, until they saw this.

Baseball fights, though often considered predictable dramas—especially once the Greek chorus arrives from the distant bullpen to assist in the standing around and milling about—at least provide a new perspective on the use of the field. It is estimated the average ballpark field contains ninety thousand square feet, and most of the time, the same ten thousand square feet or so are in use. When tempers flare and scuffles break out, the TV cameras and eyes of the fans follow the scrum into uncharted sectors of the diamond and its skirt of foul territory. There might be a lengthy pile-up near one of the fungo circles, or a mobile shoving match that uses the batboy's stool as a Three Stooges–style trip hazard; the mundane dugout rail (now dressed with advertising, usually the home team's Web address) can be transformed into a wrestling ring turnbuckle. And who in the park doesn't get nervous when the mass of grappling players starts to centipede its way toward the vast ammunition dump known as the bat rack? It is almost as much fun to watch the photographers scrambling in their solitary confinement pen, juggling howitzer lenses for a better angle of the dispute.

The ultimate spot for a fight, and many feng shui experts would agree, is directly behind home plate up against the protective screen, a venue rarely used except when managers Tony LaRussa and Buck Showalter got together for pre-game discussions at Yankee Stadium back in May of 1992. The Yankees and Mariners also occupied this special spot at Seattle's Kingdome when the brawl known as *O'Neill vs. Marzano* boiled over from a batter-catcher home plate scrap to a full-scale dance party courtesy of some extended play from Darryl Strawberry.

If sportswriters paid close enough attention to the athletes walking among them, they'd find several ballplayers with boxing backgrounds or penchants for the martial arts. Well-traveled outfielder Reggie Sanders is a black belt in tae kwon do and seems to follow its principles. Dodgers outfielder Willie Davis followed the peaceful precepts of Buddhism, despite having been on the field during baseball's most notorious brawl—the *Marichal vs. Roseboro* bat-wielding incident in 1965. Davis, known for his speed, was a free-wheeling, happy-go-lucky card player at the time. Around 1972 however, he discovered chanting and Buddhism, and even talked teammates Willie Crawford (of *Crawford vs. Greif*) and Lee Lacy into joining him on his new spiritual trek. Go figure.

Hall of Fame catcher Rick Ferrell had a brief boxing career before taking up baseball. Art Shires of the Chicago White Sox, and later the Boston Braves, actually fought bouts during his baseball career, which spanned from 1928 to 1932. Shires made great efforts to set up an official fight with Hack Wilson in a promotion that had the Midway buzzing. The baseball commissioner at that time, Judge Kenesaw Mountain Landis, stepped in, demanding that "The Great" as Shires was nicknamed, choose between the squared circle or the diamond. Landis reportedly said any ballplayer participating in "professional boxing will be regarded by this office as having permanently retired from baseball."

In the 1950s, the Yankees settled some internal differences after an exhibition game at West Point. Pitcher Jim Coates was considered a racist for his habitual buzzing of black ballplayers' chins and for his open hostility toward Elston Howard, the first black Yankees player. After the exhibition game, Mickey Mantle talked the team into playing some basketball at a nearby gym. Noticing a boxing ring in the facility, the players then coaxed Howard into a boxing match with Coates. Howard floored the pitcher.

In the tradition of Pirates firebrand infielder Don Hoak, who was an unsuccessful teenage boxer, catcher Manny Sanguillen mastered the sweet science in his native Panama before taking up baseball and becoming popular among Pittsburgh fans.

In the true spirit of manliness and mutually assured self-destruction, Brooklyn Dodgers hurler Hugh Casey had a boozy boxing match with Ernest Hemingway while the Dodgers visited Cuba during wartime spring training. The bout was at Hemingway's house after a full day of drinking and skeet shooting with Billy Herman, Augie Galan, and Larry French. The exchange of blows was said to be pretty even, with Casey rallying at the end amid plenty of broken furniture. The next morning, as Herman tells it, Papa Ernesto's wife made the scribe apologize in person to the Dodger players in the lobby of the team hotel. The Cuban combatants would meet their demises in eerily similar ways decades later. On July 3, 1951, at the age of thirty-seven, Casey killed himself with a shotgun blast to the neck in a hotel room in Atlanta while on the phone with his estranged wife. A friend was rushing to his room and was thirty feet from the door when he heard the blast. Casey was despondent about a paternity suit back in New York, his separation from his wife, and a downturn in business at Hugh Casey's Steak and Chop House, his restaurant at 600 Flatbush Avenue, a few blocks from Ebbets Field. Ten years after Casey's death, almost to the day (July 2), Hemingway killed himself with a shotgun blast to the head in Ketchum, Idaho. He was sixty-one, and his obituary ran on the front page of the *New York Times*, with his wife claiming the gun went off accidentally while he was cleaning it.

Pundits have occasionally placed hockey goons and heavyweight boxers into the context of "walking the streets" for comparison purposes. Flyers goon Dave Schultz, a psychologist once said, could not walk the streets pushing people around like he did in the ice rink, because he would be arrested. Columnist Jimmy Breslin, asked for a sound bite on late night television after one of Mike Tyson's early one-punch victories, said yes, Tyson can fight, but the real story is he is no longer walking Atlantic Avenue in Brooklyn beating up old ladies to steal their grocery change.

Baseball players usually do not have to worry about that type of context. There are a few louts who would be considered criminal elements while in street clothes, and there are the obvious egomaniac gladiator types, but even they do not have to humiliate themselves in the arena and turn to the crowd to ask "Are you not entertained?" Baseball is romanticized, nationalized, and fetishized all in one fell swoop ("Baseball, hot dogs, apple pie, and Chevrolet" the ad jingle said), despite its burly beginnings filled with bruisers and nut jobs such as Art Devlin, Ty Cobb, and Leo Durocher. Ballplayers bake their brains all summer long, enduring heat and humidity and a grind like no other in the sporting world, which makes it surprising there are not more fights in baseball.

Television, the de facto owner of the sport, uses perpetual highlight orgies to fast-forward baseball history. The Nostalgia Department has granted these players their own channel, bathed in a comical sepia tone, filled with period costumes, and fast-motion magic lantern footage, to re-create an aura of the olden days. Few fans of the video era can recall the antics of New York Giants third baseman Devlin, who was involved in at least two incidents attacking fans in Brooklyn. One was in June of 1910 in Washington Park where Devlin was arrested with a pair of teammates for thrashing a fan who had been razzing them during the Giants 8-2 win over the Superbas. In 1922, a few blocks away at Ebbets Field, Devlin punched a fan sitting in the box seats. He was not arrested, but got a five-game suspension. Four years later, as a coach for the

Boston Braves, Devlin was credited with starting one of the heartiest brawls of the century. He was verbally abusing Reds third baseman Babe Pinelli at Crosley Field. When Pinelli was coming off the field, he brushed against Devlin and the fists started flying. Braves outfielder Frank Wilson was arrested for hitting a police inspector, according to at least one writer's rendering of the incident. After that fight settled, the two teams went at it again in the following inning after a collision at home plate between Boston's Jimmy Welsh and Reds catcher Val Picinich.

If Major League Baseball wants to close the generation gap that leaves geezers who remember Devlin out in the cold, it should officially incorporate old-timey players into today's video games. The kids would gobble them up and future generations would know if they send Carl Everett sliding hard into third against Devlin, chances are a fight will ensue, and then they will soon be redlining the fun-meter. From then on, the updated credo will be "Those who do not remember the past are condemned to hit reset." Imagine a little bio box onscreen pop-up showing Devlin's brief enrollment at Georgetown University, or how sportswriter Grantland Rice named Devlin the third baseman on his all-time Giants team. "Dude, he picked him ahead of Pedro Feliz?" would be the response of a modern teen. And the debates would begin anew and probably last as long as the eyeblink attention span of the average gamester. If these gamesters are prone to frequently use players with violent personalities, then EA Sports would be forced to name its neo-retro title "Cobb 2008."

Cobb's twenty-three-year black eye on the game in the early twentieth century is well documented by at least six biographies and a major motion picture featuring Tommy Lee Jones as the Georgia Peach. Among baseball's sensationalist storytellers, Cobb's excesses have been shamanized, putting him up there with comedic mythical figures such as salesman deity Bill Brasky from the *Saturday Night Live* sketch, or actor/martial artist Chuck Norris, who has seen his own tall tale biography turn cancerous with a string of hyperbolic factoids propagated by the Internet's volunteer army of snarky busybodies.

Among Cobb's more fabled and colorful brouhahas, most of them sparked by racial slurs:

- In June of 1908 near Detroit's Hotel Ponchartrain, Cobb jumped out of the path of an oncoming car and landed in the freshly-spread asphalt in front of laborer Fred Collins. An argument ensued, and

Cobb attempted to take on Collins and his fellow workers. A mob of one hundred gathered before Cobb was pulled away by teammate "Scranton Bill" Coughlin.

- In 1909, at the Hotel Euclid in Cleveland, Cobb had a late-night altercation with a black elevator operator. A night watchman soon got involved and struck Cobb twice with his night stick. After a lively wrestling match between the two, the watchman pistol-whipped Cobb, who then fled to his room. Criminal charges and an outstanding warrant would keep Cobb from traveling through Ohio for many months. For the 1909 World Series which began in Pittsburgh, Cobb and his wife had to take a circuitous train route through Canada to avoid the Buckeye state.

- On May 15, 1912 at New York's Hilltop Park, Cobb leaped into the stands to go after a heckler twelve rows up who turned out to be disabled—he only had two fingers on one hand and was missing his other hand. Cobb didn't care and kept stomping him. American League president Ban Johnson was at the game and gave Cobb an indefinite suspension. The punishment prompted a one-game mini-strike by Detroit players the next day, when replacements were called in and lost to Philadelphia 24-2. The next day, Cobb urged his teammates to return to action and his suspension was reduced to ten games.

- In August of 1912, Cobb said he chased one of three men who attempted to rob him and his wife. He was slashed in the back during the fracas, but used his malfunctioning revolver to beat one of his assailants to death, Cobb said. There is no police or coroner record of anyone killed in such a manner, and like many of the Cobb incidents, details are sketchy and disputed.

- Cobb's revolver also played a part in his trashing of a Detroit butcher's shop in June of 1914. His wife had purchased fish in the shop and had Cobb go back to the shop to get fresh perch. As he was about to leave the shop, Cobb and the butcher's assistant exchanged words. A meat cleaver was pulled, and Cobb got out his gun. By the time the police came to break up the skirmish, Cobb had hurt his thumb and missed several games due to the injury.

• In 1919, Cobb clashed with a black chambermaid at the Pontchartrain, kicking her in the stomach and knocking her down a flight of stairs. The local press supposedly covered up the story and the maid, who suffered a broken rib and was hospitalized for more than a month, agreed to a settlement out of court after filing a suit for $10,000 in damages.

The vast Cobb lore also includes the old-time baseball fight staple: the post-game, under-the-grandstand gentleman's bout. Cobb supposedly got umpire Billy Evans to agree to a fistfight, quickly roughed him up and pinned him to the ground, before Cobb's teammates broke it up. Despite the scores of Cobb horror stories making up his self-created "monster" aura, there are "other side of the coin" anecdotes, such as the time the humorless competitor gave $5 to a fan after Cobb inadvertently crushed his straw hat pursuing a foul pop during a game. When he was a player/coach, Cobb was lauded for benching himself for hitters more appropriate for the game situation despite his stellar batting average.

Hughie Jennings, Cobb's manager in Detroit for fourteen seasons, wrote in a magazine article that Cobb never intentionally spiked a player during a game. Jennings, a Cornell law school graduate and no slouch himself on the diamond as his Cooperstown credentials confirm, would have a tough time convincing a jury that statement was true. Jennings was one of only a handful of major leaguers who would attend Cobb's funeral. Despite his Ivy League background, Jennings suffered skull fractures after the ultimate leisure-time bonehead play: diving headfirst into an empty swimming pool. Until Craig Biggio and his boxcar-sized elbow pad overtook him in 2007, Jennings was the all-time hit-by-pitch leader, getting plunked 287 times. One quote that sums up Cobb's approach to the game: "Baseball is a red-blooded sport for red-blooded men . . . a struggle for supremacy, survival of the fittest." This from a man who slept with his favorite sidearm, a Luger.

Art Fletcher, an infielder for the New York Giants at the dawn of the roaring 20s, made the team based on his haranguing abilities that were admired and sought after by manager John McGraw. It was hardly surprising Fletcher led the league in the hit by pitch category several times. Oddly, he was known off the field as a devout Christian who never swore, unless the writers of the era were duped by a Bowery Boys style twisting of the facts, which is entirely possible. Fletcher was self-conscious about his oversized mandible, a fitting physical tribute and cradle for his talent that won over the feisty Giants skipper. There were scores of on-field brawls prompted by a few choice lines from Fletcher, who would go on to manage the Phillies for a few seasons before signing on as a coach for the Murderer's Row Yankees.

Fletcher preceded a baseball character he is often compared to—a man who mastered the now-lost art of heckling—Leo Durocher. He was dubbed "The Lip" and "the most hated man in baseball" during his expansive career as a player and manager. A sharp dresser who was as at home among the Hollywood elite and organized crime figures as he was around a big league clubhouse, Durocher pulled no punches. He was a light hitter, but a flashy fielder, and legend has it he fought Babe Ruth in the Brooklyn clubhouse during the 1937 season when the Bambino was a first base coach for the Dodgers. While they were briefly teammates on the Yankees, Ruth had called Durocher "The All-American Out" and picked on him because of his diminutive size. But soon Ruth was encouraging Durocher to ride opposing stars from the bench. After Durocher was talked into calling Ty Cobb a "penny pincher" the Babe had to save Durocher from a post-game licking by the Tigers firebrand. In his autobiography *Nice Guys Finish Last*, Durocher also recalls Ruth saving him from the large fists of slugger Fatty Fottergill.

During the 1929 season, Durocher's third with the Bronx Bombers, the legend of Babe Ruth's missing watch emerged with Leo's name attached to it. It has never been confirmed Durocher stole Ruth's watch, or his five marked $100 bills during a drunken evening at a Detroit hotel. There was also talk concerning Durocher making off with Lou Gehrig's World Series ring, which may or may not be another tall tale surrounding the pugnacious pool hustler from western Massachusetts.

The story of Durocher sending Dodgers pinch-hitter Joe Gallagher into an instant fight with Cubs pitcher Claude Passeau has also made the rounds. Passeau is known for having the nail on the middle finger of his throwing hand knocked off by a line drive from the bat of Detroit's Jimmy Outlaw in Game 6 of the 1945 World Series, so whether he was considered tough as nails is a matter of debate. Durocher had the Dodger bench riding Passeau pretty hard, and someone called him a "dirty S.O.B"—words strong enough to lure Passeau to the top of the Brooklyn dugout and challenge the man who said that to come out onto the field. The bench fell silent, but Durocher instructed Gallagher to grab a bat and pinch-hit. Gallagher had not been paying attention to the incident and stepped onto the field reporting for duty only to be greeted by an immediate blow to the jaw from the Cubs hurler. Stunned, Gallagher took another punch before using his own 240-pound frame to grab Passeau and end the conflict, convinced that the Waynesboro, Mississippi native with the French moniker had gone crazy.

Durocher also observed in his book that in a major league clubhouse, "no fight is going to last more than ten seconds." In his famous scuffle with Ruth during the sad Dodgers campaign of 1937, his time limit held true. Durocher lunged at Ruth in an attempt to get in the first blow and hope for the best. Durocher's momentum carried them both into a locker behind Ruth. Teammates quickly pulled the two apart, and for years, Ruth and Durocher would have a rollercoaster relationship in the public eye and in the press, though privately the word was the Bambino couldn't stand Durocher, making Ruth a part of a club with a very crowded membership indeed.

Making up the third entry in a triptych of Evil Arts along the game's brawling timeline, Art Ditmar joins Devlin and Fletcher in the infamy file. Ditmar was throwing skull-high pitches at American League color-line breaker Larry Doby of the White Sox in June of 1957. The resulting fight was loud and large, highlighted by former Purdue football standout Moose Skowron of the Yankees putting a hard tackle on the enraged Doby. Inexplicably, Ditmar was allowed to stay in the ballgame while four other participants were ejected and fined, including Yankees outfielder Enos "Country" Slaughter, Chicago's Walt Dropo, Doby and New York's Billy Martin, who reacted to Doby mentioning a knife and sparked a second round of flailing limbs once the umpires had finally calmed things down. After the twenty-eight-minute fracas, Slaughter—who left the field with his uniform in tatters and his hat on backward thanks to a solid thrashing by Dropo—told a United Press sportswriter it was the first fight that he'd "seen them swing like they meant it."

Meanwhile, on the same day at Ebbets Field in Brooklyn, pitcher Don Drysdale and Milwaukee shortstop Johnny Logan went toe-to-toe after Drysdale hit Logan in the back, with both benches clearing. Their fight started dramatically with a Wild West–style showdown walk during which Drysdale tossed off his Dodgers cap and Logan chucked aside his Braves batting helmet. Unfortunately, first baseman Gil Hodges, Milwaukee coach John Riddle, and Eddie Mathews quickly muddled the showdown scenario. Dodgers manager Walter Alston and shortstop Pee Wee Reese were divided as reinforcements/peacemakers, and it was Don Newcombe who finally escorted his livid teammate Drysdale back to the Brooklyn dugout.

Drysdale and Logan were both no strangers to the frequent fracas, with the latter earning a nod on Joe Garagiola's "All-Star Team for Brawls" in his 1960 book *Baseball Is a Funny Game*. Two sizeable fights on the same day prompted the presidents of both leagues to warn all sixteen teams to put a halt to the fisticuffs trend. In a statement that would be repeated dozens of times over the next five decades, the leagues vaguely threatened "action" to prevent the controversial "dust-off pitch," which a United Press sportswriter called the "spark which touches off almost all baseball fights."

Chapter 2: PITCHED BATTLES

Though a UPI writer used the term "dust-off" pitch to refer to the villainous element in the pitcher-batter relationship, it is easy to see why that mild term faded in favor of "brushback," "chin music," and, in the case of the assassin landing a headshot, the "beanball." There is also the watered down term favored by many announcers: "message pitch." "Dusting off" is what happens after the pitch buzzes a batter's sideburn and he whiplashes out of the way and then, while regrouping, makes the crucial decision about charging the mound or standing his ground in the erased chalk confines of the batter's box.

In yet another failure of the MLB rulebook, batters getting put on their asses is a violation of Rule 8.02(d) which states: "The Pitcher shall not intentionally pitch at the batter." It also says that pitching at a batter's head is unsportsmanlike and highly dangerous. Once again, reading the rulebook only proves that the reader should never stop using it solely as a doorstop or to level off the short leg of a bistro table.

The advent of "body armor" has contributed to batters' tendencies to lean over the plate, elbows armadillo-like with protection. So the old-school territory claimed for decades by intimidating pitchers such as Bob Gibson has been usurped by enterprising equipment managers dressing a battalion of Craig Biggios, Jason Kendalls, and Andres Galarragas, all of whom have been cited by hurlers for "diving" out over the plate as the delivered pitch arrives in the strike zone.

The scores of frustrated batters who charge the pitcher's mound each season should know they are ignoring the ancient advice of the Chinese general Sun Tzu, *The Art of War* author whose words make frequent cameos in any number of Oliver Stone movie scripts. Tzu would have made a hell of a bench coach, and his book is fine road trip reading for MLB's underground cerebral elite. There are at least two references in Tzu's ancient tome about how it is not wise to wage war against an enemy who has gained the high ground. "Do not climb heights in order to fight," he puts it plainly in one of his later chapters. Tzu also wisely advises against opposing an enemy who is coming down a hill.

Strategically, the batter who has chosen to ignore Tzu has an open road toward the hurler, whose momentum has usually carried him to the front of the eighteen-foot diameter pitcher's mound after delivering the insulting throw. Most of the time, the pitcher still carries two enormous advantages. The first is he is at least ten inches higher than his victim, as the standard MLB pitcher's mound can be ten or more inches higher than home plate. Second, he's got five guys in his immediate vicinity backing him up, while the batter has himself and two typically geriatric base coaches—in the toy world, these two are the equivalent of the surrendering guy and the minesweeper in the bag of little green soldiers.

Closest to the attacking batter are two fellows behind the plate, both traditionally slow as beetles and encumbered by iron masks, Kevlar chain mail, and all manner of desperate fiberglass and plastic padding. The catcher and the umpire, given the physics of the pitch delivery, are moving slightly in the opposite direction of the lunging batter, allowing a millisecond or two advantage for the targeted player to escape their pudgy grasps from behind. Being caught and restrained by either of them can be a shameful experience for the enraged batter.

The interloping third party has also been known to be an alert corner infielder whose job description requires decent reflexes. Their intrusions from the flanks throw off the balance of the ensuing battle, turning the confrontation into a disorganized joust that usually results in a messy pile-up, where the real injuries take place.

Organizing a list of mound-charging incidents can warp itself into an oddball version of studying for the bar exam. One weighs the shaky foundation of *Steinbach vs. Thigpen* relative to the precedent setting *Cobb vs. Herzog*, or even the revenge ambush theme of *Cowens vs. Farmer*. The pitcher's height advantage on the mound was never as clear as the body slam served up in *Nevin vs. Pittsley* in Kansas City in June of 1998. That fight was followed a few innings later by a lengthy, extremely boring rugby scrum that somehow brought the number of ejections between Anaheim and Kansas City to twelve. Angels catcher Matt Walbeck wisely removed Jose Offerman's bat from his hands after pitcher Mike Holtz buzzed him. Both team's managers got eight game suspensions, and Troy Percival made a lame attempt to pound Felix Martinez who had already been tenderized by Gary DiSarcina and Damon Mashore in foul territory in the ninth inning melee. Anaheim's Cecil Fielder yelled a lot at Hipolito Pichardo and Kansas City pitching coach Bruce Kison tried to revive his old career as an instigator but was talked down by Anaheim coach Marcel Lachemann, who completely upstaged fellow Anaheim coach Larry Bowa.

Then there are third party incidents when a catcher, corner infielder or umpire restrains the charger, like Pete Rose (of *Rose vs. Harrelson*) vacating the hot corner to keep Bill Russell from delivering an urgent memo to Tug McGraw, or George Bell (of *Bell vs. Kison*) being faked out by an Aaron Sele bob-and-weave and immediately falling into the hefty embrace of first baseman Mo Vaughn, who also played a key interference role in *L. Frazier vs. Gunderson.*

Not to be forgotten is the bookend version of the mound-charge, as displayed in *C. Hayes vs. T. Stottlemyre,* when the Giants' Charlie Hayes charged the Arizona mound *from second base*, which was a refreshing change of pace.

Let's take a page from a personal injury law class syllabus and examine a few of these cases and their merits, beginning with one of the most famous cross-generational clashes in the history of the game.

ROBIN VENTURA vs. NOLAN RYAN
(CHICAGO WHITE SOX)   (TEXAS RANGERS)
August 4, 1993, Arlington Stadium, Arlington, Texas

Maybe it was the courage oozing from the "for display only" unofficial gold medal Ventura won as a member of the 1988 USA Olympic baseball team? Maybe it was the fact he had more than doubled his salary from the year before, putting him in the seven-figure club for the first time in his career? Maybe he knew he was facing a pitcher who also had a girly first name? Maybe his elbow was still sore from getting hit in the same place two weeks earlier by Milwaukee's Cal Eldred? Maybe he knew he had sizable reinforcements on the bench in the terrible trio of Frank Thomas, Bo Jackson, and Joey Cora?

Speculation was indeed rampant following the events of August 4, 1993, yet another steamy night in Arlington, Texas. With one out in the third inning and the Chicago White Sox up 2-0, Texas starter Lynn Nolan Ryan, the "Ryan Express" and baseball's all-time strikeout leader, was facing Robin Ventura, the White Sox third baseman who had an RBI single in the first inning. Starting off the second inning, White Sox pitcher Alex Fernandez clipped Juan Gonzalez with a fastball. But the word on the streets (in this case, the stadium parking lot) was Ventura might be a target not as retaliation for Gonzalez getting hit, but for a baserunning play from the previous night's game when Chicago was winning 11-6 in the ninth inning. Ventura singled, giving him a 3-for-5 night. He then attempted to steal second base. Red flags went up in the minds of the Texas dugout dwellers and apparently Ventura's name was written into the team's family Bible as a violator of unwritten baseball rules.

The White Sox already had Ryan's name in their family Bible, dating back to August 1990 when the Ryan Express plunked Scott Fletcher in Texas a week after light-hitting rookie Craig Grebeck and Ozzie Guillen hit back-to-back home runs off him in a 5-1 White Sox victory in Chicago. Oh yeah, there was also that time in April of 1990 when Ryan tossed a one-hitter against the ChiSox, striking out sixteen . . . and the August 17, 1990 contest when Ryan went ten innings and struck out fifteen White Sox batters in a thirteen-inning loss in the first game of a twin bill. Going up against the first-place White Sox in early August 1993, Texas manager Kevin Kennedy, whose last name befits his brief tenure at the helm of the Dallas-area pro baseball team, had called it a "do or die" series for the Rangers. In his final season of a Hall of Fame career, Ryan needed no motivational speeches or bulletin board material to get him up for his start.

Losing the first game of the series dropped the Rangers from second to third place, five and a half games behind Chicago and one game behind Kansas City in the AL West—back when it was a real division instead of the four-team country club it would later become. *Ventura vs. Ryan* also serves to—at last—provide a shard of relevance to Olympic baseball.

Though few fans really care or remember the winners of the every-four-years marketing hype machine, there is an ironic point to be made in noting the number of Olympians involved in baseball fights. Jeff Weaver (*Sweeney vs. Weaver*) and Jim Parque (*Palmer vs. Parque*) were teammates on the 1996 bronze team in Atlanta. Ben Sheets (of *A. Ramirez vs. Sheets*) won a gold medal in 2000 at Sydney, and Graeme Lloyd (*A. Benitez vs. New York Yankees*) was on the silver medal squad in 2004 in Athens. Add to this pantheon of punchers the pulp moniker of Robin Ventura, who has somewhere in his residence—or perhaps dangled on eBay—a gold medal from the U.S. Olympic baseball team that prevailed in 1988 at Seoul. Baseball was still a "demonstration" sport then, so Ventura's medal is not considered official. If the rulebook is used as a doorstop, it follows that Ventura's medal might serve well as a drinks coaster.

Regardless, had Ventura been wearing his ersatz medal when he charged the mound against Ryan on August 4, 1993, it might have gotten in the way of the perfectly-executed headlock employed by Ryan. As Ventura half-staggered out of the left-hand batter's box after getting hit, he made his decision by dropping the bat, then shedding his batting helmet, and making a beeline for Ryan. The forty-six-year-old Lone Star state legend, cattle rancher, restaurateur, future bank president, and minor league franchise co-owner stood waiting for the charge on a direct line. As Ventura, the twenty-six-year-old native of Santa Maria, California, advanced with his head up, Ryan waited until his attacker was about one yard away and used his right hand to methodically remove the glove from his fielding hand in what looked like a rehearsed motion. Ventura's hands—covered in white batting gloves—would transform quickly into Mickey Mouse cartoon mitts as he reached Ryan, who turned his upper body to receive Ventura into the perfect loop of his left forearm pulling him against his chest. Ryan's right hand then formed a fist and took care of business, this time without a baseball.

In do-it-yourself Texan auto care vernacular, it was as if Ryan was a strap wrench and Ventura's head an oil filter that needed a-changin' in that dang ol' truck in the side yard. After one blow to Ventura's scalp, Texas catcher Ivan "Pudge" Rodriguez arrived and tried to pull Ventura away from Ryan, a natural reaction for any right-thinking backstop. Rodriguez's protective headgear, a visorless shell bearing a slight resemblance to a Roman cavalry helmet, added to the battlefield aura of the scene unfolding in the center of the Arlington infield. Closer examination shows

Pudge's chocolate-hued Wilson catcher's mitt framing the other side of Ventura's head, as if to provide a cushion for any of Ryan's errant blows. But the man who tossed seven no-hitters in his twenty-six-year career went six-for-six with his right fist, including a coup de grace uppercut to nail Ventura's face with punch number six.

Prior to the landing of punch number four, an Associated Press photographer snapped a shot qualifying the photojournalist for membership among the Carravagisti. The composition belies Titian, or even a detail from Theodore Gericault's masterpiece "The Raft of the Medusa." Ryan's clenched fist, the same hand used for gladhanding the locals in Alvin, Texas, is the focal point on the left side of the frame. Tendons used for two decades to deliver his trademarked heat are strained to deliver blunt blows. Ryan is the tallest in the frame, followed by the hunched form of his victim Ventura, and then Pudge at the low-point with his taped glove hand lobster-like in his effort to bear hug the attacker away from his teammate. All three bodies are in contact, the home whites of the Rangers making a Ventura sandwich out of his road grays. Had there been more horizontal striped shirts with collars, this could have been any scene from a rugby match. The background is a colorful blur of filled box seats as the crowd of 32,312 got some value added to their entertainment dollar for the evening. When the players were finally separated, the fans chanted "Nolan! Nolan!"

The AP photo also stands out because these are not the usual baseball postures, and the viewer can feel the forward momentum of Ventura and his passenger Rodriguez. Ryan's Rangers cap is only slightly askance on his head, a gray sideburn of tasteful length dropping down. His tongue is out, but folded in concentration and his brow is knit like a ploughman's. In a sense, Ryan was doing what he'd been doing for twenty-five years—torturing a batter with his right hand. His economy of motion and advanced pace allowed him to get in a record half-dozen clouts before the obligatory mob arrived. Texas third baseman Dean Palmer (of *Palmer vs. Parque*) was the fourth dance partner on the scene, but he peeled away in order to perhaps set a pick to allow Ryan to continue. Palmer might have been too ashamed to participate, since it was his two errors in the first inning that helped Chicago go up 2-0. White Sox coach Terry Bevington got in close and attempted to grab Ryan by the head as he spun away, still holding Ventura. Texas shortstop Mario Diaz, moving in from his position at a slight canter, examined the pile and then veered off, perhaps with second thoughts about tangling with the heavyweights who were in transit, including Ron Karkovice, the aforementioned Thomas and Jackson, Carlton Fisk and Dan Pasqua.

Of course, most of the heavyweights managed to avoid action, with the exception of Jackson who was active in the center of the scrum. Somewhere in the pile, courageous White Sox manager Gene Lamont, mild-mannered and with a slight resemblance to the cartoon character Droopy Dog, was punched and had his trick knee give out. He would limp for several days. Texas coach Mickey Hatcher also emerged from the pile with a bleeding head wound. And just when the scene was beginning to quiet down, the homunculus known as Joey Cora darted toward the pile in what some sportswriters claimed was an effort to "get a piece of Ryan."

Cora's presence meant the situation had deteriorated into a puckish comedy, so it was time for the umpires to issue the ejections. Like the frontier days, it was the men in the black caps who would get tossed from the saloon. The locals were spared as Ventura and Lamont were sent packing, the latter for his vehement protest when Ryan was inexplicably allowed to remain in the game.

After recovering his cap and buttoning up the top three jersey buttons that came undone during his session on the Ventura heavy bag, Ryan went on to shut down the White Sox for the next four frames, while the Rangers would score five off Fernandez in the sixth inning. When Ryan struck out Karkovice for the third time, it was his 5,700th career strikeout. Before the night was through, Ryan would also have some choice words for White Sox ace Jack McDowell, who apparently continued a verbal tirade from the comfort of the bench. Ventura's replacement at third was none other than Grebeck. When he came in to run for the ejected Ventura, Pudge Rodriguez promptly picked him off first with one of his patented throws from behind the plate

Ryan not getting tossed from the game was a longstanding tradition throughout MLB. He was ejected for the first and only time one year earlier, on August 6, 1992. He'd hit Oakland's Willie Wilson on the leg after Wilson had tripled off him in the previous at bat. The Wilson-Ryan shouting match emptied both benches and prompted a garbage shower from the Arlington faithful, delaying the game for ten minutes with two outs in the ninth inning. Among the umpiring crew for that game was Rich Garcia, who would also be present as the crew chief in Arlington when Ventura made his ill-fated charge. Ryan told the *Chicago Daily Herald* he was just trying to pitch inside to Ventura. "I don't have anything against Robin Ventura," Ryan said before uttering the quote that would essentially follow every baseball fight: "It's all part of the game."

Lamont defended his previous night's choice to send Ventura with a five-run lead late in the game, citing the potent Texas batting order as a constant threat to put quick runs on the board. "I hope I do it tomorrow," said the manager whose team would be hamstrung in October by Michael Jordan's rather public retirement hoopla during the ALCS against Toronto.

Ventura, who would accomplish a great deal in another crowd-pleasing baseball realm (his eighteen grand slams are tied for third on the all-time list), defended his actions. "I'll do what I have to do, I don't care who it is," he told the *Daily Herald*. "I'm all right. He gave me a couple noogies." Aside from his penchant for delivering thrills when the bases were loaded, Ventura was otherwise noted for the Ryan incident and his gruesome Spring Training injury in 1997 when he suffered a compound fracture and dislocated ankle after sliding into home plate.

Up until September of 1995, Ventura was vociferously jeered when he played at Arlington Stadium. It was a two grand-slam, eight-RBI night against the Rangers that finally turned the Texas tables. After he'd hit his second grand slam, the crowd of 18,036 at the new Ballpark at Arlington applauded his feat. They would add more applause when the Oklahoma State alum batted again in the ninth inning. The hatchet, apparently, was buried.

For Ryan, he would win only two more games in 1993, finishing his career with 324 victories. He hit 158 batters in 803 career games (averaging six per season), with fifteen HBPs coming in his 1971 campaign with the Mets. In 1992 with the Rangers, he hit twelve opponents. The last time anyone charged the mound against Ryan was August 4, 1980, when San Diego's Dave Winfield took umbrage after getting buzzed by a pitch from the Express. Needless to say, there was no headlock and Winfield fared much better than Ventura. In fact, Ryan said after the Ventura fight he learned from Winfield's fierce approach and powerful first blow not to be passive if someone charges the mound in the future. "You have to protect yourself," Ryan said.

Winfield said in his autobiography that Willie Montanez advised him not to take brushback pitches in stride and to charge the mound to command some respect. Winfield had already taken two under the chin from Ryan in that game—the third time was the charm. The resulting melee saw Winfield bite the finger of Houston's Enos Cabell, whom he considered a pal, and the arrival of Winfield's agent on the field. In what was probably a first during a baseball fight, the agent—known to be suffering from heart disease—jumped the railing and bolted toward the battle to make sure his client was treated fairly.

In 1983 at Yankee Stadium, Winfield charged A's pitcher Mike Norris in the first inning and put a stranglehold on him. This was a year after Norris suffered nerve damage in his hand while throwing down in a brawl with the Seattle Mariners.

During his farewell season of 1993, Ryan plunked but one batter—Ventura. And both players made the occasion as memorable—as Ryan's fellow Texans might put it—"as a skillet full of rattlesnakes."

BILLY NORTH vs. DOUG BIRD
(OAKLAND ATHLETICS)   (KANSAS CITY ROYALS)
May 18, 1973, Oakland-Alameda Coliseum, Oakland, California

One player's elephantine memory was key to an odd incident in Oakland in May of 1973. The defending World Champion A's—a franchise nicknamed the "White Elephants" when John McGraw noted the number of National League players on the American League's Philadelphia Athletics back in 1901—were hosting the Kansas City Royals. It was just another American League West contest until the eighth inning when Oakland speed merchant Billy North came to the plate. Perhaps taking a page from teammate Bert Campaneris' famous ALCS bat-as-helicopter toss at Detroit reliever Lerrin LaGrow (*Campaneris vs. LaGrow*) from the previous October, North let his bat lead the way down memory lane, with a detour toward the pitcher's mound where he had some old business to settle with Royals reliever Doug Bird.

Flashback to three years earlier in a Midwest League game at the Class A level of the minors: North, wearing the Quincy (Illinois) Cubs uniform, was facing Bird, who was on the mound for the Waterloo (Iowa) Royals. Bird had surrendered back-to-back home runs and was in no mood to face the pesky North. After a brushback, North gave the Waterloo catcher an earful, proclaiming it was not he who had struck the pair of mighty home run blows that had apparently humiliated Bird. Privy to this heated home plate conversation, Bird applied the next pitched baseball to the earflap of North's batting helmet. In the dust of the Waterloo's Municipal Stadium batter's box, North, suffering from a swollen ear on his way to two weeks in the hospital, made a solemn vow to seek revenge against Bird . . . some way . . . *some day.*

That day finally came on May 18, 1973. North swung at Bird's first pitch leading off the eighth inning. He let the bat fly out of his hand toward the shortstop and calmly walked out as if to pick it up. When he got a few feet away from the mound, he veered to ambush the pitcher, wailing away with three punches—at least one of which landed squarely on Bird's beak. The pair fell to the ground and began grappling as the benches emptied and stunned Royals rushed to help out their fallen hurler. The umpiring crew, including Don Denkinger—who would invaluably assist the Royals in Game 6 of the 1985 World Series—was quick to break up the tangle on the mound. North was ejected.

Some reports indicated North had first thrown his bat at Bird, but the fleet of foot center fielder insisted it was just a way of getting closer to his intended target. Admittedly, North's surprise charge on Bird was as premeditated as they come. "I was glad to see his name on a big league roster, glad to see him called up a couple of weeks ago," North told the *Oakland Tribune.* "I was waiting for a chance and I did what I wanted to do. I don't think I could live with myself and not challenge that dude. I'd made my mind up that one day we'd see each other again. They can hit me in the side, hit me in the legs, but they can kill me hitting me in the head." Amping up the water-under-the-Bay Bridge drama, North further invoked the Grim Reaper: "Two inches more and I would have been dead."

A's manager Dick Williams gave North a stern lecture after the game for forgetting the "team" in favor of a personal vendetta. He pointed out North drove in the tying run, stole a base and scored the winning run in the A's 5-4 victory. "Next time, just knock on the other guy's door or something," Williams told North.

The Royals seized on the North ambush as an opportunity to target the mighty A's through the rest of the season. "That hot dog is a marked man," said Royals pitcher Bruce Dal Canton, who was to pitch the fourth game of the four-game series, which opened with the late-inning rhubarb that rewarded the "crowd" of 7,535 ticketholders inside the spacious home of the NFL's Raiders. "It's going to be a long summer," said Royals hurler Wayne Simpson. He was right about that, at least as far as Kansas City was concerned. They finished in second place, six games behind first-place Oakland, with several frustrating losses to the Swingin' A's along the way.

Bird, however, agreed with North in that the Waterloo grudge was now a closed matter. He didn't recall the beaning until someone reminded him of North's penchant for memorizing minor league lore. "He just walked into it," Bird told the *Oakland Tribune* of the original incident. "I don't throw at a guy. It's his living." Bird agreed with his teammates that it was going to be a long season, however, he agreed with North about their relationship. "I guess we're even now," Bird said. North would get at least two hits off Bird in games later that season. The teams split the four-game series without further incident, including Dal Canton's Monday start which fell into the large shadow of Catfish Hunter's complete game, 5-0 shutout of the Royals. Dal Canton did hit Oakland DH Deron Johnson with a pitch, but nothing escalated.

In late August, North and Royals infielder "Dirty" Kurt Bevacqua (of *Bevacqua vs. Brett* and a beer shower victim toward the conclusion of *Pascual Perez vs. San Diego Padres*) got in a tussle at third base and both were ejected in a 10-7 Oakland victory. Sal Bando, who was at the plate during the scrap, came to North's aid, giving Bevacqua a violent scalp treatment he would remember for several years to come. Bando was not ejected, much to the Royals' horror, which increased to H.P. Lovecraft proportions after he hit an inside-the-park home run two pitches after the fight.

The Royals-A's game on September 10 provided Kansas City with a welcome entry in the "best served cold" department of revenge. Starter Steve Busby, who took the loss back in May the night of *North vs. Bird* (which was just a few starts after his April 27 no-hitter against Detroit), scored the angry pitcher's quiniela against North: He drilled him with a pitch, then promptly picked him off first base.

In the immediate wake of *North vs. Bird*, flamboyant A's owner Charlie O. Finley called the three-game suspension and $100 fine levied against North for his unlicensed Bird hunting "grossly unfair." He objected to AL president Joe Cronin's failure to consult manager Williams regarding the details of the incident. North, meanwhile, said he was in favor of a bigger fine without a suspension. Finley, in his comments to the Associated Press, certainly didn't forget the team. "This suspension is unfair to the other twenty-four Oakland players. We already have Billy Conigliaro in the hospital and Joe Rudi is hurt," Finley noted. "I'm not condoning what North did, but I think the penalty is too severe."

The Rudi injury Finley referred to occurred in the same game as *North vs. Bird* and involved North. In a partial collision with Rudi in pursuit of a fly ball, North stepped on Rudi's foot and the A's star had to leave the game with strained ligaments.

North's prized skull—which took the fateful pitch back in Waterloo—would be fine the rest of his career. His hands, feet and ankles were another story. Frequent injuries to these body parts eventually made North's career go south. After a stint with the Dodgers and three seasons with the Giants, the Seattle native retired in 1981.

BILL "MAD DOG" MADLOCK
(CHICAGO CUBS)
VS.
JIM BARR
(SAN FRANCISCO GIANTS)

GARY "SARGE" MATTHEWS
(SAN FRANCISCO GIANTS)
VS.
GEORGE "THE BARON" MITTERWALD
(CHICAGO CUBS)

May 1, 1976, Candlestick Park,
San Francisco, California

Ah, May Day in San Francisco. The reclined kids rise up off the sidewalks in the Haight-Ashbury district and attend demonstrations on the international day of worker's resistance. The abundant pagan population celebrates the end of winter, the fertile soil and the return of the sun. On

May Day 1976, The Ramones' first album had been released just a week earlier. On April Fool's Day, a month earlier, some nerds started a company called Apple computer in a garage in Cupertino. And as spring was springing, the Rev. Jim Jones was steadily moving his People's Temple congregation from his Geary Street church headquarters in San Francisco to an agricultural encampment in the jungle of Guyana, South America. (Jones—like Braves owner/media mogul Ted Turner and Turner Field two decades later—would name the encampment after himself.) May Day is usually a big deal in the Bay area, so that might explain why only 4,701 souls had checked in to witness afternoon baseball at the wind and fog machine known as Candlestick Park. If it wasn't the May Day distraction, the unimpressive attendance number was just another San Francisco mystery, much like the abundance of Dutch doors present in the city's bars and taverns.

The Cubs were in town, and the bottom of the first inning gave the tiny crowd a prelibation of the diamond disorder that would mark the day. Giants leadoff man Derrel Thomas was plunked by Cubs starter Ray Burris, perhaps as punishment for the 1-0 lead the Cubs built up in the top of the inning. Jim Barr, the Giants starter, was known as "the control pitcher." In the top of the third, when he brushed Jose Cardenal off the plate with some inside heat, home plate umpire Ed Runge marched out to warn the former USC standout. At the time, a warning was an automatic $50 fine. But before Runge could finish his business, Cardenal threw his batting helmet at Barr. His toss missed the target, but was a clarion call for the dugouts and bullpens to empty. Cardenal headed for the mound still carrying his bat—the famous cupped-end model prominent in Japan and making its National League debut in the hands of Cardenal during this very season. Third base umpire Nick Colosi was able to grab it away from Cardenal. His teammates finally restrained the Cuban and Runge ejected him from the game. Pete LaCock would finish the at bat and take a called third strike from Barr. Years later as a coach in the 1990s, Cardenal was twice struck in the head during pre-game drills; the first incident involved a line drive that put him in the hospital. He had to have metal plates installed in his cranium. The second mishap was a thrown ball during batting practice that knocked him unconscious for almost ten minutes.

In the coverage of the ensuing chaos of May Day, 1976, two of the four baseball fight clichés would make their way to the forefront. The first is the automatic sleuthing carried out by players to determine who was a "cheap shot" artist or who was throwing "sucker punches." The second is that someone—*anyone*—involved in the scrap must utter the post-game phrase: "Just part of the game." There also must be a descriptive making the incident in question stand out from the dreaded "typical baseball fight" and an announcer who says "you just hope nobody gets hurt" with a phony hangdog tone to his voice. The Candlestick Park party that began with Cardenal's aborted mound charge was characterized by at least one sportswriter as players taking "real" swings, connecting, and drawing authentic ballplayer blood.

Enter: Bill Madlock. On the way to his second consecutive National League batting title in 1976, "Mad Dog" was on deck when LaCock did his window shopping. Madlock had an RBI single in the first, and the first pitch from Barr was way inside. Madlock gestured and urged Runge to make good on his warning and take Barr out of the game. The umpire stood his ground.

Barr's next pitch was fouled off by Madlock, whose bat somehow escaped his grasp and flew in the direction of the pitcher. With his bat retrieved, Madlock stood in for the third pitch that struck him on the elbow, which prompted an urgent mound visit from the angry canine. Runge decided to go along with him and actually got between Madlock and Barr, but Madlock managed to get a swing over the ump's shoulder and struck Barr's chin with the back of his fist.

Four or five other fights blossomed from the second emptying of the benches and bullpens. Giants catcher Marc Hill, whom Madlock had steamrolled on his way to the mound, stood up bloodied just in time to see teammate Gary Matthews squaring off with Cubs back-up catcher George "Baron Von" Mitterwald. A left from "The Sarge" put Mitterwald, a Vietnam veteran who got his nickname after a three-homer game against Pittsburgh in April 1974, flat on the ground. Sarge had more orders for the Baron, straddling the fallen backstop and delivering consecutive left-right combinations to his head. Though he was not in the starting lineup, Mitterwald left some blood on the field that day. The Berkeley native had a few interesting ties to San Francisco Giants lore. He was the backup behind Johnny Roseboro (of the infamous *Roseboro vs. Marichal*) while with the 1969 Minnesota Twins. In April 1976, rookie pitcher Mike Krukow reported for duty with the Cubs, and upon entering the clubhouse, he was called "meat" by the veteran Mitterwald. Krukow would use that word decades later as his signature term during a fruitful broadcast career for the Giants—a term that would quickly catch on and stick among the Giants' fan base. ("Meat" was also what manager Bob Lemon called all players.) Mitterwald went on to coach for a few seasons in the Oakland system and was Mark McGwire's first professional manager.

Barr, who on May 6, 1973 was involved in a tit-for-tat hit batsman war with the Cubs (known as *Barr vs. Pappas*, featuring dirty work done by teammate Bobby Bonds), would later go on to play in a professional "over forty" league with fellow brawlers Cardenal, Bert Campaneris (of *Campaneris vs. LaGrow*), Mike Marshall (of *Garner vs. Marshall*) and Bret Saberhagen (of *Saberhagen vs. New York press corps*), was protected under the pile by two Cubs and two Giants serving as inadvertent human umbrellas. "Rick Monday was the only one I could identify who was covering me," Barr told the *Oakland Tribune*. In 1972, Barr had set the record for consecutive batters retired with a string of forty-one spread over two appearances.

It had already been a colorful week for Monday. Just a few days before during the Cubs west coast trip, he swashbuckled his way toward a father and son who had stormed the Dodger Stadium outfield intent on setting an American flag on fire. Monday swiped Old Glory away from their faulty lighter and earned folk hero status and White House recognition. Monday reportedly still has the flag hanging in his den.

Despite plenty of blood on the carpet, Madlock was the only other ejection after the May Day brawl. He would finish the season with the Cubs and then be traded to the Giants for Bobby Murcer and Steve Ontiveros and would go on to play for four more teams and live up to every ounce of madness associated with his nickname (see *Madlock vs. Zaske*; *Madlock vs. Montefusco, et al*).

Matthews's day was not done after pummeling Mitterwald. As if they were not busy enough with routine May Day situations, eight San Francisco policemen had to be called to the clubhouse runway beneath the stands at Candlestick to prevent more fisticuffs. Matthews was after Cubs outfielder Champ Summers (also a Vietnam vet) who accused Sarge of "sucker punching" Mitterwarld even though the pair were clearly squared off like old-fashioned boxers. Matthews said he went toward the Cubs clubhouse to ask Chicago manager Jim Marshall why he was kicking him in the back during the melee. The manager replied he was doing all he could to get Matthews off of his backup catcher. The police called in a backup unit of fifteen to twenty more officers to man the player's parking lot, but the excitement appeared to be over after the runway tussle.

Matthews was noted for his aggressive style, spending his first four seasons with San Francisco and chalking up the NL Rookie of the Year award in 1973. In 1975, he sent Johnny Bench for a loop in a hearty home plate collision during a 4-3 win over the Reds. By autumn of that year, Bench would require surgery on the shoulder that took the brunt of the charging Sarge. Following the 1976 campaign with the Giants, Matthews signed with the Atlanta Braves as a free agent after some tampering controversy involving the aforementioned Ted Turner. Matthews would eventually join the Cubs and become a Wrigley Field fan favorite as both a player and coach, long after Baron Von Mitterwald had hung up his spiked helmet.

*Some enraged batters, bayonets fixed and preparing for hand-*to-hand combat, launch a projectile when charging the mound. Bikers (of the ilk known to associate with David Wells) call them "brain buckets" and "skid lids." On the ballfield they are called batting helmets. For these adrenaline-shocked batsmen, off they come and into the air they go as a reply to the flying cowhide that so offended their person and fired the neurons leading to a melee.

Hitting a pitched baseball has been called the hardest task in sports. Throwing a batting helmet at the pitcher with any accuracy while running uphill might be even harder. The irregular, almost elliptical shape of the helmet has an aerodynamic dysfunction that affects the flight of the object. The advent of earflaps with earholes turned the once symmetrical helmet into an odd, L-shaped mass. The four forces of aerodynamics used to play nicely over the old fashioned batting helmet with no earflap. But lift, thrust, weight, and drag have been known to play havoc with the newer model and its greater mass and density. The lift to drag ratio has obviously been skewed, vector quantities have been compromised, and the flying helmet is more susceptible to barometric pressure than it used to be.

Add to this a new wrinkle: the introduction of the Rawlings "Coolflo" batting helmet to at least eleven MLB clubs in 2006. The high-tech design features fifteen individual vents and raised contour ridges and resembles a futuristic sketch done circa the original *Battlestar Galactica* television series. Coolflos winged at pitchers by screaming batters were few and far between in 2006, but it might in fact take a rocket scientist to figure out if the fifteen vents will help a batter's accuracy when throwing the helmet, or further hinder the difficult task of hitting an elevated target while running forward, possibly with a bat in the other hand. In one online sporting goods catalogue touting the merits of the Coolflo, an ironic blurb was found: "The cooler headed you are, the better focused you can be." This advice could apply to many facets of the mound-charging slugger's A-game.

With batting gloves and pine tar entering the picture, it is hard for the helmet tosser to get a reliable grip and establish an effective release point. When gripped by the visor, the helmet usually winds up diving down and away from the target, sometimes straight down, which puts the batter at an embarrassing risk of being hoisted by his own petard. Having a weak arm can be embarrassing for helmet-tossers. In *Justice vs. Percival*, Cleveland's David Justice made up for a limp lefthanded helmet toss at the Anaheim closer by landing a strong right hook during the brouhaha.

Points for efficiency should be noted in *McLemore vs. Yan*, in which Seattle's Mark McLemore, while at full sprint, delivered a near-perfect helmet throw that just missed Esteban Yan's back. The mound charge was prompted by an unfortunate failure by the Tampa Bay hurler to realize time had been called at the plate before throwing a low fastball between McLemore's legs as he stood upright and at ease in the batter's box. McLemore's ensuing tackle of a crouching Yan was also a thing of beauty, which could have had Seahawks scouts buzzing had they not been so busy dealing with Jeff Nelson's insistent Bo Jackson fantasies. The following airborne batting helmet gems carry a bit more drama than *McLemore vs. Yan* and warrant closer examination.

DEAN PALMER vs. JIM PARQUE
(DETROIT TIGERS)   (CHICAGO WHITE SOX)
April 22, 2000, Comiskey Park, Chicago, Illinois

If Ty Cobb ever wore a batting helmet, there's a good chance he might have thrown it at someone during his career. In fact, Pete Rose (of *Harrelson vs. Rose*), who broke Cobb's record for most hits, might even take wagers on that theory. A year prior to the *Sweeney vs. Weaver* incident, Cobb's old team was at the heart of another throw-down at Comiskey Park against the White Sox. Dean Palmer did the tossing, trying to expose Chicago pitcher Jim Parque to the feel and texture of a plastic helmet with the Olde English "D" on the front. Viewed from an aerial vantage or drawn up as a schematic, *Palmer vs. Parque* is an interesting study in brawl movement. Many times the testosterone storm front swirls toward either dugout or even to the backstop area. This particular gathering eventually moved instead out into right field where prairie justice lives. It is a space usually reserved for drunken fan loonies trying to kiss or embrace their favorite pasture-dwellers. Like a turf race at Saratoga, the grass underfoot gives the fighting ballplayer a different feel and the crowd is treated to a unique sound, and much less dust than the usual infield skirmish. The outfield brawl also calls for people in the stands to don the binoculars, a move that can either provide rich detail, or jumble the whole mess of untucked jerseys and warmup jackets into an even more uneven picture.

On April 22, 2000, the nation was celebrating Earth Day, and 16,410 fans had filed into Comiskey Park where the vibe would eventually become out-of-this-world. Five hit batters, two benchclearing brawls, and eleven ejections would provide sideshow dramas fit for the Windy City's Steppenwolf Theater, which was offering *The Drawer Boy* starring John Mahoney that same afternoon. On offer at Comiskey was a pitching match-up featuring two former Olympians from the 1996 USA team that won the bronze medal in Atlanta. Southern California golden boy Jeff Weaver (of *Sweeney vs. Weaver*) was starting for Detroit, and Vietnamese-American Parque, also no stranger to Southern California sunshine, drew the assignment for the White Sox.

The crowd that opted not to attend the theater would instead, by the end of a raucous afternoon, be taunted by the opposing team's catcher. And being proper Southsiders, the throng responded by heaping a beer shower upon the head of the antagonist wearing the road grays of the Detroit squad. The scoreboard, which read Chicago 14, Detroit 6 at the end of the game, also had but one message for the Tigers: *exeunt.*

Of the five batters hit in this game, all five would come around to score. There were twenty runs and twenty hits, one error, ten runners left on base, and eleven pitchers used. The first batter as victim was Paul Konerko in the fourth. The always-cantankerous Weaver hit him after giving up a double to Frank Thomas and walking Magglio Ordonez. In the sixth, after an Ordonez double and a Konerko walk, Weaver plunked Carlos Lee, who gave the lanky hurler a death stare on his way to first. Tigers manager Phil Garner then lifted Weaver for reliever Jim Poole, who promptly threw gas on the fire. By the end of the inning, Poole gave way to Danny Patterson and the Pale Hose were up 8-1.

The fun began in the top of the seventh inning. Staked to a comfy lead, Parque hit Tigers third baseman Dean Palmer in the arm with his first pitch. Palmer bolted for the mound and threw his batting helmet at the bronze medalist. Dugouts and bullpens were vacated, and for thirteen minutes there was all manner of mayhem. There was choking, punching, and kicking. Cheap shots were alleged, stitches were required, fans were taunted, and yes, beer—probably Old Style—was thrown. Tigers coach Bill Madlock, a veteran of numerous fights, said he'd never seen one this dangerous. The postmortem on *Palmer vs. Parque* also included some groundbreaking media criticism, courtesy of Tigers broadcaster Kirk Gibson and his beef with ESPN's coverage.

The brawl also covered each base as the main mob congregated near third, while another led by Weaver in a T-shirt skirmished near second base, and a bullpen posse was having a grab-fest near first. From the upper deck, the hats strewn across the infield grass were strangely reminiscent of the crowd scene gag featuring blown off hats in the Marx Brothers film *A Day at The Races*. After a short pause in the action, the whole standing crowd of players then moved toward right field where the action continued on the grass.

White Sox reliever Keith Foulke was bloodied by what he said was an attack from behind courtesy of Karim Garcia (of *Nelson/Garcia vs. Fenway bullpen worker Williams*) and Bobby Higginson, who denounced ESPN's Rob Dibble (of *Dibble vs. Piniella*, among others) for calling him out on cheap shots during the brawl. Foulke's right hand was stepped on and gashed, and he got five stitches to close a cut under his left eye. Garner was hoarse the next day after he was put in a stranglehold from behind while foolishly trying to pull Frank Thomas off the pile. Umpires Jerry Crawford and Joe West ejected Tigers catcher Robert Fick and teammates Palmer, Weaver and Patterson. Crawford also sent Chicago players Bill Simas and Magglio Ordonez packing, the latter for kicking his way through the fracas, aiming his cleats at Weaver, the umpire said.

On his way off the field, Fick taunted the White Sox faithful, waving his arms upward. ESPN's *Baseball Tonight* crew said it was an obscene gesture, but thanks to Gibson's campaign for accuracy, Fick was able to point out that he was not flipping the bird to the crowd. "I was just having fun with them, waving my hands as if to say 'bring it on,'" Fick told Knight-Ridder newspapers. The bringing it on would include several $6 cups of beer raining down on Fick before he hit the showers.

There were more fireworks in the ninth inning. Deivi Cruz, who came into the game as Palmer's replacement, was hit by Tanyon Sturtze leading off the inning. Crawford, a hardened ump who lists H.O. trains as his hobby, again had to modify his ejection flow chart, sending Sturtze to the clubhouse with an automatic accompaniment from manager Manuel, as per the warnings issued to both benches after the seventh inning rugby scrum. Bobby Howry relieved Sturtze and promptly threw two wild pitches before getting an RBI groundout by Juan Encarnacion. After walking Wendell Magee and striking out Tony Clark, Howry hit Shane Halter and, with only one out to go, the pot was stirred again as pitcher Doug Brocail, the former high school linebacker—aided by some top-step verbal preliminaries from Todd Jones—led the Tigers charge out of the dugout for five more minutes of brawling. Palmer—the firestarter of this Earth Day temblor—bolted out of the clubhouse and back onto the field to rejoin the festivities. When the smoke cleared, Brocail was ejected, as was White Sox coach Joe Nossek.

Crawford also tossed Howry, who was replaced by Scott Eyre, who surrendered a two-run triple to Luis Polonia (he of the helmet-swing move in *Polonia vs. Gunderson*). With the first-place White Sox lead shaved to 14-6, catcher Brad Ausmus, Fick's replacement after the first fight, killed the rally with a game-ending strikeout.

The loss dropped the Tigers to an MLB worst 4-12, and they were out-ejected by Chicago by a count of 6-5, which truly meant they could not win for losing. It took until the following Thursday for MLB muck-a-mucks to sort out the fines and punishments. At the time, it was believed to be the harshest penalty for fighting in baseball history. In the pot and kettle department, league disciplinarian (VP of on-field operations in cubicle-speak) Frank Robinson said, among other boilerplate comments: "Altercations like the one that took place in Chicago last week show a lack of sportsmanship. It sends the wrong message to our fans—particularly the young people. Fighting is not an acceptable part of the game." He then issued the first penalties of his career as MLB's elementary school principal.

Twenty-five players were fined, sixteen of them suspended. Palmer was slapped with a $3,000 tab and an eight-game suspension. Managers Garner and Manuel were suspended eight games each, while Detroit coach Juan Samuel—apparently landing the most blows during the scraps—was ordered to sit out fifteen games. Parque got a meaningless three game suspension and Ordonez and his active footwear had to sit out for five. To go with his five stitches, Foulke was handed a three-game mandatory rest. With the line for appeals forming on the left, Howry and Lee of the White Sox each got three-game suspensions. The lowest fines were $500 setbacks to Detroit hurlers Patterson and Poole. The White Sox were none too pleased to find Weaver, whose pair of hit-batsmen lit the fuse, was only fined $750.

As for the namesake instigators in *Palmer vs. Parque*, nagging injuries—none related to this fight—would end both of their careers in 2003. Palmer made a few comeback attempts after that, but his neck, shoulder and spinal problems were considered too risky for him to get back in the game. Parque's torn labrum after his most successful 13-6 campaign in 2000 would require surgery and after just six seasons in the Bigs, the former first round pick out of UCLA retired. He'd made the obligatory stop in Tampa Bay and then finally called it quits among the obscurity of the Arizona Diamondbacks minor league system, where Parque's pursuit of a comeback as a "crafty" left-hander turned out to be a mirage.

ARAMIS RAMIREZ vs. JAVIER VAZQUEZ
(PITTSBURGH PIRATES)   (MONTREAL EXPOS)
July 17, 1998, Le Stade Olympique, Montreal, Canada

ARAMIS RAMIREZ vs. BEN SHEETS
(PITTSBURGH PIRATES)   (MILWAUKEE BREWERS)
April 17, 2002, Miller Park, Milwaukee, Wisconsin

During his early years with the Pittsburgh Pirates (and it gets no earlier when you are called up at age nineteen), Aramis Ramirez seemed to take his namesake among the Three Musketeers quite literally. The Alexander

Dumas classic contains this line from chapter four, in which Aramis is angered by swashbuckling partner D'Artagnan over a handkerchief dispute: "Ah, monsieur, permit me to observe to you that you have not acted in this affair as a gallant man ought." Precisely what was on Ramirez's mind as he bolted for the mound against Javier Vazquez of the bilingual Montreal Expos on Friday, July 17, 1998? Well, based on the location of this incident, at least the French part might be right.

While heading north of the border for the weekend series, the Pirates traded starter Esteban Loaiza to Texas. Reliever Mike Williams had to make the emergency start at *Le Stade Olympique* against an Expos squad that had won three in a row. A crowd of 9,380 people were on hand to endure Expos mascot Youppi, and watch a game containing three bench-clearing incidents. The last time Williams had started a game, he was with the Phillies in September of 1996. He was ejected and later suspended five games for throwing at Montreal's Pedro Martinez twice, prompting Martinez the batter to rush the mound and kick off a brawl at Veterans Stadium. Pedro got docked eight games for his trouble, which was meant to teach him not to bean Gregg Jefferies anymore or charge the mound when Philly pitchers retaliated.

In his second start, Williams again had problems with his Montreal mound opponent as Vazquez stroked a double in the bottom of the fifth. Orlando Cabrera then followed with a grounder back to the mound. Williams whirled and threw to shortstop Lou Collier, who was between Vazquez and second base. Caught in a rundown, the native of Ponce, Puerto Rico, made a mad dash for third where Ramirez waited with the ball in his glove. As Ramirez tagged him out, Vazquez took a swipe at his glove and heated words were exchanged. Both benches cleared, and Pirates manager Lloyd McClendon was ejected from the game by first base umpire Wally Bell.

With two outs in the top of the sixth, Mark Smith was on third with one out. Vazquez then nailed Ramirez square in the back on a 2-1 pitch and the Dominican youngster was off to the races, launching his helmet with inaccurate aim at his human target. Vazquez appeared to throw a punch at the angry third baseman, but the pair of rookies were quickly surrounded by teammates. Vazquez was ejected and replaced by Australian hurler Shayne Bennett. Ramirez was also tossed from the game, and replaced by the diminutive "Polish Prince" and Pittsburgh fan favorite, Kevin Polcovich.

The benches would clear a third time in Montreal that night when Pirates reliever Elmer Dessens buzzed Rondell White up and in, but the players did not go beyond their own foul lines. Later on, Pirates first baseman Kevin Young (of *Young vs. DiFelice*) was hit by Anthony Telford in the ninth, but by then the Expos fate was sealed as the Bucs were up 5-1, thanks to the three runs scored in the inning featuring the clash of hot-headed rookies known as *Ramirez vs. Vazquez*.

After the game, Vazquez played dumb, telling the Associated Press he had no idea why Ramirez charged the mound. He was suspended five games for the incident. Ramirez, who also received a five-game suspension, chalked up his trip up the middle to Vazquez not throwing too many pitches inside in the previous innings. Having made his Major League debut only two months earlier in Milwaukee, Ramirez thought he was growing up fast on a Pirates team that had surprised a few people the year before but was still on an extended stretch of losing seasons. Would the one they call "A-Ram" learn not to lose his head and helmet so quickly? Pirates officials thought so, at least for the next three seasons. But another Ramirez "head case" signpost was up ahead, in the city (decidedly less French than Montreal) where the Musketeer made his precocious debut.

Sheets Feels the Wind

It was the first afternoon game of the 2002 season and the roof was open at Milwaukee's Miller Park. Thousands of kids were in the bleachers for the midweek matinee, and Olympian Ben Sheets was taking the hill for the Brewers, coming off an 11-10 rookie campaign. Fans of the Beer-makers had large expectations for the Louisiana native who had shown flashes of fireballing brilliance as the potential ace of the staff after being selected in the first round of the 1999 draft.

April of 2002 had been a nightmare for the Brewers, while the Pirates were riding high. McClendon had his Buccos on a six-game winning streak, and with a win against Sheets they would be in first place having swept the three-game set in Milwaukee. Davey Lopes, meanwhile, was managing the Brewers to the worst start in franchise history, with only three wins spread over the first two and half weeks of the season. Something had to give.

Ramirez, who had been hit by Sheets on May 13, 2001, stepped in against Sheets who was down 2-0 thanks to his mound opponent. Not only had lefty Dave Williams knocked in two runs with a broken-bat bloop with two outs in the second inning, Williams had plunked Brewers slugger Geoff

Jenkins, who angrily barked at the hurler as he walked to first base in the bottom of the second. Not known for throwing heat, Williams had hit Jenkins in June of 2001 during another Pirates sweep of Milwaukee, an incident that apparently left a mental bruise still fresh on Jenkins' psyche as he unleashed the verbal barbs.

Home plate umpire Ted Barrett, an amateur boxer who restores Harley Davidson motorcycles and has since become an associate pastor at an Arizona church, had a situation brewing: home team brimming with tension and frustration trying to avoid a sweep, a boisterous crowd of kids with parents fresh off a federal income tax filing deadline, a nice sunny day after a long Wisconsin winter, and plenty of the local product flowing. While the Brewers carried a palpable air of desperation, the red hot Buccos were resting regulars such as Brian Giles, Jason Kendall and Kevin Young—normal day game after a night game procedure for a team that rarely wins six games in a row.

The top of the third started with Abraham Nunez, captain of the Bucco "B" team, taking his usual called third strike. Super sub Rob Mackowiak singled to right. Up came Ramirez, who had doubled to right off Sheets before being "driven in" by the Williams bloop. As a kid in the Dominican Republic, Ramirez had dreamed of being a basketball star. He didn't take up baseball until age thirteen, but still managed to get drafted at age sixteen. It looked like the 2001 campaign was his blossoming season—he had batted .300 with 34 HR and 112 RBI. He was seen as a key to any Pittsburgh success—a homegrown youngster rising up as a power-hitting corner infielder, sorting out his temper and concentration issues with the help of the Pirates coaching staff.

After charging Sheets, the Pirates found they had lost their cleanup hitter. "It's swollen right now, we'll know tomorrow," Ramirez told MLB.com. He was not talking about the Pirates run production. He was referring to his sprained ankle, which would nag him and the Pirates the rest of the season, bringing his 2002 final numbers down to .234, 18 HR and 71 RBI.

Exactly who landed on Ramirez's ankle is not clear. What is clear is Ramirez was nailed on his left hip and he bolted for the mound, head down. Halfway there, he took his helmet by the visor and fired it at Sheets as hard as he could, missing him. Sheets threw his glove at Ramirez, in reflexive retaliation. Sheets then completely dodged the Ramirez juggernaut, moving to the first base side of the mound as his catcher, Raul

Casanova, got a piece of the attacker wearing the road grays, spinning him around slightly and opening him up for a tackle by Brewers first baseman Richie Sexson. Before the pair landed on the grass, the arriving hordes slammed into the scrum. The second wave hit with much more force—the Bucco brigade running from the dugout on the third base line. Sometimes the longer run helps to move some bodies, and odds are Ramirez's sprained ankle might have been from friendly fire.

The center field camera shows a veteran umpire at his most unfazed. Second base ump Tim McClelland, he of the George Brett pine tar incident (*Brett vs. umpire McClelland*) and more than two decades wearing the blue in the majors, is seen walking ever so slowly toward the churning pile of National League Central ballplayers, as if he was approaching a shop window filled with spring blazers. His arms are crossed until he gets a few yards closer to the action. As Sheets was ejected and left the field, the gold medalist from the 2000 Olympics received a standing ovation, quickly followed by boos rained upon the umpires. Ramirez was also sent to the showers and later punished with a seven-game ban as a repeat helmet tossing offender. Mike Buddie took over pitching chores for Milwaukee. After the Brewers rallied to tie the game, Buddie threw a gopher ball to Adrian Brown in the fifth, whose solo shot bounced off the top of the fence and over, making the difference in a 3-2 Pirates win.

MIKE SWEENEY vs. JEFF WEAVER
(KANSAS CITY ROYALS)   (DETROIT TIGERS)
August 10, 2001, Kaufman Stadium, Kansas City, Missouri

One of the more dramatic mound charges in recent history occurred thanks to several elements, including the role of the innocent rosin bag, a grip enhancement device introduced to the sport in 1925. Though several pitchers throughout the history of the game have abused the cloth sack of rosin to doctor the baseball, prompting rule changes, the bag has rarely been the centerpiece of a brawl. Mets reliever Turk Wendell used to rile the Shea Stadium crowd by slamming the rosin bag to the mound to end his warmup routine with puffs of rosin "smoke" rising behind him. But on August 10, 2001 in Kansas City, devout Christian Mike Sweeney's request that home plate umpire Mike Fichter ask devilish pitcher Jeff Weaver to move the rosin bag in the sixth inning would prompt a pitcher-batter rhubarb with the unusual twist that no pitch was thrown.

Sweeney came up with two outs and Carlos Beltran on second base. Fichter, a reserve umpire working behind the plate, went out to the mound at Sweeney's request. Weaver said he was not going to move the bag because he didn't put it there. And there it remained. Fichter turned around to head back to the plate, and Weaver turned his back on Sweeney, who claims the pitcher called him profane names. As Sweeney began his charge, Fichter, mask in hand, was quickly in front of him but could not get hold of the dependable Royals slugger from Orange, California. Sweeney seemed to shed Fichter much like a football linebacker disposing of a decoy receiver's attempt to block him. Though some newspaper accounts had Sweeney firing his batting helmet and then charging, video replays clearly show Sweeney carrying his helmet until he got to the mound. Then he fired it viciously at Weaver, who, with his back still turned, had sauntered off the back of the mound in what he thought was a nonchalant snubbing of Sweeney. Weaver not only surrendered his high ground, but Sweeney gained it as he crested the hill with downward momentum as he pursued Weaver into the middle of the grass infield.

Radar guns unfortunately did not pick up the fired helmet's speed, which appeared to graze Weaver's forearm on a sharp downward vector. Once on the ground, the helmet would do some damage. The combined weight of Sweeney and his dance partner Weaver—totaling around four hundred twenty pounds—toppled backward and right onto the royal blue helmet, which put a dig into Weaver's back and a gash into Sweeney's head. And then the pileup began, with baserunner Beltran arriving first and rather cautiously, like he was awaiting instructions from a coach on whether to proceed with breaking up or joining the violent tangle. Within seconds, reinforcements arrived from the Detroit and Kansas City dugouts. Tigers catcher Robert Fick was especially harsh upon arrival, digging through bodies for Sweeney. After Sweeney was separated from Weaver and the rank and file was distracted by a shouting match between Tigers center fielder Wendell Magee and Royals manager Tony Muser, Sweeney would again pass on the biblical option of turning the other cheek, instead deciding to tackle Fick, with the catcher's head ironically striking home plate on impact. With Sweeney now doing a St. Vitus dance around Fick, it was probably a good thing Kansas City hurler Paul Byrd (of *Eddie Perez vs. Byrd*) pinned the exhausted Tigers catcher to the plate, protecting him from further damage from heaven above and the once-angelic Sweeney, who by the end of this battle had his hair standing straight up, a la Klaus Kinski.

Sweeney vs. Weaver lasted twelve minutes, according to press accounts. Tigers manager Phil "Scrap Iron" Garner, a Tennessean who lives up to his nickname, called it "the most vicious thing I've ever seen." In the end, *Sweeney vs. Weaver* contained an all-star cast of established brawlers. Among the Detroit coaches fined by MLB for their participation in the battle were Juan Samuel, Ed Ott and Bill Madlock, while Kansas City pitching coach Al Nipper checked in as a fellow ejectee along with Detroit bench coach Doug Monsolmo. At one point, Monsolmo was the only person holding Nipper and Madlock apart as they screamed and clawed at each other.

Sweeney was issued a ten-game suspension and a $3,000 fine by MLB VP Frank Robinson (of the famous *F. Robinson vs. E. Mathews* in 1959). Fick, who got an eight-game suspension, had also been involved in a massive donnybrook accompanying *Palmer vs. Parque* in Chicago the year before. Garner denounced the unbalanced punishment dealt by Robinson in *Sweeney vs. Weaver*. "That's a joke," Garner told the Associated Press. "We didn't start this but we've got six people fined or suspended and they have three . . . it doesn't add up." Ott (of *Ott vs. Millan*) was fined, Samuel (of *Samuel vs. N. Charlton*) was suspended one game, and Madlock (*Madlock vs. et al.*—fights too numerous for a parenthetical of reasonable length) got a two-game rest. Magee also was fined by MLB for his animated conversation with Muser. Aside from Nipper (of *Nipper vs. Bradley, et al.*) and Sweeney, catcher Brent Mayne was the only other Royal to be punished as he also received a monetary penalty for his involvement.

Garner's team was winning 2-1 at the time of Sweeney's charge, and the Detroit manager sarcastically lauded the effort to physically knock out a pitcher if he's throwing a good game. Dave McCarty replaced Sweeney after the fight, drew a walk, and then Raul Ibanez would tie the game, driving in Beltran with a single. Despite an inside the park home run by Detroit's Shane Halter, the Royals put this one in the win column by a 7-3 score.

Weaver, who was also fined, would stay in Detroit until July of 2002 when the former first-round draft pick of the Tigers and his marketable anti-authority tendencies were dealt to the Yankees as part of a three-team deal that included Oakland getting Ted Lilly. The A's overrated GM Billy Beane provided the final piece of the five-man deal by sending the Tigers the "player to be named later"—none other than Jeremy Bonderman. Weaver went from New York to the Dodgers in 2004 for Kevin Brown, then left as a free agent for Orange County and the Angels in 2006. He was dealt halfway through a so-so season to St. Louis to make room for his brother Jared in the Anaheim rotation. With the Cardinals, Weaver would square off against Bonderman and his original team in the Fall Classic, with the Northridge, California native spinning a gem to seal the Cardinals world championship in Game 5. On the way out of the dugout to celebrate with his teammates, Weaver appeared to be apologetic to a policeman whom he almost plowed over. Muser, meanwhile, employed a great metaphor regarding his player with the churchgoing tendencies, elevating Sweeney to apostle status. "When Michael Sweeney tells me something, I take it as gospel," Muser said. Sweeney hurt his wrist in the melee, and after serving his ten games, he would gingerly finish out the season with only three home runs and seventeen RBI.

Sweeney vs. Weaver would also serve as a warm-up to these two franchises meeting again for a dance around the Detroit diamond in 2005 (*Runelvys Hernandez vs. C. Guillen*), though Sweeney would have a more predictable choirboy role in that fracas. Prior to both of those incidents, these franchises made some noise in July of 1994 when Royals heavyweight Bob Hamelin charged the mound occupied by Detroit reliever Greg Cadaret. Hamelin would also make a spirited run at Tigers third baseman Travis Fryman during the melee.

Here's a quote from Sweeney several months after the fight: "The night after the brawl, I couldn't sleep and two things stuck in my mind: Number one, have I embarrassed the name of God in what I did? And number two, have I embarrassed the name of the Kansas City Royals?" Sweeney should know by now, given the recent years of cellar-dwelling by the Royals, that number two is next to impossible, even with God's help.

Chapter 4:
NINETY FEET OF MAYHEM

Though most baseball fights involve the invasive arrival of the actual ball—thrown by one human being at another—a large portion of on field disputes occur in the paths leading to the bases and on the bases themselves. Most sportswriters through the years have written off these incidents, along with any other type of baseball fight, as what the British would call "handbags." The image of two elderly women swinging purses at each other in a crowded department store comes to mind, a kind of harmless, if not pedestrian, altercation. There is a good deal of incidental contact between baserunners and infielders. Basically, the runner's desire for the small square haven of the base clashes with the duty of the fielder to eliminate his foe either by preceding him to the base for a force out, or by application of the leather appendage containing the baseball—commonly known as being "tagged out." When overapplied or done too zealously, tags themselves can be a form of violence. For infielders, the double play, known in the cliché-heavy announcer's booth as "a pitcher's best friend," can in fact be more of a *danse macabre*, especially when the fielder at second base is distracted by an errant or tardy throw, leaving him open and sometimes blind to the onrushing runner whose top priority is preventing the completion of a double play.

In a July 20, 1982, game at the Metrodome, for example, the Twins and Brewers got into a "double play" war in the middle innings that resulted in a benchclearing. In the sixth, lumbering rookie Kent Hrbek took out Milwaukee second baseman Jim Gantner with a monster slide while Gantner was turning two on a Gary Gaetti grounder. Gantner left the game with a bruised thigh and Brewers manager Harvey Kuenn screamed his head off at Hrbek as he returned to the dugout. Kuenn later said Hrbek's slide was a "cheap shot."

The next inning, Milwaukee's Robin Yount tried to break up a twin-killing being turned by Minnesota shortstop Lenny Faedo. Yount slid into second way out of the baseline, tangled up Faedo and was called out for interference. When he got up, the 1982 AL MVP had words with Twins second baseman John Castino. As the discussion heated, the dugouts spilled forth onto the AstroTurf and soon both teams were staggering around second base holding each other's jerseys and engaging in a group shove. As Hrbek, Milwaukee's intended target, rushed to help teammate Faedo, Brewers pitcher Bob McClure sought him out and squared away to fight him. Four more Milwaukee players jumped in, and it was catcher Ted Simmons who ended up pounding on Hrbek's head a little bit. Hrbek said he hadn't intended on hurting Gantner and was appalled at being assaulted in the next inning. "I was just playing peacemaker," Hrbek said. "I hate fighting. But tempers flare and things happen."

One of the most famous base path battles was a result of the game's challenging 3-6-3 double play: The grounder to first base is fielded by the first baseman who pivots, throws to second base to force the runner and quickly retreats to his own base to receive the return throw that will elimi-nate the batter. Economy of motion is required, as is lively footwork and precise throws. Many things can go awry on this play. Someone gets in the runner's way, or he is struck with the throw, or a spike catches a misplaced ankle back on first base. Throws can sail into left field or the photographer's cage along the dugout behind first. More often than not, the second baseman can only be an oafish spectator as the first baseman and shortstop share the defensive limelight. When it is completed successfully, the 3-6-3 is an exhil-arating play. When it is botched, it is downright painful to watch.

PETE ROSE vs. DERREL "BUD" HARRELSON
(CINCINNATI REDS)   (NEW YORK METS)

October 8, 1973, NLCS Game 3,
Shea Stadium, Queens, New York

The story of how Pete Rose got the nickname "Charlie Hustle" involves another player known for carousing and not entirely wholesome off-field activities. It was Spring Training of Rose's rookie year—1963. Rose drew a walk and sprinted to first base, a process he would repeat 1,566 times in his twenty-four-year career. He'd seen Enos "Country" Slaughter (a combatant in *Doby vs. Ditmar*) do it and agreed it was a good idea. When Mickey Mantle saw Rose's quickened pace to first base during the exhibition game, he asked who "Charlie Hustle" was. (Some reports have Whitey Ford posing the question about Rose.)

Rose was, in fact, all about hustle. A Cincinnati native who was signed by the Reds out of high school, Rose made it to the big leagues after a few seasons in the minors and settled in as the Reds regular second baseman. By 1973, Rose had shifted to left field with the arrival of Joe Morgan. But not before making the 1960s an unforgettable decade of quality performances. He took the NL Rookie of the Year Award in 1963, won back-to-back batting titles in 1968–69, became an All-Star regular after 1965 and collected a pair of Gold Glove awards in 1969–70.

Many say 1973 was Rose's best season. He hit .338 to earn his third batting title, was named NL Most Valuable Player and had a career high 230 hits. His image evoked quintessential "hard-nosed" baseball: the lantern jaw, crew cut, extreme crouch for a batting stance, headfirst slides and frequent collisions with catchers and infielders on close plays.

The 1973 Reds battled the Giants and Dodgers through mid-summer and took over the NL West lead as September dawned. They finished 99-63, which was well ahead of the sluggish NL East division. The Mets took the East crown with an unimpressive 82-79 record. They were in last place on August 27, but would hurdle over five teams languishing around .500 to edge the Cardinals at the wire. Who knew they would see their starters twirl three consecutive complete games in the NLCS? The third complete game was a 9-2 domination by Jerry Koosman in game three, which was somewhat overshadowed by the pyrotechnics surrounding *Rose vs. Harrelson*. It was not only a fairly heavy brawl in the center of the diamond, but the fans added some danger by unleashing projectiles from the stands in the following inning.

Koosman, whom the Mets had signed in 1964 after seeing him pitch for the U.S. Army during his Vietnam era military service, was not the only military man on the Amazin's. Harrelson served in the National Guard reserve on many a weekend during his career. He grew up in Niles,

California, and longed to play for the Giants. But San Francisco's front office saw Harrelson as too small, and he signed with the Mets out of San Francisco State. By 1966, Harrelson was on his way to becoming a fan favorite through his quality fielding and quick feet on the base paths. Nothing wins over the fans better than stealing home and successfully pulling off the "hidden ball" trick—two thrilling feats executed by Harrelson during the 1966 season.

Like Richard M. Nixon and Spiro T. Agnew in the White House, in 1973 the Reds seemed to know their autumn days were numbered after splitting the first two games at home and heading for Queens for games three, four, and—if necessary—five. Jon Matlack had mastered the Reds with a two-hit, 5-0 blanking in Game 2, which followed Tom Seaver's complete game 2-1 loss in the series opener.

When Harrelson and Rose met at second base at Shea Stadium in Game 3, the mighty Reds were under Koosman's thumb. The atmosphere was already a bit charged as Harrelson had reportedly upset a few Cincinnati players by comparing the "Big Red Machine" to his own light-hitting self. One account had Morgan confronting Harrelson about the remark.

In Game 3, Koosman had brushed Rose off the plate in one of his early at-bats. No one is certain whether Rose had stored up rage from this incident, or he just didn't care for the words exchanged between the two switchhitters. Rose had a single in the fifth inning with one out and was moving to second on Joe Morgan's grounder to Mets first baseman John Milner, who turned to throw to Harrelson at second base. Rose was forced out. Harrelson returned fire to Milner to get Morgan and the twin-killing was in the books. After his throw, Harrelson fell on top of Rose, who employed the "pop-up" slide in trying to break up the double play. As they were untangling, Harrelson said Rose bumped him with his elbow. Profanities were exchanged, then a shoving match and some upright wrestling that ended with Rose, roughly forty pounds heavier than his foe, lifting Harrelson and then pinning him in the Shea Stadium dirt. Mets third baseman Wayne Garrett arrived first and began flailing at Rose as the dugouts and bullpens emptied. Morgan also made his way to the scene as 53,967 fans at Shea were buzzing with extracurricular excitement.

Harrelson suffered a three-inch scrape over his left eye. "Maybe I did lose the fight," he told AP after the game. "But we won the ballgame. That's what really counts." Harrelson said he didn't think the incident would result in further animosity in game four, and he held no hard feelings toward Rose and his aggressive style of play. Rose issued another of his classic quotes in the wake of his toppling the Mets shortstop. "I'm no little girl out there. I'm supposed to give the fans their money's worth and try to bust up double plays—and shortstops."

Playing the roles of restarters as the fight was about to calm down were Pedro Borbon, the Reds workhorse reliever, and Buzz Capra, a solid contributor in the Mets bullpen. (The two right-handers had twenty-one wins between them in 1973.) Borbon allegedly "sucker punched" Capra on the fringe of the mob. The two relievers then exchanged haymakers, and Borbon, who in 1974 would be nicknamed "Dracula" after biting a Pittsburgh player during the ugly *Kison vs. Billingham* brawl, again demonstrated the strength of his teeth. He had once bitten the cover off a baseball to impress a Reds teammate. This time, he took out his anger on a Mets cap. After the fight was finally disbanded and teams returned to their dugouts, the players collected their caps from the ground. Borbon inadvertently picked up a Mets cap and was wearing it. When a teammate pointed out his transgression, he took off the blue cap and tore it to shreds with his teeth.

An AP photo of Rose and Harrelson squaring off shows them standing with perfect posture in a dreamlike cloud of dust. The hatless Rose has his right arm extended, forearm muscles flexing, with a square fist an inch from Harrelson's chin. The shortstop looks agitated and somewhat defenseless with his flip down sunglasses under his brim, his glove bent awkwardly inward by Rose's arms which are seen extended almost in Frankenstein fashion. Rose is captured in perfect profile, with lettering from an outfield billboard giving his famous mop of black hair a religious halo of some kind. Harrelson's eyes are closed, and his right hand is open with his pinky slightly extended. Rose is wearing the elastic-belted road gray pants, Harrelson has the old-fashioned leather belt through the belt loops of the Mets pinstripes. Rose is bare armed, free of accessories. Harrelson is wearing a long-sleeved blue undershirt. Rose's fighting stance captured in the photo resembles the fixed postures of the "Rock 'Em Sock 'Em Robots" toy, featuring chiseled red and blue (appropriate colors for *Rose vs. Harrelson*) robots with triangular heads that pop up on a metal rod if the chin is struck with enough force.

Rose finished his historic career with the most hits of any player in the history of the game—4,256. Harrelson, who briefly tried amateur softball after leaving the Mets in 1977, finished with 1,120 hits. The two men would be reunited as Philadelphia Phillies in 1979, Rose playing first base and Harrelson used frequently at second base. Harrelson was correct about no hard feelings—both players have made appearances together to happily autograph photos of their 1973 playoff fracas.

Rose did, however, continue to bash the Shea faithful in the wake of the donnybrook. When the Reds relievers tried to return to the bullpen after the fight, fans showered them with cups, fruit, bottles and any trash they could get their hands on. A beer can caught Gary Nolan in the face, cutting him slightly. Pitcher Clay Carroll said he feared for his life. It got worse when the Reds took the field in the bottom of the fifth.

When Rose made his way out to left field, a whiskey bottle whizzed dangerously close to him and manager Sparky Anderson took his players off the field. "They're supposed to be human beings they sell tickets to out there, and they were throwing whiskey bottles," Anderson said. The angry Shea mob was calmed after Mets manager Yogi Berra sent Willie Mays, Tom Seaver, Rusty Staub, and Cleon Jones out to left field to plead for peace.

Rose came up big in Game Four, homering in the twelfth inning to bolster a 2-1 Reds victory. In game five, which the Mets won 7-2 to send them to the World Series against Oakland, the mob invaded the field after the final out. The terrified Reds brandished bats in the dugout in case things really got out of hand. Team officials and family members had to be taken to a special area under the stands as the fans crowded the railings along the field late in the game. Rose, who was on base when the game ended, managed to make it through the chaotic swirl of gnashing teeth and reached the clubhouse unscathed. "They brought the fans from the zoo to the ballpark and they bring them back after the game," Rose said. Rose's wife, who greeted the Reds at the airport in Cincinnati, told the AP: "It's a good thing I wasn't there. I would have been in jail for fighting."

CHAN HO PARK vs. TIM BELCHER
(LOS ANGELES DODGERS)   (ANAHEIM ANGELS)
June 5, 1999, Dodger Stadium, Los Angeles, California

Interleague play was in its third season when the Anaheim Angels and Los Angeles Dodgers met at Chavez Ravine on June 5, 1999, for more of what the MLB marketing department has boldly dubbed "The Freeway Series." The novelty of American League pitchers having to stand in and face live ammo from senior circuit hurlers had but a scintilla of appeal remaining. The novelty of Asian pitchers had long ago worn off, especially at Dodger Stadium. But Park was the first Korean to make the Bigs, and definitely the first Korean to be fined $3,000 and suspended for seven games by the league office.

Park vs. Belcher carries a thick file of cross references. The colorful scrap joins other interleague brawls worthy of "doozy" status (*Barrett vs. Pierzynski, F. Rodriguez vs. Grudzielanek* aka *Dodgers vs. Mariners*) and a number of pitcher-on-pitcher conflicts (*Gooden vs. Combs, P. Martinez vs. Mike Williams* and the aforementioned *Kison vs. Billingham*), as well as the always-entertaining karate kick incidents (*Corrales vs. D. Stewart, G. Bell vs. Kison*). It is also interesting because it did not involve a pitch, but instead a tag. This exact same formula was the cause of a fight between Houston's Don Wilson and southpaw George Stone of Atlanta, who fielded Wilson's lame bunt in the Astrodome in June of 1969. After Stone's tag knocked down Wilson in the base path, Wilson got up and charged Stone and the two exchanged punches. The ten-minute brawl brought out Astros John Edwards and Doug Rader, while the Braves pitcher was backed up by the illustrious trio of Rico Carty, Orlando Cepeda and Hammerin' Hank Aaron.

Tim Belcher was born in central Ohio. He attended Mount Vernon Nazarene University, which was known as Mount Vernon Nazarene College during his days there in the early 1980s. The small campus in football-crazed Knox County adheres to the Nazarene church's belief in abstaining from alcohol, dancing and wearing jewelry. USC it ain't. When the university retired Belcher's baseball uniform number, it did so "in a private ceremony," according to a university press release, befitting Belcher's rather reticent nature and therefore avoiding the crush of humanity that surely would have attended any public event marking such an occasion in so glamorous a location. Belcher bounced around after being drafted by the Yankees and finally made his debut with the Dodgers in 1987. He made serious noise in the Dodgers defeat of the Mets in the 1988 NLCS. He was thirty-seven-years old and with his seventh and final team when he and Park made their own noise along the first base line at Dodger Stadium in 1999.

Park's college days were spent at one of South Korea's largest, most prominent schools—Hanyang University in Seoul. The university cranks out a lot of engineers, which makes its motto, "Love in truth and in deed" almost as strange as its founding philosophy. The Hanyang Web site states: "The founding philosophy . . . is to foster individuals who understand love in terms of practicing the virtues of diligence, honesty, modesty and service, ultimately to make a leading contribution to the community, society, nation and all humankind." It says absolutely nothing about karate-kicking your opponent after being tagged out on a bunt play.

Earlier in the game of June 5 against the Angels, apparently frustrated at giving up a grand slam to light-hitting Anaheim catcher Matt Walbeck, the twenty-five-year-old Park brushed back Randy Velarde. A few innings later, he knocked Velarde down again with a head-high pitch.

In the fifth inning, down 4-0, Park was trying to help his own cause by laying down a one-out sacrifice bunt. Belcher fielded the bunt on the first-base side of the mound and proceeded toward the baseline, eschewing the throw to first in order to tag out Park.

The play unfolded innocently enough, so much so that first baseman Mo Vaughn could be seen casually ambling back to his position as Belcher, ball in hand, moved toward the base path where he would await the oncoming Park.

Park began to slow down his jog to first as he neared Belcher, the successful sacrifice (one of six executed by Park in 1999) having moved the runner over. Belcher, still slightly in motion, applied the tag to Park's chest with the ball gripped in his right hand. The tag looked routine, and certainly was nothing on the scale of the sledgehammering issued by catcher Dave Valle on Chad Curtis in the tag-inspired battle royale *Valle vs. Curtis*, or the claymore mine unleashed by Carlton Fisk on Lou Piniella in *Fisk vs. Piniella* at Yankee Stadium in 1976. Belcher's glove hand swung around as his momentum forced him to revolve around Park as the pitcher took his medicine. For a millisecond, the two pitchers embraced in the style of a senior prom photo—Belcher behind the shorter Park, both facing forward. But there was no corsage in sight, especially as Park did an abrupt about-face, his left elbow striking Belcher's sternum. Words were exchanged as Belcher objected to the unnecessary sharp-boned contact.

Belcher then assumed an usher-like air, pointing with his glove hand in the direction of the Dodger dugout, issuing Park specific directions to his reserved seat on the bench. Park shoved Belcher away, creating an adequate gap of personal space between them. More words brought Park's left forearm upwards, directly into Belcher's grille, the follow through knocking his winged-A Angels cap off the back of his head. His halo having vanished, the reeling Angels hurler clearly made a mental note that it was indeed "go time" as they say back in Knox County. Park had moved away from him in the direction of home plate, where umpire Charlie Reliford was making his way up the line.

Vaughn's casual stroll back to first was interrupted, and the first baseman made a feeble attempt to grasp Belcher as the pitcher took a futile swipe at Park with his glove hand. His other hand still held the precious cowhide, which he would finally toss backward as he rushed forward to get at Park, who planted his right foot and elevated and extended his left foot toward Belcher's upper thigh. With Reliford looming directly behind him, it looked as if Park was trying to plant his left foot and pivot around to strike Belcher with his right foot. As both feet were in the air, Belcher grabbed Park's left foot and halted the blender-blade spin move.

The still photo most newspapers selected to use from this melee depicted Park as a rad dude skateboarder—his curved, airborne posture connected only by his feet to Belcher's midsection. Park looked like he was attempting an ollie grind on Belcher's belt buckle. Belcher's head was down, and it appeared Park's right knee might have grazed the pitcher's forehead as gravity took over and Park fell to the ground with Belcher on top of him.

With Park face down and still helmeted, Belcher began the first of five blows with his right fist. Having concluded his tae kwon do kicking portion of the program, Park seemed to be switching to a ground fighting strategy. He tried to rise from his slumped position as his helmet finally fell off and Belcher continued to rain punches inward on his prostrate foe, even with Dodgers first base coach John Shelby attached to his back. By this time, Vaughn had reasserted his initial slippery grip and other Angels players, led by catcher Grebeck, arrived to aid and abet in *Park vs. Belcher*. Troy Glaus, in his first full season with the Angels, scampered mouselike around the pile, looking for a low opening where he could get a grip on someone or perhaps deliver some blows of his own.

Park was ejected. Belcher stayed in the game and saw his 4-0 lead dissolve into a 7-4 Los Angeles triumph, keyed by Devon White's grand slam in the next inning. He was relieved in the sixth by Mark Petkovsek (of another interleague scrap known as *Damon vs. Petkovsek*).

Park told the AP Belcher used an obscenity in telling him to make his way to the dugout. Teammate Eric Young credited Park with earning some respect throughout the clubhouse, citing *Park vs. Belcher* a spark for the victorious Dodgers. At least this pitcher-tagging-out-a-bunter dispute did not follow the ugly path of *Randle vs. Wilcox*, a 1974 melee in Arlington, Texas, which would eventually pit several Cleveland Indians against Texas Rangers fans, with police having to separate the two rather sorry groups.

The fine and suspension came down on Park three days after his meeting with Belcher. He said he was expecting three or five games, and that seven was too long. Belcher avoided reporters, issuing a terse statement after the game in which he forwarded his respect to the umpiring crew for allowing him to remain in the game (and therefore absorb his fifth loss of the season).

Two years earlier, Park had faced the wrath of another Angel when he buzzed the head of Tony Phillips (*Phillips vs. fan Hovorka*) during an interleague contest in Anaheim. Phillips was restrained by catcher Tom Prince and first baseman Eric Karros, who did most of the fighting on Park's behalf. Suffice it to say, when a certain South Korean hurler is involved in the "Freeway Series," road rage seems to be the order of the day.

GEORGE BRETT
(KANSAS CITY ROYALS)
VS.
"DIRTY" KURT BEVACQUA
(MILWAUKEE BREWERS)

May 11, 1975, Royals Stadium, Kansas City, Missouri

Unfortunately, some baseball fights cannot be dissected frame by drama-filled frame and ultimately converted into the chariot race from *Ben Hur*. Some are just as mundane as advertised, and such was the case one May afternoon in 1975 late in a shutout game at Royals Stadium when a future Hall of Famer, coming off his AL Rookie of the Year season, unsuccessfully tried to break up a double play against a second baseman nicknamed "Dirty" Kurt.

George Brett is probably best known among baseball anarchy scholars for his lead role in *G. Brett vs. umpire McClelland*, aka "The Pine Tar

Incident" at Yankee Stadium in July of 1983 (removing the existing stigma and heckling material related to his public hemorrhoids during the 1980 World Series). He was also part of a rare postseason fight in *G. Brett vs. G. Nettles* in the 1978 ALCS. Brett made the Hall of Fame in 1999, six years after his retirement in 1993. He spent all of his twenty-one seasons wearing Royals blue and manning third base as a fixture among the mod confines of Royals Stadium.

Bevacqua, a Miami Beach native who played for six teams in his fifteen seasons in MLB, was Brett's teammate in Kansas City for half of the 1973 campaign and half of Brett's stellar 1974 season. Aside from his participation in the grudge legacy of *North vs. Bird* with the Royals in 1973, "Dirty" Kurt was known far and wide for bringing a slight element of on field sleaze to the national pastime. Dodgers manager Tommy Lasorda, never short on hyperbole, loved to cajole Bevacqua on his lack of hitting skills (lifetime average: .236).

On May 11, 1975, with Steve Busby well on his way to a 4-0 shutout win over the Brewers, the Royals batted in the bottom of the seventh. Frank White stroked a lead off single and was moved to second by a Buck Martinez sacrifice bunt. After Jim Wohlford walked, Brett came to the plate against Bill Champion. He promptly singled home White and Wohlford advanced to third as the Royals went up 4-0.

Champion was lifted by manager Del Crandall, who brought in Eduardo Rodriguez. He induced Amos Otis to hit a double-play grounder to shortstop Tim Johnson, who threw to Bevacqua covering second, who relayed on to George Scott at first, retiring the side as fans busied themselves penciling in the 6-4-3 on their scorecards. But before the 11,163 in attendance could finish their scorecard paperwork (which also included Harmon Killebrew's nineteenth and final career stolen base), there was commotion at the keystone. Brett had been forced at second, but went barreling into the pivoting Bevacqua, tangling his leg and bringing him downward. Brett said Bevacqua purposely buried a knee in his chest. "I hauled off and slugged him, and he slugged me," Brett told the AP after the game. "He's known as a dirty ballplayer." Both Brett and Bevacqua were ejected from the game.

Yes, this is the same Bevacqua who was hailed as the winner of the 1975 Bazooka Bubble Blowing contest, appearing on a special card with Joe Garagiola and featured on the television show *This Week in Baseball*. So to youthful fans, Bevacqua was a cuddly guy who chewed the same brand as they did and could blow a 14-inch bubble. To the adults making up the MLB player's circuit, he was indeed "Dirty" Kurt.

In *Brett vs. Bevacqua*, Mr. Big Bubble claimed Brett grabbed his leg and tripped him. "I turned around and hit him. That's the thing to do, isn't it?" Bevacqua was quoted in the AP game story. Bevacqua added he was too quick for Brett and was able to avoid the punch of the man nicknamed "Mullet." He said he didn't look for trouble, and yet he'd been in other fights. Bevacqua said his clash with Sal Bando (a by-product of *North vs. Bird* in '73) was "like being hit by a freight train." When asked about the other fights, Bevacqua paused and laughed. "Yeah, a couple," he said, "with my wife." Odds are, if Bevacqua was playing in 2008, he would be given his own reality TV show.

RAY KNIGHT VS. ERIC DAVIS
(NEW YORK METS)   (CINCINNATI REDS)
July 22, 1986, Riverfront Stadium, Cincinnati, Ohio

Advancing the Mets-Reds brawl legacy from second base (*Rose vs. Harrelson*) to third, this incident is one of at least five major conflagrations during a colorful championship season for the Amazin's. It is also a case where one combatant eventually became a manager with the other combatant occupying a spot on his player roster. In addition to *Knight vs. E. Davis* on this date, there was also the five-minute uprising known as *V. Coleman vs. F. Williams* in the Cards-Giants game in St. Louis. It would be another decade before Vince Coleman would don a Mets uniform and bring his own brand of pyrotechnic trouble to Shea Stadium, but in July of 1986, he was still second fiddle as the brash Mets had already been making headlines well before the July 22 extra-innings circus at Riverfront Stadium.

Four days earlier in Houston, a quartet of Mets players led by Ron Darling and Tim Teufel clashed with a pair of off-duty policemen working security outside a nightclub with the slightly sci-fi moniker "Cooter's Executive Games and Burgers." The dispute apparently involved the players drinking beer outside the establishment. Legal troubles surrounding the incident would extend well into the following season; meanwhile a Cooter's manager told a restaurant trade magazine his business was up twenty percent after the highly-publicized Mets tussle with the authorities. Apparently, the Mets players were not able to resist the allure of one of the club's specialty cocktails called the "Betcha Can't"—an assemblage of light and dark rums and fruit juices intended to be shared by six patrons with six straws dipping into a sixty-ounce champagne glass. Despite the off-field distractions, the Mets had built a giant lead in the National League East and rolled into Cincinnati to face an inconsistent Reds team featuring player/manager Pete Rose.

When Rose left the Reds for Philadelphia in 1979, his replacement at third base was a Georgian named Ray Knight, who had his work cut out for him in attempting to win over the Cincinnati fans. Despite good numbers, the fans were reluctant to embrace him, and he was eventually traded to Houston for Cesar Cedeno in December 1981. By late 1984, Knight was playing for the Mets.

Eric Davis came out of Los Angeles as yet another youth with the ubiquitous "next Willie Mays" label. His skills were well-rounded, and before long he'd earned the nickname "Eric the Red" from the Cincinnati faithful. Part of his game was terrifying opposing catchers by stealing bases almost at will.

The Reds were up 3-1 heading into the ninth inning, with the only controversy along the way being Davis's old Los Angeles boyhood buddy Darryl Strawberry's ejection for arguing balls and strikes in the sixth. (Just eleven days earlier, Strawberry had charged the mound at Shea, angered after getting hit by Braves hurler David Palmer, who put an abrupt end to *Strawberry vs. D. Palmer* with a well-placed throw of his glove, nailing the Straw right in the gob and knocking him off course. The same glove-throw was also used less effectively by St. Louis pitcher Allen Watson in *Destrade vs. Watson* in which Orestes landed a sharp right after taking some leather to the face from Watson.) With two men on base and two outs, Reds closer John Franco watched in astonishment from the mound as outfielder Dave Parker dropped a routine fly ball, allowing the Mets to tie the score—one of a gazillion breaks that would go the Mets way all season long and well into the cliffhanger 1986 postseason. Parker was among several Cincinnati veterans who were not pleased with the Mets arrogant demeanor in 1986.

The trouble started when Davis, pinch-running for Rose, stole second and then third base, which put him at forty-seven for the year on the way to 349 in his career. As Davis executed a Rose-style pop-up slide into third, Knight was taking the throw from catcher Gary Carter which was a hair late. Standing after his slide, Davis's backside slightly bumped into Knight and they seemed to brace each other to maintain balance. On top of the play, umpire Eric Gregg executed three emphatic safe signs as he marched forward toward Knight and Davis a few steps. As Davis seemed to react to a slight bump, Knight brought his glove hand up into Davis's face. Gregg, not as voluminous as he would become later in his career, was still marching forward and was about to step between the two players. Knight's glove knocked Davis's helmet off, and like Rose thirteen years before in the play-offs, the husband of golfer Nancy Lopez threw a right cross from a perfectly upright position to the jaw of Davis, spinning his head backward. Gregg took another step and had embraced the reeling Davis, completely cutting him off from his attacker as Knight followed his perfect right with a left from his glove hand, leather still employed, which might have grazed Gregg's beefy shoulder. On May 27, Knight had been the centerpiece in *Knight vs. Neidenfuer* in which the Mets third baseman charged the mound against the Dodgers pitcher, fists flying with catcher Mike Scioscia in pursuit. The Mets, of course, won the game 8-1 and Darling ran his record to 6-0 and no one was ejected following the old NL West rivals' rhubarb. Knight was fined $300, and Neidenfuer had to take out a loan to pay his $250 fine. It was during the pile-up on the mound that Neidenfuer called for big league manicures. "There was just a lot of scratching going on underneath that pile," he told the press. "There are a lot of long fingernails in this league."

As *Knight vs. E. Davis* escalated into a fifteen-minute event, the first back-up and reinforcements to arrive included batter Eddie Milner, who went in the direction of pitcher Jesse Orosco, and catcher Gary Carter, who pulled a smooth move with his equipment. Having escaped umpire Gregg's embrace, Davis was immediately felled by Carter who first put his catcher's mask on Davis' stomach. When he brought the Cincinnati gazelle to the Astroturf, he fell on top of his own mask, was immediately winded, and therefore out of the fight. With the benches and bullpens emptied, mellow Met Mookie Wilson found himself squared off with Bill Gullickson, one of several Cincinnati pitchers intent on starring roles in this particular brouhaha. Gullickson freed himself off Wilson long enough to join Reds ace Mario Soto in grabbing Mets rookie Kevin Mitchell, a product of San Diego's street gangs who was being sought after by Parker, who himself had four or five Mets clinging to him. Both Gullickson and Soto paid dearly for their attempt to throttle Mitchell as he shed Gullickson quickly and tossed Soto like a rag doll. Reds starter Tom Browning then stepped in against Mitchell and managed to remove Mitchell's gold chain in an abbreviated skirmish among the throng.

Meanwhile, Reds pitcher John Denny (of *Reggie Smith vs. Denny*) who had a belt in karate, apparently got to Carter and enacted a *Star Trek*–style nerve pinch to his shoulder which took him out of the tussle, according to some reports. This would turn out to be the grandest gesture in the final season of Denny's career, just three years after his unlikely Cy Young Award with the Philadelphia Phillies.

Knight would later say he acted on Davis because of his pop-up slide and the fact that Davis looked him in the eye, which Knight interpreted as a challenge. When the smoke finally cleared along the Ohio River that July night, Knight, Mitchell, Davis, and Soto were ejected from the game. As the Mets returned to their dugout, they found a sole figure sitting on the bench in the form of ex-Reds slugger George Foster. He said he didn't want to fight because it set the wrong example for kids. No one, especially manager Davey Johnson who was bent on team unity, was buying Foster's story. By mid-August, he had been released despite his giant contract. While the Mets seemed to get the better of the Reds in this fight, and eventually won the game in fourteen innings on a three-run homer by Howard Johnson, the post-game mood after the five-hour marathon was not one of celebration but of disdain for Foster. The Mets also could have celebrated the tactical calisthenics of their manager, who, after the ejections, was forced to juggle two pitchers rotating as outfielders. Orosco and Roger McDowell would stay in the game simultaneously and switch positions as needed, with each being granted warm-up tosses during each re-entry to the mound. This sent player/manager Rose frantically to the rule book where he unsuccessfully sought a point of protest for Johnson's unorthodox switcheroo system. Orosco actually made a catch in the outfield, and Carter, who was not ejected, and had to take over third base, started a double play from his new position.

Foster's reluctance to leave the dugout has to rank up there with the other most lame nonbrawl scenario: Tom Glavine being forced to "throw" at ex-Brave Dale Murphy—the result being an unintentional intentional walk on inside pitches—with Glavine being ejected automatically and practically crying in the dugout afterward. All of it chalked up to a Braves-

Phillies grudge match stemming from *Nixon vs. W. Ritchie* several games earlier. Foster did hit 244 of his 348 career homers with the Reds, but still, sitting on the bench with your arms folded during a full-scale brawl can only lead to a fresh entry in the transactions column soon after the skirmish.

Knight, of course, would manage Davis when he returned to the Reds in 1996 after spending time in Los Angeles (reunited with his childhood bud Strawberry) and Detroit. Following his comeback in Cincinnati, Davis would thrill Baltimore fans with an heroic postseason home run against the Indians that was made more dramatic by his early return from colon cancer chemotherapy. Davis then went on to St. Louis, and San Francisco would be the final stop of his career marked by many injuries, including a lacerated liver suffered after diving for a ball during the Reds incredible 1990 World Series sweep of Oakland. As of 2007, Davis was active in cancer education and prevention based on his own experience with the disease, maintaining a website and releasing a DVD about his triumph.

Knight, thanks mostly to his timely home runs, went on to become the 1986 World Series MVP, scoring the winning run after the infamous Bill Buckner miscue in Game 6 against Boston. After retiring in 1988, Knight tore up the LPGA circuit as a caddy for his wife Nancy Lopez in the late 1980s. As yet another *Knight vs. E. Davis* tangent came full circle, Knight would return to the Queen City as a coach under none other than Davey Johnson, who managed the Reds from 1993 to 1995, before yielding the reins to Knight in 1996. The Reds played .500 ball under Knight that year, and the thirty-four-year-old Davis won Comeback Player of the Year honor that season with twenty-six home runs and twenty-three steals. Unlike Davis, Cincinnati fans were still simmering with anger about Knight's extra-innings punch-up ten years earlier at Riverfront's hot corner, and they seemed to let him know about it every chance they had.

Chapter 5: KICKING ASH

A walk through any sporting goods store is a stroll through the prop house for baseball fight dramas. (A hardware store will also do, especially from the spectators' point of view.) Golf balls have anonymously been rained down on the field from upper deck seats for decades, batteries travel well through the air, and the rosin bag played a major role as an instigator (see *Sweeney vs. Weaver*). Combat tools, mostly used by batters and pitchers, have included helmets (both authentic and souvenir), gloves, and baseballs (both game-used and promotional giveaway types). Martial arts moves are not unusual. An open folding knife was thrown from the stands at Comiskey Park in 1959, aimed at Detroit's Al Kaline; the handle end of a Bowie knife—heaved from the upper deck— grazed Wally Joyner of the Angels as he was walking off the field at Yankee Stadium one August night in 1986. Teammate Gary Pettis, playing center field and apparently out of range, picked up the blade and gave it to Angels manager Gene Mauch, a man who had certainly cornered the market on frustration (see 1964 Phillies collapse, 1986 Angels playoff heartbreak) and might be prone to using it on himself. When the Yankees next visited Anaheim, kooky fans at the Big A tossed rubber knives in the direction of outfielder Dave Winfield.

In the blink of an eye during a Giants-Cubs game on August 13, 1997, Jeff Kent of the Giants removed Tyler Houston's catcher's mask, then the Cubs catcher promptly returned the favor, sending Kent's batting helmet for a loop. Kent had been walking up the first base line, escorted by Houston for nine intense strides, after pitcher Jeremy Gonzalez hit Kent in the armpit with a pitch. Kent had apparently made fun of Gonzalez the week before. With the sporting goods items out of their way (Kent had gestured with and then flipped his bat away before starting his staredown trek to first) and home plate umpire Charlie Williams glued to Houston's back, the pair began throwing punches but were soon consumed by a pile of sizeable fellows, including Mark Grace, Barry Bonds, Dusty Baker, Gene Clines, and Glenallen Hill.

The most obvious weapon—the one Kent tossed away—has made thankfully few appearances during diamond skirmishes. Men carrying war clubs tend to use them. Shillelaghs, cudgels, quarterstaffs. Prehistoric highlight reels clearly show early man enjoying the use of wood to do damage to other creatures. Yes, Theodore Roosevelt said "speak softly but carry a big stick." But to carry the phallic symbolism another ninety feet, Roosevelt also said: "All daring and courage, all iron endurance of misfortune—make for a finer, nobler type of manhood." When someone brings a baseball bat to a baseball fight, there had better be plenty of iron endurance.

If a batter decides to use his bat to take care of personal business on the field, the stakes are immediately raised. Once they start swinging or throwing that thing at other players, the donnybrook becomes a high-profile case study in psychotic rage among athletes. The story then moves off the sports pages and onto the editorial page where the national pastime suffers its three thousandth "loss of innocence" and again is accused of failing in its duty to provide unwavering refuge from societal woes.

There have been times when the bat escorts the player charging the mound, but is not used, such as the incident during Spring Training of 2003 when Vladimir Guerrero of the Montreal Expos went after Florida Marlins pitcher Brad Penny while toting a club made of the hardwood known as ash. Guerrero used his free hand to swing at Penny, somehow resisting an ancient temptation to brain his foe with the hard cylinder in his other hand.

Sometimes bats escape the batter's grasp and do their own damage, as if the ash or maple wood has a mind of its own. When Claudell Washington of the Braves let his bat fly past the mound after swinging at a Mario Soto pitch in June of 1984, he detoured on his way to retrieve his bat and charged Soto, who immediately threw the ball, striking Washington and home plate umpire Lanny Harris at point-blank range. Harris would then pay dearly for trying to break up the fight as Washington tossed him to the ground during his pursuit of Soto. Washington was fined $1,000 and suspended three games for that action, while Soto was fined $5,050 and suspended five games by the league because it was his second offense—he had bumped an umpire during a brawl with the Cubs at Wrigley Field in May. A side tussle during *C. Washington vs. Soto* involving Bob Watson and Tony Perez resulted in the Big Red Machine legend seriously injuring his shoulder.

In his one season with Baltimore, Reggie Jackson let fly with his bat in the direction of White Sox reliever Clay Carroll, who was on the mound at Memorial Stadium celebrating the bicentennial year of 1976 by throwing behind Reggie's head. Jackson followed his bat to the mound, everyone spilled forth in a reenactment of the Fort McHenry bombardment, and Reggie and Chicago DH Lamar Johnson were thumbed after the fracas.

Ex-Yankee Scott Kamieniecki could teach Roger Clemens a thing or to about picking up stray bats and tossing them at the opposition. In the final game of the 1999 regular season with Baltimore, Kamieniecki was working a no-hitter against playoff-bound wildcard Boston at Camden Yards. He plunked John Valentin, and when Troy O'Leary batted later in the inning, O'Leary let his bat fly toward the mound after a swing. He then walked toward the mound and Kamieniecki picked up the bat and hurled it in the direction of the Boston dugout, where Red Sox players were spilling forth for some early October roughhousing. It was a hearty fling by Kamieniecki, turning a meaningless game into a bit of a nail-biter. With so many equipment bags packed and ready in the Baltimore clubhouse, it was surprising the middle of the diamond flooded with ballplayers playing shirt-grab. Inexplicably, Boston regulars such as Jason Varitek and Trot Nixon got overheated and veered toward an actual fight as Red Sox broadcasters decried the stupidity of a pre-playoff donnybrook with a loose cannon team like Baltimore. Cooler heads did prevail as O'Leary and Kamieniecki were ejected and the Red Sox, finally getting a hit in the eighth inning, won the game 1-0.

Several unfortunate fans have felt the wrath of flying bats. Gary DiSarcina of the Angels and Carl Everett of the Texas Rangers both injured spectators after losing control of their bats. And there wasn't a game that went by without Dave Winfield letting go of his business partner, keeping front row fans, base coaches and dugout dwellers on full alert during his at-bats. Winfield also carried his bat halfway to the mound when he charged Nolan Ryan at the Astrodome in August of 1980, shedding Houston catcher Luis Pujols, then resisting home plate umpire Jerry Dale's grasp before dropping his lumber and connecting with The Express, sparking a 10-minute rhubarb.

Sometimes the bat warfare is more sublime. In 1981, Oakland catcher Mike Heath picked up the bat used by "Disco" Dan Ford of the California Angels and asked home plate umpire John Shulock to inspect it. Ford had just hit a home run, and when he finished his trot around the bases, he objected to Heath's handling of his bat and made it known in no uncertain terms, grabbing the catcher. ("Nobody likes to be grabbed. I had to react," Heath told the AP.) Both benches emptied for five minutes of AL West argy-bargy that featured a sequel confrontation after the game in a clubhouse runway. The peacemaker during the initial donnybrook? None other than A's manager Billy Martin, who peeled Angels catcher Ed Ott away from the scrum. Martin would, however, pin former Yankees teammate and Angels pitching coach Tom Morgan during the post-game runway scuffle. Martin had established a routine with Heath whenever sluggers hit towering home runs off Oakland pitchers, or when the ball seemed to have some extra jet fuel behind it leaving the park: check the bat, this time, not for pine tar.

The same game also saw Rod Carew ejected in the second inning after he argued with umpire Bill Kunkel over impeding a baserunner, then insisted the arbiter remove a knife from his pocket . . . a knife he had asked a batboy to deliver to him two nights earlier during another bat challenge involving a search for cork.

It was a big year for Ford. He bared it all in the July issue of *Playgirl* magazine, sharing the cover with Sylvester Stallone, and, for the second time in his career, he led all AL outfielders in errors. He also co-starred in an incident in August against Cleveland when he was restrained from charging Cleveland pitcher John Denny, who had just hit him with a pitch. Though Ford was held back, Disco's teammate Carew stormed out of the dugout to clash with Denny on the mound.

In the off-season, the Angels dealt Disco Dan to Baltimore for Doug DeCinces.

The multifaceted *Ford vs. Heath* certainly appears to be outright folly when compared to one of baseball's most heinous moments, which happened across the bay at San Francisco's Candlestick Park during the torrid summer of 1965.

JUAN MARICHAL vs. JOHNNY ROSEBORO
(SAN FRANCISCO GIANTS)   (LOS ANGELES DODGERS)
August 22, 1965, Candlestick Park, San Francisco, California

Johnny Roseboro thought he had experienced the worst thing that could ever happen to a catcher. He had knelt down to give the sign, like he did a hundred or so times per game. Behind him he heard a gurgle. It was umpire Paul Pryor. His nickname was "The Puker" according to Leo Durocher in his autobiography *Nice Guys Finish Last*. Within seconds, Roseboro and his protective gear were covered in a greenish vomit apparently caused by Pryor's consumption of some discount green beer before the game, Durocher claimed. Of course, colorful heckling ensued. As it turned out, being a victim of the Puker was only the second worst thing to happen to Roseboro on the ballfield. The worst would come courtesy of San Francisco Giants pitcher Juan Marichal in the final game of a tense four-game series between the two ancient rivals whose bitterness and disdain for one another dates back to when both franchises played their home games in New York.

Roseboro lived near the Watts section of Los Angeles. For six days beginning August 11, 1965, the neighborhood was the scene of a race riot that began when police pulled over a black motorist suspected of drunken driving. The death toll of the riots was thirty, with more than one thousand injured and six hundred buildings damaged as many Americans watched the burning and looting on television. A local radio DJ's catchphrase "Burn, baby, burn!" was popularized during Watts, and eventually became the chorus of the 1977 hit song "Disco Inferno" by The Trammps. Many years later, "Burn, baby, burn!" was the expression used by Yankees radio broadcaster John Sterling whenever Bernie Williams hit a home run. In Vietnam, American troops were engaged in bloody battles with body counts on the rise.

When the violence in Watts erupted, the Dodgers were homestanding at Chavez Ravine, hosting the Pirates and the Phillies. Dodger Stadium attendance dipped slightly during one of the most notorious weeks in the city's history. The Dodgers then embarked on a seventeen-game road trip that began in San Francisco. With tension from the Watts riots still simmering, many in Los Angeles found themselves once again in front of a television, staring mouths agape as the horrors of August 22 unfolded at Candlestick Park where 42,807 fans—the season's largest crowd at Candlestick—were set to witness baseball infamy.

The Dodgers had won two of the first three games in extra innings. They occupied first place in a tight race in the National League, ahead of the Milwaukee Braves by half a game. The Giants were one and a half games out. On Friday night, Maury Wills, the Dodgers speed merchant and base path instigator, tapped Giants catcher Tom Haller's mask while at bat in the fifth, drawing what many considered an intentional catcher's interference call that awarded him first base. Matty Alou had tried the same thing on Roseboro, but the umpire did not take the bait. Marichal worked Roseboro over with some verbal barbs from the dugout; the pitcher known as "The Dominican Dandy" was supporting his countryman Alou. Reports indicated Roseboro told other Giants players that Marichal should clam up or expect some retaliation from the catcher. The teams taunted each other throughout the contest, adding yet another chapter to the vast collection— a healthy row of leather-bound tomes—documenting hatred between Dodgers and Giants. In May of 1965, Marichal told reporters he would "get" Don Drysdale after the Dodgers pitcher upended Willie Mays twice in one game. Drysdale returned fire in the press, saying "If he gets me, I'll get four Giants and they won't be .220 hitters."

Saturday's game three of the series was relatively uneventful as the Dodgers won 6-4 in eleven innings. Sunday, however, Wills presented his peskiness in the first inning, when he beat out a bunt and eventually came around to score. In the third, Marichal with his trademark high leg kick working and in search of his twentieth win of the season, had seen enough of Wills and threw one at his head, sending him dancing from the plate. Ron Fairly, the Dodgers MVP during their championship year, was also sent down to the dust with a head-high pitch earlier in the game. Marichal, it was noted, was due to bat in the bottom of the third with Los Angeles leading 2-1.

Dodgers starter Sandy Koufax was looking for his twenty-second win of the season. He had thrown his second career no-hitter against the Giants two years earlier. A week after the no-no, the Giants pounded him in the first inning of their next meeting, sending the fireballer to a rare early shower. Koufax-Marichal was a matchup of the league's premier pitchers, and Marichal seemed to own the Dodgers when he faced them at

Candlestick. There was also the expected mini-drama of the battle of wills between Wills and Marichal, with the pitcher throwing over to first repeatedly to keep Wills from stealing at will, which he did in the 1965 season to the tune of ninety-six swipes. As Roy Campanella's replacement, Roseboro had a tough time hitting Marichal—though an All-Star noted for his defense, he never excelled with the bat.

Roseboro knew Koufax would not avenge the knockdowns of Wills and Fairly on that Sunday afternoon, so he had to take matters into his own hands. After a harmless strike one to the batting Marichal, Roseboro received the next pitch low and inside and dropped it. He picked it up and zipped it back to Koufax, possibly grazing (ever so slightly) Marichal's ear. The stunned Dominican turned to Roseboro and asked him why he did that.

Obscenities were employed. Accounts have Marichal moving slightly toward the mound as Roseboro came out of his crouch and appeared to be reaching for his mask. The varied reportage on whose neurons fired next is the stuff of debates, some of them quite scholarly among sociologist types.

Marichal, bat in hand and fearing the iron mask of Roseboro, panicked and brought the bat down on top of the catcher's head a few times as Koufax charged in from the mound, the ball still in his glove as Roseboro was spun around with his back to his pitcher. Giants third base coach Charlie Fox raced in and home plate umpire Shag Crawford, dubbed the "bravest man on the field" by several sportswriters, moved forward. Roseboro's head was gashed and bleeding.

From the on-deck circle, bat also in hand, Tito Fuentes charged toward the scene, and veteran Orlando Cepeda, who once wielded a bat unsuccessfully in a 1958 skirmish in Pittsburgh (he was tackled by teammate Willie Mays), was moving out of the Giants dugout brandishing a third bat. Crawford then got his hands on Marichal and tackled him to the grass as both teams crowded together for fourteen minutes of violence along the first base line. Mays, again the peacemaker, crossed Giants-Dodgers lines and cradled the injured Roseboro, escorting him to the Dodgers dugout. Along the way, he tackled Dodgers outfielder Lou Johnson, who had designs on getting a piece of umpire Crawford. Johnson somehow managed to kick Mays in the head during their encounter.

Roseboro required 14 stitches to close his head wounds, but there was no concussion. Crawford ejected Marichal, if only because he used his bat and not his fists during the incident.

Koufax, rattled by the incident, struck out Marichal's replacement batter Bob Schroder, got Fuentes to fly out deep to left, but then walked the next two batters. Mays stepped in with Roseboro's blood on his jersey and clubbed a 450-foot, three-run homer, his fourth in the four-game series, sixth in six games and thirty-eighth of the season, putting the Giants up 4-3. Mays would go on to win the NL MVP award, but the Dodgers won the National League by two games and then beat Minnesota in the World Series.

The Giants went on a bit of tailspin after *Marichal vs. Roseboro,* and as part of his punishment, Marichal was not allowed to accompany his team for their next series in Los Angeles in its post-Watts charred tinderbox condition. Mays, however, was given a standing ovation at Dodger Stadium when the Giants arrived to renew old vows and exchange wooden nickels.

In the days immediately following *Marichal vs. Roseboro,* a boxing matchmaker invited the combatants to enter the ring at San Francisco's Civic Auditorium to settle their differences in a three-round preliminary bout with proceeds going to the winner's favorite charity. The novelty fight would have been on the undercard of the Elmer Rush-Todd Herring main event, courtesy of matchmaker Bennie Ford.

Marichal was fined a then-record $1,750 by NL president Warren Giles and suspended for nine days, which meant he missed two starts. Koufax, who had to let his catcher do the dirty work and pay the price with a sliced scalp, went on to win his second of three Cy Young Awards with a record of 26-8.

Roseboro did file a $110,000 damage lawsuit on September 1 against Marichal and the Giants in Los Angeles Superior Court, but the case was settled out of court for $7,500 some five years later. On September 30, 1965, Marichal suffered a hairline fracture of his left thumb after a collision with Reds shortstop Leo Cardenas. As he entered the empty clubhouse in pain during the seventh inning, Marichal was served with the court papers, apparently using his right hand to collect the official document.

In September of 1971, more Dodgers-Giants fireworks included an incident in which Bill Buckner—bat in hand—charged the mound against Marichal at Candlestick. Dodgers pitcher Bill Singer had already plunked a few Giants. The oddity wasn't the Giants and Dodgers fighting—it was the Dodgers beating Marichal in San Francisco for only the second time in twenty-three opportunities.

Like Pete Rose and Bud Harrelson a few years later, Marichal and Roseboro would eventually become friends, with Roseboro forgiving the Dominican Dandy. Appearances at Old-Timer's games and golf tournaments followed on a steady basis, and they were always asked the same questions. Some reports said Marichal missed his ticket to Cooperstown on the first two ballots because of lingering shock from the incident. But once the Dodgers catcher and Giants pitcher mended their ways, the Hall of Fame came calling for Marichal. At Roseboro's funeral in 2003, Marichal said being forgiven by Roseboro was one of the best things to happen to him. As anniversaries of the incident came and went, Roseboro always confessed to sparking the whole affair; Marichal did not favor talking about it and still harbored some sadness about the day he mistook the Los Angeles catcher for a baby harp seal.

PEDRO GUERRERO VS. DAVID CONE
(LOS ANGELES DODGERS)   (NEW YORK METS)
May 22, 1988, Dodger Stadium, Los Angeles, California

Sometimes batters decide they've had their fill of brushback pitches, and they become men of action. Dodgers slugger Pedro Guerrero said he wanted to brushback David Cone with the bat during one of ten Los Angeles losses to the Mets during the 1988 season. It was the sixth inning of the May 22 meeting between the Mets and Dodgers. Guerrero had just faced two inside fastballs from Cone, one of which he managed to foul off. He was then hit in the shoulder by a seventy mile per hour curveball from Cone. The ball glanced off his shoulder upward, striking his batting helmet, no doubt ringing his ears as the slightest impact registers mega decibels inside the helmet. Guerrero responded by swinging his bat with both hands, purposely releasing it in the direction of Cone. Had the bat been the ball, it would have been an easy 6-3 putout as Guerrero's lumber missed Cone by a dozen feet or so and landed in front of shortstop Kevin Elster.

Quick action by Mets catcher Barry Lyons (Gary Carter's backup who played fifty games that season) denied Guerrero the satisfaction of successfully charging Cone on the mound. As Guerrero walked toward Cone, the catcher from Biloxi, Mississippi, grabbed him from behind, with third baseman Howard Johnson helping out with the restraining order. Both benches then emptied for a lot of standing around, with Los Angeles' Mike Marshall helping to hold back his angry teammate. Guerrero was quickly ejected by home plate umpire John Kibler and later suspended four games and fined $1,000 by the league office.

In the previous game, Doc Gooden, on his way to raising his record to 8-0, plunked Alfredo Griffin, fracturing his right hand and putting the Los Angeles shortstop on the disabled list. Dodgers pitcher Brian Holton then dutifully nailed Johnson of the Mets, setting the stage for the Sunday matinee when the Mets would be going for their seventh straight win—a sweep of the three game set—and a chance to knock the Dodgers out of first place in the NL West.

The Mets knocked Fernando Valenzuela out of the game after one inning in what was then the quickest exit of Valenzuela's career while Cone was in a successful pursuit of raising his record to 6-0, which he did when the Mets prevailed 5-2.

Guerrero later acknowledged Cone was not trying to hurt him with the slow curve, but still emphasized he did not like to get hit by pitches. Guerrero was third in the league in batting average at .326, on his way to celestial praise from stats guru Bill James who cited him as the best hitter of the 1980s. Guerrero was also on his way to the trading block as the Dodgers dealt the four-time All-Star and 1981 World Series co-co-MVP on August 16, 1988, to St. Louis for pitcher John Tudor. The year before, Tudor had his leg broken by the seldom-used Mets catcher Lyons as he pursued a foul pop and crashed down the Cardinals dugout steps at Busch Stadium. Lyons string of strange luck would continue with one blogger honoring him for having his bald pate struck by seagull dung during the National Anthem, and then in 2005 when his house in Biloxi was destroyed by Hurricane Katrina, his 1986 World Series ring lost in the storm.

Karma would be the theme of *P. Guerrero vs. Cone* as manifested in the 1988 NLCS. Despite winning ten of eleven regular season meetings against Los Angeles, the Mets would lose in seven games to the Dodgers, who would go on to dramatically defeat the Oakland A's in the World Series. Few predicted the outcome of the 1988 NLCS, except for Cubs broadcaster Harry Caray, who warned of Dodger postseason supremacy on an obscure WGN afternoon broadcast in late September with the Cubs nestled in fourth place, twenty-four games behind the first-place Mets.

Cone, whose colorful career would include hurling a perfect game with the Yankees in 1999, was named in an $8.1 million suit during a wacky 1992 spring when a group of women said in 1989 he masturbated in front of them while in the bullpen at Shea Stadium and in a hotel room in Montreal.

Mets manager Davey Johnson had some of the team's trademark 1986 swagger lingering, apparently, as he told AP after *P. Guerrero vs. Cone*: "The melee was a courtesy show of support. I like it when they are not too long, and no one gets hurt on the bottom." Comments weighted with such flippancy tend to come from managers whose teams are 30-11 at the time. The time of the game, by the way, was three hours and eighteen minutes.

BERT CAMPANERIS vs. LERRIN LAGROW
(OAKLAND ATHLETICS)   (DETROIT TIGERS)
Oct. 8, 1972, ALCS Game 2, Oakland-Alameda Coliseum, Oakland, California

Drop in on any youthful wiffle ball game in the mid-1970s. Wait awhile. Sooner or later, the observer will witness a young boy (or girl) unleashing a "Campaneris." Usually boredom or bad pitching prompts the move, and the plastic bat poses little authentic danger to its intended human target. Basically, a kid pulls a "Campaneris" by helicoptering the bat at the pitcher's head. It's fun. Try it sometime.

Untold thousands of young fans were among the many shocked by the televised events of October 8, 1972, as the Swingin' Oakland A's battled the somber, heavy-legged Detroit Tigers for a trip to the World Series. The contrasts were many—the A's with their garish green and gold rayon garb, replete with toothpaste white cleats and goldenrod socks that had viewers constantly adjusting their color TVs. The Tigers wore the same shirts and hats they'd worn since the Crusades, or the Battle of Trafalgar, or however far back the archives go. Dick Williams managed a cadre of mustachioed zanies going by Rollie, Catfish, Campy, Blue Moon and Reggie. Detroit skipper Billy Martin—in his permanent state of slump-shouldered hands-in-back-pockets discomfort—was in charge of a collection of gas station attendant types with names like Al Kaline, Ed Brinkman, Norm Cash, Dick

McAuliffe, and Lerrin LaGrow. It was jazz-fusion versus doo-wop; a Corvette against a Ford Falcon; mint-pistachio taking on vanilla (even the most youthful wiffle ball player gets the idea at this point.)

The A's had taken Game 1 of the best-of-five series with a comeback 3-2 victory in eleven innings, with the winning run scoring on a Kaline throwing error. As A's outfielder Joe Rudi noted in many interviews, agitation between these two clubs dated back to the Tigers championship season of 1968, when Jim Northrup was beaned. In August of 1972, Detroit reliever Bill Slayback had thrown at Campaneris' head, and then threw behind Angel Mangual, who charged the mound and floored Slayback with a flying punch. The ensuing chaos saw Willie Horton lay out Oakland's Mike Epstein, Detroit backup catcher Duke Sims exchanging blows with A's coach Jerry Adair, Martin pursuing Mangual and Oakland coach Irv Noren getting a hurting from Tigers reliever Tim Timmerman. *Mangual vs. Slayback* went down as a hate-filled quarter of an hour punch-up, with Detroit fans clearing the Tiger Stadium aisles of every scrap of garbage which they promptly hurled onto the field.

During the Tigers-A's 2006 ALCS, there was much reminiscing about *Campaneris vs. LaGrow*, but little coverage of *Mangual vs. Slayback*. Martin told his biographer Peter Golenbock in *Wild, High and Tight: The Life and Death of Billy Martin* that he thought throwing at Latino players was a good way of intimidating them. Campaneris was having a big ALCS Game 2. He led off the game with a single, stole second and third base, and scored on Rudi's single. He had two more hits before coming to the plate in the seventh with the A's up 5-0. Martin had reportedly conferred with his rookie reliever LaGrow, the fourth of five pitchers Detroit used in Game 2, who was about to pitch the only postseason inning of his ten-year career. The old adage of throwing at a speedster's legs was soon to be engaged. LaGrow's first pitch nailed the Cuban shortstop's left ankle bone, even as he tried to avoid what he knew was coming. Campaneris staggered and spun away from the plate, where a lumpen and dingy duo of Duke Sims and umpire Nestor Chylak—with his cumbersome heart-shaped balloon of a chest protector—stood like scarecrows. Campaneris grabbed his bat slightly up the handle with his right hand—his A's jersey too tight around his torso—and performed an impressive hammer-throw style heave. The wood was quickly spinning and rising toward LaGrow. An AP reporter, obviously sitting miles away in the rear of the Coliseum press box, inaccurately wrote that the "bat sailed harmlessly over LaGrow's head." The lanky 6-foot-5 pitcher from Phoenix, who had pitched only twelve innings for Detroit as a call up the season before, ducked toward the dirt of the mound as the bat whooshed overhead and landed well behind him. It was only a matter of inches as it roared over his skull, and the velocity of Campaneris' heave looked to be anything but harmless, with a distinct possibility of a pair of road gray Detroit trousers being seriously soiled at that very moment.

Among the 30,088 fans in the distant stands of the Coliseum was AL president Joe Cronin. He watched as Chylak ejected Campaneris and LaGrow, while three umpires were required to restrain Martin, who was the first out of the Tigers dugout seeking to work on the other end of Campaneris now that his ankle was appropriately battered. Ike Brown was keeping pace with his manager, and managed to retrieve Campy's bat, which he quickly splintered.

Post-game hyperbole from Martin included this statement (worthy of a stand-up act at the airport hotel, considering his own rap sheet): "That was the dirtiest thing I ever saw in the game of baseball." The words "gutless," "idiot," and "disgrace" were also attributed to Martin's assessment of Campaneris' actions. "The next thing he ought to do is carry a knife. Or does he fight with his feet?" Martin is quoted in Golenbock's book, inadvertently citing Rod Carew's dilemma in *Ford vs. Heath* and the action of *Park vs. Belcher* in one fell swoop. Of course, being old school, Martin attempted to get at Campaneris in the clubhouse runways, conjuring the ghosts of Durocher and Stengel, among others.

Cronin suspended Campaneris for the remainder of the playoffs and fined him $500, but he remained eligible for the World Series, as per the decision of commissioner Bowie Kuhn. The commissioner also suspended Campaneris for the first seven days of the 1973 season.

When the smoke cleared with LaGrow, Campy was taken to a hospital for X-rays on his ankle, and was replaced by Dal Maxvill. Without Campy, though, the A's dropped the next two games. Martin had successfully found a way to rid his team of the pest who tortured them in the first two games with his speed and his hot bat. And with Reggie Jackson out with a serious hamstring injury, Oakland had to squeak out a nervous Game 5 victory aided by sudden relief pitching by Vida Blue, who replaced a stressed and nauseous Blue Moon Odom halfway through the crucial contest. The two pitchers almost came to blows among the tense, rather forced celebration in the A's clubhouse after clinching the

AL pennant for their hated owner, Charles O. Finley, who had been feuding with Blue and kept him from starting the game. All Blue had done the year before was go 24-8 with a 1.82 ERA to become the youngest Cy Young Award winner—and he had the *nerve* to ask the penny-pinching Finley for a pay raise.

Campaneris, who would finish his MLB career playing under Martin with the 1983 Yankees, helped the A's defeat Cincinnati in the 1972 Fall Classic. His 649 stolen bases were good enough for twelfth on the all-time steals list. The Cuban also has the oddball distinction of having played in nine no-hitters.

LaGrow, who was also suspended for the rest of the 1972 ALCS, stayed with Detroit through 1975 and then bounced around with the Cardinals, White Sox, Dodgers and finally the 1980 Phillies, who released him in July before going on to win the World Series.

The Oakland win over Cincinnati in the 1972 World Series would launch a three-year Athletics dynasty that began with their first World Championship since 1930. That's when a twenty-two-year-old Jimmie Foxx and the Philadelphia Athletics, compiling a little dynasty of their own, beat St. Louis in six games, uncorking their celebratory champagne at Shibe Park on October 8—exactly forty-two years to the day before *Campaneris vs. LaGrow*.

A glance (using a magnifying device) at the back of any given MLB game ticket spells out the rules of conduct for those attending ballgames. The language, legal boilerplate probably cooked up during the early days of the Kuhn regime, is called "Terms and Conditions" and usually reads something like this: *"Management reserves the right, without the refund of any portion of the ticket price, to refuse admission to or eject any person whose conduct is deemed by management to be disorderly, who uses vulgar or abusive language or who fails to comply with the terms and conditions herein. The license granted by this ticket is revocable and may be terminated by tendering to the holder the purchase price of the ticket. By use of this ticket you consent to a reasonable search for cans/bottles, drugs, weapons or other prohibited items and you agree that you will not transmit or aid in transmitting any description, account, picture or reproduction of the baseball game or event which this ticket grants admission. Breach of the foregoing will automatically terminate this license."*

Oh yeah, the rest of the stanza: "I don't care if I ever get back. So it's root, root, root . . . ." Groucho Marx couldn't have written a better blurb to print on the back of tickets, the reading of which can lead to blindness. Umpire Nestor Chylak, who had the best possible view of *Campaneris vs. LaGrow*, almost lost his eyesight after being hit by shrapnel during World War II's Battle of the Bulge. A Silver Star and Purple Heart later, Chylak became an American League umpire in 1954. In 1999, the Veteran's Committee voted him into the Hall of Fame, one of eight arbiters enshrined at Cooperstown.

A Penny an Ounce

As if Campaneris hadn't provided enough excitement for Chylak in 1972, the venerable ump was behind home plate as the crew chief during "Ten-Cent Beer Night" at Municipal Stadium in Cleveland on June 4, 1974. Billy Martin's Texas Rangers were in town for a bit of a grudge match as the two teams had brawled six nights earlier in Arlington, Texas, when Lenny Randle (of *Randle vs. Lucchesi*) went after pitcher Milt Wilcox (of *G. Brett vs. Wilcox*) who had just fielded Randle's bunt. Wilcox had thrown behind Randle on a previous pitch, and instead of charging the mound, Randle decided to put one in play and send a forearm to the head of the pitcher who was about to retire him unassisted. Randle's momentum unfortunately carried him head down into the groin of John Ellis, the Tribe's massive first baseman. In the off season, Ellis worked in personal debt collection for bailbondsmen and usually was awarded the "Employee of the Month" plaque. Ellis punished Randle on the spot and the brawl was on, emptying the benches of both dugouts. Martin, surprise of surprises, was in the middle of the mix and was downed twice by Buddy Bell. Indians manager Ken Aspromonte was tackled from behind and pinned by the North Country duo of pitcher Steve Foucault (Duluth, Minnesota) and future Hall of Famer Ferguson Jenkins (Chatham, Ontario).

The Rangers had staged their own discount beer night, and as the Indians left the field after the eighth inning brawl, they were doused with suds. Catcher Dave Duncan was infuriated and was restrained by teammates as he tried to get over the dugout to reach a fan in the stands who was armed with ten cups of beer. One Texas columnist reported the beer-slinging fan was wearing a T-shirt that read: "Eat More Possum." The Rangers won 3-0 behind a three-hitter by Jackie Brown. After the game, Toby Harrah of the Rangers compared the Texas fans to those in Venezuela, known for chasing umpires and soccer referees out of arenas.

The following week the Rangers were due to enter the hulking confines of the WPA fortress known as Cleveland Municipal (sometimes Lakefront) Stadium, just a lamprey eel's throw from the shore of Lake Erie. Like Aqueduct racetrack in Queens, New York, Municipal Stadium was built for nonexistent hordes, its yawning chasm set to welcome tens of thousands eight-fold who would never materialize out of the leisure time ether. Though the football Browns would certainly fill the ballpark, the Indians rarely came close to capacity crowds, especially in 1974, just four years after Kent State and its long-lingering malaise made northeast

Ohio a prominent entry in the world almanac of Vietnam era protest angst and social unrest. Not long before Kent State, the polluted surface of Cleveland's Cuyahoga River caught fire, an incident which plagues the city's reputation to this day. The flaming river story has no doubt suffered from urban legend exaggeration and usually results in countless mispronunciations of Cuyahoga.

In late September of 1940, Birdie Tebbetts of the visiting Detroit Tigers was struck with a large basket of green tomatoes that had been thrown into the Tigers bullpen from the upper deck of Cleveland Stadium. It was Ladies Day at the stadium, and the left field stands were well stocked with not only women, but eggs, fruits, and vegetables that were hurled at the Tigers for much of the game. In the late innings, police were called in to comb the stands looking for the produce-throwing culprits. The man with the bushel basket of tomatoes was looking to quickly jettison the evidence, and the Detroit bullpen down below was as good a place as any to dump the goods. The Tigers won the game and the police reportedly caught the basket thrower and he was served justice by being placed in the hands of a groggy Tebbetts in the Detroit clubhouse. The odd scene found the Tigers not only celebrating their survival of the demented salad bar experience, but their clinching of the AL pennant.

Aside from the sheer height of its upper deck, another one of the cool things about Cleveland Municipal Stadium was its Gate M, the "media" gate, which had a tree growing right up against the cream brick façade. It was also featured prominently in the Jack Lemmon movie *The Fortune Cookie* in which he played an injured cameraman covering the Browns. The underlying sadness of the place was also visible in the screwball comedy *Major League*. Its cream brick exterior did little to brighten up the gray mass that had been dubbed "the mistake by the lake" even before it was finished. In the early 1970s, the Tribe was averaging around eight thousand fans per game in a house that could seat almost eighty thousand. So a kid from the football-crazed plains of central Ohio attending an Indians game during that era would probably smell his first whiff of cigar (and pot) smoke, see pigeons nesting in wooden slat box seats covered in layers of dust and untouched since the days of Lou Groza, and hear the mercurial echo of the tom-tom player apparently serving a lengthy detention in the outfield seats. Homeless men in raincoats—perhaps ticket holders from a previous homestand—slept in luxuriously abandoned long rows of the upper deck, undisturbed except for the occasional Rick Manning foul ball. This sensory overload managed to exist within the slightly East German atmosphere of the massive ballpark. And topping off the parade of urban grotesqueries (including Indians baseball) was the piano grimace of Chief Wahoo.

But any startling sights taken in by wide-eyed bumpkin children were immediately nullified by the fact Major League baseball was being played in front of them on a professional diamond, which made it all good, no matter how dreary the atmosphere. On the field, in their oddly gothic head-to-toe maraschino uniforms, Indians players—even ersatz heroes like "Joggin'" George Hendrick—still loomed larger than life. For decades, the team reflected the depressing vibe of the city and endured the Frankenstein-like embrace of its ballpark.

The first night of the three-game Texas at Cleveland series was Ten-Cent Beer Night. The midweek set would also include a souvenir bat giveaway. Had the two promotions been combined on that first night, the Texas Rangers (and most of the Cleveland Indians) would have suffered fates not even conceivable by rugby teams flying low over the Andes in rough weather.

It was a Tuesday night, sixty-eight degrees and a full moon, and the crowd of 25,134 might have caught the forty-eight police officers on duty at the stadium off guard. The evening began with an already well-oiled crowd lighting off firecrackers (enhanced by the stadium's cavernous acoustics) and a large woman who charged onto the Indians on-deck circle in the second inning to flash her breasts to fellow fans. The pitching matchup was an intriguing one: 1971 NL Cy Young Award winner Ferguson Jenkins, on his way to a twenty-five-win season in his first AL campaign with Texas, against Fritz Peterson, traded from the Yankees to Cleveland in the Chris Chambliss deal after the red-faced wife swapping scandal with Yankees teammate, roommate and pal Mike Kekich.

Things remained on a kooky level, even as Tom Grieve hit his second homer of the game in the fourth, adding to the Rangers early lead. That's when a naked man streaked onto the field and slid into second base as Grieve was completing his home run trot. In the fifth inning, a father-son duo took the field and mooned the crowd, getting a less enthusiastic reaction than the shirt-lifting woman who had raided the on-deck circle earlier. In the sixth inning, Leron Lee, who had hit Jenkins in the stomach with a line drive earlier in the game, was called safe on a close play at third base. When the Rangers argued the call, debris rained onto the field.

More fans entered and exited the playing field at will, with police offering futile chases and adding a failed authority figure to the sloppy spectacle. Public address announcer Bob Keefer issued a warning about throwing objects onto the field, which predictably brought new salvos of stuff onto the diamond, with some fans turning to hurl sundries in the direction of the press box.

Lines were still moving toward the beer trucks beyond the outfield fence, where refills were the order of the day for two nickels or ten pennies. Amateur mathematicians figured sixty-five thousand cups of beer were moved on this Tuesday night on the shores of Lake Erie.

When firecrackers and cherry bombs continuously detonated around the Texas bullpen along the left field line, Chylak called the Rangers relievers in to stay in the dugout and away from the explosions, telling them they'd have as much time as needed to warm up on the mound if they were called into the game.

At this point, fans were making group forays on and off the bluegrass playing surface of Municipal Stadium. The grounds crew was trying to salvage the padding along the left field fence, which was being pulled off by souvenir seekers or perhaps fans who were overserved by the Stroh's truck and sought some type of bedding for the night. Pasty streakers continued to dot the landscape, and hot dogs and a gallon jug of wine (said to be Thunderbird) were thrown at Rangers first baseman Mike Hargrove, who had entered the game in the fifth. "Grover" would go on to win the AL Rookie of the Year award at the end of the season and would later play for and manage the Cleveland Indians. As the fire-brewed Stroh's suds began to really kick in, the ignored scoreboard said the Indians were losing and the fans were starting to lose the kookiness in favor of mob violence. Fights were breaking out all over the stadium, with the undercard having been a first-inning sparring match between a vendor and a customer, a dispute centered on spilled beer. Cleveland's radio announcers reported by the sixth inning fathers were ushering their kids out of the ballpark, and the Indians front office staff was also seen trying to reach the last helicopter out from the roof of the embassy.

Jeff Burroughs, the Rangers rookie right fielder, would play the role of Archduke Ferdinand in this particular baseball war. In the ninth inning, with Cleveland having staged a dramatic rally to tie the game at 5-5 and with the winning run on base and Leron Lee at the plate, a fan ran up to Burroughs and tried to swipe either his cap or his glove, or both, depending on which media account is cited. As he turned to pursue the grabber, Burroughs slipped and fell down.

In the Rangers dugout at that very moment, manager Billy Martin briefly lost sight of his prized right fielder, who was destined to win the 1974 AL Most Valuable Player award. So Billy took action—he grabbed a fungo bat and told his players to do the same. He then led a Texas Ranger charge worthy of a Tennyson poem (or at least an Iron Maiden song) toward their fallen comrade in right field. Pouring over the fence were hundreds of drunken fans, many armed with knives or chains, according to witnesses. The field was pelted with rocks, golf balls, batteries, and chair back slats. There were no warriors in face paint, horses or elephants, but it was clear there was going to be a player-fan clash of the first order. The Indians, who had brawled so heavily with these Rangers the week before, also raided the dugout bat rack and rallied along in the effort to prevent Burroughs from serious injury.

Like a professional wrestling match, baseball facilities seemed to provide throwable chairs of all types for drunken hordes to use against their targets. Indians reliever Tom Hilgendorf and umpire Chylak were both struck in the head with a chair and both were bleeding. Chylak, who denounced the crowd as "animals" and "uncontrollable beasts" after the game, was also hit with a rock. Umpire Joe Brinkman, who later estimated ten thousand fans eventually took the field to fight each other, the players, and anyone they could grab, said he helped a man who had been kicked in the head and was bleeding. It was the human equivalent of a burning river. Reports indicated there were nine arrests and seven injuries, according to a local hospital. Dave Duncan and Rusty Torres of the Indians made futile attempts at peacemaking with their own fans during the riot, but eventually had to resort to fisticuffs to flee the field. Hargrove brawled openly for his own survival, as did good old Duke Sims, the Rangers backup catcher who had a front row squatting seat for *Campaneris vs. LaGrow*.

It wasn't until Cleveland police outside the ballpark heard the description of the melee on the Indians radio broadcast that back-up officers were sent in. When all the players were found to be off the field, Chylak, who had almost stepped on a hunting knife lodged blade down in the grass behind him, declared the game a forfeit, awarding Texas a 9-0 win. The previous forfeit in MLB had come on September 30, 1971, when the Washington Senators played the Yankees at RFK Stadium for the final game in D.C. before the Senators were moved to Texas and became the

Rangers. Fans in D.C. stormed the field in the ninth inning on an extended souvenir binge, ignoring the ballplayers, instead going after bases, slabs of turf and any other fixtures commemorating the Senators tenure in the capital. The umpires could not clear the field and declared the forfeit in favor of the Yankees.

Hargrove pointed out the fungo bat Martin carried into battle on Ten-Cent Beer Night was later seen broken—one of Ten-Cent Beer Night's unsolved mysteries. Martin, like he did after *Campaneris vs. La-Grow*, was astounded by the shocking display of violence he'd seen in Cleveland. "That was the closest you're ever gonna be to seeing someone get killed in this game of baseball," Martin said, perhaps forgetting the grave of Ray Chapman, the Cleveland player killed by a Carl Mays fastball in August of 1920, was only a few miles away in the historic Lake View Cemetery. "They had knives and every damn thing. We're lucky we didn't get stabbed," Martin added. Martin was even more eloquent when he scoffed at the unsuccessful appeal filed by the Cleveland front office. They didn't think the forfeit was appropriate action, and Martin had fanned the flames of the fan's anger. "They should do what the President (Nixon) didn't do," Martin said. "Just come out and admit they made some mistakes and they will do everything they can to prevent it from happening again." Without the abundant Stroh's the following night, Cleveland beat Texas 9-3 in front of the usual eight thousand people, and Martin was booed when he visited the mound for a pitching change.

The Tribe had two more Ten-Cent Beer Nights scheduled, and like the Milwaukee Brewers and the Minnesota Twins (who had a Five-Cent Beer Night), the plan was to continue with the promotions. Those same amateur math guys, using the insane inflation of ballpark concessions and outright price gouging to victimize a captive audience, figured the modern equivalent of a Ten-Cent Beer Night would be a team holding a $3.25-Beer Night.

On July 19, 1974, the pitching matchup of Oakland's Catfish Hunter against Gaylord Perry of the Indians drew 41,848 fans to the second Ten-Cent Beer Night in Cleveland. The crowd was described as "well-mannered" and most sportswriters, without a riot to watch from the press box above, opted for "fans cried in their beer" imagery as the A's beat the Tribe 3-2 and things appeared to be back to normal in "the mistake by the lake."

Kill the Umpire

Chylak can be thankful he wasn't at Ebbets Field in Brooklyn in September of 1940 when a 5-foot-5 Dodgers fan named Frank Germano stormed the field immediately after a 4-3 loss to the Reds in ten innings. Umpire George Magerkurth, who had a longstanding feud with Dodgers manager Leo Durocher, had been having a rough game at Ebbets. Germano went after Magerkurth and fellow umpire Bill Stewart had to pull the fan off him.

Germano, who said he was an unemployed truck driver, was charged with assault in a Brooklyn court. It took some forty ushers and policemen to quiet down the donnybrook. Other reports said Germano was a parole violator who caused the ruckus so his partner could work the stands as a pickpocket during all the excitement. Germano said he was angry at Magerkurth's performance, and that the umpire had cursed him and that prompted the attack. In any case, Germano picked the wrong ump to attack as Magerkurth, known for his short temper and aversion to the nickname "Meathead," was a former pro boxer with seventy bouts under his belt. He was also known for several other on field incidents when he did not hesitate to let his fists do the talking.

Raising the bar of politeness for irate fans attacking umpires was a fellow named Boyd Michael Owens, who ran onto the field in Kansas City in July of 1960 to make his views known to home plate umpire Bob Stewart. He tapped Stewart on the shoulder and floored the ump with a punch, then punched an usher who tried to break it up. It was a 3-3 game going into the tenth inning, and the Orioles had a big inning to make it 9-3. The inning had been extended when Stewart ruled Walt Dropo was hit by Bud Daley's pitch to load the bases. After the third out and with the Athletics heading to the dugout to hit in the bottom of the tenth, Owens took the field to howls of approval from the Municipal Stadium throng. The 6-foot-tall fan required four umpires, a pair of Civil Defense patrolmen, an auxiliary policeman, several more ushers, and at least three policemen to subdue him. Somehow, umpire Ed Hurley received three spike wounds during the battle.

Owens' surrender was even more polite than his initial assault. According to the AP, Owens had this to say when he gave up on the field: "All right, boys. I've had my fun now. I'm willing to pay for it. I'll go quietly."

At Yankee Stadium during a 1981 playoff game, a man named Frank Kuraczea, Jr., from Ansonia, Connecticut, jumped over the rail along the third base line and tackled umpire Mike Reilly, who had earlier called

Dave Winfield out on a close play at third. Yankees third baseman Graig Nettles came to the rescue, getting the fan in a headlock as stadium security workers dragged the maniac spectator into the Milwaukee dugout. It took four New York City cops and a few Brewers to restrain Kuraczea, and it was later discovered he was carrying a blackjack the whole time. Kuraczea was charged with illegal possession of a dangerous weapon, criminal trespassing and disorderly conduct.

Again with the Folding Chairs

Umpire Joe Brinkman, having survived Ten-Cent Beer Night in Cleveland, was also on the job when the Texas Rangers took on the Oakland Athletics (and their fans) on Monday, September 13, 2004. Brinkman would again see a folding chair take center stage, even though technically it was stage right, along the right field line where the Texas bullpen sits on a bench mere inches from spectators in the front row. Four years earlier at Wrigley Field, a certain backup catcher for the Dodgers, not exactly displaying Moe Berg type brilliance, was baited into entering the stands when a fan stole his cap and ran (see Chapter 7).

Proving that Chicago does not hold the copyright on ugly fan incidents, the Bay Area has checked in with more than its share. The most demonstrative was probably when Texas reliever Frankie Francisco, just two days from his September 11 birthday, briefly lost his marbles in the ninth inning after he and teammate Doug Brocail were heckled to the boiling point. Brocail sparked the rumble by getting visibly agitated in a verbal battle with the heckler just after Alfonso Soriano hit a solo homer with one out to tie the game 5-5. In a court hearing later, the main heckler, identified as Craig Bueno, said the banter included fans asking the bullpen "Who is going to take the loss?" and "When are you going to lose?"—both legitimate questions as Oakland prevailed 7-6 in ten innings and Francisco Cordero (3-2) took the loss. This was not 2003, when Texas outfielder Carl Everett was beaned by a cell phone tossed from the upper deck by an Oakland supporter. This was worse because it was an incident with a face attached to it, a female face, and a more injurious outcome. Raymond Chandler couldn't have compiled a case with as many tasty tangents: an arrested rookie relief pitcher, husband-and-wife season ticket holders with a penchant for heckling, a large chunk of bail money, press conferences with lawyers, private investigators showing nudie photos around firehouses, and of course the last gasp of Texas playoff hopes. If only it was more of an AL West noir whodunnit worthy of discussion in taphouse joints like the Pop Inn in nearby Alameda. In this case, the videotape does not lie.

The incident was not without precedent in Oakland. Travel back to September 28, 1976, at the Coliseum to find members of the Kansas City Royals bullpen being showered with beer and garbage following a Dennis Leonard–Don Baylor tilt on the mound. Several Kansas City players ventured into the stands for what the AP called "an umbrella-swinging battle." Royals manager Whitey Herzog noted the fans along the right field stands in Oakland "used the worst language in the majors." Apparently, the death of Chairman Mao and the resulting end of China's cultural revolution in the weeks before were not topics being discussed between the hydrophobic A's fans and Royals relievers.

The 2004 clash saw Rangers players flood the bullpen area. Shirts were grabbed, and Francisco—almost mimicking a European soccer player's overhead throw-in—raised a white plastic and metal folding chair above his head and lobbed it into the first few rows. His lawyer said Francisco was merely getting in position to defend his teammates when he was caught in the crush between those teammates, the wall of Network Associates Coliseum, and the sharpened teeth of the heckling A's fans, one of whom had grabbed his wrist, the lawyer said.

Brocail was being restrained by his manager, Buck Showalter, who had his back to the action. That meant Showalter missed seeing the chair, traveling forever in slow motion, come down at a horrible angle on the face of Jennifer Bueno, forty-one, the wife of main heckler Craig, a forty-two-year-old fire battalion chief who astutely called heckling ballplayers "an American tradition." Unfortunately for his wife, Craig ducked when the Francisco-thrown chair arrived via air mail. Her nose was broken and bloodied, and the image of her damaged face was broadcast worldwide, perhaps drawing a chuckle or two from English soccer hooligans who have been cartoonishly portrayed by the American media. She appeared at a press conference two days later with a large white bandage over half of her face. Jennifer called heckling "part of going to a baseball game."

The incident took twenty minutes to clear up, and during the delay, Brinkman, perhaps reeling from the 1974 déjà vu, said there was discussion about forfeiting the game to the Rangers. The A's public address announcer issued a stern warning that if any Oakland fans went on the field at any time, the A's would forfeit the game. Texas officials decried the lack of security near the bullpen bench. Oakland front office types said their fans' behavior was not unruly prior to the fisticuffs and flying seat, and that baseball's rules of conduct—the vaunted terms and conditions—are posted at every ballpark entrance.

Police arrested Francisco after the game and he posted a $15,000 bond. He was later suspended by MLB for the remainder of the season (sixteen games). In July of 2005, an Alameda County Superior Court judge sentenced Francisco to five hundred hours of community service and twenty days in a Texas sheriff's work program, in addition to a requirement he attend twenty-six anger management classes, pay some retribution to Jennifer Bueno and be on probation for three years. Francisco, a native of the Dominican Republic, had pleaded no contest to the misdemeanor assault charge and was concerned about his immigration status relative to any conviction.

Texas reliever Carlos Almanzar, who made some progress into the first rows during the fight after Bueno reportedly disrespected his pitching abilities and his family by saying they were better off working as day laborers at Home Depot, was suspended five games. Rangers coach Rudy Jaramillo was also suspended for five games, while Brocail, who told the *Fort Worth Star-Telegram* he was enraged by Bueno insulting his mother, was handed a seven game suspension. The whole scene, dissected frame by frame by various cable television highlight shows, certainly gave new meaning to the term "foul territory." For a $19.95 folding chair, the litigation has been impressively expensive, proving that not only is heckling an American tradition (as Craig Bueno pointed out), but so are lawsuits.

Jennifer Bueno's personal injury lawsuit against the Texas Rangers Professional Baseball Club, Francisco, two of his teammates, and the security firm working at the Coliseum, was finally settled in January of 2007 after it prompted a counter-suit from the Rangers. The *East Bay Express* newspaper reported the case was getting ugly just prior to settlement. The Texas club's attorneys subpoenaed the city of Hayward, where Craig Bueno works in the fire department, demanding his personnel file, disciplinary records, and copies of any complaints against him. The Rangers attorneys were also looking into a 2003 alleged sexual assault case at Shasta Lake and reportedly used private investigators to show pictures of the woman involved to area firefighters, inquiring about Bueno's possible involvement in the incident.

The newspaper reported the Rangers were trying to debunk the "last-ing emotional distress" portion of Bueno's lawsuit by somehow exposing misdeeds by her husband, whom the Texas attorneys also saw as depict-ing himself as an unblemished hero. An Alameda County Superior Court judge supported a motion by Bueno's lawyer Gary Gwilliam to prevent the Texas attorneys from trying to produce improper character evidence against the husband of the plaintiff. Gwilliam told the *East Bay Express* that if his client was awarded punitive damages in the Francisco case, the payout could easily be in the "high seven figures." Terms of the settlement were not announced, and the Rangers issued another terse apology to Mrs. Bueno. There was also a suit filed by another fan who claimed he was injured trying to dodge the flying chair.

In the aftermath of Francisco and Brocail's uproar, Craig and Jen-nifer Bueno cancelled their A's season ticket plan. Brocail had claimed he alerted a security guard about Craig Bueno's verbal abuse more than once, but no action was taken. Perhaps facing the certainty of extra innings after Soriano tied the game in the ninth, Brocail stood up on his own be-cause he knew that would get Bueno removed from the stadium. Oak-land officials have maintained all along there was no problem with security in the bullpen area. In the wake of the player/fan brawl they can now refer to as 9/13, Coliseum officials established an internal hotline for the reporting of excessive verbal abuse as it is happening inside a build-ing renowned for being the home of Oakland Raiders football fans, who don't always say "please" and "thank you."

Beer Showers

As Oakland's Coliseum underwent its twenty-third name change in 2005, there would be another arrest on May 14. This time it was a fan sitting just behind the visitor's dugout. The Yankees were in town, and Jason Giambi, who won the AL MVP award while playing for the Athletics as a tattooed, long-haired feller in 2000, had become a clean-cut, yet slump-plagued Yankee. Regardless, he was the target of a thrown beer as he returned to the dugout after a routine fly out. It was a rare Kevin Brown win for New York, a 15-6 triumph during a horrid stretch of losing by Oakland. The thirty-year-old fan who drenched Giambi was promptly arrested, and the slugger had no hard feelings after the game, instead praising security for their quick action. In that same series against the Yankees, outfielder Eric

Byrnes of the A's assisted security by holding back a fan who had run onto the field and was attempting to escape by scaling the outfield wall. It was an assist Oakland management wished they hadn't seen, as the policy for players is to avoid contact with fans running onto the field. (Byrnes dog-catcher act pales in comparison to Mets catcher John Stearns, who on the night of June 12, 1980, ran from his position behind the plate all the way to left field to tackle one of two drunken fans who had made a mockery of Shea Stadium security and police who could not seem to catch them.)

Before Bob Watson became MLB's disciplinarian, he played nineteen seasons in the Bigs and was involved in his share of scrapes (*Watson vs. Enzo Hernandez* comes to mind). In 1974, he was on duty roaming center field for Houston in a game against Cincinnati at Riverfront Stadium. After crashing into the center field wall, he slumped to the warning track, injured and bleeding. Fans high above him in the center field seats proceeded to dump expensive beer on Watson—probably Hudepohl—as part of some bizarre, Southwestern Ohio holistic medicine practice which called for the use of lager to stop any bleeding.

In April of 1987 at then-named Candlestick Park, Mike Marshall of the Dodgers provoked a more serious beer shower from the Giants faithful, about seventy-five of whom were ejected and several arrested. San Francisco manager Roger Craig ordered Scott Garrelts to intentionally walk Pedro Guerrero to get to clean-up hitter Marshall with two outs in the tenth inning of an 8-8 game. With two men on, Marshall hit a home run to put Los Angeles up 11-8. As he rounded the bases, Marshall pumped his fist and gestured repeatedly at Craig in the Giants dugout, gloating in his success in the face of such blatant disrespect. It was Marshall's personal response to the Shot Heard 'Round the World, apparently.

Of course, the next pitch from Garrelts—facing Dodgers reserve catcher Alex Trevino—sailed over the batter's head and both benches emptied as is the tradition between these two old rivals. Guerrero and the Giants Chris Brown locked horns and required heavy restraint as the disruption lasted a quarter of an hour. As the entire Dodgers roster made its way back to the dugout, Giants fans showered them with gallons of draft beer apparently stored throughout the game for such an occasion. They also hurled coins, cups, ice, garlic fries, and any Candlestick debris they could find at the hated blue team from SoCal. Some fans said a few Dodgers spit at several spectators in retaliation. Dodgers manager Tommy Lasorda was beside himself (yes, there was room), calling the Giants fans a "disgrace to the U.S.A." He also said he lost all respect for Garrelts after he threw at Trevino's head.

After the game, Marshall had come down from his home run high and apologized to Craig. "My emotions got carried away," Marshall said. "I regret I made those gestures. It was sheer emotion and frustration." Marshall was 0-for-5 as he stepped in against Garrelts. The Dodgers 11-8 lead held up as Ken Howell struck out the side in the bottom of the tenth after all the crap had been cleared off the field.

In any case, a beer shower is always preferable to the one Houston pitcher Dave Smith got in Queens, New York. He was in the bullpen of Shea Stadium, situated next to the left field stands. Apparently, a Mets fan relieved himself off the edge and drenched Smith with some urine. It was after this incident Smith issued his immortal quote: "It was the first time I've ever been used for long relief."

And if Mets fans weren't busy peeing on the opposition from the loge, they were busy impersonating reporters to get clubhouse access. In January of 2007, an eighteen-year-old man pleaded guilty to second-degree criminal impersonation and was fined $1,000 and banned from Mets home games for three years. He had used a forged press pass to gain entry to the visiting clubhouse at Shea because he wanted to meet his longtime hero Mike Piazza, who was in town with the Padres. The fake reporter was booted from the clubhouse when he asked Piazza to pose for a picture with him. He was arrested a week later when he tried to use the forged pass at the press entrance for a game against Colorado.

Practice Makes Perfect

The Marshall fist-pumping display in San Francisco came five years after the famous Reggie Smith invasion of the Candlestick stands. On September 24, 1981, Smith of the Dodgers was stretching in front of the dugout in the sixth inning and engaged in an insult battle with thirty-seven-year-old Giants fan Michael Dooley. As the conversation heated up, Dooley threw his souvenir batting helmet at Smith. That was the last straw for Reggie who bounded into the stands and administered a beating on Dooley, an insulation parts salesman from Redwood City, California. Other fans tried to aid Dooley, which prompted Jay Johnstone and Davey Lopes of the Dodgers to jump in. A strange tug-of-war ensued as Smith was trying to pull Dooley onto the field and police and security guards were pulling Dooley in the opposite direction. His front-row seat became a theater of unrest with the authorities crowded into the aisle, fellow fans dodging thrown beers and other objects aimed at Smith and the police. Under it all was a helpless Dooley, his white jacket pulled up over his head and shoulders. Five minutes later, with calm restored to the expensive seats, eight fans were detained by authorities and Smith was tossed from the ballgame. As Smith was being walked off the field by police officers (he was carrying two of his bats and his *authentic* batting helmet), an inaccurate beer bottle thrower missed him and the officers by ten feet. Dooley, who took several blows from a San Francisco police officer's truncheon during the tussle, suffered three broken ribs and a broken hand. The following March, he tried to sue the Dodgers for $5 million. By then, Smith had signed with the Giants as a free agent. Charges against Dooley were eventually dropped, while Smith was suspended for five days, fined $50 by the Dodgers and $5,000 by the National League.

In possibly the most constructive use of Spring Training ever, in April of the same year, Smith had pummeled a fan on the final day of Dodgers camp in Vero Beach, Florida. Smith was playing catch with consultant/coach Sandy Koufax, taking it easy on his surgically repaired shoulder, when a trio of young men began taunting him. After ten minutes of sun-splashed ribbing within the ever-quaint confines of "Dodgertown," Smith was pushed too far when one of the lads started blowing kisses at him. So he charged at the guy and landed a hefty blow to his jaw, sending him straight to the ground. Koufax was probably relieved to see there were no bats involved.

In 1996, White Sox outfielder Tony Phillips did manage to chase down a heckler in the stands of Milwaukee's County Stadium. He clocked him twice, claiming the fan was yelling racial epithets. Though the Milwaukee County sheriff's department wanted Phillips to be charged with battery for landing two to the jaw of fan Chris Havorka, twenty-three, of Racine, Wisconsin, both player and fan got the same citations. The county charge was disorderly conduct, one step above a speeding ticket, with Phillips and Havorka ordered to pay $287 each. Phillips would face more serious charges in August of 1997, at a motel in Anaheim where one of the guests was a drug called crack.

Chapter 7:
MY KIND OF TOWN

The song made famous by Frank Sinatra fails to mention them.
And Carl Sandburg may have captured many of Chicago's traits in his
Windy City verse, but he also left out the psychotic baseball fans dotting
the big (tattooed) shoulders' populus. Sandburg mentioned the wicked,
the crooked, the brutal, and even brawling, in his most famous poem. He
also referred to a "tall, bold slugger set vivid against the little soft cities"
(hear that, Milwaukee?) but he never got around to naming the Ligues,
the Visgars, the Murrays or a guy called Eric Dybas. These were all bold
fans who attacked a Royals first base coach, a Houston outfielder, a Cubs
reliever, and an ex-Marine umpire, respectively. Not to mention the corporate ticket holder who felt it was necessary to steal Chad Kreuter's cap
while the backup catcher was sitting on the Dodgers bullpen bench at
Wrigley—an incident that Chad saw as an invitation to walk among the
Cubs faithful on an ill-advised headgear retrieval mission. There was also
the time in 1971 when Don Buford of the Orioles was so incensed by debris tossed at him from the Comiskey upper deck that he departed the
on-deck circle and went after a fan along the third base line, bloodying the
taunting spectator's face. The ammunition used by White Sox faithful
that night included rocks and a jagged wooden slat torn from a seat. It was
thrown at Buford, missed him, and stuck into the ground in front of the
on-deck circle. Sometimes, the Comiskey ammunition, like *Soylent Green*,
is *people*. There was the time in 1980 when Texas Ranger Mickey Rivers
got in a fight with fans outside Comiskey. Teammate Danny Darwin, a

real Texan, came to his rescue but suffered a broken knuckle in his right hand during the rumble.

The aforementioned attacked umpire was Laz Diaz, who was working the White Sox–Royals game in April of 2003 at Comiskey Park, which had just been renamed U.S. Cellular Field. Three fans ran onto the field early in the contest, and the fourth, Eric Dybas of Bolingbrook, Illinois, grabbed Diaz around the legs in a drunken attempt to perform an open-field tackle. The twenty-four-year-old fell face first into the grass. Royals right fielder Brandon Berger had just caught Carlos Lee's fly ball for the last out of the eighth inning, and was the first to reach Diaz and Dybas. Diaz, a former Marine, was able to shed Dybas with relative ease, and the swarm of Royals players and red-faced park security officers did the rest. It appeared Berger even landed a blow to Dybas's head with the baseball still clenched in his fist. Diaz was not hurt and was able to finish the game. Dybas was photographed in the back of a police vehicle with a bloody bandage adorning his apparently numb skull. He said later he had been drinking at a Cubs game at Wrigley Field earlier in the day, and his attorney blamed alcohol for his client's attack on Diaz. The Dybas beer count for the Northside-Southside ballgame combo: one dozen sixteen-ounce cups.

The Dybas incident rattled the Royals, as their visit to Comiskey the previous September resulted in a bizarre attack by a shirtless father and son duo on first base coach Tom Gamboa. "Every time we are here, something crazy happens," said Mike Sweeney of the Royals. The Gamboa attack resembled an al fresco version of *The Jerry Springer Show* as thirty-four-year-old William Ligue Jr. and his fifteen-year-old son ambushed Gamboa from behind, wailing away on the mild-mannered fifty-four-year-old coach in the ninth inning. The Ligues had reportedly been heckling Gamboa from the front row the entire game and claimed he responded with an obscene gesture at one point. Ligue called a female acquaintance on his cell phone to see if she was watching the game. When she said she wasn't, he told her to watch the news. He handed his cell phone, keys, and jewelry to one of his cousins, then he and his son leaped over the rail. Royals outfielder Carlos Beltran saw the pair running onto the field and figured they would try to run the bases, like many other crazed fans do. Instead, Gamboa was blindsided and went down in a heap, with the Ligue family doing their best to inflict some quick damage with their fists.

With Gamboa on the ground swiveling to see his attacker, he said he was surprised to see two of them. The Ligues suffered from inadequate traction as both father and son could not get solid footing and were falling over each other as their momentum sent Gamboa sprawling. When the coach was turned around, he was able to show them his spikes and push off of the legs of the younger Ligue. The shirtless Ligues certainly violated the innocence of the first base coach's box, giving it a rare atmosphere of a dime store mosh pit manned by two loser guys who showed up to see a local thrash metal band and were determined to make the most of it.

Gamboa suffered some facial abrasions and a cut to his forehead. A pocket knife was found on the ground after the fight, but was never put to use by either Ligue.

The image of a defiant Ligue being led to the police car, covered in tattoos with a scraggly mustache—resembling a demented Ken Burns in one photo—became a symbol of concern for ballplayers who suddenly felt vulnerable on the field, especially when Ligue said, "He [Gamboa] flicked [sic] us off. He got what he deserved." Gamboa, who played a few seasons of pro ball in Canada in the early 1970s and managed a half-dozen years in the Puerto Rican winter leagues, suffered impaired hearing in his right ear as a result of the attack. He later went on to become a spokesman for the Florida-based personal safety advocacy group called Survive a Violent Encounter (S.A.V.E.).

The younger Ligue was charged with two juvenile counts of aggravated battery for his attack on Gamboa and a ballpark security guard who was an off-duty cop. In the weeks after the incident, Papa Ligue underwent a cleanup transformation for the ages. In June, he was spotted working as a catering official at the 2003 U.S. Open golf tournament at Olympia Fields, Illinois. The press got a good look at the new Ligue when he appeared for a hearing in August. Gone was the demented Ken Burns look. Ligue walked into court clean-shaven, with his black hair trimmed short, looking pensive behind spectacles and wearing a plaid collared shirt tucked neatly into khaki trousers. Though initially sentenced to 30 months probation, Papa Ligue would end up in jail in 2004 after breaking into a car near a pizzeria where he worked as a deliveryman, leading police on a brief chase before being captured. He was sentenced to fifty-seven months in prison. In March of 2007, the littlest Ligue—Michael, who was fourteen when he stayed behind in the Comiskey seats to watch his older brother and dad go after Gamboa—faced felony gun charges after being involved in a drive-by shooting in suburban Chicago.

Disco Inferno

During the height of the disco era, the city of Chicago and its baseball fans struck a blow for rock 'n' rollers whose mantra was "Disco sucks." In 1979, while the Pittsburgh Pirates were forging a rallying cry with "We Are Family" by the disco act known as Sister Sledge, Chicago disc jockey Steve Dahl was staging a promotion between games of a Tigers–White Sox doubleheader at Comiskey on July 12. It was called "Disco Demolition" and fans could be admitted to the game for a mere 98 cents (98 was the FM frequency of his radio station) if they surrendered a disco record at the gate. Ninety-eight was almost the temperature that night on the Southside. The floundering White Sox were six games under .500 and drew the usual fifteen thousand or so customers the night before. After a bland 4-1 loss to the Tigers in game one, most of the listed 47,795 anti-disco fans had packed into the ballyard, many still carrying disco records that were no longer being collected at the gate. This was not the usual Thursday night baseball crowd. There might have been a stoner keeping a scorecard, slowly noting that the White Sox had a third baseman named Jim Morrison (whoa!) and he struck out against Aurelio Lopez (of Mexico—peyote, dude!) to end the first game. The extra vinyl discs doubled as Frisbees throughout the game as fans sailed them off the upper deck, turning Donna Summer recordings into shrapnel as they hit seats, pillars, and fellow fans.

In between games, Dahl was to take the field and detonate a crate inside a Dumpster filled with the donated disco records. Dressed in military garb, he delighted the crowd by maintaining the chant of "disco sucks!" and then the explosion rocked the pile of records in center field. Smoke filled the already airless stadium, and the crowd went nuts. Game two starter Ken Kravec was trying to warm up in the bullpen, but a barrage of fireworks moved his pre-game pitches to the Comiskey mound. After a couple of tosses, he noticed Dahl had beaten a hasty retreat out of the ballpark in a mock military vehicle, and hundreds of fans were pouring over the right field fence. Several were sliding into second base when Kravec did his evac, and got the hell out of there, running to the dugout with his White Sox cap in hand.

The ten thousand or so turned away at the gates were finding ways into the ballpark via drainpipes and the famous arched windows of the place locals called "Sox Park." The freeways and sidewalks around the park were jammed with more angry customers, and the police closed at least two exits on the Dan Ryan Expressway. The foul poles were being used as ladders for fans trafficking to and from the upper deck, not always with success.

Channeling the Ligues of the future, many of the young, white male field invaders were shirtless, but without as many tattoos and with no bone to pick with an obscure first base coach. Photos of the crowd of at least five thousand on the field show some sitting like sunbathers, in circles, lighting cigarettes, and other smokeables. Smoldering disco records were regrouped for an impromptu bonfire in right-center field, with stoners jumping through the flames. Homemade "disco sucks!" banners were burned, perhaps even the one seen earlier that asked: "What do Linda Lovelace and disco have in common?" Some witnesses said they saw couples fornicating on the Comiskey turf. The bases were lifted and gone, including home plate and the pitcher's rubber. Chunks of turf and infield dirt had been gouged out as souvenirs as Harry Caray was pleading from the announcer's booth for fans to "regain our seats" so more baseball could be played. Announcer Jimmy Piersall, who famously clashed with a pair of teenage hecklers on the field at Yankee Stadium in 1961, relayed to his audience notations of disgust with the promotion and the behavior of the young, rock 'n' roll crowd that came to the ballpark to make musical history. The forty minutes of anarchy brought on by Dahl's detonation meant the second game would be cancelled and later forfeited, giving the Tigers a midsummer sweep of the twin bill. White Sox president Bill Veeck, famous for his legacy of zany promotions, was incensed that the umpires ruled the field unplayable. Sparky Anderson, in his first season managing in the American League, was concerned for the safety of his players, noting the crowd was even more unplayable than the field. Among the umpires was Dave Phillips, who would later title his autobiography *Center Field On Fire* in honor of this blessed event. Also in the house for disco's loud death was none other than Nestor Chylak, grizzled veteran of baseball's landmark upheavals. He was serving as an umpire supervisor when the crew of arbiters was suddenly given the rest of the night off thanks to the cultural Battle of Hastings being waged at old Comiskey.

Chylak probably wasn't surprised. All he had to do was think back to the game he worked at Comiskey in September of 1960, when he saw Chicago shortstop Sammy Esposito attacked by one of his own fans after bobbling a surefire double-play grounder hit by Moose Skowron in the eighth inning, helping the White Sox blow a lead against the Yankees. There certainly wasn't a Skowron flattop haircut in sight as the anti-disco denizens discovered the batting cage beyond the center field wall. It was wheeled back onto the diamond and all but destroyed by the mob like the uprights on a football field. "It was the sickest thing I've ever seen in my life," White Sox pitcher Ross Baumgarten, apparently the leader of a sheltered life, told the AP.

Mounted Chicago police in full riot gear finally cleared the field with a slow march from home plate to the outfield. The anti-disco demonstrators, known as members of the Dahl-created gang Insane Coho Lips, dispersed quickly at the sight of batons from a rather famous police force. Arrests numbered near forty, not bad for a crowd estimated to be well over sixty thousand by the end of the night. Injuries were less than a dozen, according to reports, and many of them involved fractured ankles and various forms of broken landing gear resulting from ill-advised leaps from misjudged heights.

If Ten-Cent Beer Night had captured the height of Nixon-era angst, Disco Demolition provided a bookend for an itchy, polyester-clad decade finally coming to a close. If anything, the botched promotion firmly placed one evening of disjointed baseball among scores of sociology textbooks and pop culture highlight reels for many years to come.

As of late 2006, Dahl, a prototype of the modern-day "shock jock" who was twenty-four-years old on Disco Demolition night, continued to espouse on-air zaniness to Chicago radio listeners. His Web site promotes the sale of a twenty-fifth anniversary DVD documenting the disco destruction, as well as a self-help book Dahl credits with helping him kick his problem drinking habit. But for baseball fans in Chicago, especially on the Northside, the party never stops.

Wrigley's Mad Hatter

Game-worn or game-used equipment—nomenclature born as a byproduct of the memorabilia industry that has flourished beneath the sport like Bartertown in the third Mad Max movie—never had a more unspectacular moment than Chad Kreuter's cap from May 16, 2000, at Wrigley Field. It was removed from his head, before or after a punch was delivered to the backup catcher's skull, as he sat on the bullpen bench along the brick wall running along the first base line and into the right field corner of the facility referred to as "the friendly confines." Thousands and thousands of ballplayers through the years have resisted, despite great temptation, the quintessential "bad idea" that Kreuter subscribed to that night in Wrigley. Cobb did it, but he was Cobb. Jim Rice did it with the help of Don Baylor. Tony Phillips and Reggie Smith were experts at it. The bad idea: climbing into the stands to physically settle a score with a paying customer.

With one out in the ninth inning on a chilly May evening, the Dodgers lead had been cut to 6-5 by a pinch-hit RBI double by the Cubs Julio Zuleta. The Cubs were not going to go down without a fight. A fan named Josh Pulliam, an employee of the Tribune Company—the corporate owners of the Cubs—left his corporate seat and decided the Dodgers bullpen bench was his personal souvenir stand. He said he calmly approached Kreuter from behind, but did not hit him, Pulliam's attorney emphasized later. Kreuter, along with several other Dodgers bullpen staff, was seated on the bench up against the chest-high brick wall with his back to the fans. Pulliam was quick to flee after grabbing the hat, and Kreuter wasn't about to give up his cap and dignity sitting down. It was then Chadden Michael Kreuter, backup catcher in his first of three seasons with the Dodgers, processed decision-making synapses in his cerebral cortex, prompting his relaxed (yet check-cashing) muscles to move his skeleton over the wall and into the sea of cup-holding, hooded sweatshirt wearing fellows. Moving among the cramped seats in pursuit of his vanished attacker, and briefly grabbing him, Kreuter was soon in trouble. He could see a few teammates and coaches following his ill-fated charge, leaping in to help their man overboard. Coaches John Shelby (of *Shelby vs. Clemens*) and Rick Dempsey (of *Dempsey vs. Dykstra*) plumbed the depths of agitated fans. The rubbernecking crowd was forced to stand quickly, with extra effort required not to trip over nine innings worth of detritus on the treacherous Wrigley floor. Todd Hollandsworth got in an extended tussle just over the wall, with Lilliputian Alex Cora and brawnmeister Gary Sheffield at his elbow. Half the Dodgers team seemed to relish standing in their blue warm-up jackets atop the brick wall separating the stands from the field. It was their version of attending a gymnastics fantasy camp.

Kreuter was soon surrounded and trying to get back on the field as his brave teammates clashed with fans to his left and right—the kind of awkward tussles that involve chair backs, slippery souvenir programs, dropped sweaters and cap bills jousting each other off both parties' heads. Kreuter was punched and then spit on, according to Dodgers officials. Oddly enough, the Tribune Company corporate seats are located behind the bullpen because the corporate parent thought its own workers would be well behaved and leave the opposing team's bullpen staff alone. So in terms of public relations fiascos, the Kreuter incident gave the company its second version of "Dewey Defeats Truman," the Trib's famous headline gaffe from the 1948 presidential election.

Kreuter refused comment after the game, though his agent Scott Boras made a few lawyerly remarks certainly not worthy of repeating at any cost (something about Chad being "battered" and "trying to recover his property").

Kreuter kept referring the press to Todd Hundley, whose home run bolstered the 6-5 win for the Dodgers when they were on the field. Hundley quickly hung himself and his teammates out to dry, playing the hometown card, expressing his disappointment with the fans of the team his father played for, and a team he would play for in 2001 and 2002. "If you wanted a hat that bad, be polite and ask for one. We'll give it to you," Hundley told the AP. "We've got a whole bunch of them." And they've got a whole bunch of hairshirts to be worn, as well, especially after those comments. Hundley's disappointment with Northsiders would boil over during his Wrigley tenure, when, mired in yet another slump, he was caught on camera giving the finger to a heckling Cubs fan.

Kreuter, who spread his mediocrity over eight different teams in a sixteen-year career, would go on to be named head coach of USC's baseball team in 2006, so student-athletes were assured of quality instruction on how to protect their caps at all times, especially when riding the pine. On the USC baseball Web site, Kreuter set up a column called "Kreuter's Korner" (with no apologies to Ralph Kiner, a Hall of Famer who in just ten seasons hit 369 home runs, 315 more than Kreuter's career total). In his first column, Kreuter promised to focus on, as he put it, "re-kreuting." This must have been a kinder, gentler, more cutesy Chad than the one who invaded Wrigley territory. He'd had other bad experiences in Chicago. In July of 1996 at Comiskey, he was catching for the White Sox and Johnny Damon of the Royals, scoring on a sacrifice fly, shattered Kreuter's shoulder in a home plate collision. Kreuter was out for the rest of the season, and passed out in his hotel room just prior to having surgery on the shoulder. Paramedics rushed him to the hospital where doctors found another injury from the Damon collision—a rib had punctured his stomach lining and caused massive internal bleeding. The following May, Kreuter and fellow fan-abuser Tony Phillips were traded to the Angels for Chuck McElroy and Jorge Fabregas.

Pulliam, of course, was not prosecuted, but four other fans—one who ran on the field and three who fought Dodgers in the stands—were arrested and charged with disorderly conduct. Pulliam reportedly dropped Kreuter's cap, probably a component of a pants-soiling moment when the sometimes-Dodgers catcher actually had the thief in his grasp. Therefore, with the hat no longer in Pulliam's possession, the charge would have likely been "attempted theft" and would have involved Kreuter autographing an official complaint and returning for court dates. This unlikely scenario never materialized and the Dodgers front office chose to drop the matter.

The knee-jerk reaction was to blame the whole Kreuter brawl on alcohol, but Pulliam insisted he had only consumed two beers. Security was tightened all over MLB parks, and Yankee Stadium stopped selling beer in its rowdy right field bleachers, apparently because George Steinbrenner suspected those vociferous, jet-setting fans had flown to Chicago and helped pummel the Dodgers in the stands at Wrigley.

Meanwhile, the suspensions came down heavy on the Dodgers and sent Davey Johnson's troops single file to the appeals desk of MLB's Park Avenue digs in Manhattan. Frank Robinson punished sixteen players and three coaches for a total of eighty-four missed games. Kreuter got an unnoticeable eight games, coaches Dempsey, Shelby and Glenn Hoffman also got eight games each, Sheffield got five games while Hundley, Eric Karros and the mild-mannered Shawn Green got three games each.

Bond Trader Lacks Maturity

Night games at Wrigley have had several incidents, and day games at 1060 West Addison usually feature beer, bonhomie, and bad baseball much to the delight of the sunbathing crowd. But on September 28, 1995, in a doozy of what would become an extra-innings win for the Cubs that would take almost five hours to play, a twenty-seven-year-old suburban bond trader did something extremely stupid. He charged after Cubs reliever Randy Myers, a former "Nasty Boy," military memorabilia collector, hunter, martial artist and native of rugged Washington state. Myers, rumored to carry a knife on his person *while on the field* (hinted at in former teammate Rob Dibble's column on ESPN.com), saw the man coming and dropped him with one quick forearm block.

The twenty-seven-year-old "attacker" was John Murray of Riverside,

Illinois, adding yet another chapter of psychotic Windy City fan behavior to the wrong side of the ledger. Myers had just given up a two-run homer to Houston's James Mouton, who was pinch-hitting in the eighth. The homer put Houston up 9-7. Just prior to the long ball, Murray said to his brother, "If he throws another home run, I'm going to run out there and give him what for." Mouton delivered the goods, and Murray, in his denim shirt, leaped out of the stands on the first base side and ran toward the 6-foot-1, 230-pound Myers, who calmly dropped his glove and let the man approach.

After leveling him with his forearm, Myers pinned Murray to the bluegrass and clover infield of the Friendly Confines until security could scrape him up and haul him to jail. He was charged with assault and disorderly conduct and released on a $75 bond. Myers, who didn't have time to reach into his own pocket for his little friend, said he feared Murray was about to reach into his own waistband and produce some type of weapon.

Cubs shortstop Shawon Dunston (of the hearty mound charge in *Dunston vs. Arnold*) feared for the man's life and was first on the scene, along with a Cubs ball boy brave beyond his years. "I knew Randy was going to do one of those martial arts moves," Dunston told AP. "I was afraid Randy was going to snap his neck." Had Myers done so, it would have meant one less bond trader at the Chicago Board of Trade.

Murray's occupation harkens back to the earliest days of the game's disciplinary actions. The first fine recorded on the books of professional baseball was on October 6, 1845, during a New York Knickerbockers game. That's when one Archibald T. Bourie was fined six cents for swearing. Bourie was a Wall Street broker.

In a reverse of the fan chasing after Myers, there was the incident in June of 1977, when a Wrigley Field heckler taunted Reggie Smith of the Dodgers to the point where the headstrong outfielder charged after him in the stands and had to be restrained. (He would pull the same stunt at Candlestick Park with messy results in 1981.) Smith's road trip would get even more tense a few days later in steamy St. Louis, when he charged Cardinals pitcher John Denny after getting hit by a pitch in the second inning. And upon returning home to Dodger Stadium, Smith's June swoon continued when he charged Cubs pitcher Rick Reuschel. "I'm tired of being thrown at," Smith told the AP after the game. "I will do anything to protect myself." Cubs manager Herman Franks pooh-poohed Smith's claims. "Every time a pitch is close to him he challenges the pitcher," Franks said.

Rough and Tumble Bratwurst Belt

No discussion of deviant behavior in the Chicagoland area is complete without a John Wayne Gacy reference, or, for that matter, an Ed Gein and/or Jeffrey Dahmer reference if nearby Wisconsin is to be included. Serial killers have a way of putting a city or town on the pop culture map unfurled by postmodern hipster types engaging in incessant retro-irony. Gacy was an upright businessman and a clown. Gein was a rural loner. Dahmer was a hungry drunk. Sometimes fans who run on the field are clowning upright businessmen. Occasionally they are rural loners. Usually they are hungry drunks. The majority of the time, though, it seems they all hail from the Chicago area. Their actions usually cause sports columnists to take the moral high ground (requiring a Machu Picchu type of ascent) and exaggerate the "crimes" of these haywire spectators to a status seemingly comparable and in the same transgressions ballpark as the aforementioned Messrs. Gacy, Gein, and Dahmer.

Enter South Beloit, Illinois, resident Burley W. Visgar, a twenty-three-year-old with a Dickensian name. He lived with his parents in a town on the border of Illinois and Wisconsin, almost equidistant between Milwaukee and Chicago, giving him easy access to three different major league franchises. Visgar, through his athletic performance on Friday, September 24, 1999, at Milwaukee's County Stadium and his harsh sentencing by the court in April 2000, extended the psycho-fan legacy of Chicago to its northern suburbs, into America's Dairyland and former beer capital.

The Brewers were hosting the Astros, and former Brewers first-round draft pick Bill Spiers was playing right field for Houston. According to court documents, Visgar had been drinking beer and vodka before joining the 14,092 other fans in attendance, taking a seat in the right field bleachers. In the second inning, he advised fans sitting around him that he would jump onto the playing field, run around naked, give "the number one salute" and jump on a player's back if they agreed to pay his subsequent fines. Apparently, Visgar had never witnessed what typically happens to fans captured after running onto the field; his obviously booze-inspired plan was to run into the arms of awaiting cops to avoid any beatings from angry ballplayers.

The 6-foot-3, 230-pound Visgar took action in the sixth inning with Milwaukee coming to bat. He stepped over the wall and dropped the eight feet to the field and raced fully-clothed across twenty feet of outfield grass to leap piggyback style onto an unsuspecting Bill Spiers. The Houston outfielder may have thought he was in Seattle for a moment, a place he was hated after smashing up catcher Dave Valle's knee in a questionable effort to break up a 1-2-3 double play during Spiers' rookie year as a Brewer in 1989. But "The fog of time," as Jimmy Cannon wrote, "conceals the filth of vanished years," as Visgar made impact with the 6-foot-2, 190-pound Spiers, the outfielder's neck whiplashed back, and for a split nanosecond, he saw Milwaukee sky instead of Kingdome roof tile, so at that instant he knew he wasn't in Seattle. In the back of his mind, he also knew Valle had still yet to be avenged.

Meanwhile, Spiers said he could not get the South Beloit monkey off his back. He had to swivel and fall to the ground. A member of the groundskeeping staff was closing in to help Spiers when Houston pitcher Mike Hampton, who was about to pitch to Alex Ochoa, appeared like a juggernaut as the first teammate on the scene. Hampton's sprint from the mound into right field left second baseman Craig Biggio, first baseman Jeff Bagwell, and center fielder Carl Everett in the dust. Hampton's vigorous treatment of Visgar was also noted by several teammates as the Houston starter appeared to have lost his hat in transit to right field. Billy Wagner told MLB.com: "What was amazing is that our whole team was out there, beating the guy, and he got up laughing."

It took two law enforcement officers a bit longer than usual to hand-cuff Visgar, who stood absolutely still and appeared unruffled as he awaited processing. In fact, without a single hair mussed, Visgar resembled a chubbier version of Jeff Kent. The incident delayed the game ten minutes. Spiers' had a contusion on his left eye, and had back and neck pain and left the game in the next inning. He did not start the next night's game, but did pinch hit.

Visgar, meanwhile, posted $1,250 worth of bail over the weekend and would eventually plead guilty to two misdemeanor counts of disorderly conduct. A more serious battery charge would have been possible, a district attorney said, but it would have required Spiers to return to Milwaukee to testify. Again, the rowdy fans benefit from the busy ballplayer's travel schedule. With the Astros in the thick of the NL Central Division pennant race, it was doubtful Spiers would be able to return to Milwaukee for court proceedings.

On Friday, April 7, 2000, Visgar, who had no prior criminal record, had the book thrown at him. Circuit Judge Michael B. Brennan sentenced him to ninety days in jail and a $1,000 fine. The D.A.'s office and Brewers officials said the stiff sentence was necessary because Visgar the Horrible actually *jumped on* a ballplayer. *The Milwaukee Journal Sentinel* reported Visgar brought with him to court a letter of support from his hometown police chief and a newspaper clipping of a story commending him for his involvement with the Boys & Girls Clubs. It was a nice try. The last straw, Visgar told the court, was that his home life had been thrown into a tumult thanks to his spanking of Spiers. After the incident and as a result of his newfound notoriety, Visgar was told by his parents he had to move out of their home because they couldn't stand the phone ringing off the hook with inquiries from reporters and lawyers and other interested parties. Calls by the author seeking comment from Visgar at his new apartment were not returned.

Though the television footage of Visgar's attack isn't as dramatic as the Ligue of Extraordinarily Filthy Heathens ambush of Gamboa at Comiskey, networks will grant these wayward spectators their own immortality by replaying both incidents in retrospect and for comparison every time a fan attacks a player in the future.

Fans standing up in the stands—prompted by the on field drama—is a simple gesture that has been slowly deteriorating into one of the game's many "lost art" categories, along with bunting, bench jockeying, knowing who the base coaches and umpires are, and . . . watching the game. Fights cause spectators to rise up. So does forced jingoism— at Yankee Stadium, for instance, the once fun Seventh-Inning Stretch has become a Two-Minute Hate thanks to angry "patriots" screaming "hats off!" at fellow fans during the rote playing of a scratchy Kate Smith version of "God Bless America." Thanks to west coast fans, sometimes the stoner-infantile exercise known as "the wave" does the trick, at least for a few passing seconds.

Anticipating a close play at the plate—any play at the dish where the catcher, sometimes unmasked, receives a long-distance relay that began on the synthetic clay pebbles of the outfield warning track—should get a rise out of true fans. There will be impact, sometimes shoulder to shoulder, batting helmets will fly off like stray hubcaps in a car crash, the umpire will lean in to hone his gaze onto the ball, grasped or ungrasped, and then make his call—the eagle wings for a "safe" runner, or the "out" gesture issued with the finality of an assembly line hole-punch operator. Limbs pile up, tangle and grasp in desperation for the sunken plinth, a drowning man seeking a lifesaving spar as a beetle-like foe, captain of an overflowing lifeboat, tries to prevent another salvation and protect his team.

Home plate, then, is center stage of all baseball action. Sometimes the battles are fought on-site after a beanball, or following a dirty slide, or when the sacred space is used as a soapbox by loquacious batters. Other times, the home plate brawls are a matter of personal space being invaded in the wrong fashion. Catchers, always toting their laundry list of concerns and inning-by-inning multitasking (calling the pitches, massaging the pitcher's ego, not offending the umpire, not interfering with the batter, making sure the protective cup is in place, etc.) have an understandably short fuse when it comes to tolerating the slightest shred of insolence from the opposition.

Which might explain why Dave Valle tagged Chad Curtis the way he did. *Curtis vs. Valle* from 1992 could easily have been a reincarnation of *George Vico vs. Birdie Tebbetts* at Fenway in 1948, or indeed *Hal Smith vs. Tony Gonzalez* from Connie Mack Stadium in 1961, if you throw in a Roberto Clemente throw to home plate in the second game of a doubleheader. (The Tebbetts incident, in which Detroit's Vico was punished by Red Sox players in the clubhouse runway after he was ejected, was not the result of a hard tag but a headlong collision with Tebbetts' shin guard.) After Hal Smith's heavy catcher's mitt tag, a UPI sportswriter compared the Philly ballpark to the Coliseum in Rome, especially when there were six simultaneous fights happening on the diamond between the Pirates and Phillies. In the end, it was the managers who were injured. Gene Mauch had a shiner, and Danny Murtaugh of the Pirates somehow got spiked in the neck. The Smith fight begat future home plate ugliness for the Pirates—such as the time in June 2003 when Jason Kendall clashed with Tampa Bay's Marlon Anderson (Kendall also charged Colorado pitcher Joe Kennedy, his future batterymate in Oakland, in August of 2004), or the helmet touching dispute in June of 1998 that was *Kendall vs. Sheffield*, when Gary received a visible facial contusion during a fracas at Dodger Stadium after scoring against Pittsburgh.

On a less glamorous note, there was the tangled mess of *K. Young vs. Difelice* in 2001 at Bank One Ballpark in Phoenix, which seemed to be a personal space issue between the overpaid Pirates first baseman and the former Tampa Bay backstop. Difelice, playing in one of his twelve games for Arizona during the Diamondbacks championship season, made the mistake of lingering while standing astride Young, who had the nerve to slide into home plate in an attempt to score a run. It was Difelice's second run-in with a Bucco at home plate. In 1997 with St. Louis, he and Mark

Johnson went toe-to-toe at the dish after the Dartmouth grad barreled into him and elbowed him in the face while trying to score.

CHAD CURTIS vs. DAVE VALLE
(CALIFORNIA ANGELS)   (SEATTLE MARINERS)

April 26, 1992, Anaheim Stadium, Anaheim, California

This slight mismatch between underdeveloped rookie Chad Curtis of the Angels and the physical specimen known as Seattle catcher Dave Valle is hard to leave off the baseball violence examination table. The two engaged in pious pyrotechnics under an Orange County moon, predating Mike Sweeney's famous charge on Jeff Weaver by nine years. Valle and Curtis were both involved in their share of scraps on the field and off. Later in his career, Curtis would show he was especially intolerant of rap music played in the clubhouse, as per engagements with Royce Clayton in Texas and Kevin Mitchell in Cleveland. He also didn't approve of Pudge Rodriguez leaving a game in the middle innings to go home for a family emergency. Curtis also made October headlines for his on-air snub of TV broadcaster Jim Gray, as a protest of Gray's ambush interview of Pete Rose during the 1999 World Series. A year earlier in Arlington, Valle caused a ruckus when benches emptied after he charged Bobby Valentine as the Texas manager was pleading the case for his pitcher, Kevin Brown, who was being warned by the umpires after hitting Valle with a pitch.

When Curtis met Valle at home plate with the 1992 season not even a month old, it was long before he had a chance to establish his reputation as a clubhouse ball-buster. He was a raw rookie, in the game in the eighth inning as a pinch-runner for Lance Parrish. Curtis was scoring California's fifth run of the inning to put them up 6-5. Pinch-hitter John Morris had stroked a single to left, fielded expertly by Mariners pasture-dweller Greg Briley, who hurled the orb toward the Valle of death at home. Curtis was safe after a tumbling slide, but on his way past Valle, who was a few strides out in front of home plate, he tried to get a piece of the opposition. With umpire Rocky Roe presiding and issuing a safe call, Valle disagreed with that determination on several fronts. The brash rookie (selected by the Angels in the Job-like forty-fifth round of the 1989 draft) was lying in the dust beyond the plate as Valle, in a move perhaps learned growing up on the strangely numbered streets of Bayside, Queens, marched over and applied a Van Helsing–style stake-to-the-heart tag— with the catcher's mitt coming down quite hard on the chest of the Angel.

There was a point before the scene became a mosh pit in which Seattle reliever Jeff Nelson, himself known for tempestuous behavior, and California outfielder Luis Polonia, could have separated their angry teammates. They did not.

Parrish, who had earlier in the inning tied the game with a single, arrived to do the dirty work for his pinch-runner Curtis. The veteran catcher who would wear seven different uniforms over a nineteen-year career was the main tussler, and along with Valle, the AL's 1993 hit-by-pitch leader (plunked seventeen times), was ejected in a game the Angels would win 7-5. Any fight involving the Angels always had a Chuck Finley angle as the Louisianan was the unofficial Sergeant at Arms of the organization. He was of course another main player in the swirling shove-fest known as *Valle vs. Curtis,* which, seen without the storylines and on field personalities, was not the most spectacular brawl. (Things were a little more interesting in *Curtis vs. Ed Sprague* in June 1993 in Anaheim, when Chad was trying desperately to grow a mustache, and charged out of the Angels dugout to take on the Toronto third baseman shortly after being hit by a Pat Hentgen pitch. This dusty brawl, which careened onto the third base railing, featured some second-man-in thug-work by Finley, as well as heated moments, courtesy of Toronto's Darnell Coles hitting an Anaheim cop, and Mark Eichhorn sitting on an unknown Angels player. The scrum prompted some fans to toss souvenir giveaway baseballs at the visiting Blue Jays.)

Curtis also made the papers during his New York career when he criticized Derek Jeter for chumming up to Seattle's Alex Rodriguez during a Yankees-Mariners fight in 1999, taking on the duties of pinstriped fraternization sheriff. Not surprisingly, Chad was traded to Texas for a pair of minor leaguers that December.

Finley did not hesitate in joining Parrish to defend Curtis in the Valle fight. Finley's involvement came a decade before he was a victim of domestic violence at the hands (feet, actually) of his buxom actress wife Tawny Kitaen in Newport Beach, California. Reports indicated she kicked Finley repeatedly in the head with her high-heeled boots while the couple was driving home on April Fool's Day. Kitaen, after Finley divorced her, went on to model for various hair-metal acts, including an appearance on a Ratt album cover and later in a few Whitesnake videos, thus adding a gothic heavy metal tangent to the story of a pair of Christians losing their tempers on the ballfield. In November 2006, Kitaen's name (and therefore Finley's), was back in the news when she was charged with felony drug possession at her Newport Beach home.

In a certain den of iniquity in Seattle during Valle's ten seasons with the Mariners, his presence was celebrated by the establishment pricing a mug of beer based on the catcher's lackluster batting average on a particular day. This odd communion for sad Mariners fans got even more twisted in late June of 1992, when California released Parrish and Seattle acquired him to be Valle's backup. It's enough to drive any Seattle baseball fan to drink—or start a grunge band.

RICK DEMPSEY vs. LENNY DYKSTRA
(LOS ANGELES DODGERS)　　(PHILADELPHIA PHILLIES)
August 20, 1990, Dodger Stadium,
Los Angeles, California

One was twenty-seven, the other was forty. One was complaining to the umpire about being called out on strikes earlier in the game, the other was accused of buttering up said umpire while squatting in front of him as the catcher. One was leading the NL in hitting, the other was making his occasional start behind the plate. Veteran catcher Rick Dempsey punching Lenny Dykstra began as a tableau seen countless millions of times. A left-handed batter digs into the batter's box and turns for a word or two with either the umpire or the opposing catcher. Tobacco juice is released orally, adjustments to equipment (and underwear) are made, swings are practiced, gloves are popped, and the world awaits the action as the trio of helmeted and padded figures huddled around home plate aim their eye sockets at the pitcher.

But on this night in Dodger Stadium, the fifth inning ended with Dykstra being called out on a seemingly wide strike three from Mike Morgan, as seen by umpire Ron Barnes. As the seventh inning rolled around in the tight game, Dykstra stepped in and had his say with Barnes, who stood quite comfortably with his hands in the front pockets of his blue blazer—a Spiegel catalogue pose if ever there was one. As Dykstra self-heated—Barnes seemed calm during the exchange—the Phillies outfielder known both as "Dude" and "Nails" turned his attention to Dempsey. Making one of sixty-two appearances during the 1990 campaign, a season that meant he'd played in four decades, Dempsey stood up and removed his mask. On his head was his Dodgers cap, worn backwards like only catchers are supposed to, with the bill flipped up to denote his old-school status. Words flew as Dykstra stepped to the deepest rear of the batter's box. Dykstra dropped his bat. A millisecond later Dempsey nailed Nails in the face with his left fist, which happened to be covered by his catcher's glove. It was a rising left that planted leather dead center in Dykstra's gob. Dempsey, known for his clown prince act during rain delays and his fisticuffs during one of many run-ins at Milwaukee's Pfister Hotel (a 1974 lobby scuffle with Rick Sudakis while they were both Yankees), had opened the whoop-ass can, but Dykstra would be the one spilling its contents.

With his helmet knocked off, Dykstra attempted an overhand right that ended up gripping Dempsey and pulling him down into the dirt. Dykstra landed under him but absorbed the impact and quickly flipped the 1983 World Series MVP with an impressive wrestling reverse. As the pair were prone in the Chavez Ravine dust, Dykstra's hands, covered in white batting gloves, could be easily seen going to work. He reached up for Dempsey's face and buried it into the dirt as they writhed away. Umpire Barnes, his hands at last removed from the blazer pockets, had backed off long ago as Darren Daulton arrived and embraced Dykstra, making it a three-man pile. Dodger players (like their fans coming to games) were slow to arrive on the scene, though third baseman Mickey Hatcher proved to be effective support. Soon both rosters were employing their own versions of the Jaws of Life to pry the two apart. When they did, Dykstra was restrained by Philly manager Nick Leyva and Dale Murphy. On the way to the dugout, he finally spit out his impressive chaw of tobacco. Dempsey, meanwhile, had a welt on the side of his face and had his chest protector knocked way out of whack. Being held by Phillies Dickie Thon and Don Carman, the hatless Dempsey appeared in the upright throng looking exactly like actor Hal Holbrook (of *Creepshow* fame; he also played Deep Throat in *All the President's Men*). During that post-fight pause among the locked-arm bundle of major leaguers, Dempsey looked like he only had two more seasons left in him, which would bring him to twenty-four. His feisty foe Dykstra would hit .325 in 1990—the highest average of his twelve-season career, but not enough for the batting title. Dempsey was ejected and Mike Scioscia's night off was ruined, while Sil Campusano batted for the tossed Dykstra and flew out to center. The Dodgers held on to win 2-1, and within a few days, Dempsey received a one game suspension and a $1,000 fine from NL officials. Dempsey told the AP he knew he had to take action once Dykstra dropped his bat. "When he did that, I knew he was going to hit me," he said.

As for Nails, his career would contain a famous car crash after Daulton's bachelor party, broken collarbones from outfield walls, several hundred pouches of tobacco, and a warning from the league about high-stakes poker playing. His retirement, which involved operating his chain of car wash facilities in his native southern California, also had its off-color moments involving sexual battery charges, questions about steroids, alleged drug use, rehab, and, of course, a column for the financial Web site thestreet.com.

At least he did not suffer the fate of his teammate and drinking buddy who had his back in *Dempsey vs. Dykstra*. "Dutch" Daulton was last seen on an HBO sports show talking about how he travels on metaphysical planes, including a fifth dimension, and has had a variety of out of body experiences.

A decade after *Dempsey vs. Dykstra*, Yankees catcher Jorge Posada would demonstrate the proper takedown of a left-handed batter who misbehaves. At the Tropicana Dome opening the seventh inning of a July 1, 2000 game, Devil Rays third baseman Bobby Smith was called out on strikes by home plate umpire Rick Reed on a check-swing of a Jeff Nelson pitch. On the way back to the dugout, he bumped into Posada. Words were exchanged, they grappled and Posada dropped him with a good wrestling move. But Smith and his dyed blonde hair kept his upper body in position to land several blows on a reverse move. His proper use of potential energy and leverage gave him the upper hand before the mob of teammates arrived. Apparently, like Dykstra, Smith knew it was better to have the catcher pinned to the ground before really going to work.

EDDIE PEREZ vs. PAUL BYRD
(ATLANTA BRAVES)   (PHILADELPHIA PHILLIES)
July 30, 1999, Turner Field, Atlanta, Georgia

It was, as the song goes, the night the lights went out in Georgia. With the Dog Days looming just a few dozen hours away, the Phillies and Braves went toe-to-toe on a steamy Friday night in Atlanta.

Eddie Perez vs. Paul Byrd had roots reaching back to the previous Sunday in Philadelphia, when Byrd, using his ye olde overhead wind-up and delivery, plunked Perez in a game the Braves won in ten innings. Perez was the thirteenth batter hit by a Byrd pitch during the 1999 season. Byrd would lead the NL in 1999 with seventeen, a number that would include another plunking of Perez in the third inning of the uncomfortable July 30 contest in Atlanta.

After the notorious junk-baller Byrd hit Perez for the second time in a week, the pitcher gestured at the Venezuelan catcher who served mainly as the backup for Javy Lopez. Both benches emptied, but no punches were thrown. The already-charged atmosphere on the field got another jolt when, after the umpires got everyone back to their places, the Turner Field lights went out. A Georgia Power substation had failed thanks to the hot weather red-lining electricity demand. After that sixteen-minute delay, play resumed and Perez was called out on the base paths for interference on a John Smoltz double play grounder. This sent Braves manager Bobby Cox into an on field tizzy, and he was tossed by second base umpire Larry Poncino, a Tucson resident who was more accustomed to the dry heat, not the wool blanket humidity stifling Atlanta. Byrd was due up to bat third in the top of the fourth.

As the pitcher dug his cleats into the righthanded batter's box, he addressed his former battery mate who had caught him a few times during Byrd's 1997–98 tenure with Atlanta, the franchise that waived him in August of 1998, when the Phillies claimed him.

Reports indicate Byrd told Perez that he did not intend to hit him with a pitch. From behind his iron mask, and with home plate umpire Jerry Meals ever vigilant over the catcher's shoulder fiddling with his official umpire pen in his breast pocket, Perez barked back at Byrd and began to slowly stride toward him. Meals, unlike the lounging Barnes during

Dempsey vs. Dykstra, sensed danger in their dialogue and removed his face mask. Perez walked right into Byrd's face, letting his catcher's mask collide with the bill of Byrd's batting helmet. Perez then unleashed a two-handed shove quite hard to Byrd's sternum—too hard because the recoil pushed Perez slightly backwards and knocked Byrd a full stride and half away from their initial contact. Byrd had dropped his arms to his side as Perez tried to make up the lost middle ground with another stride. The catcher stretched to make another two-handed shove aimed at Byrd's chin as Byrd, always the Kentucky gentleman, flipped his bat behind him and away from the fray. Meals, admirably still right among the action, was reaching in on Perez as if to take advantage of the momentary momentum break. But the umpire had to back off as Perez's second two-handed push landed short and actually met Byrd's defensive two-handed shove, making for an innocent "Patty Cake, Patty Cake" moment under the dodgy lights of Turner Field. Byrd had stepped back another stride, and as Perez stepped forward he attempted a crossover move with his catcher's glove, switching it from his left hand to his right, then winding up a haymaker aimed at Byrd's face. As his glove was switched, Byrd executed a devious disposal of his shiny batting helmet, using two hands to pass it like a basketball just an inch or two over the 6-foot-1 Perez (making him think "Did he throw that at my head?") and out of harm's way, clearly deciding not to transform it into a truncheon or some type of Jerry Lewis comedic distraction in the face of hand-to-hand combat. Byrd's stiff-arm left to Perez's shoulder neutralized the glove swing and the pair had quickly locked arms. By then, Curt Schilling arrived to back up Byrd, grabbing at Perez as on-deck batter (and Penn alumnus) Doug Glanville performed some strange Ivy League bunny-hop ritual over Byrd's back, as if he was trying to get his batting gloves between his pitcher and the snorting bull Perez.

Glanville appeared to take the full brunt of the wave of road gray uniforms that swept through the home plate circle and toppled the entire scrum into that standard baseball fight posture of the forward leaning squat. Players have their knees bent awkwardly as the arms try to do extraction work while the vertical hold on the TV set is jostled by late-arriving teammates, myopic bench coaches and the aftershock that is the bullpen troops pulling in with tender hamstrings, Gatorade towels, and sunflower seed bags still in hand. Atlanta's corner infielders arrived first—Chipper Jones got in from third just before the rush, trying to get some type of leverage for his fallen catcher, aided by Randall Simon, who had "sprinted" in from first base and deflected off Schilling's back. As the mass of players grew cancerous with fake testosterone, the pile edged its way onto the grass of foul territory behind the home plate circle, so at least the fellows at the bottom had a nicer texture beneath them.

The press pointed out the 9-2 Philadelphia win not only knocked Atlanta out of first place after the All-Star break for the first time in five years (the Mets took a half-game lead), but also made the Braves appear "troubled" for the first time in the past decade.

Byrd and Perez would be battery mates once again on the 2004 Braves. Perez lasted one more season after that, while Byrd continued to make his rounds on various pitching staffs. Though his uniform changes every other year, one thing remains certain: Byrd, a Louisville native, will never be his hometown's most famous fighter. That honor belongs to a fellow named Muhammad Ali.

JOHN STEARNS vs. GARY CARTER
(NEW YORK METS)   (MONTREAL EXPOS)
April 11, 1979, Shea Stadium, Queens, New York

In talking to Mets fans of a certain age, it is apparent that catcher John Stearns was the football hero that New York baseball fans never had. How a guy from Denver captured the hearts of National League baseball supporters in the Big Apple is a tale untold. Through gritty play and guts, Stearns won them over. Twice he has led a charge out of the Mets dugout (once in Montreal when Bill Gullickson threw over Mike Jorgensen's head, and the second time as a coach when Roger Clemens beaned Mike Piazza during interleague play at Yankee Stadium on July 8, 2000). He also once included in his pre-game preparations the physical banishment of Braves mascot Chief Noc-A-Homa from the Atlanta playing field. In June of 1978, Stearns was noted for not only his survival of a home plate collision with Pittsburgh behemoth Dave Parker, but for the latter's suffering of a shattered and bloody cheekbone that would require him to wear a football style facemask for weeks to come, giving the Cobra an even more menacing look on the base paths.

For Mets catchers, most of the fawning lore falls on the shoulders of Gary "Kid" Carter. The only reaction to Hall of Famer Carter and his Montreal perm clashing with the gritty Stearns at Shea Stadium in the ninth inning of the second home game of the 1979 season is to quote George Washington, who wrote to his brother during the Seven Years War: "I heard the bullets whistle, and believe me, there is something charming in the sound."

Stearns, nicknamed "Bad Dude" (take that, Dykstra), could have easily played pro football after his college career as a defensive back at the University of Colorado.

In 1979, the Mets opened the season with two wins on the road at Wrigley Field. Returning home to face Montreal for their opener, they lost in extra innings. Home game number two would also go extra innings, and Tony Perez would win it 3-2 with a home run in the eleventh. But before that Hall of Famer could make some noise with his bat, another future Cooperstown inductee—the only one to wear an Expos cap—would be involved in a collision at home plate in the ninth inning. It was future Met Carter, trying to score from first base when Mets pitcher Pete Falcone threw wildly over the bag after fielding Larry Parrish's grounder. Right fielder Elliott Maddox retrieved the ball and made a great throw to Stearns at home, and Carter was thumbed out at home by umpire Lanny Harris, keeping the game at 2-2. The two catchers rolled in the dirt of Flushing, Queens, and it was Stearns opinion that Carter threw an elbow at him during this tumble. So the former footballer who used to wow 'em in Boulder, Colorado, reacted by throwing several rights to Carter's head, emptying both benches and bullpens during a brief home plate brawl supporting the tenet that April is indeed the cruelest month. Both Carter and Stearns were ejected, and three months later they would share space on the National League's All-Star roster.

After the fight, it was the Californian Carter who was much more loquacious than the man from the Mile High City. "I thought John was out of line for initiating a fight," Carter told the AP. "I was just trying to do my job and touch home plate." Carter sound bites traditionally ramble, and his Hall of Fame induction speech included quotes from the movie *Field of Dreams*, a selection in French and Psalms 18. Stearns, meanwhile, would only say: "Nobody got hurt." Carter continued to the press: "I'm not out there to hurt anybody, I'm just trying to play good, hard baseball. The next thing I knew he [Stearns] was giving me a football tackle and

[Mets coach] Pignatano had me by the legs. What else could I do?" Ah, Joe Pignatano. The man responsible for growing the famous tomato plants in the Shea Stadium bullpen. It gets no more "New York" than that.

Stearns had been a first round pick of the Phillies in the 1973 draft and was traded to the Mets the following season along with Mac Searce for Tug McGraw, Don Hahn and Dave Schneck. After being ejected in the ninth, Stearns, who played for the Mets every season of his career except for one, was replaced by Ron Hodges. Many attributed Stearns' frequent presence on the disabled list to his football attitude toward playing baseball.

Carter, who was replaced in the game by ex-Met Duffy Dyer, would come to the Mets in a December of 1984 trade for Hubie Brooks and three other players. He would win a World Series ring with the Amazin's in 1986, and, after the 1989 season, he was acquired by the San Francisco Giants. Repulsed by the bohemian culture there, Carter fled south to the Los Angeles Dodgers in 1991 and then would finish his career with an honorary appearance back in Montreal, where they eat french fries with cheese and gravy, drink coffee from bowls and ignore their baseball team. He survived eleven seasons in Quebec, and one clash with the Bad Dude. After he retired, no Carter public appearance was complete without him handing out autographed photos of himself with Christian messages inscribed on them. He represents the Babylon-esque Expos franchise as the token Hall of Famer wearing the tri-colored hat. Like all things Expo-related—the hat, the insignia, the mascot, the stadium, the exchange rate—they can all be blamed on the 1967 World's Fair.

MICHAEL BARRETT vs. A.J. PIERZYNSKI
(CHICAGO CUBS)   (CHICAGO WHITE SOX)
May 20, 2006, U.S. Cellular Field, Chicago, Illinois

After two Chicago catchers became poster children for baseball brawling (base*brawl* in hackneyed headlinese) in the Spring of 2006, it would not be surprising if sociology grad students, perhaps at Northwestern University, began a few studies in the Windy City. The educational probe might endeavor to figure out the trends of reoccurrence for catcher-on-catcher violence (*Stearns vs. G. Carter* included) and just what the city of Chicago is putting in its drinking water to cause so many upheavals within a given baseball metropolis, Sandburg poetry notwithstanding.

It began with White Sox bullying of the Cubs during interleague play. On Friday, May 19, the Southsiders slammed the Wrigley tenants 6-1 at U.S. Cellular Field. Saturday's sun-splashed tilt was a nationally televised affair with the pitching mis-matchup of Freddy Garcia against Rich Hill of the Cubs. In front of 39,387 allegedly divided Chicagoans, the teams wasted little time before mixing it up. By the end of the summer, most baseball fans would know way more than they wanted to about Pierzynski's penchant for being a clubhouse irritant and a player they love to hate. Readers of various sports magazines would know his dog's name (Bubba), that he is pals with another fan favorite/media target (Doug Mientkiewicz), while with San Francisco chose to play cards instead of helping a disgruntled Brett Tomko prepare for a start, and had a knee-to-groin tussle with the Giants trainer.

The game was scoreless in the second, but Hill had the bases full of White Sox with one out when Brian Anderson stood in. He lofted a fly to left, which was caught by Matt Murton. Pierzynski, who "runs like a catcher," tagged up from third base and was bound for pay dirt when Murton's weak throw home bounced harmlessly behind him on the Comiskey grass. Barrett, however, was hunched over and blocking the path to the plate, waiting to receive the throw when Pierzynski arrived in a crouch, landing his shoulder against Barrett's shoulder. The impact sent Barrett perfectly backward—the flipped turtle syndrome. Pierzynski stopped dead and was seated perpendicular to the left edge of home plate. Home plate umpire Greg Gibson was slightly up the first base line, and directly behind home plate with a better view than the ump was on-deck batter Scott Podsednik, who, if he had been tagging from third, would have been seated in the dugout by the time Murton's throw arrived.

Freezing the action as the catchers' shoulders met, and seen from an overhead vantage from the backstop, the U.S. Cellular home plate circle resembled a larger Sumo wrestling ring, though Barrett appeared to be the only person wearing a ceremonial apron of any kind. The official Sumo ring is seventeen feet in diameter, while the MLB home plate circle is twenty-six feet. Barrett was not knocked out of the ring, so the match would continue. And then some. As Barrett righted himself without the ball, Pierzynski, still seated, slapped home plate with a hammer gesture worthy of Khrushchev at the United Nations. The Cubs catcher later told reporters he did not see this defiant gesture.

Pleased with himself having riled the crowd and staked his team to a 1-0 lead, Pierzynski rose triumphant and in search of his stray batting helmet. Staggering slightly, he collided again with Barrett who was walking toward him. It was an "excuse me" commuter embrace like the ones happening a few dozen times every day on Chicago's El trains full of briefcase jousters getting on and off. Barrett sensed an extra shoulder from Pierzynski and the two embraced in a classic contra dance position. There was no jig or reel, however, as the straight-legged Barrett raised his right fist—beyond the clenched fingers umpire Gibson could be seen rushing toward the pair—and Barrett hammered Pierzynski's jaw with a right cross that sent his foe staggering several feet in the opposite direction, near the edge of the Sumo ring. At this point, Pierzynski and many of Chicago's Polish citizenry must have flashed back ever so briefly to the Deluge of 1655, when the Swedes, with the help of the Cossacks and Tartars, invaded Poland and did some serious damage. Barrett, a former first-round pick of the Expos as a shortstop and native of Atlanta, is seen in photos with his arm raised to deliver the telltale blow. Photographers caught the split-second before the punch arrived; Pierzynski bears a quizzical look and Barrett's face carries a disinterested gaze as if he were sorting the day's junk mail. (There's also a shot of Barrett's fist on Pierzynski's cheek—a photo that goes down in baseball fight history as one of the few to catch fist to face contact, up there with *Rose vs. Harrelson* and the action shot of a massive Walt Dropo of the White Sox nailing the forty-one-year-old Yankee Enos Slaughter in that 1957 melee in Chicago.)

Podsednik decided it was "go time" to borrow a phrase from the late Chris Farley—Pierzynski's doppelganger, if the catcher added one hundred pounds. Podsednik lunged for Barrett and took him down in an expert Secret Service–style chokehold as the onrush of players engulfed the plate. Jacque Jones made a valiant effort to get Podsednik off his fallen teammate. The day game after the Friday night game can leave many an MLB bench riddled with somnambulists, but the alarm clocks were apparently working on both sides for this one.

Barrett's blow could have been inspired by the bases-on-balls frustration that saw Hill walk the bases full before Anderson's fly ball. The catcher was carrying the sorry Cubs with his offense early in the season. He had shown frustration before, a week earlier shouting down San

Diego's Dave Roberts as he crossed the Wrigley plate during a Padres blowout of the Cubs. In 2004, Barrett had carried a grudge against Houston's Roy Oswalt, who hit him with a pitch after Aramis Ramirez hit a three-run homer. Five days later, Barrett verbally assaulted the pitcher when he stepped into the batter's box. Benches emptied again.

Barrett vs. Pierzynski delayed the game thirteen minutes and both main participants were ejected along with sac fly author Anderson and Cubs first baseman John Mabry who tangled rather viciously. Mabry went to the hospital for precautionary X-rays after getting tossed. Podsednik, the obvious "third man in" who did some damage to the Cubs catcher with his bulldog move, astonishingly escaped punishment. When play resumed, he drew yet another walk from Hill. The following batter was Tadahito Iguchi, who crushed a 2-2 pitch from Hill into the left field seats for an out-of-the-frying-pan grand slam, putting the White Sox up 5-0. Iguchi would later slam a two-run blast, giving the Pale Hose their 7-0 junkyard dog victory and the Fox broadcasters something to talk about other than *Barrett vs. Pierzynski.*

Hill, still winless and without a leg to stand on in the post-game commentary, insisted Pierzynski's collision was "gutless" even though his own manager and several other heavy hitters called the play legitimate "hard-nosed" baseball. Barrett was suspended ten games, the largest punishment levied against a Cubs player in the history of the storied franchise. A week later, he started having back problems. And on September 2, 2006, in a game at Wrigley against San Francisco, Barrett was wondering why he ever switched from shortstop to catcher. A foul tip off the bat of Matt Cain caught Barrett in the groin. He had to leave the game and was hospitalized with the wince-inducing "intrascrotal hematoma" injury that would require immediate, season-ending surgery. Ouch.

Pierzynski, who was born in Bridgehampton, New York, of all places, had further cemented his status as a baseball rogue, Uriah Heep in a chest protector, a Polish villain in the spirit of Roaring 20s Canadian wrestler Stan Stasiak. In fact, Pierzynski made a pro wrestling cameo as the "manager" of Dale "The Demon" Torborg (son of Jeff and the trainer of the White Sox) at a TNA pay-per-view event in Orlando, Florida, in December of 2005 and again during the 2006 off-season, when he and Torborg confronted the diminutive World Series MVP David Eckstein who was promoting an upcoming book. Pierzynski's channeling of White Sox boxer Art Shires probably had Judge Landis spinning in his grave (which is just a few exits down the Dan Ryan Expressway in Chicago's Oak Woods Cemetery).

The old wrestler Stasiak, known to be well-liked outside the ring despite his ornery victory strut, died from blood poisoning after breaking his arm in a match in Toronto. Pierzynski, as he exited the gladiatorial soil of U.S. Cellular the day he clashed with Barrett, despite getting hammered so publicly, waved his arms in the air to work the sell-out crowd in his own Stasiak victory strut. He then entered the dugout for painfully robust high-fives with unfortunate teammates, his straight hair jiggling Pete Rose–like as he gathered his gear and headed for an early shower.

Providing further tests of ballplayer contract language, Pierzynski and Eckstein appeared for a February 2007 pay-per-view TNA wrestling event promoted via a surprise appearance by Yankees outfielder Johnny Damon. Dubbed *Basebrawl 2*, the match was met with chants of "baseball sucks!" by the audience. Eckstein's team won because Pierzynski "cheated" by using a folding chair to strike wrestler Lance Hoyt. During that same busy offseason, Pierzynski used his Chicago "pull" to land a security guard assignment for a taping of *The Jerry Springer Show* in January of 2007. He was called to duty to help break up a fight on the set during a classy segment entitled "Dumped and Deserted."

CARLTON FISK vs. THURMAN MUNSON
(BOSTON RED SOX)   (NEW YORK YANKEES)
August 1, 1973, Fenway Park, Boston, Massachusetts

When titans clash, the world stops to watch. On August 2, 1973, the sportspage headline in the *Reno Evening Gazette* of Reno, Nevada, read in perfect middle-line haiku: "Two Best Catchers Best Fighters." Even the most jaded gamblers and divorce lawyers out west pause when Carlton "Pudge" Fisk and Yankees captain Thurman Munson mix it up inside the small ballpark on Yawkey Way. And to add the bonus of sword-wielding skeletons to this titanic clash, it all happened on a broken version of one of baseball's most thrilling plays: the suicide squeeze. But if the "two best" catchers were asked, there was only room for one best catcher, and both believed they were it.

Fisk vs. Munson serves as the middle panel of the triptych depicting the simmering hatred between the Boston and New York catchers. The first incident was a hard slide by Fisk into Munson in 1972. Then came the afternoon tea dance in Fenway in 1973, followed by what many considered the granddaddy of Yankees-Red Sox fights between Fisk, Lou Piniella, Graig Nettles, and Bill Lee in 1976, which will be examined in a later chapter, as will the *real* granddaddy, Don Zimmer, and his meeting with Pedro Martinez on Fenway turf.

The August 1, 1973 affair was a mid-week matinee, and the Yankees were teetering atop the AL East, at risk of losing their grip on first place for the first time since June 20. It was typical Yankees-Red Sox baseball—a tight contest with plenty of tension. Munson tied the game at 2-2 in the fourth inning with an RBI groundout. It remained 2-2 as the ninth inning rolled around and Munson led off with a double against Boston starter John Curtis.

Munson's demeanor with the press was not exactly dynamic. He was described as moody and approached his job with workmanlike perfectionism. He was an anti-glam Yankee from Canton, Ohio, a first round draft pick in 1968. He was a Kent Stater with a cop mustache who became a god to generations of Yankee fans. After this game in Boston, he was excited in the clubhouse, telling reporters to go ask Fisk who "won the fight."

It started when Gene "Stick" Michael didn't get his stick on the baseball in a suicide squeeze. Without Michael's bunt, the homeward-bound Munson was a sitting duck for Fisk, who had the ball in his glove and an easy out heading right toward him. But Michael formed a human obstacle in the batter's box. Fisk throttled him out of the way to get at his nemesis wearing the number fifteen road gray jersey of the Yankees. With Michael crumpled out of the way, Munson barreled into Fisk in an effort to jar the ball loose. California's Al Gallagher had tried a similar move on Fisk back in May after the Angel was caught in a rundown. Fisk got to him later in the game, which also featured a tussle between Jeff Torborg and Rico Petrocelli.

Munson failed in his mission to jar the ball loose from Pudge, but knowing teammate Felipe Alou was also on the move from first base, The Captain let his 191 pounds surrender to gravity, smothering Fisk, who was frantic to get out from under the one they called "Tugboat." Fisk used a slight kick to flip Munson off of him, and the Yankee rebounded quickly with fists blazing as Fisk immediately responded with a haymaker of his own. Munson stepped up his punch count as the cavalries headed toward home plate. Michael, meanwhile, perhaps feeling a bit guilty about the missed suicide squeeze, also wanted a piece of Fisk and tried to get in some blows over his shoulder before a scrum frothed over the action. Carl Yastrzemski was among the first Boston players to arrive, attempting some impossible leverage by grabbing Munson around the waist from behind while Fisk was in his face, and also dealing with the pesky Michael.

Had this been a post-2000 brawl, the game delay would have been at least a quarter of an hour. But this being the economical early 1970s and the third game of a four-game set, things were cleared up in just four minutes. Fisk emerged with a scratch on his face and a mouse under his eye. The umpiring crew, which included donnybrook-magnet Nestor Chylak, ejected Fisk and Munson. When play resumed, Michael promptly grounded out to short to end the inning. The Red Sox were livid that Michael was allowed to stay in the game, but all was forgotten in the bottom of the ninth. Bob Montgomery singled off ace reliever Sparky Lyle, and Rick Miller walked. The Yankees were one out away from extra innings when Mario Guerrero singled home Montgomery with the winning run for Boston.

In his 1978 autobiography, Munson gave the busted squeeze against Fisk a terse sentence or two. He did mention the All-Star game, which was just a few weeks earlier in Kansas City. Fisk was voted as the AL's starting catcher, and Munson was the reserve catcher. They both played half the game, both going 0-for-2 in a 7-1 loss to the NL. Behind the plate, calling balls and strikes in the Midsummer Classic, was Chylak himself.

Munson, who won the AL Rookie of the Year award in 1970, earned AL MVP honors in 1976. Six years to the day after the fight with Fisk, Munson played his last game, manning first base for the Yankees in a drubbing of the White Sox at Comiskey. The next day, Munson died after crashing his private airplane while practicing landings at the Canton airport. The Yankees retired his number that same year, and August 2, 1979 is considered the most tragic date in Yankees history.

As for Fisk, the New Englander's career paralleled Munson's in many ways. He was a first round draft pick in 1967 and won the AL Rookie of the Year Award in 1972. They both endured knee injuries and icy relationships with the press. As Fisk's career developed, he took his catching duties seriously and respected the game to the point where, as a veteran, he would not hesitate to chastise young players whom he felt were not showing the proper respect for the game. Just ask "Neon" Deion Sanders. Perhaps lured by the Second City's legacy of baseball incidents, Fisk moved from Boston to the Chicago White Sox in 1981, where he would spend the majority of his Hall of Fame career. Pudge was inducted into Cooperstown in 2000, wearing a Red Sox cap on his plaque. In his induction speech, Fisk quoted the Hopi Indians ("you cannot pick up a pebble with one finger") and cited the rivalry with the Yankees as the most intense he'd experienced thanks to "comparable talent, comparable personalities, and the intensity with which we approached the game." Fisk also mentioned Munson, among others, as a member of a new generation of catchers who were true athletes.

If Sal Maglie were pitching in 2008, he would no doubt have some ridiculous nickname like "Daddy Mags" or "S-Mag" or he would have had his first name changed to Steve or Scott by a high-powered agent who runs his players through an Ellis Island politburo of Boring, Normal, and Middle of the Road. Calling him by his real nickname, earned in the 1950s spanning the hatred between the Dodgers and the Giants, would cause much hand-wringing. Using it in public would cause the tripwires of political correctness to coil up around his ankles. He was "The Barber" because he threw at batter's heads as a matter of routine, ironically sporting a permanent five-o'clock shadow of his own.

Maglie was the master of the curveball, a right-handed intimidator who as a New York Giant loved to buzz Dodgers. One of Maglie's main targets was Carl Furillo, who would later have to welcome Maglie as a Dodger teammate in 1956, when Maglie would teach a young hurler named Don Drysdale how to own home plate. Furillo, a Pennsylvanian whose strong throwing arm earned him the nickname "The Reading Rifle," won the NL batting title in '53, the same year he got into world class rumbles with Maglie, Giants pitcher Ruben Gomez, and Giants skipper Leo Durocher, whom he nabbed in a headlock during a rarely successful dugout charge. Gomez, it might be noted, would make headlines three years after hitting Furillo by plunking Milwaukee's Joe Adcock on the wrist. Adcock took first base, then decided to charge Gomez, who threw the ball at him again and fled in a high-speed chase toward the dugout, outrunning Adcock and basking in the safety of the bench. He then armed himself with a bat and an icepack in the clubhouse, and later enjoyed a police escort to his hotel. Yes, Gomez did some dirty work on the mound, but he was by no means carrying the integrity of "The Barber."

Maglie confessed many of his beanball secrets in a magazine article a year after his 1958 retirement. He said he did throw at Dodgers' heads, and that he chose the skull because at least the batters would be able to see a pitch up there and it was harder to hit a guy in the head than, say, in the ribcage.

At least Maglie didn't play it like Lew Burdette, the Milwaukee Braves hurler known to have collected more than a few scalps. Burdette used to scream "Look out!" at the batter as he delivered a slider on the outside corner of the plate. That might qualify as "dirty pool."

Baseball history has painted bold pictures of Bob Gibson and Don Drysdale, Dizzy Dean, and Carl Mays—hurlers who possessed deeds of ownership for home plate and its batter's box environs. Batting against them was perilous. At least the poor souls standing in against that lot knew what they were getting into. It's the lesser known "headhunters" that have been more perilous. Take, for instance, a Bruce Kison . . . or a Mike Proly. Not household names, but still involved in some serious brushback and beanball incidents through the years.

In 1985, Kison's final season and only year with Boston, he tangled famously with a karate-kicking George Bell. Through his years with the Pittsburgh Pirates, however, the thin hurler set a pattern of sticking up for his teammates. In August of 1971, when Jose Pagan had his arm broken by a pitch from Montreal's John Strohmayer, Kison made Expos pinch hitter Jim Fairey fear for his life with a hearty brushback that drew a warning from the umpire. One of Kison's most famous tussles, aside from his clash with Jack Billingham of the Reds in 1974, was an encounter with Mike Schmidt of the Phillies.

It was July of 1977, and Kison had surrendered a two-run homer to Garry Maddox in the seventh inning, putting the Phillies up 4-3 at Three Rivers Stadium. Kison got Larry Bowa to ground out to second, then had an 0-2 count on Schmidt when he plunked him in the back. Schmidt slowly charged the mound and threw a haymaker easily dodged by Kison. But the Washington state native was about to meet Greg "The Bull" Luzinski, who hit behind Schmidt in the Philly batting order. Luzinski tackled the 6-foot-4 Kison, who described the experience to the AP thusly: "I felt like a noodle." Schmidt would also feel like a noodle when Pirates catcher

Ed Ott arrived to tackle him and "stop the fight as quickly as possible," the former high school football star said. Schmidt was ejected after order was restored. He was joined in the eighth inning by pitcher Tug McGraw and manager Danny Ozark. They were both tossed after McGraw hit Willie Stargell following a warning from umpire Harry Wendelstedt. Stargell also did the slow walk toward McGraw, which summoned all hands on deck yet again—a sight that was quite common when these two teams played each other. Kison said later he respected Schmidt for taking action. "There's no barbed wire fence between the plate and the pitcher's mound," he said. "A lot of guys talk and don't come out to the mound, but he did and I respect that."

The dramatic game ended in tedious fashion in the ninth. Rookie hurler Warren Brusstar walked Bucco pinch hitter Jim Fregosi with the bases loaded to give the Pirates the 8-7 win. The home plate umpire was Eric Gregg, known later in his career for his wide and generous strike zone.

In fifteen seasons, Kison had sixty-eight career hit batsmen. In 1972, he finished second in the NL in HBP with nine, one behind Jerry Reuss. In 1974, Kison hit a career-high eleven batters, again good enough for second place in the category behind San Diego's Bill Greif, who plunked fourteen. Kison's brief tour in the American League saw his high and tight stuff rile Buddy Bell and Johnny Grubb of Texas, as well as Pat Sheridan of Kansas City. During his retirement and years as a coach, Kison was reluctant to discuss his penchant for the high inside part of the plate, ordering at least one interview with Major League Baseball Productions to end abruptly when producers asked him about beanballs.

Kison's teammate, Dock Ellis, who made history of his own in San Diego with his now infamous 1970 "no-hitter on acid," was also very good at plunking batters. After surrendering a mammoth home run to Reggie Jackson in the 1971 All-Star game in Detroit, Ellis waited five years until he was with the Yankees and Reggie was with Baltimore. He then shattered Jackson's cheekbone and his trademark eyeglasses with a fastball. For many years, Jackson felt numbness in his cheek and was haunted by the beanball.

In 1974, in an attempt to shake his team out of a fear of the Cincinnati Reds, Ellis wasted no time drilling the opposition. Pete Rose, Joe Morgan, and Dan Driessen were hit in succession by Ellis pitches in the first inning. He then walked Tony Perez, putting the Reds up 1-0 and bringing manager Danny Murtaugh out of the dugout to remove Ellis from the game. Dock's remedy did not work as the Buccos lost again to the Reds, 5-3. In 1975, the last year of Dock's initial run with the Pirates, Murtaugh challenged Ellis to a clubhouse fight after the flamboyant pitcher openly criticized his teammates and manager, but Ellis refused to take him on. Coach Don Leppert also jumped in, wanting a piece of Ellis, but was restrained. Despite the tumult, the Bucs went on to win the NL East in 1975 but fell apart in the NLCS, victims of a sweep at the hands of who else but their hated rivals along the Ohio River—the Cincinnati Reds.

A similar incident can be mined from the 1952 box scores, when black pitcher Joe Black of the Brooklyn Dodgers reacted to the Cincinnati bench singing the song "Ol' Black Joe" by buzzing the heads of seven straight Reds batters who had to dive out of the way. They quickly urged their teammates on the bench to cease their serenading of the 6-foot-2 Dodgers hurler with a mean fastball.

Perhaps the most aptly named headhunter to toe the slab in a long while was Danny Darwin, who pitched for eight different clubs over twenty-one seasons. The Bonham, Texas, native nicknamed "The Bonham Bullet" and "Dr. Death" was traded often, appeared as a starter and reliever at various stages in his career, and was not afraid to remind batters who was in charge. In Arlington in 1981, Darwin of the Rangers nailed A's DH Cliff Johnson and set off a memorable AL West melee. In 1996, while with Houston, he touched off a colorful brawl after hitting Montreal's Henry Rodriguez in the ribs after he had stood and admired a home run earlier in the game. Darwin was suspended six games for that gesture. In 1990 while an Astro, Darwin fought with St. Louis first baseman Pedro Guerrero after reaching base with a single. Police had to be called to the locker room door when Darwin and Guerrero vowed to continue their fisticuffs in the bowels of Busch Stadium. While with the San Francisco Giants in his final season of 1998, Darwin fought teammate Barry Bonds in the clubhouse tunnel in Pittsburgh after a dispute over the left fielder not hustling for a ball. During Darwin's rookie season of 1978 with the Texas Rangers, he was a teammate of Barry's father Bobby.

Improbable Proly

Mike Proly played only seven seasons, pitching for St. Louis in 1976, then spending a few turns with the White Sox, a year with the Phillies, and ending with two campaigns for the Cubs. The mop-up reliever from

Queens had only eight HBPs in his career. In 1980, his final year with the White Sox, Proly was involved in two fights caused by baseballs he pitched that struck the batter instead of landing in the catcher's mitt.

On April 20, 1980, a year after hitting Baltimore Orioles third baseman Doug DeCinces, Proly nailed him again. This time it was high on the back of the neck, on the edge of his batting helmet. Eddie Murray had just tripled to tie the game 6-6. DeCinces had homered in the fourth off starter Steve "Rainbow" Trout. After Proly's pitch deflected off the back of his head, DeCinces took a few steps toward the mound, hesitated, then broke in the direction of Proly. The combatants said later it was a verbal exchange during the pause that prompted DeCinces. Proly yelled at the indecisive Orioles corner man: "If you're coming, come on!" DeCinces said he then had no choice but to address Proly up close and personal. First he had to fight off the restraining effort of home plate umpire Jerry Neudecker, and when he made it to the hill, Proly tackled DeCinces. As they spilled toward the dirt of Memorial Stadium, DeCinces got in a few punches to Proly's back. DeCinces was ejected after the dust settled. In the seventh, Baltimore reliever Sammy Stewart sailed his first pitch past the head of rookie Harold Baines, but Neudecker issued no warnings and considered the matter closed.

On May 5, 1980, Proly caused a brawl against Milwaukee that made headlines because his manager, Tony LaRussa, suffered a separated shoulder in the melee at Comiskey. Though instead of hunting for heads, it was a shinbone that prompted the action—Ben Ogilvie's shinbone. After Robin Yount led off the fourth inning with a home run, Proly, who was cleaning up starter Rich Dotson's mess, got Cecil Cooper to line out to center, then Sal Bando flew out to left. Ogilvie stepped in with the Brewers up 7-6. After Proly's slider in the dirt skipped and struck Ogilvie's leg, he threw his helmet and his bat to the ground, then took a half dozen steps in Proly's direction before finishing his charge. White Sox catcher Bruce Kimm intervened, but Ogilvie was able to land a face shot against Proly over the catcher's shoulder. The fight showed off the versatility of the White Sox famous uniforms—the top half was a pajama pullover with a V-neck, simulated collar and olde tymey lettering. The shirts, worn untucked, originally went with dreaded Bermuda shorts. During *Ogilvie vs. Proly*, short pants were not worn, and Ogilvie was promptly ejected from the game. As Ogilvie made his way to the dugout, a Comiskey denizen issued a well-tossed beer shower that struck the shunned Brewer where it counts. It was yet another shining moment of fan behavior in Cook County, Illinois.

LaRussa and Proly both decried the incident in the post-game discussions, claiming the shinbone is not connected to the brawl bone. With his shoulder taped, LaRussa put his best lawyer spin on the fight. "Traditionally, when something like that happens the ball is thrown a little higher," he told the *Chicago Sun-Times*. Brewers reinforcements quickest to the scene included Jim Gantner and Sal Bando, who later mentioned to the umpires that *DeCinces vs. Proly* was a precedent-setter for this go-round. Proly, again experiencing the strange sensation of being sought out by sportswriters, told them he was getting a "bad rap" as a headhunter.

Pitchers who throw at batter's heads and connect are usually identified by a semi-permanent association with their victims, men who eventually rise from the shameful dust and take out their rage and fear on the next pitcher to breeze one by their precious gourds. DeCinces and Ogilvie are remembered. Proly, in all probability, is not.

"C" Is for Cyclops

In Boston, the mere mention of "Tony C." still brings sighs and speculation about "what could have been." His proper name was Anthony Richard Conigliaro, and he was born in Revere, Massachusetts. In 1965, his second season, his thirty-two home runs topping the AL made him the youngest home run leader in league history. Almost half a dozen times in his eight-year career, Conigliaro was sidelined by injuries suffered as a result of being hit by a pitch.

The last straw, so to speak, came against the California Angels and pitcher Jack Hamilton, who hit Conigliaro in the left cheekbone on August 17, 1967. The ball shattered Conigliaro's cheekbone, dislocated his jaw and damaged the retina in his left eye. Enjoying an All-Star season, Conigliaro would be out of action for a year and half, missing the Red Sox run to the 1967 World Series. Essentially, the Hamilton beanball was the end of his career. Conigliaro's beaning was a prologue to "The Year of the Pitcher" that was 1968, when fear was spread from the mound with beanballs and brushbacks, which became a matter of routine. It wasn't just Gibson and Drysdale; it was gents like Stan "Big Daddy" Williams, a 6-foot-6, 230 pounder whose approach to batters who had worked a 3-0 count was to hit them with the next pitch instead of issuing a walk.

With only partial vision in his left eye, Conigliaro called it quits in July of 1971 while with the Angels. During the game that prompted his quick retirement, Conigliaro had been called out on strikes, threw his helmet sixty feet into the air toward first base and then smashed it to bits with his bat. When he got to the dugout, he threw his bat in the direction of umpire George Maloney—a gesture he later called his "goodbye" to baseball. He had gone 0-for-8 with five strikeouts in the Angels twenty-inning 1-0 loss to Oakland. (His teammate Billy Rowan bested him with an 0-for-8 with six strikeouts.) Among the post-game comments to the AP from Conigliaro's manager Lefty Phillips: "That guy is ready for an insane asylum."

One of Conigliaro's most colorful mound charges came on July 12, 1970, in Cleveland. The Red Sox had been in a mini brushback war with the Indians earlier in the month, and in the second game of a doubleheader, Tribe starter Jim Lasher, who had knocked Conigliaro down two weeks earlier, nailed him in the left forearm in the first inning. Conigliaro went after Lasher on the hill, employing what the sportswriters called a "karate" kick to Lasher's hip while connecting with a punch to his nose. Conigliaro's spike cut Lasher's hip, and the sidearm hurler sometimes called "The Whip" was given a tetanus shot after the game. Lasher said Carl Yastrzemski, who was on base with a single, grabbed his arms after Conigliaro landed the surprise kick, hampering his ability to fight back. After the umpires restored order, Conigliaro was ejected and he threw a fit. He had to be escorted off the field by young teammate Reggie Smith, whose nascent career had many a baseball donnybrook lying ahead.

In 1975, Conigliaro returned for a dozen or so games as a designated hitter with Boston before he was released in September. In 1982, he had a heart attack and was in a coma for several weeks. As a result of the brain damage suffered during that coma, Conigliaro died in February of 1990 of pneumonia and kidney failure in Salem, Massachusetts. He was forty-five.

Red Glare

To the press, fireballer Roger Clemens loomed as large, if not larger, than his Texas hero Nolan Ryan. The missing element to the Rocket's mythology? There was no Robin Ventura for Clemens to pound on. Part of Clemens' routine included first pitch chin-buzzes to hitters who handled him well or had the nerve to think about getting an edge in the batter's box. It is a baseball maxim—cemented alongside excessively inflated beer prices and announcers describing any piece of debris (no matter how large or how foreign) on the field as a "hot dog wrapper": The Clemens welcome wagon always arrived inside and high.

After winning the 1986 AL MVP and hearing of Hank Aaron's disapproval of a pitcher getting the award, Clemens said, in so many words, he'd have to "crack open" Hammerin' Hank's head to show him how valuable he was. Later in his career with the Yankees, Clemens hinted at plunking Barry Bonds in his large elbow pad during an interleague contest. Clemens did just that, and clucking noises could be heard throughout the press box. His aim, if anything, was true.

The Clemens interactions with Mets catcher Mike Piazza during the 2000 season, starting with the July 8 interleague beaning and building up to the crescendo of the broken bat incident in Game Two of the 2000 World Series in the Bronx, were old-fashioned New York baseball opera ripe for embellishment by sportswriters. The fact is, Piazza and Clemens never did physically clash. Sure, John Stearns was hungry and among the first to charge out of the Mets dugout that night in the Bronx when Clemens mistook Piazza's broken bat barrel for "the ball." The benches did in fact empty, but the right people were held back and the national television audience was not subjected to any Tobe Hooper–style violence. And where Clemens is concerned in the fraternity of headhunting pitchers, there never were too many punches thrown. Maybe that is why he has enjoyed an unprecedented longevity among hurlers who hurl at melons residing beneath the opposition's batting helmets.

When Clemens threw Piazza's broken bat barrel back in the direction of the jogging Mets legend, he resembled a fussy neighbor cleaning his side yard and tossing an errant object back onto his neighbor's plot. Clemens liked to keep a tidy mound area, and he didn't need Piazza's litter getting in his way, especially during an important game. Piazza, who was painfully "sawed off" on the foul ball, took a slow walk inside the foul line and as his bat was returned near his feet, he had a simple question to Roger: "What's your problem?" Clemens looked away, as if to downplay his brash toss of the shard, or perhaps to see the train of teammates headed in his direction.

Piazza's midsummer beanball victimization by Clemens was a dramatic display of brute force on par with an American Museum of Natural History diorama of a woolly mammoth being felled by a prehistoric hunting party. The glassy-eyed expression of the Mets catcher—serving in a designated hitter capacity for the contest—in the dust of the batters box, his All-Star appearance disappearing like the vapors of the trainer's smelling salts, is easy to remember. The William Tell–like placement of the pitch by Clemens was also an uncanny sight. And the sound of a Mets batting helmet being plunked so squarely also resonated throughout the five boroughs and through Texas and echoed throughout Norristown, Pennsylvania, where every other bartender claims to be Piazza's third cousin or at least a relative of Tommy Lasorda. Piazza was finding his old stride with the Mets who were once again in hot pursuit of the Braves in the NL East. Then Clemens uncorked a doozy.

Oddly enough, in July of 1991, the Boston Red Sox experienced a similar scare of losing their All-Star pitcher who was mere days away from representing the American League. The Detroit Tigers were at Fenway, and somehow Pete Incaviglia and Rob Deer had used their first at bats against The Rocket to stroke back-to-back home runs and put the Tigers ahead on a temporary basis. Former Dodger John Shelby, who as a base coach would see significant action in *Park vs. Belcher* years later, was the unfortunate batter stepping in after the back-to-back taters. Until that date, Clemens hadn't surrendered consecutive round trippers since Jose Canseco and Dave Kingman did it wearing Oakland uniforms. Shelby, who was just a few weeks away from being released by Detroit and was carrying a .177 average, fouled the first pitch from Clemens down the left field line. Until the Inky-Deer mess in the second inning, Clemens had only surrendered three home runs all season. That might have been fresh on his mind as his next delivery struck Shelby squarely between the shoulder blades.

Shelby did what Piazza could not do on July 8, 2000, and what he might have been thinking of doing on October 22, 2000. He charged a Clemens-occupied mound—and took his bat with him. The overreaction from the Boston dugout and from the Red Sox infielders almost caused more damage than Shelby ever could have. Catcher John Marzano was able to tackle Shelby from behind before he reached Clemens, but the swirl of immediate arrivals on the mound created a deep pile that consumed both batter and pitcher, knocking off Clemens' hat and mussing his hair. When the bundle of major leaguers was sorted out, nervous Bostonians were relieved to see an unscathed Clemens emerge and a disgraced Shelby ejected. Clemens stayed in to go eight innings and win his eleventh game before heading to the Midsummer Classic in his future home Toronto where he would work an inning and give up a home run to Andre Dawson.

At the 2004 All-Star game played in front of his fellow sharp-toothed, corporate Texans in Houston, Clemens, wearing Astros colors, was the NL starter, pitching to a battery mate named Mike Piazza. He was shelled for six runs in the opening frame and absorbed the loss.

Pedro Being Pedro

At first glance, Pedro Martinez does not look like someone who would be so demonstratively arrogant. The mound presence of the skinny strikeout maestro contradicts the power he wields with his pitches. A puppy dog countenance sits atop a jersey that always looks oversized because of his request for flared sleeve cuffs. He could look bored, even sleepy, in the most crucial of situations with men on base and sluggers digging in. He had long since established the inside part of the plate as his own real estate, and he was not afraid to show the deed and title to any interested parties.

His fringe encounter during the 2003 playoffs with Yankees coach Don Zimmer, one of the game's more famous excursions into absurdist theater, will be covered in a later chapter dealing with bad blood.

For now, two incidents set the scope and range of Pedro's fearlessness and propensity for hitting batters. The first involves the dynamic that emerges when contenders play doormat teams as the season wears on. One team is in a pennant race, the other is shuffling September call-ups and making October plans for family trips and golf outings. On August 29, 2000, in the Tropicana Dome in an overly-landscaped corner of St. Petersburg, Florida, Pedro had an arduous test of his ability to concentrate—he was facing the Tampa Bay Devil Rays, who were a mere seventeen games behind the first-place Yankees and looking for their fifty-eighth win of the season on an electric Tuesday evening. The Red Sox, meanwhile, were five games back of their Bronx-based rivals and were facing Yankees castoff Dave Eiland as a less than formidable mound foe. In fact, the pitching box score for Tampa Bay in this particular odd game is an almost unmatchable collection of ham and eggers. Eiland would be joined by Tony Fiore and Doug Creek, and future Yankee Cory Lidle (who died when his small plane crashed into a Manhattan apartment building in October 2006).

The fireworks began just four pitches into the game as Gerald "Ice" Williams, another Yankees castoff, was struck in the left forearm by a Martinez pitch. The seven steps taken toward first base by Williams were almost Jerry Lewis–like as the hit batsman examined his wrist, kept walking, examined his wrist, kept walking, and made one last glance—like a commuter checking his wristwatch as the subway train arrives in the station—before deciding to charge Martinez. All the while Williams was in his decision-making stroll, Martinez was walking in toward the plate with his glove raised to nonchalantly receive a new ball from his catcher Jason Varitek. Williams didn't have to travel far to land a hard shove to Pedro's upper body, followed by a very hard right cross. As Pedro reeled backward onto his posterior, Varitek tackled Williams from high and behind while third baseman Lou Merloni arrived low and hard from the hot corner. Brian Daubach was the third Boston player to join the fray, coming over from first base too fast, his momentum causing him to crash into the three-player pile. Shortstop Nomar Garciaparra squatted in as the fourth man and "Ice" was engulfed by Boston road grays for a terrible few seconds before his teammates arrived from the first base side of the diamond. The Red Sox would suffer the most damage after the first inning chaos. Daubach hyperextended his left elbow but stayed in the game to become a target for Tampa Bay pitchers, eventually leaving in the seventh after being hit by Fiore. Daubach flew back to Boston for tests on his elbow the next day and was out of action until September 6. Merloni left the game with a slight concussion. Williams was ejected along with his manager, Larry Rothschild, who was insistent to home plate umpire Phil Cuzzi that Pedro should be sent to the showers as well.

Pedro had much work to do as he would take a no-hitter into the ninth inning. It was overshadowed, supposedly, by the first-inning brawl and subsequent benchclearings, the ejections of Eiland in the third after he hit Garciaparra, and then Fiore and acting manager Jose Cardenal in the seventh when Daubach was victimized. Greg Vaughn, who struck out three times against Pedro, was tossed after a called third strike in the seventh. Pedro, who won the AL Cy Young Award in 1999, struck out thirteen on the way to his fifteenth win of the season.

Devil Rays catcher John Flaherty busted up the no-hitter by leading off the ninth with a single off Pedro. It wasn't enough to spark a Rays rally, though, and Boston prevailed 8-0. When asked about his third career hard-luck one-hitter after the game, Pedro told the AP: "I don't really care. I've achieved enough." He added: "A no-hitter is not what's going to dictate what kind of pitcher I am. I think my career is more interesting than one game."

One game that was interesting was a complete reversal of the Ice Williams incident. It was back when Pedro was in his first year at Montreal, early in the season. On April 13, 1994, at Le Stade Olympique, the twenty-two-year-old Martinez was working on a perfect game against Cincinnati when he nailed Reggie Sanders on an 0-2 pitch with one out in the eighth inning, with the Expos up 2-0. Martinez tossed his hands in the air, apparently in disgust with himself, and then the unlikely events unfolded. Sanders bolted at Martinez and tackled him on the mound and the two teams quickly acted out their version of act two of *Les Miserables*. The perfect game was quickly out the window, and the no-hitter would die in the ninth with a leadoff single by Brian Dorsett. Martinez ended up with a no decision, and the Expos had to scratch back and win the game 3-2 with a bunch of singles in the bottom of the ninth, giving reliever John Wetteland the win.

Clearly the Reggie Sanders incident was not the work of a head-hunter, but an early instance of the bizarre fringe violence that would follow Martinez throughout his career. Unlikely scenarios would become common occurrences around Pedro. Midget mascots, dugout pranks, persuasive banter with Grady Little, stray quotes about plunking Babe Ruth in the ass, and Yankee fatherhood—Pedro was a Dominican medicine show, even in some of his most mundane starts, such as the Tuesday night in St. Petersburg in front of 17,450, most of them probably Red Sox fans.

Pedro's first start of 2006—his second season with the New York Mets—was on April 6 against the Washington Nationals at Shea Stadium. That night, Martinez enjoyed an unusual feat for a pitcher—he got to nail one of his favorite targets and take out a home plate umpire with the same pitch. After hitting Jose Guillen in the hip in the third inning, Pedro clipped him on the elbow in the fifth inning. The ball deflected off Guillen and into the throat protector of home plate umpire Ted Barrett. Despite being hit with the ricochet, Barrett sprang into action helping Mets catcher Paul LoDuca restrain the enraged Guillen, who marched toward a motionless Pedro, waving his bat at him and taking off his helmet. Mets third baseman David Wright also sealed off the path to Pedro as the umpires walked Guillen to first base with the temperamental batter still pointing and yelling at Martinez. The benches had of course emptied, and the Nationals bullpen corps made an impressive battlefield cutoff run against the charging regiment from the Mets bullpen, meeting and halting the home relievers near the lip of the infield grass several yards from the Guillen-Martinez phalanx. Meanwhile, Mets veteran Julio Franco came off the bench to play elder statesman and assist two other elders—Nationals manager Frank Robinson and coach Davey Lopes—in soothing the nerves of Guillen as he stood at first base. Though he was famous for his outbursts, perhaps the numbers vouch for Guillen's anger toward Martinez. In forty plate appearances against Pedro, Guillen had been hit by a pitch five times.

Pedro said his pitching was "erratic" after the game. He had also hit Nick Johnson in the second inning. Umpire Barrett, who was praised for preventing what could have been an ugly scene between Guillen and Martinez on the mound, left the game in the seventh inning as his neck injury from the Guillen ricochet worsened. He was replaced by second base umpire Rick Reed, who would be kept busy by more hit batsmen courtesy of Duaner Sanchez and Felix Rodriguez, the latter being ejected along with his manager Robinson after violating the warning to both teams when he nailed LoDuca in the eighth. The Mets won 10-5, and Pedro earned his first win of the season in his first start.

Runelvys Leaves the Building

An admitted student of Pedro's, Runelvys Hernandez, a Dominican fireballer who was the Royals opening day starter in 2003, had his share of the blues while with Kansas City. On July 17, 2005, at Comerica Park in Detroit, Hernandez, who oozed confidence on the mound despite his lack of stamina, disapproved of batter Carlos Guillen's behavior. The early innings of the Sunday afternoon game had featured a trio of hit batsmen, including Hernandez plunking Brandon Inge and Chris Shelton in the opening frame. In the sixth, Guillen looked at a pitch in the dirt and claimed it struck his foot. He tossed his bat toward the dugout and began his jog to first base, but home plate umpire Marty Foster disagreed. Hernandez stared at Guillen as the Detroit shortstop argued his case with Foster. Told to get back into the batter's box, Guillen eventually obliged. The next pitch from Hernandez caromed off the temple of Guillen's batting helmet and went into orbit around Comerica. Dazed, Guillen dusted himself off and began yelling at Hernandez, who reacted by coming toward his victim.

Warnings had been issued after Tigers starter Mike Maroth hit Kansas City's David DeJesus with a pitch in the second. Hernandez, therefore, was out of the game, but lingered and was quickly separated from Guillen as Kansas City catcher John Buck and umpire Foster stood between Guillen and Hernandez. Ironically, in September of 2006, Hernandez and his batterymate Buck engaged in their own embarrassing dugout dustup in Cleveland, with Hernandez taking a serious swipe with his glove at Buck's head. The internal handbags came after shouting and finger-pointing as the Royals piled into their dugout after retiring the Indians. The pair shook it off in the next inning and Kansas City went on to win 5-3 as the Royals' disastrous 2006 season slowly entered its final days.

Guillen would later say he remembered very little from the events after getting his bell rung by Hernandez. Behind him as he reacted angrily but groggily was the Little Caesar's pizza billboard reading "Hot N' Ready." That would prove to be quite true when the Detroit bullpen crew arrived. The Venezuelan shortstop was escorted to first base by a hatless Jose Lima, a former Tigers player who came out of the Kansas City dugout. Mike Sweeney (of *Sweeney vs. Weaver*, the fight that put these two teams on the map) also helped console Guillen. With the bullpen door opened down the left field line, the Tigers relievers dutifully sprinted for the infield. Kyle Farnsworth appeared to be the sixth or seventh man out the door, behind a coach or two and at least one bullpen catcher. Farnsworth was about to figure large in this scrap as Hernandez and Guillen continued to shout at each other among the controlled anarchy. Near the first upright collection of players was an enraged Jeremy Bonderman who was being restrained by coach Juan Samuel. Farnsworth apparently met Kansas City lefthander Jeremy Affeldt near the scrum and exchanged a shove and heated words with him. As Dmitri Young arrived to help contain Bonderman, Farnsworth bolted for Affeldt and tackled him, lifting him high in the air for a body slam along foul territory near the first base line. The ensuing dogpile would leave several Tigers players spiked and hurting, including pitcher Nate Robertson whose shoe came off. His stockinged foot paid dearly when it was found by someone else's cleats.

Farnsworth was extricated from the heap and escorted briefly by Emil Brown and then Matt Stairs. Lance Parrish, one of many burly Detroit coaches, patrolled the area after Farnsworth was isolated. Affeldt was saved by a quick thinking Magglio Ordonez of Detroit, who pulled him away from the *Buck vs. Parrish* sideshow that was happening atop the

Kansas City pitcher. Alberto Castillo, who thought he was being a peace-maker, seemed to anger his own Royals coaches with his loud presence and was among the six players and one manager ejected from the game. Hernandez and his manager Buddy Bell were tossed, along with Brown and Castillo. For Detroit, Guillen, Bonderman and Farnsworth were shown the door. For Farnsworth, his tackle of Affeldt was certainly ranked much lower than his colorful clash with Reds pitcher Paul Wilson in 2003 (see Chapter 12). Bell praised the way the umpires handled the extended incident, calling it juvenile but "part of the game" and credited the over-all brawl experience in one regard: "It breaks up the monotony," Bell told MLB.com.

Hernandez had been skating along in the game until the eruption in the sixth. He had surrendered just two singles and had a 4-0 lead. Kansas City coaches appreciated his worshipping of Pedro Martinez, but were insistent Hernandez learn when to buzz the opposition and know better than to wake sleeping giants when your own squad has pinned you to a tasty 4-0 lead. Known for his formidable singing voice and his persever-ance in the Kansas City farm system, Hernandez's inconsistencies and unchecked boldness fizzled in middle America. The Royals released him in December of 2006.

Eris, the goddess of discord, was definitely a baseball fan. Like a Red Sox supporter living in New York City, the Greek gods never invited her to any occasions. This led to trouble. She even named one of her sons "Strife" for crying out loud. Eris was surely in attendance at the earliest games between the Dodgers and Giants, the Yankees and the aforementioned Red Sox, and various other blood feuds and vendettas that have dotted the game's extracurricular landscape. Some are epic battles waged over decades, while others are flashes in the pan of a fortnight, conjured by bored broadcasters and press box denizens. The lingering malaise usually required a collective memory and combined effort from the press, the clubhouse "bulletin board," one or two firebrand ballplayer personalities, along with some grizzled veterans, naïve rookies, and cigar-chomping managers. Sometimes Eris blessed a pair of players with the gifts of rebuke and loathing that went beyond the usual sparks that fly during the extremes of athletic competition.

The middle years of the 1950s were heated up by the two Johnnys—Logan and Temple—who exchanged volleys of rage on a frequent basis, entertaining and horrifying the two beer-producing Midwestern cities of Milwaukee and Cincinnati. Their battles were waged both on the field and off, and were for keeps, with dental work and blood loss usually involved, according to *Bill James' Historical Baseball Abstract*. Temple was considered by many observers to be a Ty Cobb–style throwback. He retired from the Reds in July of 1964 under some duress. He was made a special scout for the organization, but that lasted about a month until Temple got into a clubhouse brawl with Cincinnati coach Reggie Otero, which led to embarrassing headlines as the Redlegs were embroiled in a tight race for the NL pennant.

Logan and Temple supposedly settled their long-running battle with an on field handshake at second base in 1958. Temple went on to a troubled retirement scarred by bad business decisions, tax trouble, and larceny charges. He died of pancreatic cancer in January of 1994. Logan stuck around Milwaukee, worked as a scout for the Brewers, operated the Milwaukee Braves Historical Association, and played golf. He turned eighty in March of 2007.

Mets-Phillies Ring in the 1990s

Like Pittsburgh and Cleveland, the distance between Philadelphia and New York City is, as the T-shirt says, "a six-pack." When the Mets traded bullpen clown Roger McDowell along with Lenny Dykstra (and Tom Edens) to the Phillies for Juan Samuel in June of 1989, the composition of both franchises changed dramatically. In the last week of the 1989 campaign, McDowell came in to a game at Shea with two outs in the ninth inning to face rookie Greg Jefferies with the Phillies up 5-3. After getting him to ground out to second base to end the game, McDowell yelled at Jefferies and the youngster charged the pitcher and tackled him. As players swarmed around them, McDowell was able to land a flurry of punches on Jefferies' noggin. Mets manager Davey Johnson said McDowell told Jefferies to "get a new bat" and that there was "bad blood" between the two players.

Umpire Randy Marsh was working that game as well as the August 9, 1990 contest at Shea that turned into a slugfest without bats. It was the fifth inning when Pat Combs, the Phillies pitcher, hit Doc Gooden above the left knee and the Doctor made a house call on the mound. Gooden had already plunked Dickie Thon (of *Thon vs. S. Fletcher*) in the second inning and Tommy Herr in the top of the fifth. Combs was either retaliating for Herr and Thon getting hit or was still sore about being the final player cut from the 1988 USA Olympic baseball squad that went to Seoul, Korea. Mets manager Bud Harrelson said Gooden's charge against Combs motivated the Mets to pull out the 5-4 win and edge closer to the division-leading Pirates.

Gooden took a few blows to the head from catcher Darren Daulton, and Combs emerged from the melee with a cut over his nose. Phillies reliever Dennis Cook had the pleasure of being wrestled off the pile by umpire Joe West and thrown to the ground. The chaos took twenty minutes to sort out and restarted a few times courtesy of Mets catcher Mackey Sasser clashing with Jose DeJesus and Darryl Strawberry going after Daulton but ending up with a handful of Von Hayes. In all, seven ejections were declared: Gooden, Strawberry and Tim Teufel of the Mets, and Combs, Daulton, Cook, and bullpen coach Mike Ryan of Philadelphia. It was a fine sendoff for the crowd of 39,240 that turned out for the Mets home finale. It was apparent the '89 Mets, a second place team, were finishing the season the way they started it. There were March fireworks during Spring Training when Strawberry charged Blue Jays pitcher Jeff Musselman, then had to deal with a bear hug from catcher Pat Borders and a tackle by Toronto third baseman Kelly Gruber, whom the Straw (who was not ejected) tangled with as an encore after reaching third base later in the game. All this because Ron Darling hit Jesse Barfield in the early innings of what should have been another sleepy exhibition game in Dunedin.

The night before *Gooden vs. Combs*, Phillies pitcher Don Carman had thrown over David Cone's head as the Mets pitcher stood at the plate and angry words were exchanged. It was classic NL East tension—the overspending Mets were bound for trying times over the next few seasons, while the ragtag Phillies were on the rise.

Self-Imploding Rangers Rarely Angelic

Handling public relations for a franchise such as the Texas Rangers was no walk in the park back in the 1970s. Aside from the famed Beer Night riot in Cleveland, the Rangers of that era also had their share of Spring Training incidents (see *Randle vs. Lucchesi*, and *Billy Martin vs. E. Maddox*). The gig didn't get any easier through the first decade of the twenty-first century. In 2004, Frankie Francisco, apparently inspired by the Maurice Sendak children's book *Pierre*, used a bullpen folding chair to tell Oakland fans he did not care. In 2005, Texas hurler Kenny Rogers, before he became a supercharged, pine tar stained self-motivator on the mound for Detroit, throttled a video cameraman in front of lots of other cameramen and most of his teammates. There had been rumors swirling that Rogers had injured his hand in order to avoid facing the Anaheim Angels. The footage of Rogers abusing the cameraman rivaled *Seinfeld* for ad nauseum reruns, and the moody hurler served a thirteen-game suspension for his impersonation of a human lens cap.

Then there was August 16, 2006, when Adam Kennedy of the Angels charged the mound occupied by Texas pitcher and Hawaii native Scott Feldman—Scott Wayne Feldman to honor the full-name lore of assassins. Rangers starter Vincente Padilla planted the seeds of the conflict the night before. He was having a bad game, and he hit Juan Rivera and Vladimir Guerrero with some of his wilder pitches in the fourth inning. He was ejected, along with Texas manager Buck Showalter. Earlier in the season, Padilla got the heave from a game after he plunked White Sox catcher A.J. Pierzynski a couple of times.

The night after Padilla's mess against Anaheim, with the game-time temperature officially listed as 101 degrees, the Angels were down 9-3 in the eighth inning in Arlington when Kevin Gregg tossed a pitch behind Ian Kinsler of Texas. Gregg then nailed Michael Young in the back and was ejected. Brendan Donnelly relieved, and after a few pitches to Rangers batter Freddy Guzman—BAM!—Donnelly chalked up the HBP and was also gone, along with acting manager Ron Roenicke, the bench coach who took over for ejected manager Mike Scioscia, who had to escort Gregg into the clubhouse because the umpires had issued warnings. (Scioscia had a famous mound charge during his playing days, against Montreal's Pascual Perez, who hit the Dodger catcher in the head with a pitch in May of 1989.) With Scioscia and Roenicke in the clubhouse, the Angels brain trust chain of command listed pitching coach Bud Black as the man in charge.

In the ninth, with two outs and nobody on base, a retaliation for the retaliation was in order when Feldman—a 6-foot-5 sidearm thrower—dealt some pain to Kennedy and the fight was on. Feldman spiked his glove and unleashed a blow to Kennedy's armpit—no doubt quite moist given the atmospheric conditions—and Rangers third baseman Mark DeRosa thrilled the 31,723 sweaty football lovers in attendance with an authentic Cowboys-style tackle of Kennedy. His teammate John Lackey played the role of "angry man" and bolted from the Angels dugout and had to be restrained by the Angels bullpen coach at the conclusion of the four-minute fracas. Feldman's lack of control meant Rangers manager Buck Showalter was ejected for the second straight game. Kennedy and Feldman were also tossed by crew chief Randy Marsh, who was suddenly one busy umpire.

Add to all this the August 6 contest when Adam Eaton of Texas was ejected for throwing at Rivera after giving up a three-run homer to Garrett Anderson. Eaton, it should be noted, was well behaved for the seven innings he threw in the August 16 game.

For those who like to place blame, the intimacy of the four-team AL West division—already a creepy arrangement that defies all logic of league structure—can be cited as a root cause for this type of extended feuding. Failing all else, fans, writers, bloggers, pundits, and assistant general managers could always take the easy way out—blame Buck Showalter. It's as easy as throwing at A.J. Pierzynski.

West Coast Not So Mellow

The bitter rivalry that began when the Giants and Dodgers were both playing home games in Manhattan and Brooklyn respectively survived the trip west in the late 1950s. The franchises left a changing Gotham landscape for the relative safety of earthquakes, wildfires, the Manson family, Hollywood executives, Tommy Lasorda, fog, smog, traffic jams, road rage, Reverend Jim Jones, mudslides, the Watts riots, Governor Jerry Brown, rolling blackouts, drought, the Heaven's Gate cult, drive-by shootings, killer bees, O. J. Simpson, and restaurant menu items such as a plate of mashed yeast with sprouts. Cultural highlights aside, the question is where to begin between these two NL entities? *Marichal vs. Roseboro* (see Chapter 5) was certainly an emblematic flashpoint between the blue and brown. The bad blood that still flows up and down the California coast has seen a broad range of disputes and subtle incidents of one-upmanship played out on the field, off the field, and in the press.

The Giants added an epilogue to the Roseboro incident in Spring Training of 1973, when Roseboro was a coach with the Angels, proof that Giant hatred of all things Dodgers occasionally spilled over to the neighboring AL squad in Orange County.

The March afternoon in Palm Springs got very ugly after Clyde Wright hit San Francisco's Tito Fuentes and Wright needed stitches to close a wound on his head after a serious pier sixer ensued. But it didn't end there. Angels catcher (and ex-Giant) Jack Hiatt, who was warming up replacement pitcher Dave Sells as the Giants prepared to bat, exchanged words with his old coach Charlie Fox, the San Francisco skipper. In an always unwise move, Hiatt charged the opponent's dugout brimming with players to get at Fox. That's when Angels coach Roseboro tried to rescue his catcher and paid dearly for his mission, when 6-foot-6 Dave Kingman of the Giants grabbed the old Dodger catcher by the throat. The outnumbered Angels were quickly pummeled, and it was Angels coach Tom Morgan who finally rescued Roseboro by extracting Kingman from the pile. Five police cars soon pulled into the ballpark lot and officers rushed to settle down both sides. Fans had littered the field with debris aimed at the Giants, and several San Francisco players, including Bobby Bonds, had to be restrained from plowing into the tiny grandstand to duke it out with sun-baked exhibition game patrons. Roseboro's old Dodger teammate, Don Drysdale, was in the Angels TV booth during the melees and the Hall of Famer—still hungry for Giants blood—said he was itching to get down on the field and join the tumult.

A random sample of a more recent semi-rhubarb between the clubs—a two night period in June of 2004—provides a microcosm of the bitter rivalry that might or might not have been mentioned on one of the Dead Sea scrolls. But such ancient history is uncalled for when MLB.com arrives and gives its readers this brilliant, flashy headline from June 24, 2004: "Dodgers-Giants Rivalry Still Intense."

At the center of the Giants late June coup in 2004 was Michael Tucker. The Giants had won the opener of the series 11-5. The second game was on a Wednesday night at SBC Park and was much tighter. Tucker led off the fifth inning against Dodgers starter Jeff Weaver, a baseball violence parolee if ever there was one. The Giants outfielder tried dragging a bunt down the first base line, but struck it too hard. Dodgers first baseman Robin Ventura fielded the ball moving in toward the mound and made a glove flip to Weaver covering first. Tucker arrived as Weaver was getting to the bag and there was a moving collision, a tag, and then Weaver followed Tucker with some harsh words. The benches emptied. First base umpire Andy Fletcher separated Weaver and Tucker before any real action could start. Barry Bonds did his best to curtail the on-deck batter, Marquis Grissom, from starting any fires among the throng as the sellout crowd howled in delight and anticipation of another chapter of Dodgers-Giants angst. No punches were thrown or served at this particular old-school clam bake.

The next night, Tucker was facing cult figure Eric Gagne, the Canadian closer who was festooned with the annoying slogan "Game Over" as part of his overproduced entrance from the bullpen. It was garbage time for Gagne—he was simply getting work in during the bottom of the eighth with his team trailing 9-3. Gagne, the 2003 NL Cy Young Award winner, threw a 2-2 fastball high and tight to Tucker, sending him for a loop. As he recovered from the experience, Tucker stepped toward Gagne and pointed at the 235-pound Montreal native who was smiling back at him. Gagne then threw down his glove (hockey style) and marched toward Tucker. Dodgers catcher David Ross frog-marched Tucker out of the way as teammates were called to duty for another punchless spectacle.

First base umpire Tim Welke, perhaps a bit hasty in his decision, ejected Tucker and Gagne on the spot, further enraging the Dodgers closer. Third baseman Adrian Beltre, realizing his teammate suddenly had a new target in mind, sprinted over to intercept Gagne. He'd forgotten Tucker and seemed to want a piece of Welke and his fellow umpires, who were just a few bodies away in the stand-up scrum.

Cooler heads—and the Giants—prevailed. When Gagne finally made his way to the dugout, Giants fans serenaded him with jeers. Somehow, he had recovered the ball and flipped it over his shoulder toward the mound. He then sarcastically doffed his cap to the hooting crowd.

San Francisco used the three-game sweep in late June to overtake Los Angeles for first place in the NL West. But by late September, the Dodgers would reclaim first and win the division by two games, clinching against the Giants at Dodger Stadium on the next to last game of the season. The bilingual Gagne had two stories: One said it would be "ridiculous" to think he was throwing at Tucker; the other, in a radio interview, said he was sending a message to Tucker for his lack of respect for Weaver on the play at first base the night before.

Omar's Book Club

Another famous punchless spectacle: the ongoing blood feud between San Francisco Giants shortstop Omar Vizquel and well-traveled reliever Jose Mesa. As teammates back in October of 1997, they had a meeting on the mound of Pro Player Stadium in the ninth inning of Game Seven of the World Series. Mesa's job was to protect the lead and close the game so Cleveland could hoist the spikey flagpole trophy, instead of allowing the Florida Marlins to come back and steal the hardware and get to brush up against commissioner Bud Selig's cheap blazer during the post-game ceremony. As Vizquel noted in his premature autobiography with the enigmatic title *Omar! My Life on and Off the Field*, Mesa had a vacant look in his eyes. Like he wasn't there. "Nobody home," Vizquel wrote with the help of Akron sportswriter Bob Dyer. Mesa and Vizquel were the best of pals at one time while playing for the Tribe, their lockers side by side.

The bad blood had started during a spring intrasquad game in 1998. Vizquel homered off Mesa and did a cartwheel while crossing home plate. Mesa was extremely pissed off by the clowning and vowed to drill Vizquel the next time he faced him. That chance came the following season when Mesa was with Seattle. He knocked Vizquel off the plate with some inside heat, and the two exchanged words. Mesa was fined $500.

At Jacobs Field in August of 2000, Mesa, still with Seattle, threw at Vizquel's head and buzzed him inside with the following pitch. Vizquel threw his arms in the air and approached the mound and the benches emptied. Resuming the at-bat, Vizquel grounded out to second but on the way back to the dugout had a mini-skirmish and second verbal battle with Mesa near the baseline. Their now-exhausted teammates again performed the obligatory spilling out of the dugouts and bullpens. Mesa, pointing at Vizquel, had to be restrained by fellow Mariners. Physically, the mismatch went in Mesa's favor. The closer is 6-foot-3, 225 pounds, while the shortstop checked in at 5-foot-9, 165 pounds.

The last straw came in the form of Vizquel's published written word, which hit bookstores in 2002 and indirectly blamed the Indians loss of the '97 World Series on Mesa's lack of intensity in Game 7. Mesa saw red when he saw Vizquel's book and what the slick-fielding Venezuelan wrote about him. The book, which in video form could be adequately reduced to a three-minute cornball segment on *This Week in Baseball*, had upped the ante significantly. Mesa said he wanted to kill Vizquel. Yes, that's right, he told a Philadelphia sportswriter "*kill*."

In a game in Cleveland in June of 2002, having done his reading of Omar's book, Mesa hit Vizquel in the back with a fastball. He was again fined $500. Vizquel told writers he didn't go after Mesa for two reasons: he was hitting well and didn't want to face a suspension, and he didn't want to get his ass kicked. Mesa again vowed to hit Vizquel every time he faced him. He also said he still wanted to kill him.

In April of 2006, with Mesa wearing a Colorado Rockies uniform and Vizquel having settled in with the San Francisco Giants, Mesa hit Vizquel again, and the shortstop calmly went to first base. He later decried Mesa's refusal to move on. "He's the one with the problem," Vizquel told reporters.

MLB disciplinarian Bob Watson, who had already looked into the whole death threat angle of this dispute and had seen the feud jump leagues, gave Mesa a four-game suspension for his April foolishness. The Dominican pitcher, one of nineteen relievers in the three hundred-save club, persuaded Watson to reduce the penalty to three games.

The game after Mesa plunked his old pal and got no reaction from him, there were retaliations galore in Denver as the HBPs flowed between the two NL West squads. A rookie umpire was hasty with the warnings and subsequent ejections. Rockies manager Clint Hurdle reportedly lectured Mesa on cooling down the almost-ten-year-old feud. The reliever said he would just get Vizquel out in the future and perhaps it was time to move on. Vizquel said he didn't believe a word Mesa said. "It's just stupidity," he told AP.

In December of 2006, the AL Champion Detroit Tigers signed Mesa after the Rockies passed on bringing him back for a 2007 campaign and its schedule dotted with frequent games against Vizquel's Giants.

Get Your Mota Runnin'

The informal March madness that is Major League Baseball Spring Training in Florida—the Grapefruit League, as it is known on the T-shirts—is both the perfect and most unlikely place for players to duke it out. It is also the time of year when college basketball squads compete in a large bracket format for the NCAA championship—a tournament that provides a Wonkaville of wagering for both the wagering types and the rank-and-file office drone. As one of a thousand courtesies extended to those lucky enough to be in attendance, the PA announcers at quaint ballparks from Winter Haven to Fort Myers to Vero Beach always provide early round NCAA scores as the lazy, tropical afternoons drag onward. If thoroughbred ponies are preferred over student-athletes playing basketball, the tasty Kentucky Derby warm-up race called the Florida Derby is a late March tradition at Gulfstream Park.

But the sure bet every March in Florida is that the New York Mets will conjure some type of colorful controversy. Motel date rape charges, pissing and brawling in pizzeria parking lots—tips of a few icebergs to scrape the hull of moribund public relations fellows such as Jay Horwitz. As a relief to the spin doctors, sometimes the skullduggery happens *on* the field.

In March of 2002, the Mets were visiting Dodgertown in Vero Beach for an exhibition tilt against Los Angeles. Pitcher Guillermo Mota, a 6-foot-4, 205-pound former Mets shortstop prospect then with the Dodgers, hit Mike Piazza in the hip in the seventh inning. Piazza was taken out of the game and stayed on the Mets dugout bench (the dugouts are "open air" benches in Dodgertown). When Mota left the game in the eighth inning and was walking past the Mets dugout bench, Piazza yelled at him and grabbed him by the jersey, throttling his neck until the two were separated by teammates. Mota's plunking of Piazza marked the 4th HBP for the Mets catcher in March of 2002, including a nasty high fastball off his forearm a few weeks earlier courtesy of Dodgers fireballer Eric Gagne.

On March 12, 2003, the Dodgers were visiting Port St. Lucie as part of a split-squad contest against the Mets. In the sixth, Piazza stepped in against Mota, who was working his second inning of the night. Mota's first pitch was inside and tight against Piazza. His second delivery nailed Piazza in his shoulder blade. The result was a Bill Bixby-to-Lou-Ferrigno type of transformation by Piazza. He slammed his bat and helmet to the ground and flew toward the mound with his right fist cocked Marvel Comics style. It was, as Ben Grimm of the Fantastic Four might have put it, "clobberin' time!" His red face clashed with his orange Mets jersey as he dodged the glove thrown by the Dodger hurler who quickly began backpedaling away from Piazza. Mota's flight to the safety of the Dodgers bench was described as rabbit-like by Mets manager Art Howe, who later theorized that Jim Tracy kept Mota in the game so he could settle some scores with Piazza. Jeromy Burnitz and Joe McEwing made a great effort to catch Mota before he reached his blue sanctuary, but to no avail, especially after Dodgers reserve Mike Kinkade impeded Burnitz. Again, Dodgers catcher David Ross was pressed into duty and made feeble attempts to corral Mad Mike. Adrian Beltre assisted, as did several coaches and umpires. Piazza made a few attempts to charge the Dodgers dugout and extract Mota, who, incidentally, hit a three-run homer off fellow madman reliever Armando Benitez in the top of the sixth.

Mota and Piazza were both ejected. Both left the stadium during the game, but for Piazza, the dispute was far from settled. He dressed and got into his black BMW, which he drove to the other side of the stadium parking lot. He gained access to the visitor's clubhouse, much to the chagrin of Dodgers GM Dan Evans, and demanded out loud "Where's Mota? Where's Mota?" Piazza then searched the premises, including the trainer's room, the showers and the lockers. Mota had in fact been driven away from the ballpark by teammate Brian Jordan, a known Met-killer himself, who had also helped tackle Piazza during his on-field pursuit of the skinny Dominican pitcher.

Mota and Piazza were given five-game suspensions that were the talk of Spring Training right through St. Patrick's Day. They were another entry in what had been a particularly violent Spring Training in 2003, thanks to an ugly incident involving Vladimir Guerrero carrying his bat while charging the mound against Brad Penny, and a wild brawl in Arizona between the Padres and Angels that featured four major suspensions to be served during the regular season.

Luckily, by the time Mota joined the New York Mets in 2006, Piazza had moved on to San Diego. Through his final seasons in New York, he weathered minor storms of controversy about his sexual orientation, his reaction to the beaning by Roger Clemens, ill-fated moves to first base and left field, and a brilliant April Fool's media hoax involving a rumor that he secretly co-starred in the movie *Teen Wolf.*

In November of 2006, Mota was suspended fifty games for violating MLB's drug policy when it was found he had taken a performance-enhancing substance, reportedly a steroid. He was a free agent when his suspension was announced, and, according to Mets brass, they were *so* impressed with his public apology they resigned him to a two-year deal in December. Mota still holds the unofficial record for the fastest time by a pitcher running backward off the mound.

Breaking News for Cave Dwellers

A certain cable television sports network owned by a theme park conglomerate that has "cast members" instead of "employees" has done its best to turn every game played between the Boston Red Sox and New York Yankees into a retelling of Gettysburg, Stalingrad, Falkirk, Vicksburg, San Juan Hill, Wounded Knee, Midway, Dunkirk, Gallipoli, etc., with subplots stolen from various soap operas and reality shows.

The awful truth was sometimes the televised contests were more like New York City mayor Ed Koch against TV journalist Gabe Pressman, or a reclined William F. Buckley dissecting a point made by Art Buchwald, or the semifinals of the Mohegan Sun trick-shot billiards tournament over on ESPN2, or a typical day in traffic court in Scarsdale. Apparently, there is some type of "rivalry" between these two AL East clubs. They don't like each other, and because of that, the drama of this particular athletic competition has to be rammed down everyone's throats.

The Yankees have lots of money and stars and a big city known as Gotham and crass fans who are never satisfied. The Red Sox have a bunch of college students in an old town they call the "Hub." They've also got scores of media types, erstwhile academics, and L.L. Bean fanatics who have over-romanticized the franchise to the point where one more shot of Ben Affleck in his "disguise cap" at Fenway is enough to turn every eight-year-old into Travis Bickle. If ESPN had been in existence back in May of 1938, footage of Jake Powell charging Boston's Happy McKain only to be intercepted by player/manager Joe Cronin would be seen on a nightly basis for two weeks straight following the occurrence. There would be overused catchphrases and an opening montage showing the reaction of the more than eighty thousand fans at Yankee Stadium as Cronin, the player/manager, charged in from his position at shortstop to make sure Happy stayed that way. Later, on ESPN Classic, a Powell documentary filled with amber-tinted interview footage would tell the story of his life as a racist cop in the off-season who ten years after charging McKain committed suicide with a gun after being arrested on charges of writing bad checks in Washington, D.C. Powell was also known for throwing empty bottles at fans he deemed unacceptable.

Play the Powell dispute forward to the pre–designated hitter era and a pitcher named Thad Tillotson is unearthed, wearing Yankee pinstripes, standing at first base and screaming at Boston starter Jim Lonborg during "Gentleman" Jim's Cy Young season of 1967. Lonborg, a Stanford graduate and bachelor extraordinaire known for attending the symphony, had just hit Thad with a pitch and was being verbally abused to the point where the benches emptied. Soon enough, the hirsute Joe Pepitone ended up losing a wrestling match with a Boston rookie named Reggie Smith, who also mixed it up pretty good with Tillotson.

And poor Bill Lee—the outspoken New Englander and Boston pitcher who lost his shoulder during a dandy of a donnybrook in the Bronx in May of 1976 thanks to the shifty efforts of Mickey Rivers and Graig Nettles—well, Lee was just backing up a play at the plate that should have seen Sweet Lou being tagged out by Pudge thanks to a bullet throw from Dewey. For those who don't speak Yankees-Red Sox, designated hitter Lou Piniella was trying to score from second on a looping single to right field handled by Dwight Evans, who threw home ahead of Piniella, who was to be greeted by Hall of Fame catcher Carlton Fisk, ball in hand. Lee claimed in one of his nine autobiographies that Piniella was just playing to the crowd with the futile collision with Fisk. Replays show Lou simply rounded third base too wide and had no choice but to lower a shoulder and hope for some type of Fisk juggling act on impact.

Yankees outfielder Otto Velez, who had taken Lee's low and away sinker into right field for the base hit, was making a beeline for Fisk, who had flipped Piniella over while tagging him and then pounced on him to deliver blows with home plate umpire Terry Cooney on his back and first baseman Carl Yastrzemski just seconds away from grabbing both combatants. The spark igniting Fisk's first blow was captured in a dramatic May 31, 1976 cover of *Sports Illustrated*. The shot showed Piniella prone in the chalky dust, Fisk all business with one arm pinning Piniella and the other holding the ball in his glove, and Cooney looking resplendent in his claret blazer and short-billed umpire's cap, leaning over Fisk. Masks are off, Fisk's hair looks bouncy and alive, and Piniella has his right fist at the ready, even while on his back. It is an invigorating glimpse of AL East baseball under the headline: "Head-On Collision in the East." Inside is an excellent shot of Boston shortstop Rick Burleson taking a flying leap onto Piniella's back, wedged in front of Lee. Fisk's shin guard covered leg appears to be bearing the weight of the pile, and Cooney has backed off holding his balloon chest protector and mask.

Lee said his intent was to prevent Velez from getting to his catcher, so he tackled him high, which didn't work. He was spun around and nailed from behind by a blow from Rivers. Nettles, who had been on first base when Velez singled, grabbed Lee and body-slammed him to the ground, shoulder first. When a semblance of calm began to set in and the roving throng began to resemble a committee meeting without enough chairs, Lee sparked Nettles with one of his many witty barbs—something tangential and spacey about playing with Nettles's brother in Alaska, followed by the word "asshole"—and the Yankee third baseman landed a Joe Frazier–style right cross to the pitcher's jaw and down he went, stirring the pot again for more Bronx chaos. When Lee was finally scraped off the dirt of the home plate circle, his pitching arm visibly sagged as he was escorted off the battlefield and to a local hospital. But not before a Yankee fan tried to get at him as the Boston trainer, a sideburned blond fellow wearing tomato red slacks, began to assess the damage. (This was the 1970s, when fans spent a lot of time on the field.) The damages included a bruised thigh for Yaz, a swollen finger for Piniella and an injured toe for Rivers. *Sports Illustrated* reported that a batboy was struck with debris thrown from the stands. Yes, the Yankees and Red Sox were fighting again, which was important even in the pre-cable era. The big difference for this one—only 28,418 fans had checked in to the old ballyard to witness the beautiful disorder unfold.

In addition to the incident at Fenway in August of 1973—*Fisk vs. Munson,* covered in chapter eight—there were the events of July 24, 2004, when another Yankees third baseman stirred the beanpot against the Carmines. His name was Alex Rodriguez.

It had been a rainy midsummer morning in Boston, so much so the Fenway Park playing surface appeared to be suffering a great deal as game time approached. It was to be "national television" as Fox foolishly called it, meaning the game was on network television in a vast Northeastern market served by one team's very own cable network in addition to the other's regional sports network. The afternoon start was delayed fifty-four minutes, with many of the Yankees shedding their uniforms and leaving the ballpark convinced of a Saturday rainout.

The pitching matchup of Bronson Arroyo against Tanyon Sturtze was not exactly the Saturday matinee of Pedro Martinez versus Roger Clemens that Fox Sports would have preferred, but that is the way this particular rivalry cookie crumbled. There was also the matter of the Yankees having almost a double-digit lead over Boston in the standings. The early innings introduced the sloppy Boston defense that would be on display all afternoon, and the Yankees took the early lead in the second. The fireworks would begin in the top of the third. After Bernie Williams scored when Gary Sheffield grounded into a double play, A-Rod stepped in. Fox cameras showed Red Sox GM Theo Epstein yawning in his Fenway seat. Seconds later, the Red Sox season and march to a curse-lifting World Series victory was about to be set on its course by the actions of catcher Jason Varitek, the man who would soon be named captain of the Boston squad. Arroyo hit A-Rod on his padded elbow, and the high-salaried glamour boy began his walk to first base with several harsh words hurled in the direction of the pitcher's mound. The act of removing protective gear has turned the typical base on balls or hit batsman into a housekeeping venture for the player and the bat boy who must come out and retrieve the accoutrements heavy with Velcro and fiberglass. Once A-Rod had shed his elbow spacesuit he was almost halfway up the line, and Varitek had come forward to escort him to make sure the verbal provocations did not escalate to the point where the scrawny Arroyo would be punished by a bulky Yankee. Varitek was also telling A-Rod to proceed to first base, in no uncertain terms, while in the background Arroyo taunted Rodriguez with his usual cerebral brand of humor—a crotch tug. (While with the Pirates, the juvenile Arroyo wore uniform number "69"—*get it??*)

A-Rod stared at Varitek, annoyingly called "Tek" by certain literary-minded Red Sox fans, and said "Come on!" The boiling point had been reached. Taking a page from the NHL's "facewash" glove maneuver, Varitek used his catcher's mitt to swipe the moisturized and pampered skin of A-Rod's face at extremely close range, with his throwing hand bracing the glove and applying further pressure on A-Rod's brow. Catcher's mask still on, Varitek then took a return blow from Rodriguez that sent the mask and the two of them tumbling to the ground where they would quickly be concealed in a haystack of MLB player personnel humanity. Several splinter groups would form around the pile halfway to first base. Kevin Millar, Trot Nixon, Gabe Kapler and David Ortiz seemed to extract Yankees starter Tanyon Sturtze from the pile, with Nixon and Kapler roughing up the former Devil Rays star in a mini-pile closer to the dugout while Ortiz remained upright, making a rudimentary effort to remove fallen bodies. Ortiz did manage to pull Sturtze off of Kapler, freeing his teammate from a chokehold and probably cutting Sturtze's ear in the process.

When the proverbial dust settled, Sturtze was standing around hat-less with his left ear looking slightly . . . menstrual. A thick trickle of dark blood was lowering onto his ear lobe, giving the fight a certain science-fiction edge, as if Ortiz had planted some type of parasite into Sturtze's skull, one that would cause the pitcher to hang curveballs for the rest of his life and be relegated to mop-up work out of the pen.

Sturtze and his inner-ear alien would leave the game in the fourth inning thanks to a bruised pinky, of all things. He was upset because he was pitching a decent game with the Yanks leading 3-2. Bruce Froemming, the crew chief in his thirty-fourth season of umpiring who tried to stay between Varitek and Rodriguez, had by then sorted out the ejections. Varitek, A-Rod, Kapler and Kenny Lofton were dismissed. Red Sox manager Terry Francona would get the thumb in the fifth inning from umpire Mike Winters after arguing a force play at second base.

The image of Varitek toe-to-toe and right up in A-Rod's face, and the robust brawling which followed, became a signature moment for the curse-lifting Boston club. After Bill Mueller hit the walk off homer in the ninth off Mariano Rivera to give Boston the 11-10 win, the Red Sox would go 46-20 the rest of the way.

Photos of A-Rod, his face obscured by Varitek's leather and his Yankees helmet embarrassingly askew, were soon plastered everywhere. In October, the Red Sox would again meet the Yankees in the ALCS and find a way to come back and eliminate them after being down 3-0 in the series. The 2004 Red Sox also performed a greater service—spoiling the hackneyed franchise storyline of continuous "heartbreak" forever, and not a moment too soon, because people were wondering: How much Doris Kearns Goodwin kvetching can a populace endure before tumbling into anarchy? The A-Rod fight photo also graced the cover of Stephen King and Stewart O'Nan's diary of the 2004 Boston season called *Faithful.*

The machismo oozing from the hard-fought elimination of the Yankees somehow diminished by the time Varitek and several of his teammates had their looks "redone" by the television show *Queer Eye for the Straight Guy* the following March. The makeover included photo opportunities at Spring Training that gave the hardscrabble Red Sox a Yankee-like vainglorious air of metrosexuality and irony-free glam. Varitek, who was named Boston's captain after the 2004 World Championship put to rest the "1918!" chant in the Bronx, refused to autograph photos of his tango with A-Rod.

Yankees fans had seen a similar—though less spectacular—incident in August of 1996 when Seattle catcher John Marzano took a disliking to Paul O'Neill's commentary after reliever Tim Davis brushed him back in the Kingdome. (The catcher's glove punch had also been seen prominently in the National League in *Dempsey vs. Dykstra* and when Atlanta's legally deaf Curtis Pride barreled into Cubs catcher Sandy Martinez and the latter punched him in the face with his catcher's mitt during the ensuing rhubarb.)

It was one game from October of 2003 that turned many pages in the Yankees-Red Sox tension tome. Postseason baseball in a cramped yard near Kenmore Square. A ticket to the World Series was at stake. Regional celebrities, authors, and FOX television B-listers were on hand in the fancy seats. It was Game 3 of the ALCS on the afternoon of Saturday, October 11. Some three hours after the first pitch from Pedro Martinez, the day would have seen infamous scraps in foul territory near home plate on the first base side, and beyond the right field fence in the Yankees bullpen.

The first confrontation resembled something that might be seen in the parking lot of a bowling alley. A seventy-two-year-old coach charging at a thirty-one-year-old superstar pitcher, with the latter taking the old man's large head in both of his hands and throwing the senior citizen to the ground, like a soldier unloading cannonballs from the back of a Jeep. In a video collage on MLB.com before the ALCS, New York bench coach Don Zimmer was interviewed about the Yankees-Red Sox rivalry. He said it was still intense, but there was less "hatred" now between the players. As he said that, the editor cut to footage of New York shortstop Derek Jeter and Boston shortstop Nomar Garciaparra giving each other a handshake and awkward "thug hug" on the field.

Zimmer was beaned while in the minors in 1953 and was unconscious for almost two weeks. Doctors inserted four metal "buttons" in his skull to stabilize his injuries. In 1956 with the Brooklyn Dodgers, Zim was hit in the cheekbone by Reds pitcher Hal Jeffcoat. As a manager of the Cubs in 1990, Zimmer once professed an idea to reduce injuries during baseball fights. He told the *Chicago Daily Herald* MLB should follow the NHL model and keep fights on a man-to-man basis, instead of allowing "fifty guys on the field." Zimmer's question: "With four umpires out there, how much can they [the fighters] do to each other?" Perhaps too much Wrigley Field sun was responsible for Zim's Stan Mikita solution?

The travails of Zimmer's fifty-four-year career in professional baseball were quite visible on his ruddy face and his lumpy, bald dome—which Jeter frequently rubbed for good luck. Jeter would later mistake Zimmer's bald dome for David Wells, whom he thought had charged Martinez when the benches emptied after Roger Clemens threw a head-high pitch to Manny Ramirez leading off the bottom of the fourth. Despite the pitch being over the plate, Ramirez reacted by yelling at Clemens and walking toward the mound brandishing his bat. This was after Martinez had struck Karim Garcia high on his back in the top of the fourth. Garcia took his base, but not before a shouting match with Martinez and help from the top step of the Yankees dugout, where Zimmer, Jorge Posada and Clemens were letting Martinez have it. When Martinez stared at Posada and made a gesture at his own temple, the players spilled out of the undersized dugouts but didn't venture too far onto the field. Home plate umpire Alfonso Marquez then warned both teams.

Martinez had already plunked Jeter and Alfonso Soriano during the regular season—facts which were certainly on file in the Yankees dugout.

Before the top of the fourth would end with the Yankees up 4-2, Garcia slid hard into second base trying unsuccessfully to break up the double play. He and second baseman Todd Walker got into a shoving match, causing the dugouts to froth once again.

So with Ramirez toting the bat toward Clemens, all hell broke loose. David Ortiz came out to restrain Ramirez, and Zimmer made a run across the field to get at Martinez, who was walking toward the plate in his warm-up jacket. Stunned to see Popeye coming at him and leading with a right and then a truncated left hook, Martinez reacted with the quick throw down and quickly attention was diverted from shirt-grabbing around Clemens and Ramirez to the health of the old man face down in the grass. A police officer tended to him as fellow Yankees and team staff rushed to his side. He had a cut on the bridge of his nose. He would stay on the bench for the rest of the game, but would be rushed to a local hospital afterward, telling reporters he had nothing to say because "we won."

It was a tight 4-3 win for the Yankees, putting them up 2-1 in the best of seven series they would eventually win when Aaron Boone hit a walk-off home run at Yankee Stadium in Game 7. But the Game 3 fireworks were not over. As darkness fell on the Hub, a Fenway Park grounds crew member assigned to the Yankees bullpen in right field was, like everyone else on the field, caught up in the emotional battle. He was rooting for his employer by waving a white "rally" towel and pumped his fist facing the crowd after Hideki Matsui grounded into a double play to end the top of the ninth. Yankees reliever Jeff Nelson had asked the worker—Paul Williams—to move to the Red Sox dugout if he wanted to continue his moonlighting gig as BoSox cheerleader. Somehow, the two ended up face to face, each claiming later the other acted first in the fisticuffs that followed.

Warming up in right field was Garcia, who noticed Nelson getting shoved in the bullpen. He ran to the short fence, scaled it like Napoleon Dynamite and volunteered his services to the Nelson cause. Witnessing the altercation was none other than baseball violence magnet Jeff Weaver, relegated to the Yankees bullpen. He told the press Williams had made the mistake of cussing at Nelson and getting in the reliever's face when asked to move.

FOX cameras struggled to pick up details of the distant dust-up beyond right field. Police and security staff could be seen scooting about the dark bullpen. Garcia would leave the game after cutting his left hand.

His dodgy explanation was he lacerated it either while climbing over the fence or "someone's spikes." The latter would have to be considered friendly fire because bullpen grounds crew cheerleaders usually don't wear spikes, nor do Fenway security staff or Boston police officers, at least during working hours. Williams, meanwhile, would be taken to a hospital with spike wounds to his back and arm, with a police investigation of the incident pending. Fines for ALCS Game 3 totaled $90,000. Martinez was docked $50,000, Zimmer $5,000, Ramirez $25,000 and Garcia a painful $10,000.

Yankees president Randy Levine played the role of drama queen as the events of ALCS Game 3 unfolded. First he engaged in a shouting match with MLB exec Sandy Alderson about Fenway not having enough police or security. Then, after the ninth inning bullpen tizzy, Levine played the role of stunned Bronx aristocrat, denouncing the heathens of the Old Town. "A security incident like this would never be tolerated at Yankee Stadium," he told the AP. "Unfortunately, there was an atmosphere of lawlessness that was allowed to be perpetrated all day long. The events of the entire day were disgraceful and shameful, and if it happened at our ballpark, we would apologize, and that's what the Red Sox should do here." And with that, Levine adjusted his powdered wig as footmen prepared for his ascent into his gilded carriage pulled by noble steeds onto the southbound lanes of the Olde Post Road also known as I-95.

"Great theater, whatever you want to call it," Clemens told the press after the bizarre contest had ended.

Chapter 11:
MISMATCHES

On a cold day in late January of 2007, with the denizens of the Windy City around him caught up in Bears Super Bowl XLI fever, John Cangelosi was thinking about what it was like to be at the bottom of a pile of Major Leaguers. He was recalling his encounter with Braves pitcher John Smoltz at Shea Stadium in May of 1994. "You're on the bottom and it just gets heavier and heavier and heavier. Frank Howard was on top of me. He's 6-8, 300 pounds. Needless to say it was a little claustrophobic down in the pile," Cangelosi said from his home in suburban Chicago. "You can't breathe, your face is in the dirt and you're just waiting for the bullpen to get there. Once the bullpen's there, then they finally start taking guys off."

It was Cangelosi's only season with the Amazin's, but even the most miserable Shea Stadium dwellers seem to crack a smile when recollecting the afternoon when the little guy from Brooklyn took matters into his own hands against the vaunted rulers of the NL East who had tortured the Mets for so long. The clash on the Shea mound made the cover of *Sports Illustrated*, one of the most graphic baseball front pages the magazine has ever run. The image served as a reminder to Cangelosi as to who hit him as he and Smoltz were bound for the ground after bulldogging each other on the first base side of the mound. Cangelosi had just watched Ryan Thompson's fifth-inning grand slam from the on-deck circle, a towering drive that guided the proverbial bee into Smoltz's bonnet.

"He [Thompson] kind of Cadillacked it a little bit. But again, my feelings are if a guy hits a grand slam and it's a bomb, then he should enjoy it," Cangelosi said, using the automotive brand name invoked on the diamond when a batter takes his time rounding the bases after hitting a home run, as if proudly driving a luxury car. Thompson, who had struck out in his previous five at-bats (known as a Ford Pinto?), had put the Mets up 7-0. Enter, the 5-foot-8, 160-pound whipping post.

"I got in the [batter's] box and all of the sudden when he released the ball I saw him change his arm delivery so his arm slot was coming across his body so I knew he was throwing at me intentionally," Cangelosi said. "I pretty much started running after him before I even got hit. I kind of ran into the ball a little bit and then I ran out there . . . and the last thing I can remember was thinking 'just don't embarrass yourself.'"

Vindication came in the form of a compliment delivered from Mets first base coach and baseball legend Frank Howard while the two were in the pile. "That's good hard baseball, son," Howard told Cangelosi.

"I threw a punch and missed," Cangelosi recalled of the hard baseball. "I threw a Hail Mary, he went down, I went down on top of him [Smoltz] and that's all I remember. Then *Sports Illustrated* came out with Charlie O'Brien hitting me in the back of the head, which I thought was kind of cool. To each his own, he's got to protect his pitcher."

The *Sports Illustrated* cover of May 23, 1994, features Cangelosi's back, showing off his home pinstripe Reggie-esque forty-four jersey. He's neck-to-neck with a bowed Smoltz. Atlanta third baseman Terry Pendleton looms open-mouthed as an arrival in the background, his flip-up shades flipped up. Intruding into the magazine's logo is the bellicose image of former Met Charlie O'Brien, who was catching Smoltz that day. His fist was cooked at an odd angle—like a larger, healthier version of Joey Ramone's clench during a "Hey, ho, let's go!" chant—and looked to be aimed at the back of Cangelosi's helmet-free head. O'Brien's right knee—a gleaming red shin guard covering it—was aimed at Cangelosi's buttocks. Charlie's goateed face is a grimaced study in concentration. His chest protector was about to get a workout. The editorialized headline is "Enough Already!" with the subhead "Another round of ugly brawls gives baseball and basketball a black eye." Inside, the magazine delivered a tut-tutting trend piece about the latest round of brawls in baseball and the NBA. It has become what editors call an "evergreen" piece as the same story with different names and photos could have been published every spring since 1902 through the present.

Meanwhile, back in the pile, Cangelosi said he always protected his assets. "I'm on the bottom and I try to rearrange my legs," he said. "That's my game, I can't afford to get hurt." Cangelosi said he was somewhat surprised by Smoltz throwing at him. "When I went up there reporters asked me 'what were you thinking?' Coming from John Smoltz I didn't think—you know if it's a Danny Darwin or someone else that is a headhunter, of course—but John Smoltz, with his temperament and personality—that was the last thing on my mind," he said.

The memories of the incident were amazingly fresh in Cangelosi's mind some thirteen years later, even as he busied himself with his fifth year of running the Cangelosi Baseball Academy in the Chicago suburbs. "I'm not one that causes confrontation," Cangelosi said. "If I had to do it all over again I would. The circumstances were he was throwing at me, I reacted. It wasn't done with malice intent. It was just baseball." And Baseball, from its offices on Park Avenue in Manhattan, said Cangelosi had to sit out four games for his mound charge, while Smoltz paid for his bad aim with an eight-game detention.

The undersized Cangelosi charging the mound against the 6-foot-3, 210-pound Smoltz was an odd mismatch in many ways, but not the biggest mismatch in Cangelosi's thirteen-year career. The Brooklyn native, who grew up in Hialeah, Florida, once clashed with the 6-foot-8, 265-pound Jeff Juden as part of a sideshow attached to an Astros-Expos donnybrook at Le Stade Olympique in August of 1996. The brawl started when Houston's Danny Darwin (of *Pedro Guerrero vs. Darwin*) punished Henry Rodriguez with a pitch for admiring a homer he'd hit earlier in the game. The benches emptied. Derrick May went wild with Ugueth Urbina, Moises Alou and Rondell White danced around with Shane Reynolds, and a stray batting helmet crashed into the lip of Houston manager Terry Collins, leaving the skipper in need of several stitches to close the cut. Alongside it all on the turf was the gargantuan Expos hurler Juden, born in the gothic environs of Salem, Massachusetts, a first round draft pick of the Houston Astros in 1989. He'd come off the bench, as had Cangelosi, who back in 1982 was selected by the White Sox as the 433rd pick in the 1982 draft.

"All of a sudden there's a 6-8 bastard running at me," Cangelosi recalled. "What am I gonna do? I just put my head down between his legs, picked him up and we fell down and while we were down I got about ten to twelve rabbit punches in on him." The pair would rise up from the pile once, then fall back down again as F. P. Santangelo tried to separate them and Cangelosi barely avoided an iron fist thrown at the last second by

Juden. Cangelosi was among several players given a four-game suspension after the Montreal melee, while Darwin received a six-game sentence. An unusually large crowd of 35,458 got their Canadian dollar's worth in witnessing what was perhaps a sequel to the Expos-Astros tilt from May of 1989 known as *Spike Owen vs. Larry Andersen,* a smackdown featuring multiple ejections in the Astrodome.

Cangelosi, who has a World Series ring from his days with the 1997 Florida Marlins, also recalled an encounter with a brawny man during Spring Training. Cangelosi was with the Pirates. Testy pitcher Don Carman of the Phillies had thrown behind Barry Bonds during an exhibition game, and the benches at Bradenton emptied. Having just played winter ball with Carman, Cangelosi went to him in the mild scrum that formed on the field. "Just a few guys wrestling, no punches really," Cangelosi said of the skirmish. Innocently enough, he had come off the bench to make small talk with Carman in an effort to keep things calm. But he was too near the prized possession during any fight—the pitcher—thus provoking an automatic response from the battery mate. Before he knew it, Cangelosi was lifted from the ground from behind—by his neck. "He was choking the hell out of me," Cangelosi said. "I could see my parents and my girlfriend in the stands, and my feet were dangling off the floor," Cangelosi said. His hangman that day in March was future Marlins teammate Darren Daulton, who has since told ESPN he travels between dimensions of space and time from his home in Tampa, a city where, coincidentally, traffic is a nightmare. Daulton also said he believes the world will end on December 21, 2012, as it is written in the Mayan calendar. Perhaps out of respect for Fernando Valenzuela, the Mayans at least had the courtesy to schedule the apocalypse during the offseason and after the Winter Meetings.

Two seasons after he and Daulton helped the incomparable Jim Leyland raise the World Series trophy in the Miami suburbs, Cangy retired knowing he never backed down. He even pitched several innings of extreme mop-up duties at the tail end of blowout losses. In four career innings pitched, Cangelosi surrendered one hit and no runs. Not one batter dared to charge the mound against him.

"My mentality was always to be very tough mentally. I never had a problem with me being small. I never had a chip on my shoulder," Cangelosi said. "I wanted to prove to people that I belonged, so I just worked harder." The David vs. Goliath tale is not necessarily among the lessons learned for students of the game at the Cangelosi Baseball Academy. Being taller than actors Tom Cruise and Al Pacino counts for something, but not on the baseball diamond. "I don't recommend fighting. I'm not proud of it. Would I have done everything the same again? Of course, because I was totally in the right," Cangelosi said. "I don't look for a fight, it was something that happened, and it got a lot of attention because of my size, especially the one with Juden. The one with Smoltz was more because it was Atlanta and Shea Stadium. I would do it all over again."

Sausage Abuse, Gross Indecency

Cangelosi is not the only man to wear a Pirates uniform and be part of a mismatched battle. One in particular happened in Milwaukee's Miller Park on July 8, 2003 and gave headline writers across the globe a chance to cut up. Randall Simon, the Curacao-born outsized first baseman, was leaning on the dugout rail holding his bat. The popular sausage races were taking place in the seventh inning, with anthropomorphic participants such as the Hot Dog, Italian Sausage, Polish Sausage, and Bratwurst competing in a footrace wearing large, top-heavy foam costumes depicting each particular menu item. (A Chorizo character was later added to the races.) The longstanding promotion has drawn interest from players mired on the disabled list (Pat Meares donned one of the costumes in 1999, as have Hideo Nomo and Geoff Jenkins) hoping to combat boredom. The Miller Park tubesteaks, as well as other "zany" mascot types, have been frequently exploited for ironic laughs in countless ESPN commercials.

As the Italian Sausage, replete with trademark mustache, ran past Simon at the dugout rail, he stuck out his bat in a half-swing and hit the character on the backside. The impact sent the meat product to the ground. Inside the costume was eighteen-year-old Mandy Block, an employee of the Brewers. Her stumble also brought down a fellow employee dressed in the Hot Dog suit, leaving only the Polish Sausage and Bratwurst to complete the race. Both Block and her coworker suffered scraped knees from their fall.

Simon, who indeed had nowhere to hide in this sausage affair, was initially charged with misdemeanor assault by the Milwaukee County sheriff's department. The Man reduced the charges to disorderly conduct after Simon was led from the ballpark to the sheriff's office in handcuffs. The disorderly charge carried a $432 fine, which was up from the $287 fine for the same charge the sheriff slapped on Tony Phillips back during his 1996 fan run-in at County Stadium (see Chapter 6). MLB was decidedly tougher on the smiling, free-swinging Simon. Commissioner Bud Selig called the act "wholly unacceptable." Simon was suspended for three games and fined $2,000. A few weeks later, the Pirates traded him to the Cubs.

On August 24, 1993, a full decade before Simon's SausageGate, the Buccos were visiting Dodger Stadium. Bob Walk was facing off against Los Angeles' Kevin Gross. In the third inning, Gross plunked rookie Kevin Young in the back of the head with a pitch. Observers said manager Jim Leyland and reserve outfielder Lloyd McClendon were shouting at Gross from the dugout after Young was beaned. Gross batted in the bottom of the third and was promptly hit in the leg by Walk. He was immediately tossed from the game by home plate umpire Mike Winters. When Leyland came out to complain to crew chief Bruce Froemming, the Pittsburgh manager was ejected.

Having no other recourse, Leyland charged at Gross, who was taking his base, telling him to throw the ball over the plate. Gross responded with a choice obscenity. The 5-foot-10, 170-pound Leyland had to reach up with his forearms to get in the face of the 6-foot-5, 210-pound Gross. Both Leyland's arms came up, as if he couldn't decide which fist to throw at Gross. Before Leyland could decide, the pitcher pushed the manager away, and Bucs catcher Don Slaught arrived to shove Gross away from his manager, knocking the batting helmet off the pitcher's head. On-deck batter Brett Butler (of *Butler vs. Danny Jackson*) was the first Dodger in, pulling Slaught away from Gross. Tom Foley of the Pirates checked in for more Leyland support, and then the Dodgers designated "rescue" man for all fights—coach Joey Amalfitano—answered the bell, trying to keep a shouting Jay Bell away from his starting pitcher. Leyland was bear hugged by an umpire and the scrum moved from the mound area to the plate with everyone in attendance. Mike Piazza and Eric Karros—the latter who had a big night in the 13-4 Dodgers rout—showed off their swell hairdos and heated up the fringes of the mob by grabbing any available Pirate player and trying to throw them to the ground. It was a 0-0 game until right after the brawl. When Mark Petkovsek (of *J. Damon vs. Petkovsek*) took over the ejected Walk, the Dodgers put a 6 up on the board and the laugher was on.

The teams had some beanball history going back to 1989, and Leyland and Walk were both around back then to remember that some payback might have been necessary.

Andy Van Slyke finally led Leyland away from the excitement. "He believes in us, maybe more than he should," Van Slyke told a suburban Pittsburgh newspaper. Leyland later told ESPN his attack on Gross was "stupid" and that he had since made peace with the Dodgers hurler.

Leyland's polar opposite on the personality and likeability scale—Dodgers manager Tommy Lasorda—had this to say to a Pittsburgh sportswriter: "Leyland made a mistake going after that guy. I'd say one thing about Kevin Gross—he showed respect and didn't hit him. That was good, because I certainly didn't want to see Jimmy get hurt."

Leyland was suspended five games and fined $7,500.

Beware All Who Enter Skull Island

His middle name? Arthur. His nickname was "Kong." It is no wonder he still has an underground following of worshippers. Gargantuan slugger Dave Kingman was one entertaining ballplayer. Very few of his career 442 home runs were cheapies. Many of them were things of beauty. His strike-outs were gawky displays of flailing limbs bound to an elongated torso. His attitude, however, was a constant problem, especially the time in 1985 when he sent a rat in a box to a female sportswriter. That type of behavior might explain his travels—four different teams in one season (1977) and eight teams played for in his sixteen-year career. Kingman's painful throat-grab of Angels coach (and former Juan Marichal opponent) Johnny Roseboro during Spring Training was touched on as a touching moment in Chapter 10. Kingman, who stood 6-foot-6 and weighed 215 pounds, always stood out when baseball fights erupted.

One of the better quotes about facing an enraged Kingman came from St. Louis pitcher Lynn McGlothen. "I was ready to fight. He's 6-foot-6, but I'm no midget," said the 6-foot-2, 195-pound McGlothen. McGlothen had just been thrown out of a game by Bruce Froemming after hitting Mets pitcher Jon Matlack as part of a beanball war at Busch Stadium in April of 1976. Before McGlothen could leave the field, Kingman led a charge of Mets players out of the dugout. With Kong bearing down on him, McGlothen threw off his red cap and dropped his glove. But Cards first baseman and future Mets legend Keith Hernandez tackled Kingman before he could reach the mound.

A year later, on August 7, 1977, at Wrigley Field, Kingman was visiting his future stomping grounds wearing a Padres uniform. In 1976 while with the Mets, he stunned the Wrigley faithful with a majestic 550-foot blast that struck a house well beyond the Friendly Confines. This time around, the business at hand unfolded in the second game of a twinbill. San Diego took the first game 8-6, and Kong hit a two-run homer to add to the pair he'd hit the day before.

The nightcap got a little testy from the start. Padres starter Bob Shirley plunked Larry Biittner and then surrendered a three-run homer to Jose Cardenal. Kingman led off the second inning against Steve Renko, who promptly nailed Kong with a pitch. Home plate umpire John Mc-Sherry issued warnings. With Kingman on first, George Hendrick grounded to short and the double play was on—until Kingman crushed second baseman Mick Kelleher as he was turning the twin-killing. It was an impact worthy of action at Soldier Field. When the Kelleher-Kingman pile of limbs sorted itself out, the two came up fighting, and after bullpens and benches emptied to join the fray near the keystone, Kingman and Kelleher both were tossed from the game.

Kelleher, at 5-foot-9, 176 pounds, was known as a light-hitting, slick-fielding middle infielder. He was famous for never hitting home runs, even at Wrigley. But after his brutal tussle with Kingman, Cubs fans knew him from then on as "Killer."

Kelleher injured his neck and ribs in the battle with Kingman. Team-mate Steve Ontiveros was kicked in the back during the melee that followed the broken double play and had to leave the game in the seventh. "The way Kingman came in on Kelleher he could have broken him in half," Cubs manager Herman Franks observed. Renko, who told the AP he wasn't throwing at Kingman, accused Kong of taking a cheap shot on Kelleher. Of course, the Kong and Killer became teammates in 1978, playing three seasons together as Cubbies.

There was another Chicago manager who had a low opinion of a Kingman performance. White Sox skipper Tony LaRussa wanted Kong suspended for his actions at Oakland Coliseum on September 10, 1984. That's when Kingman, playing for the A's, charged the mound against pitcher Rich Dotson, who had hit Kong with a pitch in the third inning. Some said the A's were sensitive regarding Dotson's pitch placement after he buzzed Rickey Henderson's gourd in a game the week before. Kingman landed several blows to Dotson's gourd after he got to the mound and grabbed the 6-foot, 215-pound hurler. White Sox first baseman Greg Walker finally got Kingman off his pitcher as both teams made the long journey from the dugouts on the horizon of the Coliseum's Sargasso Sea-like foul territory. After the fight, Kingman was tossed from the game. Dotson was allowed to stay in, and promptly put himself in a position to take the loss as the A's prevailed 3-0. "I don't think he was throwing at me intentionally," Kingman told the AP, "but the pitch last week to Rickey could have killed him. It was right at his head." During that same series at Comiskey, Kingman was plunked by Floyd Bannister, one of a half-dozen HBPs for Kong during the 1984 campaign. LaRussa's grounds for demanding a Kingman suspension were dodgy, even for a lawyer, especially when Dotson himself told the press he wasn't surprised Kong came out to give him a beating on the mound. After scaring Henderson in Chicago, Dotson had made an oddball remark to the press regarding Oakland players whining about his aim. "If they can't take it, they should get a seeing eye dog at the plate," Dotson said. Head scratching ensued, then some king-sized revenge would be served by the big man wearing the Oakland uniform.

Horton Serves Up a Tanana Split

The California Angels were visiting Tiger Stadium on June 12, 1975, and Frank Tanana, a Detroit native, was looking in on the Virginia-born Detroit legend who was Willie Horton. It was the first inning of the opening game of a doubleheader. The flame-throwing Tanana knocked Horton to the dirt. For the past three weeks or so, "Willie the Wonder," as he was known in the Motor City, had been hitting the dirt quite frequently.

In the fourth inning, with the Angels up 2-1, Tanana skimmed one inside on Horton again. The 5-foot-11, 210-pound Horton—all muscle and possessing Herculean strength—thought the pitch nicked his thigh. So he charged the mound to take out his anger on the 6-foot-3, 195-pound Tanana. Horton later said he was simply going to the mound to "talk" to Tanana. Home plate umpire Marty Springstead and Angels catcher Ellie Rodriguez were shed like gnats when they tried to restrain Horton. Springstead told the AP Horton "is the strongest man in the league. Nobody can hold him."

Second base umpire Larry Barnett was also thrown aside like a piece of lawn furniture when he tried to restrain Horton as the fight moved from the mound toward the first base dugout. Angels infielder Denny Doyle, all 5-foot-9, 175 pounds of him, managed to keep Horton away from Tanana for a few seconds. Detroit manager Ralph Houk, who said he noticed pitchers had been buzzing Horton on a frequent basis, clashed with Angels pitcher Dick Lange, who suffered a scratch and threw the tough Tigers skipper to the ground.

Springstead ejected Horton after the brawl. "I don't like to get mad," Horton said after the game. Though he claimed Tanana had thrown near his head, the pitch in question was alleged to have struck him in the thigh. Springstead said he would not recommend a suspension for Horton, also known in Detroit as "The People's Champion." He was signed by the Tigers off the city's sandlots. He was the youngest of nineteen kids. During the 1967 riots in Detroit, he put on his uniform and stood on a car among the rioters, trying in vain to restore peace. The fans also loved him because of his penchant for hitting grand slams and having multi-homer games.

In 1974, he hit a foul ball directly above the plate that struck and killed a Fenway Park pigeon, which fell dead at the feet of Boston catcher Bob Montgomery. Those birds can get revenge on Horton by visiting his statue, which stands beyond the wall of Comerica Park next to the Ty Cobb statue. Imagine the conversations between those two monuments during the wee hours? And if Horton's batting helmet could talk? He wore the same one his entire career, repainting it whenever he changed teams. The helmet got five more coats of paint after Detroit, as he made stops in Texas, Cleveland, Oakland, Toronto, and finally Seattle. That helmet was there when Horton made some noise in 1967 when Chicago's Tommy John mixed it up on the field with Tigers shortstop Dick McAuliffe. The helmet was there when rookie pitcher Rich Hinton of the White Sox hit Horton in the eye with a pitch in August of 1971, causing Willie to sit out twenty-eight games. The helmet got very lonely in May of 1969, when Horton left the Detroit bench and went AWOL from the club for four days. It was also atop his head in 1979 when he was named "Comeback Player of the Year" after a fine season as DH for the Mariners.

A week after his encounter with Horton, Tanana would strike out seventeen Texas Rangers on his way to leading the AL in strikeouts that season. Tanana would eventually join his hometown club in 1985 when the Texas Rangers traded him to Detroit for minor leaguer Duane James. Three years later, the name "Willie Horton" would be used for mudslinging in the 1988 Presidential campaign, when George H.W. Bush used the case of an unrelated rapist and murderer furloughed in Massachusetts to slight his opponent Michael Dukakis.

By that time, ballplayer Horton had done a stint coaching for the Yankees in 1985, when he was unofficially serving as Billy Martin's chaperone. In 2005, Horton and Tanana—the two players who clashed viciously at Tiger Stadium in June of 1975—did a promotional appearance together at the opening of the new Kar's Nuts facility in Madison Heights, Michigan. The Tigers mascot—Paws—was sent along just to make sure they didn't rekindle any old disputes.

"The Demon" Scares "El Pulpo"

Circus music would have been appropriate in March of 2002 at the Carl Barger Baseball Complex in Viera, Florida, the Spring Training home of the Florida Marlins. Not because of the garish teal covering the seats and walls of Space Coast Stadium, but more so for the interaction between the team's Dominican-born closer and his conditioning coach. One had six fingers and six toes on each appendage, earning the nickname "El Pulpo" (The Octopus), and the other moonlighted as a professional wrestler known as "The Demon" who wore makeup styled after the glam-metal band KISS.

Antonio Alfonseca, the 6-foot-5, 260-pound reliever, was tipping the scales on the heavy side and was under strict instructions to get his weight down during Spring Training. The Marlins wanted him to lose fifteen pounds to avoid stress on his surgically repaired back. This meant daily weigh-ins with conditioning coach Dale Torborg, son of then-Marlins manager Jeff Torborg and no stranger to folding chairs, cage matches, and foes with names like "Vampiro" and "The Wall."

One March afternoon in Viera, Alfonseca did not want to get on the scales and cursed at the insistent Torborg in Spanish. He made fun of the 6-foot-6, 280-pound Torborg's *curriculum vitae* in the wrestling trade. An argument developed, and Torborg got so mad he threatened to hurt Alfonseca and the chase was on, according to the *Fort Lauderdale Sun-Sentinel*. Alfonseca, who does have six fingers on each hand and six toes on each foot (a condition known as polydactylism), fled in fear to a nearby office, and locked the door. There was great clamor as Torborg yelled for Alfonseca to unlock the door and show himself. Other Florida players—assuming the role of inept wrestling referees—soon intervened, and calm was restored without any punches thrown or sleeper holds employed. Who emerged from this incident looking like the "heel" is a matter of online debate for wrestling Web logs and Marlins fan message boards.

Torborg would go on to work as a conditioning coach for the White Sox and would pair up with A.J. Pierzynski to make a few appearances on pro wrestling's famous Orlando soundstages. Try as he might, Dale Torborg still had trouble upstaging his brother Greg, who worked briefly as a bullpen catcher for the White Sox when his father managed Chicago in 1990. Greg was disciplined by the league for taking part in the *Buechele vs. Hibbard* melee in Texas, mixing it up in the pile alongside such luminaries as Barry Foote and Donn Pall. Soon after, Greg gave up the non-roster life for Fordham Law School, and by 2006 he was busy winning salary arbitration cases against ballplayers such as Alfonso Soriano.

As for Alfonseca, he was traded along with Matt Clement to the Cubs just a few days after his 2002 run-in with the Marlins house wrestler ("The Demon"—according to World Championship Wrestling—was involved in a Boiler Room Brawl known to be the lowest rated segment in the history of the entertainment franchise). In return from the Cubbies, the Marlins received head case Julian Tavarez, Ryan Jorgensen, and a future All-Star named Dontrelle Willis.

Haselman Hassles Moose

Sometimes the mismatches in the baseball fighting arena do not feature physical discrepancies. Some are vastly distant points on the Cooperstown radar suddenly converging (*Shelby vs. Clemens*). Others involve talent, salary, and career path. Or, a journeyman catcher takes it upon himself to charge a pitching legend in the making. That was the case at Baltimore's Camden Yards on June 6, 1993. The anniversary of D-Day to many, the day back-up catcher Bill Haselman charged quiet boy Mike Mussina to some.

In the abstract realms of this dispute, even the home ballparks were polar opposite mismatches. Haselman's Mariners played home games under the roof of the Kingdome, a building resembling a pale version of the Death Star. In 1993, the Orioles were in their second year of playing in Oriole Park at Camden Yards—the much-loved prototype for retro-futuristic nostalgic forward-thinking fan-friendly manufactured nook-and-cranny ballparks that would soon be the norm. Quaint little things called bricks—instead of precast concrete rings—were used in the construction of Camden Yards.

With Sunday personnel written on both team's lineup cards, Seattle starter Chris Bosio threw behind two Baltimore batters early in the game.

This put the ball squarely in the court of mild-mannered Mussina, a self-confessed crossword puzzle addict and master of stone-faced professionalism and mannered public appearance. Haselman, playing most of the season behind Dave Valle, homered off Mussina in the fifth to cut the O's lead to 3-1.

In the seventh, after Jay Buhner and Mackey Sasser struck out, the Mussina-bot apparently downloaded the "Protect Your Players While Getting Revenge on Home Run Hitters" software, and threw a pitch that hit Haselman on the top of his shoulder. As the 6-foot-3, 220-pound Haselman ran toward the mound, the 6-foot-2, 185-pound Mussina stood motionless. He dropped his glove . . . and was tackled. Suddenly, the sleepy Sunday matinee had a serious edge. Two teams mired in the middle of their respective divisions were putting up their dukes on getaway day.

Baltimore manager Johnny Oates watched in horror as the franchise player Mussina, earning $450,000 per season in 1993, buckled under the weight of the Mariners catcher drawing $122,500 in yearly pay. Mussina had multimillion dollar contracts in his future and by 2007 was closing in on 250 career wins. Both combatants were first round draft picks. Mussina came out of rural Pennsylvania to attend Stanford to study economics; Haselman's legacy was pure Jersey Shore transplanted to USC. The catcher would bow out after thirteen seasons and a .259 career average that lit up the transactions column with stops in Boston, Texas, and Detroit. The only time Haselman was paid more than a million dollars was the 2000 campaign with Texas.

As of this writing, Mussina was still notching wins for the Yankees in his seventeenth season of pro ball, cashing checks the size of Lake Michigan, watching the likes of Randy Johnson, Roger Clemens and Andy Pettitte come and go in the predictable tide of George Steinbrenner/ television contract money.

On June 6, 1993, the hourglass would be drained of twenty minutes worth of sand before *Haselman vs. Mussina* would cease to be an unfolding drama. It started slow, with Baltimore players making a greater effort to keep the peace. But several micro-fights broke out on the fringe, marquee clashes like Seattle's Fernando Vina going after Baltimore's Leo Gomez, with Valle, who thought he had the afternoon off, trying to split them up. Meanwhile, David Segui and Jay Buhner heated things up with O's catcher Jeff Tackett, who suffered a gash on his right cheek. Baltimore pitchers seemed especially eager after things got started. Reliever Mark

Williamson got a cut on his nose after the running of the bullpen, and Arthur Rhodes, already on the disabled list, was quick to throw down. And yes, Alan Mills went insane looking to exchange blows with anybody wearing Seattle garb.

Rick Sutcliffe, who was the Cubs protagonist out of the dugout to lead the assault on Eric Show after he beaned Andre Dawson back in 1987, told the press he wished he had better speed to get out of the dugout quicker and take out his rage on Haselman. "We protect our players around here," Sutcliffe cryptically told the press after the game.

Umpire Durwood Merrill said his crew was taken by surprise at the ferocity and length of the on field battle. Camden Yards security offered to help the umps restore order after a while. Before long, the Orioles made Bosio pay, even if it was via the use of a pile of players. Bosio was at the bottom when things got heavy and he aggravated a collarbone injury and earned a trip back to the disabled list.

But the real concern on the Orioles version of *The Longest Day* was centered on the Baltimore shortstop—the one trying to break Lou Gehrig's record for consecutive games played. Cal Ripken Jr. was suddenly favoring a knee after failing to keep the peace on the manicured diamond. The next day, Ripken considered sitting out. "It's the closest I've come to not playing," he told the press. But he played, and he went on to break Gehrig's streak. Baltimore police officers had walked on to the field to help contain the skirmish, but umpires quickly instructed them to keep fans from getting involved.

Seattle manager Lou Piniella got the heave-ho after he learned Mussina was not being ejected. His subsequent fit included kicking dirt onto home plate and declaring Seattle was playing the game under protest. Mussina, who was warned by the umpires after the marathon brawl, went on to win his eighth game of the season as the Orioles swept the Mariners and ascended into fifth place in the AL East. Seven players were ejected. Sutcliffe, Mills, and Segui were the Baltimore bad guys, while Seattle's red carded personnel included Bosio, Haselman, Mackey Sasser, and reliever Norm Charlton. "The ones we threw out were the most combative," Merrill said after the game. "The ones who prolonged it."

American League president Bobby Brown spent a good deal of time watching videotape of *Haselman vs. Mussina* and its hefty aftermath. All seven ejected players were slapped with $1,000 fines. Then he issued suspensions. For the Marylanders: Sutcliffe got five games, Mills got four games, Segui got three games. The team representing Kurt Cobain had Bosio with a five-game sit, Charlton four, Sasser and Haselman three games each. "I'd rather it be a $2,000 fine than miss a start," Sutcliffe told the *Baltimore Sun*.

Seattle brass was still chapped about Mussina dodging all the bullets. Piniella insisted he had exhibit A after the game when he said "Mussina told one of our players he was instructed to hit him." For the pitcher nick-named "Moose" known for pinpoint control and hitting an average of four batsmen per year, there would be no Nuremberg. Mussina's post-game quotes said it all: "I was just trying to pitch him in. I thought we could get him out by going inside." As for the fisticuffs, Mussina's report included this action: "Once we were on the dirt I tried to hang onto him. I tried to cover up so he didn't get in any shots. We had a few words, but you can't print them." Golly.

Have Dunn, Will Travel

A 10-0 lead can be a dangerous thing in a baseball game. On June 13, 2003 in Cincinnati, the Reds were up by that score over the Phillies. Adam Dunn, a former college football player at Texas, had homered in the third off Kevin Millwood to end an 0-for-18 slump. In the fourth, Millwood plunked Dunn with a pitch. In the fifth, Dunn was on second base when Ken Griffey, Jr. singled. Pitcher Jimmy Haynes, who had singled ahead of Dunn's walk, scored ahead of Dunn as the tenth run. The Bobby Abreu to Jimmy Rollins to Mike Lieberthal relay was flawless, and as Dunn lumbered toward the plate, the ball had beaten him there by an Ohio River mile. The 6-foot-6, 240-pound Dunn did not surrender. Instead he put his shoulder down and barreled into Lieberthal, much to the horror of the Phillies. He really wanted to be the eleventh run. He was out. Catchers are used to this kind of thing. "It's fine, as long as it's not a cheap shot to the face with a forearm," Lieberthal told the AP. His starting pitcher did not agree. "If it's a close ballgame, that's what should happen," Millwood told the AP after the game. "But when it's 10-0, you stop or give a cour-tesy slide. You don't run over a guy."

With Millwood gone and Carlos Silva on the hill, Dunn stepped into the box in the sixth a little suspicious of what would unfold. Silva threw a fastball just under Dunn's knees, which drew a warning from home plate umpire Doug Eddings, a native of New Mexico who said in his media guide bio he would be a Secret Service agent if he wasn't an umpire. Silva fired the next pitch from behind a stockade fence on a not-so-grassy knoll—it went behind Dunn, belt-high. Eddings ejected Silva and his previously-warned manager Larry Bowa on the spot. Dunn stood motionless for a moment or two, let go of his bat, tightened his batting glove and then bolted for the 6-foot-4, 225-pound Venezuelan on the mound. Any time a player of Dunn's size charges the mound, or travels with the intent to pound on another position player, it is a bona fide mismatch. (Philadelphia fans might remember the time Greg "The Bull" Luzinski charged San Diego headhunter Bill Greif in June of 1975.)

Lieberthal, making like an Oklahoma Sooner linebacker, took down Dunn before he could hook his horns into the Philly reliever. As Lieberthal and Dunn formed an awkward dogpile on the front slope of the mound, Silva stepped forward to ambush the fallen Reds outfielder, taking a sizeable swing at his head. An enraged Sean Casey arrived quickly to defend his towering teammate but was restrained. The swirling mess that ensued was a confusing collection of red caps, red uniform trim, red shirtsleeves and red socks, so it was difficult to tell the sides apart. The similar color schemes also elevated the risk of friendly fire incidents.

Silva finally emerged from the chaos with his jersey torn open. Dunn and Casey had joined him on the ejection list, as had Philly closer Jose Mesa, who somehow got in the middle of the action. Silva was booed off the field at Great American Ballpark. In December of 2003, the Phillies traded him to Minnesota in the Eric Milton deal.

Dunn received a three-game suspension, but Reds general manager Jim Bowden talked MLB disciplinarian Bob Watson into reducing it to two games because of Dunn's otherwise clean record. A week later, Watson would be reviewing more facts about Reds blood flowing on the ballfield, courtesy of a hothead Cubs reliever named Kyle Farnsworth.

Chapter 12:
TEMPER, TEMPER

The majority of the incidents covered in this book naturally involve "hotheads," but some players have a higher propensity for shit-starting, to paraphrase some rural Ohio vernacular. And Ohio has seen its share of hotheads, from Woody Hayes on the sidelines of Ohio State football games to Rob Dibble, Albert Belle, and Paul O'Neill wearing the baseball uniforms of Cincinnati and Cleveland. That's not to say the Buckeye State has cornered the market on bile. Not by a long shot, @#$+%#*!

There's a whole world out there filled with Billy Martin's exploits (that's why he gets his own chapter) and many of Darryl Strawberry's unsavory actions have been documented so far. The rest of the nasty nation includes role models such as Leo Durocher, Jimmy Piersall, Bill Madlock, Jose Guillen and the riled gamesmanship of Milton Bradley, to name a few. It is a land where lids are flipped as well as wigs, the fecal matter always strikes the blades of the cooling device, and fuses are never more than a few centimeters in length. What follows is a look at some hotheaded practitioners who have spiced up the national pastime in one way or another.

Type O from Generation K
Roughly a week after the *Dunn vs. Silva* spectacle on the mound of Great American Ballpark in Cincinnati in 2003, Reds fans were treated to another fight courtesy of the visiting Chicago Cubs. The Associated Press

called it a "much tamer" fight than Dunn's run and Lieberthal's tackle during the Reds blowout of Philly. Apparently, the AP writer didn't see his agency's own photos of Paul Wilson, the Reds starter who got the win but definitely took one on the chin in the seventh inning of the June 19, 2003, NL Central clash.

Things got testy in the middle innings of this contest. Reds catcher Jason LaRue was standing in against Cubs fireballer Mark Prior, who threw a pitch behind him. In the top of the seventh, Wilson plunked Moises Alou in the leg. Many on both teams thought the tit had been issued for the tat, and that was to be it on a Thursday afternoon in Cincinnati.

After the wholesome Seventh-Inning Stretch program, Ray Olmedo led off the bottom of the seventh with a single to center off new Cubs pitcher Kyle Farnsworth. Wilson came to the plate with the bunt sign on. When he squared to bunt he found himself looking at a heater from Farnsworth that tailed so far inside it eluded Cubs catcher Damian Miller, zipped past home plate umpire Lance Barksdale, and struck the backstop.

Wilson began barking at Farnsworth, stepping slightly forward in the batter's circle. Farnsworth, his momentum having carried him to the front of the pitcher's mound dirt, continued walking as if to expedite getting a new ball from Barksdale. Wilson dropped his bat, and both batter and pitcher charged forward. (Both would later claim the other guy did the charging. Reds manager Bob Boone said Farnsworth charged Wilson, while Cubs manager Dusty Baker said his pitcher was acting in self-defense as Wilson charged Farnsworth.) In any case, it didn't take long for the 6-foot-4, 235-pound Farnsworth, a forty-seventh-round draft pick by the Cubs in 1994, to meet the 6-foot-5, 215-pound Wilson—a first round draft pick of the Mets in that same 1994 draft. "What's your problem?" was the question from Wilson, and it was answered by Farnsworth using his right shoulder to body slam the Reds pitcher into the ground. Farnsworth also threw a sloppy right, with catcher Miller in close enough range to perhaps interfere with the accuracy of the punch. With Farnsworth and Miller descending upon him, Wilson was clearly in trouble as he waited an eternity for the benches and bullpens to spill forth. Farnsworth, the Fightin' Latter Day Saint, was busy turning home plate into Wilson's personal Garden of Gethsemane—the biblical site of great shedding of blood, sweat, and tears the night before Christ's crucifixion.

As the fracas was sorted out with ten minutes of milling around, and players holding onto each other, Wilson emerged from the pile with blood spattered on his home pinstriped vest jersey and a gash on the bridge of his nose. The image would be broadcast and printed throughout the land for many weeks to come. For Wilson, who along with Jason Isringhausen and Bill Pulsipher was lauded by the Mets as being part of a triumvirate of youthful star pitchers (dubbed "Generation K"), the moment was emblematic of his disappointing career, given the initial hype from Mets marketers. None of the trio of Generation K evolved into successful Mets marquee players as promised. With the exception of Isringhausen who eventually became a top-notch closer, Generation K floundered around the majors, their suffering ranging from elbow injuries to bouts with depression. The Mets traded Wilson and fellow first round pick Jason Tyner to Tampa Bay in 2000 for Bubba Trammell and Rick White.

As Wilson was walking off the field, several smaller skirmishes were escalating. Reds coach Ray Knight and Cubs skipper Baker exchanged some heated words, as did Cubs first baseman Eric Karros and Cincinnati's Russell Branyan after Karros was very active in the pile of players at home plate. Barksdale ejected Wilson and Farnsworth.

With the game reset and ready to go, Olmedo had moved up to second on Farnsworth's most wild of pitches. Barry Larkin stepped in against new pitcher Todd Wellemeyer and promptly singled Olmedo home to put the Reds up 3-1, a score that would stand. With so much of Wilson's blood flowing in the pile, apparently some of it got onto Farnsworth's hat. Teammate Kerry Wood would secure the cap and get it into the hands of Cubs fan and Pearl Jam front man Eddie Vedder, who added it to his vast collection of Cubs memorabilia. Vedder, who was aided by White Sox pitcher "Black Jack" McDowell (of *Whiten vs. J. McDowell*) in a New Orleans tavern brawl in 1993, told Gene Wojciechowski in his book *Cubs Nation* that the Farnsworth cap "adds a bit of violence" to his collection. In 2005 with the Tigers, Farnsworth would add a little violence to the *C. Guillen vs. R. Hernandez* brawl by tackling and pounding on Royals pitcher Jeremy Affeldt at Comerica Park.

A Very Naughty Nasty

The book *Cubs Nation* also contains a telltale quote from hot-blooded reliever LaTroy Hawkins, who in 2004 took a page from the 1992 Mets and held his very own media boycott. "They should know we're fucking crazy, so leave us alone. If I was sane, I'd still be starting," Hawkins said of his disposition.

Reds reliever Rob Dibble had similar sentiments about reporters during his playing career. Oddly enough, Dibble's father worked in television news. In Rob's retirement, he placed the media shoe on the other foot, working for ESPN and Fox Sports. Words such as "outspoken" and "irreverent" appear in his online biography for *The Best Damn Sports Show, Period*—a program where he often simply sits in a leather armchair staring into space while the multi-host talk show babbles its way forward. His hobbies are listed as hunting, fishing, golf, playing the drums, and Tan Su Do—a form of karate.

Dibble was one of the "Nasty Boys" bullpen trio that bolstered a period of excellence in Cincinnati in the late 1980s and early 1990s. He was joined by Norm Charlton and Randy Myers, both no strangers to donnybrooks themselves. Charlton is one of the few hurlers to confess to the crime of intentionally throwing at batters, and Myers was known to carry a hunting knife while on the field.

Dibble's minor league history contained an incident in Nashville where he peppered the dugout and press box area with pitched baseballs. Up with the Reds and racking up strikeouts in 1989, he was fined for plunking Willie Randolph of the Dodgers after giving up four straight hits. That was the same year he picked up Terry Pendleton's bat and heaved it onto the foul screen behind the plate after surrendering a run-scoring hit during Spring Training.

Dibble nailed the Mets Tim Teufel in the back when the Reds were being blown out at Shea Stadium in July of 1989. Teufel charged the mound and was joined by teammate Juan Samuel, who clashed with Norm Charlton in a shirt-grabbing incident that turned into a kick-boxing exhibition. Teufel managed to bloody Dibble's lip. The chaos continued after the game as the clubhouse phone lines were burning with threats—Darryl Strawberry challenged Charlton to come across to the Mets lair, and while Tom Browning and Danny Jackson were preparing to invade, five security guards cut them off in the bowels of Shea. "That guy is crazy," said Mets coach Bill Robinson, talking to the AP about Dibble. After helping the Reds go wire-to-wire in first place in 1990, including a crushing sweep of the arrogant Oakland A's in the World Series, Dibble seemed to hit the emotional skids the following season.

April of 1991 was very eventful for the Bridgeport, Connecticut, native. On April 11 against Houston at Riverfront Stadium, Dibble gave up an RBI single to Astros reliever Curt Schilling in the ninth inning.

Schilling was at the plate for his first Major League at-bat and put Houston up 4-1 in a game they would win, knocking the Reds out of first place for the first time in more than a year.

Eric Yelding stepped in after Schilling's rip. Dibble's fastball—usually in the high nineties in terms of speed—sailed more than a foot behind the shortstop's back. Yelding charged at Dibble and threw his batting helmet at Dibble's left shoulder and fanned with a punch. A deluge of players swamped the mound before any significant damage could be done by either player. After the game, Dibble bellowed at reporters, using a double-negative to boot. "I don't got nothing to say. Don't even come near my locker," he said. Houston manager Art Howe demanded Dibble be suspended for headhunting. The league obliged. NL president Bill White, whose manila folder marked "Dibble Incidents" was about to expand threefold, slapped a three-game suspension on him. Yelding, meanwhile, was fined $1,000 for his sprint to the mound.

On April 23, with the Reds visiting the Astrodome, Dibble struck out six straight Astros to tie the NL record for most Ks in a row for a relief pitcher. He notched his second save of the year.

Five days later back in Cincinnati, he earned an awkward save against the Cubs, surrendering five hits and two runs in two innings of work in a 4-3 win by the Reds. After striking out Ryne Sandberg to end the game, Dibble took the ball from catcher Joe Oliver's glove, wheeled and fired it over the center field fence. But he put too much on the toss—it sailed into the stands and struck twenty-seven-year-old school teacher Meg Porter on the elbow. Mrs. Porter's first-grade class would have a substitute teacher for a few days as she needed medical attention after her elbow swelled up. The Porter family did not sue but did expect compensation for her missed work and medical bills. "I don't think they have any great animosity toward Rob Dibble," said attorney Don Moore, probably aghast at what he was saying. "I don't think they're that type of people . . . maybe the most important thing is, it's not a huge matter. Mrs. Porter is upset and hurt, but her injury is relatively minor."

Dibble quickly apologized when he visited the Porters' home and vowed to pay their expenses. "I just thank God she wasn't seriously hurt," Dibble told the AP.

White suspended Dibble four games for injuring the school teacher. It was his fourth suspension over a three-season span. Reds manager Lou Piniella said he hoped his hotheaded reliever was learning from his experiences. "It's hurting the ballclub and it's hurting Rob Dibble at the same time," he said.

Coming off one of his suspensions in late July of 1991, Dibble took the mound at Wrigley Field. On the way to an 8-5 Cubs win, Doug Dascenzo laid down a suicide squeeze bunt. Dibble fielded it, and with the run having crossed the plate, he focused on retiring the baserunner. So he honed in on Dascenzo's legs and fired the ball at him, as if the goateed Dibble was playing in some hipster kickball league in Wicker Park. Home plate umpire "Cowboy" Joe West did not like what he saw, and ejected Dibble immediately. Dibble claimed the ball slipped out of his hand. There was no suspension from White this time, but there was the usual fine.

Andre Dawson of the Cubs, perhaps inspired by Dibble's shirtsleeve emotions, argued a called third strike with West, bumping the umpire in the process. After being ejected along with Chicago skipper Jim Essian, Dawson threw several bats onto the field from the Cubs dugout. "The Hawk" was fined $1,000 and slapped with a one-game suspension.

After his tumultuous 1991, Dibble finally admitted to the press he needed some type of anger management counseling. In late June of 1995, Dibble was slapped with one last suspension after he threw a brawl-inducing fastball at the head of Milwaukee's Pat Listach. Dibble was with the Chicago White Sox at the time. They released him a few weeks later, and before August rolled around, the Brewers picked him up and he and Listach were suddenly sharing a clubhouse.

In December of 1995, the Cubs showed interest in free agent Dibble, but the "Nasty Boy" was done. He retired to a life of wearing stiff suits and disagreeing with Tim Kurkjian on the set of ESPN's *Baseball Tonight*, followed by untucked dress shirts and boot-cut jeans favored on *The Best Damn Sports Show, Period*.

Mr. October's Scrap Heap

Bad things have happened to superstar Reggie Jackson. He had his cheekbone and trademark eyeglasses shattered by a vengeful Dock Ellis pitch. He was falsely accused of stomping a teenage autograph seeker in a Bronx parking lot after the 1977 All-Star game. Billy Martin lifted him from Fenway Park's right field during an inning when he let a ball drop in front of him, sending in Paul Blair as a replacement on national television. He threw his bat into the stands in Oakland out of frustration and struck two kids, who then had to be given season tickets. He had a clubhouse fight with Oakland teammate Mike Epstein in 1973 over ticket allotments. He fought with Yankees teammate Graig Nettles at the team's 1981 AL pennant celebration in Oakland after Nettles' wife Ginger mistakenly thought Jackson's entourage stole her purse. He was officially warned by commissioner Bowie Kuhn to stop being mean to sportswriters. He was shot at twice during a dispute with an irate motorist at Third Avenue and 83rd Street in Manhattan in 1980. He appeared in the film *Richie Rich*, the 1994 Macalay Caulkin vehicle that marked the young actor's first box office flop. Jackson's collection of vintage cars was destroyed in a warehouse fire. He was depicted as a Claymation figure in an iced tea commercial. In March of 2005, he rolled his SUV on a Tampa highway after being run off the road by a drug-crazed motorist. Oh yeah, there was the time he fought with teammate Billy North in the A's locker room at Tiger Stadium—*naked*—after North had accused him of trying to steal his girlfriend, and then followed that up with ballplayer logic by calling Reggie "faggot." When teammate Ray Fosse tried to break it up, he injured vertebrae in his neck and was out three months. Fosse had stepped in as a substitute peacemaker, telling that night's starting pitcher Vida Blue to steer clear and avoid injury.

So life wasn't always the glory of hitting three consecutive home runs on three pitches in a World Series game against Los Angeles in 1977, a year which Reggie—in one of his many autobiographies—called one of the worst of his life.

Despite his "superduperstar" label given by *Sports Illustrated,* his household name status, his many commercial endorsements and steady presence under the game's spotlight, Jackson was your basic hothead. The difference between Reggie and the Belles, Piersalls and Farnsworths, etc., is Jackson outweighed them all on the celebrity scale. Except for Belle, he's the only one who had a candy bar named after him. The Reggie! candy bar was rolled out as a promotional giveaway to each fan attending Opening Day of the 1978 season at Yankee Stadium. Fittingly, Jackson homered during the game, and fans affectionately rained the orange-wrapped confection down upon him as he took his position in right field. The delay of the game to clean them up was rather sweet in terms of being a publicity goldmine, and Reggie's agent beamed with pride as he sat in luxury box seats with executives from the candy company. This was the same agent who got the candy bar idea from a headline in one of the New

York papers alluding to Jackson's quote about playing for the Yankees when he was with Baltimore in 1976. He said if he played in New York, they'd name a candy bar after him. So it is spoken to New York sportswriters, so it shall be done.

On the other hand, his infamous "I'm the straw that stirs the drink" quote (cue: a spit take from teammate and Yankee captain Thurman Munson) was inaccurate, according to Reggie, who delivered a version of it to an obscure sportswriter during a lonely moment at the Banana Boat Bar in Fort Lauderdale during Spring Training. Jackson said he wasn't aware his conversation with the writer was on the record. Neither had any idea how the article in a May issue of *Sport* magazine would make Jackson's life so miserable with his new team. Cocktail lounge metaphors were probably not the wisest choice for a team being managed by Billy Martin, but when it comes to drinks, straws, swizzle sticks and clubhouse tiffs, who's countin'?

Along with his calendar-oriented nickname "Mr. October," Jackson also could have been called "Mr. Mound Charge." Somewhere, at some time during his twenty-one-season, Hall of Fame career, an observant fan, janitor, day porter, or groundskeeper *had* to have seen Jackson practicing his mound charge in the bullpen before the game, or maybe on a distant Spring Training practice field. What follows is a Jackson hit parade, of sorts.

Reggie Takes Woodson Behind Woodshed

Early in Reggie's career with the A's, his rage against Minnesota on a late April day in 1969 certainly heated up the chilly environs of Metropolitan Stadium. Jackson had already stroked two homers in the massive ballpark (off future Billy Martin punching bag Dave Boswell), and as he stepped in against Twins reliever Dick Woodson in the fifth, many of the 7,085 in attendance had to know what would happen next. Woodson, a righthander standing 6-foot-5 and weighing 195 pounds, threw behind Jackson, who was standing in the left batter's box. Woodson's next pitch sailed over Jackson's head to the backstop. That was enough for young Reggie. He put both hands on his batting helmet and bolted for the mound. Woodson tossed his glove aside. Jackson arrived and put a solid tackle on Woodson who was soon flat on his back in the dirt. "I kept waiting for him to straighten up and start throwing some punches," Woodson told the *Oakland Tribune*. "Instead, he tackled me. It was a lousy tackle." Woodson suffered a scratched eyelid for his trouble.

The brawl that ensued saw A's manager Hank Bauer looking for his old Yankee roommate Billy Martin, manager of the Twins and official Jackson hater. Jackson's teammate Dave Duncan was the first on the scene to rescue Reggie from the lopsided number of seven Twins against one Athletic. Martin was quickly all over Duncan, grabbing his throat. Bauer, the ex-Marine, grabbed at Martin.

Home plate umpire Cal Drummond, working his final season, had but one ejection to announce—the temporarily insane Jackson who continued shouting madly at any Twins player who came within earshot. "It didn't matter whether they threw him out or not," Bauer told the *Tribune*. "He couldn't have played anymore anyhow. He just went berserk." Jackson was escorted to the A's clubhouse, which meant he missed some more pain administered to Woodson. It came in the form of a sharp spiking by Rick Monday, who had doubled in the sixth A's run later in the fifth. Monday was trying to score in the midst of a broken pitcher-to-catcher-to-first double play (1-2-3 in the scorebook) that morphed into a pitcher-to-catcher-to-first-back-to-pitcher-covering home twin-killing by the Twins. Monday, who was idolized by Jackson when they were both at Arizona State, was out, but he made Woodson pay by opening a five-stitch gash on the hurler's left leg.

In the clubhouse after the 6-4 Oakland win, Jackson spoke of being a man. "What can you do?" he asked the gathered throng of teammates and reporters. "If I don't go out, then I'm less than a man." Jackson added he felt so good at the plate that another homer was eminent. He was also appreciative of support from teammates. "I'll tell you one thing," he told the *Oakland Tribune*, "it was great to see the guys come out there to help me out."

Woodson, it might be noted, went on to become the first ballplayer to enter into salary arbitration when he won his case in 1974 asking for $29,000 from the Minnesota Twins, who were offering $23,000. Thus was opened the can of worms that would become one of the ugliest processes in all of organized sports.

Reggie Clouds Sonny's Day

Almost a year to the day after *R. Jackson vs. Woodson*, the A's were in Boston to face an old nemesis named Sonny Siebert. In the fifth inning, Siebert went up and in on A's pitcher Chuck Dobson, who then plunked Siebert in the shoulder in the bottom of the inning. Siebert started toward Dobson, dugouts emptied, but order was quickly restored before any blows were exchanged. The Red Sox had built a 4-0 lead by the sixth, and Siebert, who was trying to end an April skid of his own, nailed Jackson in the forearm with his first pitch to Reggie. It was on.

Umpire Bill Haller caught up with an incensed Jackson as he made for Siebert. But three renegades from the Oakland bench ambushed the veteran Boston hurler, knocking him to the ground. The benches cleared and a series of shoving matches dotted the Fenway infield. A relative calm descended after a short while—until Jackson's fuse relit itself and he charged Siebert with another solid tackle. The pair wrestled on the infield grass with teammates standing around them, gawking at the display, with a few joining in. Boston's Mike Andrews took a wild swing at A's catcher Dave Duncan, who took the field wearing his shin guards. Mingling through it all was Red Sox catcher Tom Satriano, who kept his mask on during the melee. Siebert and Jackson were tossed from the game, as were Blue Moon Odom and Boston coach George Thomas.

In his last year in the Big Leagues, Siebert ended up as a teammate of Jackson's when the pitcher signed on with the 1975 Oakland A's. Reggie was traded to Baltimore in 1976, and like Siebert, would end his career with the A's, signing on for a farewell campaign in 1987 after five years with the California Angels.

Reggie's Foul Mood in Milwaukee

Brewers starter Mike Caldwell had the Yankees number in the late 70s. He pitched the Brewers 1979 opener against the Yankees, entering the contest with a 4-1 lifetime record against the Bronx Bombers. Milwaukee took the lidlifter 5-1, upping Caldwell's success to 5-1. On July 3, 1979, Caldwell chalked up another win over the Yankees, a 7-2 Brewers victory that put him at 6-1 against New York. At County Stadium on Friday, July 27, Caldwell smelled more Yankees blood. He brushed Jackson off the plate in his first two at-bats. Facing Jackson for the third time in the fourth inning, Reggie hit a pop fly to the left side of the infield. It drifted into foul territory near third base, where Sal Bando gathered it in for the first out of the inning. The frustrated Jackson, on his way to first base, tossed his bat in the direction of Caldwell. In shades of the Clemens-Piazza incident twenty-one years in the future, Caldwell picked up Reggie's black bat and flung it angrily to the ground. Jackson, already in the scorebook as a foul out to third, changed direction quickly and went after Caldwell. He grabbed the

Tarboro, North Carolina, native by the throat and they hit the ground rolling. After the benches cleared and the bodies were sorted out, Jackson was ejected from the game for throwing his bat, prompting Yankees skipper Billy Martin to play the game under protest because Caldwell was allowed to stay in the game. He went seven innings and got a no-decision as the game entered the ninth inning tied 5-5. The Brewers pulled it out when Cecil Cooper stroked his third homer of the night, a walk-off solo shot in the bottom of the ninth off Goose Gossage, delighting a healthy crowd of 47,298.

Reggie Orders Fisticuff Omelette at Denny's

The sight of Yankees Oscar Gamble and Bobby Brown carrying Reggie Jackson off the field like a cardboard cutout—somehow holding him horizontally—was startling enough. The fact that Jackson was clapping his hands, nodding and laughing maniacally added to the disturbing sight. It was a Wednesday night game in the Bronx against Cleveland. It was late September in the strike-torn season of 1981. Indians pitcher John Denny (of *Reggie Smith vs. Denny* and *D. Ford/Carew vs. Denny*) had knocked Jackson down in the second inning before striking him out. After the K, Jackson barked in anger at Denny, striking a dangerous pose in front of the plate. The dugout floodgates opened and teammates streamed onto the field, but there was no physical clash.

In the fourth inning, Jackson put the Yankees up 6-1 over Cleveland with a towering two-run homer. He enjoyed himself around the bases, doffed his helmet to the crowd after rounding third base, then touched home plate where he was greeted by Dave Winfield, who scored ahead of him. On-deck batter Graig Nettles was there, hand extended for a handshake that never came. Keeping a cautious eye on Jackson was Cleveland catcher Ron Hassey. Home plate umpire Dale Ford had begun to walk toward Denny, motioning for him to stay back, anticipating what would come next.

In what would be oft-replayed footage, Jackson followed his step onto home plate with a complete left turn and dead sprint toward Denny, who had walked toward home plate during Jackson's celebratory trek. He grabbed the pitcher into a headlock and crashed him to the grass, with Hassey and Winfield quickly piling on top of them. After the Gamble and Brown extraction, Jackson was ejected from the game, as was Denny.

To add to the asylum-like atmosphere, Yankees owner George Steinbrenner made perhaps his most bizarre post-game statement: "From here on, any pitcher who throws at a Yankee batter will be served with a lawsuit within twenty-four hours or during his next visit to New York—be it for pleasure or work," he said. Steinbrenner was in one of his most vocal periods of his stormy ownership of the Bronx baseball team. In legal circles, the Yankees hadn't heard anything this strange since 1975 when Elliott Maddox, then a law student at Hunter College, filed a $1 million negligence suit against New York City. The suit was a response to torn knee ligaments suffered by the Yankees outfielder while sliding on the soggy Shea Stadium turf—the Yankees city-owned home ballpark used while the House that Ruth Built got its official facelift.

Oddly enough, the man Steinbrenner had vaguely threatened with litigation would be the object of his desire in 1982. But Denny turned down a deal that would have made him a Yankee, and instead he was traded to Philadelphia.

Reggie Loses Cool at Major Goolsby's

Jackson was back in Milwaukee for some trouble on July 22, 1986. It was his final season with the California Angels. He'd appeared as a pinch-hitter in the eighth inning of the Angels 4-2 loss to the Brewers. With a man on base, he struck out against Milwaukee reliever Bryan Clutterbuck.

Later that night, at a downtown Milwaukee tavern called Major Goolsby's, Reggie encountered an autograph hound named Donald Weimer. He was a twenty-six-year-old unemployed office worker from Racine. Weimer obtained Reggie's signature, then tore the paper to pieces and threw it onto a table. Jackson grabbed Weimer and during a skirmish Weimer hit his head on the table. Weimer's forehead was bruised and his chin was cut, requiring several stitches, according to reports. Jackson was cited for disorderly conduct and was later cleared of all charges, so he was spared the ridiculously obscure *Price Is Right* type of monetary punishment usually issued to ballplayers by the Milwaukee sheriff's department.

Milwaukee Madness Rings Belle

It was hard not to laugh upon seeing the meeting of Albert Belle and Fernando Vina during the Indians-Brewers tilt of May 31, 1996. Call it *schadenfreude*, or maybe it was simply the oddball juxtaposition of brawny slugger and pesky middle infielder, a linebacker meeting a guy with a new wave haircut in the parking lot of a college town bar, perhaps.

Mariners catcher John Marzano has the upper hand against Yankees slugger Paul O'Neill at the Kingdome in August of 1996. O'Neill was upset after being brushed back by Seattle hurler Tim Davis.
AP PHOTO/LOREN CALLAHAN

In one of the game's most famous fights, San Francisco pitcher Juan
Marichal wields his bat over Dodgers catcher Johnny Roseboro as Sandy
Koufax tries to intervene on August 22, 1965 at Candlestick Park.
AP PHOTO/ROBERT H. HOUSTON

His eyeglasses still intact, Texas outfielder Jeff Burroughs flees the field with
bat-toting teammates at Cleveland Stadium after the crowd stormed the
diamond on 10-Cent Beer Night on June 4, 1974. The Indians forfeited the
game after a raucous night of on-field incidents fueled by the bargain beer.
AP PHOTO/CLEVELAND PRESS, PAUL TEPLEY

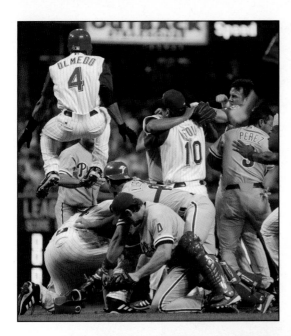

In June of 2003 at Cincinnati's Great American Ballpark, the Reds and Phillies brawled after Reds slugger Adam Dunn charged the mound to get at pitcher Carlos Silva, who is restrained at center by Cincinnati coach Tim Foli.
AP PHOTO/TOM UHLMAN

Mike Sweeney of the Kansas City Royals finishes his mound charge against Detroit pitcher Jeff Weaver in Kansas City on August 10, 2001. Weaver's teammates Deivi Cruz and Damion Easley approach from the rear during a hearty fight that was sparked by the positioning of the pitcher's rosin bag.
AP PHOTO/ED ZURGA

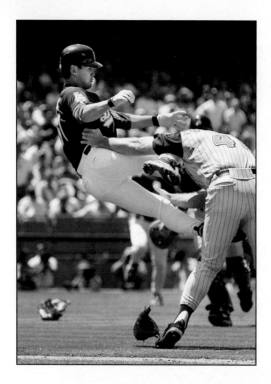

Dodgers pitcher Chan Ho Park employs a martial arts move against Anaheim pitcher Tim Belcher in an interleague donnybrook from June of 1999 at Dodger Stadium. Park was suspended seven games and fined $3,000 after the incident. **AP PHOTO/REED SAXON**

More pitcher-on-pitcher violence went down in Cincinnati in June of 2003 when Reds pitcher Paul Wilson objected to Cubs reliever Kyle Farnsworth brushing him back as Wilson attempted a bunt. Both were ejected after Farnsworth bloodied Wilson's face. **AP PHOTO/AL BEHRMAN**

In July of 1986, Braves pitcher David Palmer paid dearly for hitting Mets slugger Darryl Strawberry in the ribs at Shea Stadium. After fleeing from Strawberry, Palmer was tackled by Mets first baseman Keith Hernandez, who is seen here driving the Atlanta pitcher hard into the infield grass.
AP PHOTO/RAY STUBBLEBINE

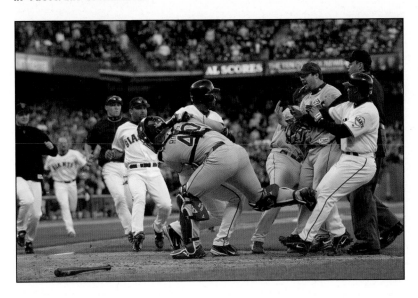

Dodgers catcher David Ross holds back Michael Tucker of the San Francisco Giants as he tries to get at Los Angeles reliever Eric Gagne, who is flanked by teammate Adrian Beltre and Ray Durham of the Giants. Gagne had knocked Tucker down with a pitch late in the game on June 24, 2004.
AP PHOTO/MARCIO JOSE SANCHEZ

Texas pitching legend Nolan Ryan is grimly determined to pound White Sox infielder Robin Ventura, who made an ill-fated mound charge against The Express on August 4, 1993 at Arlington Stadium. It was Ryan's farewell season, and during this incident, he landed six sharp blows to Ventura's head. **AP PHOTO/LINDA KAYE**

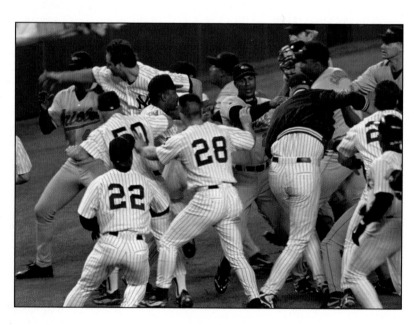

Yankees reliever Graeme Lloyd escalates the violence at the start of a wild brawl between the Yankees and Baltimore Orioles on May 19, 1998 at Yankee Stadium. The melee, which would spill into the Baltimore dugout, began after Orioles reliever Armando Benitez nailed Tino Martinez in the back with a fastball. **AP PHOTO/LOU REQUENA**

Cubs catcher Michael Barrett lands a hard right to the face of White Sox catcher A.J. Pierzynski after a testy play at the plate on May 20, 2006. The incident cost Barrett a ten-game suspension. **AP PHOTO/DAILY SOUTHTOWN, DAVID BANKS**

Houston's Derrick May gets a hand in the face from a Montreal player after Astros pitcher Danny Darwin hit Expos slugger Henry Rodriguez with a pitch on August 12, 1996 in Montreal.
AP PHOTO/ROBERT GALBRAITH

In July of 1998 at Olympic Stadium, Pirates third baseman Aramis Ramirez is sandwiched between an angry Javier Vazquez, the Montreal hurler, and his batterymate Chris Widger. Ramirez charged the mound after Vazquez hit him in the back with a pitch.
AP PHOTO/RYAN REMIORZ

Sand to be kicked in the face of the poorly drawn "weakling" in the back pages of a vintage comic book. The result of the basepath pyrotechnics would bring out not only Belle's best behavior, but that of a teammate residing in the Tribe bullpen. Julian Tavarez would have at least a decade of on field incidents ahead of him after this eventful evening in Wisconsin.

In the eighth inning, an Eddie Murray ground ball was hit right to second baseman Vina. All he had to do was tag Belle and toss to first base to complete an easy double play. But Belle, who was on first base because pitcher Marshall Boze had plunked him, had a forearm shiver addressed to Vina with a postmark reading Whoop Ass, USA. Belle, at 6-foot-2, 210 pounds, planted one leg and detonated the blow onto the head of the 5-foot-9, 170-pound Vina who went flying backward and down. Stunned silence was quashed by howls of protest from County Stadium as Belle—at least acknowledging he was out—trotted off the field with his batting helmet in hand. Vina had quickly scraped himself up off the dirt and had a few choice words for Belle who was soon standing at the ersatz dugout barroom that is the Gatorade cooler, cup in hand, trademark scowl affixed fieldward. The stage was set for retaliation in the ninth inning, when, in fact, Milwaukee pitcher Terry Burrows hit Belle with a pitch. He took his base with some discussion and interference by home plate umpire Tim Welke, who, wearing his red shirt, walked him halfway up the first base line.

With the Indians up 10-4, the Brewers came to bat in the bottom of the ninth facing Tavarez. He threw a fastball behind Mike Matheny, and the Milwaukee catcher charged the mound. Tavarez sidestepped him to the third base side of the mound and, with his glove still on, threw a solid right to Matheny's head. Matheny had shed his batting helmet on the way and slipped as he reached the mound. Falling forward, Matheny seemed to graze Tavarez with a strong right hook just as the pitcher landed his blow. Matheny grabbed Tavarez's knee and they were both swallowed by the mob.

After wriggling free of the pile, Tavarez pulled an elaborate reverse flip takedown of umpire Joe Brinkman, who was trying to restore some order. The official umpire media guide lists crew chief Brinkman's hobbies as golf, fishing, boating, and hunting. It says absolutely nothing about enjoying being thrown to the ground by apparently demented Dominican relievers. Tavarez was escorted off the field with his Indians jersey bunched up around his neck, looking like a juvenile delinquent being walked into a precinct house.

American League president Gene Budig handed out five-game suspensions to Belle and Tavarez, as well as to Matheny. Budig told the AP Tavarez was suspended "for placing the safety of an umpire at risk—which is inexcusable." There was some surprise as to Belle's punishment—technically he hadn't broken any rules. Two weeks earlier, Budig had ordered Belle to undergo counseling to control his temper.

Victim Vina would go on to make his living trying to get hit by pitches and slapping bunts all over the place—the type of anything to get on base undersized player that can rub lots of fans the wrong way—unless of course he plays for your favorite team and jumpstarts rallies on a routine basis.

In September of 1996, Belle told filmmaker Spike Lee in an interview for an HBO sports show special that he was just following orders when he clocked Vina. Cleveland first base coach Dave Nelson had reprimanded Belle for not taking Vina out in the second inning during a similar play that grew into a twin-killing. It just so happened the exact same sequence repeated itself later in the game, and Belle was able to correctly handle the situation, he said. He meant no harm to the one called Fernando with the Scritti Politti haircut.

Tavarez, who has had some interesting haircuts of his own, is probably the game's categorical leader in Spring Training fights. He's bounced around eight different teams in his fourteen-year career. While with the Cubs in 2001, he tried a flying karate kick against Russ Davis of the San Francisco Giants. Davis had just struck out and thought Tavarez was celebrating with hand gestures. The two exchanged words and soon everybody was kung fu fighting under the Arizona sun. In May of that season, the Cubs would have to fine Tavarez and send him to sensitivity training after he used a profanity and a word derogatory toward homosexuals to describe San Francisco Giants fans. Tavarez wasn't available for comment after that incident because he was finally serving his five-game suspension for his martial arts move against Davis. His nasty remarks also earned a visit from commissioner Bud Selig. While with Boston in 2006, Tavarez punched out Tampa Bay's Joey Gathright on a close play at home plate during a Spring Training game. His suspension for this incident was the fifth of his career.

Tavarez's rap sheet also included a suspension served after a brawl against the Devil Rays while he was with Pittsburgh in 2003, an eight-game suspension for having pine tar on his hat while pitching for St. Louis in 2004, and a $10,000 fine for throwing over Jeff Bagwell's head in Game 3 of the 2004 NLCS against Houston. That was the same playoff series in which Tavarez broke his hand punching a telephone after giving up a tie-breaking home run.

Three years before the Vina incident, in 1993, Tavarez was a rookie with Cleveland. During the lusty month of May, Tavarez witnessed Belle showing off his athleticism with a dogged pursuit of a Kansas City pitcher, only to end up landing his fists repeatedly on the head of a Kansas City catcher who caught him along the way. The jaded and cynical suburban Cleveland press was typified by this yawning headline in the *Elyria Chronicle-Telegram*: "Belle is One 'Crazy Guy'; Livens Up Dull Game Won by K. C."

The Royals were in town on the sunny afternoon of May 13, 1993, at Cleveland Stadium, which was in its final season as home to the Tribe. In the third inning, Belle tried to break up a double play at second base with a hard slide possibly out of the baseline into the legs of shortstop Greg Gagne. He turned the double play, then complained to umpire Al Clark about Belle's slide.

In the sixth, Belle came to the plate and the Royals dugout was collectively on the top step. He flew out to left without incident.

In the eighth, with Wayne Kirby aboard and two outs, pitcher Hipolito Pichardo hit him with a 2-1 pitch. The bat dropped, the helmet was quickly removed, and off went Belle in a full sprint toward Pichardo. The pitcher's fight or flight reflex favored the latter. Pichardo backpedaled as Belle almost caught up with him, and was throwing punches into the air while running, almost like the final scene of *Texas Chainsaw Massacre* when a frustrated Leatherface is left behind in the center of the highway thrashing the air with his motorized saw. Pichardo's survival compass failed him slightly as he made a sharp turn toward the Indians dugout.

With Belle on his heels, Royals catcher Mike Macfarlane tackled the slugger from behind, getting an arm around his waist and tumbling them both into a pile on the first base line. To followers of the baseball fight game, Macfarlane's tackle was reminiscent of the takedown of Dave Winfield by Cubs catcher Barry Foote in San Diego in May of 1980. Foote was protecting hurler Mike Krukow at the time. With Macfarlane secured beneath him, Belle unleashed three solid hammer blows to the back of the catcher's head before the swarm took over the scene. Unlike Neal Heaton, the Royals pitcher whom Belle charged on the mound in 1992, Pichardo let his catcher face the music during this fight. Macfarlane and other Royals claimed Pichardo was not trying to hit Belle because he'd already had an at-bat without incident after the Gagne meeting.

Tribe manager Mike Hargrove deconstructed the pain threshold/occupational hazard scenario quite ably, telling the jaded Elyria newspaper: "If you get hit by a baseball, first, it hurts and, second, if it hits you in the wrong spot, it could end your career." The track meet–style brawl was said to overshadow a career milestone from George Brett, who hit his three hundredth home run in the sixth inning.

After the 1996 season concluded, the Indians didn't have Albert Jojuan Belle to kick around anymore. He took his corked bat and degenerative hip to Chicago, where he was supposed to team up with fellow large man Frank Thomas and bring Jerry Reinsdorf a championship on the Southside. That failed effort lasted two seasons. Belle closed out the century, and his colorful career, with two final years for the Baltimore Orioles. The five-time All-Star finished with 381 career homers over his twelve-year career.

But headline writers would stay in touch with Albert. Felony stalking charges, GPS devices, and a child custody battle kept the wires buzzing, with datelines scattered from Arizona to Florida's Gulf Coast. The word "volatile" always seemed to be somewhere in each news brief documenting his latest travails.

Belle shares membership in the same club as Dibble, having injured someone in the stands with a thrown baseball. He did it in May of 1991 after a fan in the outfield taunted Belle about his alcohol problem. The throw earned Belle a six-game suspension.

In early 2007, Belle appeared slightly pensive in front of a judge in Bradenton, Florida, where he was battling for visitation rights with his six-year-old daughter.

"You know what, I haven't made a good impression on people my whole life," Belle told the judge, according to an AP report. "But I've been a success. I'm a fighter, I've always been a fighter and I'm going to continue fighting." Belle wanted regular visits with the child. His Roy Hobbs impression didn't work: The judge awarded him a fifteen-minute phone call each Sunday night.

Irate Canine Nickname Well Earned

Along with Hal McRae, Bill Madlock was noted among his peers as among the best at breaking up the double play. McRae is certainly more famous for his 1993 managerial tantrum in front of Kansas City's pleasant press corps—the phone-throwing tirade that saw one writer get a facial cut and McRae earn a permanent spot on every sports show featuring a list of "Top Ten Meltdowns."

Having already examined the May 1, 1976 double-feature assault at Candlestick Park that included *Madlock vs. Barr*, another several thousand words could be carted out to cover additional Madlock incidents, transgressions, and bruising tirades. He used the minor leagues to hone his fighting skills, as witnessed in the 1971 Eastern League game in Pittsfield when a S.W.A.T. team was almost needed to break up a Madlock-led brawl that saw the future four-time batting champion wielding a bat against his Waterbury foes. A fourteen-day suspension and $75 fine followed that incident.

Just a few days before the Giants traded him to Pittsburgh in 1979, Madlock threw an elbow at Braves pitcher Bo McLaughlin while running to first base. In the fight that followed, Mad Dog (nickname given to him by Cubs fans) pounded on Atlanta pitcher Larry McWilliams.

Then there was the time he was among the wrongly accused in the "Pittsburgh Drug Trials" of 1986, the time in 1987 as a Detroit Tiger when he crushed Toronto infielder Tony Fernandez with a hard slide, putting Fernandez on a shelf of Madlock victims along with Cubs rookie Steve Macko, whom he demolished with a slide in 1980. He had a few physical run-ins with teammates which further added to the strain he placed on team brass. Toss in a couple of arrests on charges of writing bad checks and a former agent who got him into trouble with the Internal Revenue Service, and Madlock appears as a classic baseball "malcontent."

In May of 1981, Madlock found a way to top his fourteen-game Pittsfield suspension with the fifteen-game punishment he received after his glove-poking incident with umpire Jerry Crawford. In a tight game against the Expos at Three Rivers Stadium, Crawford called Madlock out on strikes on what appeared to be a check-swing against Montreal pitcher David Palmer in the fifth inning. The bases were loaded in a 1-1 game. It was May 1 (May Day, the same date as his famous fight with Jim Barr in San Francisco). Madlock protested loudly to Crawford, and the two went face to face. Standard baseball courtesy is for teammates to bring gloves from the dugout to their comrades who are on the field when the final out of an inning is made. In this case, it was probably not a good idea for a fellow Pirate to hand Madlock his glove as the conversation with Crawford heated up. While making his point with hand gestures, Madlock used his glove for emphasis and basically plowed it into Crawford's mug. The Philly native whose father was an umpire and whose brother is an NBA referee lost his temper, and Bucco manager Chuck Tanner had to separate his player and the veteran arbiter.

As one NL flack mentioned in the press, the last time someone was suspended for hitting an ump with part of their uniform or equipment was Giants manager Dave Bristol, who swung his brown cap too close to Crawford back in 1978. Bristol got eleven games.

Madlock's fourth career suspension was a well-publicized fifteen games, with a $5,000 fine which combined with his lost pay amounted to more than a $20,000 price tag for giving Crawford a face full of leather. Had he spit in Crawford's face, apparently, he would have only been suspended five games, as was the case with Baltimore's Roberto Alomar and his liquid treatment of umpire John Hirschbeck in late September of 1996. Alomar was allowed to play in the postseason that year, much to the displeasure of the umpires, and instead served his time at the beginning of the 1997 campaign.

From Mad Dog to Beheaded Cat

The story about Kevin Mitchell cutting the head off his live-in girlfriend's cat in front of a horrified Doc Gooden and a guest has, in the city of baseball, reached urban myth status. It was chronicled in Gooden's autobiography *Heat* written with Bob Klapisch. The story goes that Gooden dropped in on Mitchell at his Long Island home in 1986. Mitchell was drunk, and angry, and fighting with his girlfriend. He was also holding a large kitchen knife. The cat happened to pass by his feet during a rage and Mitchell supposedly picked it up and severed its head.

If the Mitchell cat story is true, he set the stage for a second feline death at the hands of someone from the Mets organization. In April 2007, former Mets farmhand Joe Petcka—who gave up baseball for acting— allegedly punched his girlfriend's cat to death in her Manhattan apartment in a fit of jealousy. The thirty-six-year-old Wisconsin native was charged with a felony count of aggravated cruelty to animals. Petcka's lawyer insisted the cat, named Norman, was the aggressor and his death was a result of biting his client.

In 2002, when Mitchell finally confronted Gooden about the fabricated beheading story, Gooden simply said he didn't write it. Regarding the cat, that settled that. Maybe everyone involved was on too many drugs and the whole incident was a hallucination—something cooked up by regulars at Long Island's Trees Lounge?

It would take thousands of obscure indie movie references to match all the Mitchell stories abounding on the fringes of the game. He grew up in a San Diego ghetto, was shot when he was fourteen, and reportedly ran with gangs. The bullet scar, as well as a burn scar on his wrist from a fight with his father and skillet full of grease, were quite visible on Mitchell. His "badass" status is stuff of legend. Mets lore had him pummeling Darryl Strawberry when they were both in the organization's instructional league in Florida in 1981. It was during a pick-up basketball game in St. Petersburg, witnessed by fellow Mets prospects Lloyd McClendon, Randy Milligan and Mike Davis. Strawberry was incensed by a "pussy" foul from Mitchell and let him know. Mitchell didn't know who Strawberry was, and clocked him three times before body slamming him to the pavement. Mets coach Bill Robinson was credited with getting Mitchell to settle down and not ruin his shot at big league success.

Like Madlock, Mitchell earned his fighting stripes in the minors. In Mets AA ball in 1983 after a teammate was beaned, Mitchell, who was on base, got into a shouting match with the opposing club's manager. He made the mistake of running out to third base to confront Mitchell. The manager received a severe beating. Mets brass liked Mitchell's intensity, perhaps seeing how he would fit in nicely with the brash bunch that would win the World Series in 1986.

After he got his World Series ring with those '86 Mets, Mitchell was dealt to San Diego for Kevin McReynolds. On July 5, 1987, the Padres traded Mitchell and two pitchers to the Giants in a multiplayer deal that brought Chris Brown and Mark Davis to San Diego. Mitchell would make some noise with San Francisco. In 1989 he won the NL MVP Award and bashed forty-seven homers, leading the Giants to the World Series against Oakland.

Also like Madlock, Mitchell had a bushel basket full of off-field scandals and arrests, ranging from domestic abuse charges, rape allegations, going AWOL from teams in Japan and Ohio, weight problems, and a plethora of strange injuries.

One well-known incident was the time Mitchell and the Giants were visiting San Diego and facing Bruce Hurst. It was the second game of the season—April 10, 1991—and Mitchell hit a home run leading off the second inning. He'd also hit one in the opener, and by May 1, he'd be leading the NL in taters with seven. It should also be noted Mitchell owned Hurst—his April 10 blast was his fourth roundtripper in seventeen career at bats against the Mormon hurler from St. George, Utah. When Mitchell batted in the fourth, Hurst greeted him with a knock-down pitch high and tight. The two exchanged angry words. The glaring Mitchell had to be restrained by home plate umpire Bob Davidson and the benches and bullpens emptied, but Mitchell was restrained by teammates.

With everyone settled back into their dugout and bullpen perches, Hurst used his next delivery to hit Mitchell in his back foot. An enraged Mitchell charged after Hurst and threw a full-scale body block on him. Hurst and his teammates were a bit surprised at the level of anger Mitchell showed. Padres first baseman Fred McGriff, who pulled Mitchell off Hurst, said it looked like Mitchell really wanted to kill the San Diego hurler. Mitchell was suspended two games for trying to hurt Hurst.

The reactions to Mitchell's outburst poured forth from the pages of Larry Stone's article in the *San Francisco Examiner*. "I've never seen him that mad," said Giants hitting coach Dusty Baker. "He had fire in his eyes, even after it was over," noted Will Clark. "The old tank blew a gasket. He sort of overheated."

Crew chief John McSherry told the paper he didn't think Mitchell wanted to charge the mound, but he forced his own hand and the proverbial horse was out of the barn. "I mean, If Kevin Mitchell wants to go . . . unless you've got Ronnie Lott, he's going to go." For a few milliseconds as Mitchell sprinted at him, Hurst was very much alone. About to become a charter member of baseball's Fightin' Latter Day Saints (along with Kyle Farnsworth, John Buck, and Jeff Kent), Hurst's religion with its seagulls saving the Utah crops from cricket swarms could do little to halt the former San Diego street gang member headed his way. "It's not on your Top Ten list of favorite things to happen to you during a baseball game, that's for sure," Hurst told the *Examiner*.

Mitchell's last year with the Giants would be 1991 as they dealt him to the Seattle Mariners in December. The 5-foot-11, 210 pounder began to have weight issues that would haunt him through the rest of the 1990s. After stops in Cincinnati, Cleveland, and Boston, Mitchell finished his career with the Oakland A's in 1998. That was the same year he was diagnosed with diabetes.

Mitchell's retirement years were not exactly quiet ones. Playing independent league ball as a designated hitter for the Sonoma County

Crushers of the Western League in 2000, Mitchell charged the mound after a pitcher threw behind him. The brawl soon involved some taunting fans, and when the owner of the opposing Solano Steelheads went onto the field to help restore order, Mitchell decked him after a heated argument. Mitchell claimed that, like Strawberry during the pick-up basketball game almost twenty years earlier, he had no idea whom he was punching. In 2002, the Western League's penultimate season, Mitchell again had a problem against Solano. This time he was managing the Crushers and thought the Solano third base coach was stealing Sonoma's signs. So he ran onto the field and punched the coach in the face.

Chapter 13:
BRONX BIRD HUNT

One mild Tuesday night in May, when the Yankees juggernaut season of 1998 was in an early larval stage, a sales rep from a New Jersey trucking company was entertaining some clients in the left field main boxes at Yankee Stadium. Disclosure: I was among the small group as a friend of one of his clients. We called the sales rep "Millennium Mike" because he was obsessed with the year 2000. He was an old-fashioned "T & E" (travel and entertainment) account stretcher who spent three nights a week making sure the clients of his trucking company were enjoying themselves, had enough to eat and drink, and were adequately entertained.

The Bronx outing was nothing fancy—no Scores Testosterone Challenges or Alabama Slammers at some Amsterdam Avenue frat bar. Just drinks at Ted's News Room on Gerard Avenue before the 7:35 p.m. first pitch from David Cone, and plenty of food and beverage during the game. There were warehouse guys with us, one named "9:30 Dave" because he always came into work at 9:30 instead of the prescribed 9:00 a.m.

As we sat in Section 34, Box 342, Row H on the evening of May 19, we looked to our left to see the Yankee bullpen arrangements. We were complete afterthoughts with our not so desirable seats wedged into the Siberia beyond the left center field formerly known as Death Valley. I told Mike how I got to a game very early once and instead of visiting Monument Park I sat in my tier box with binoculars and witnessed Jeff Nelson killing a Bronx rat with a push broom along the farthest edge of the Yankee bullpen. It was not clear if he then ate it.

We estimated during our surveillance that the run from the bullpen to the mound was about 541 feet, based on the location of the fence with its number of feet to home plate painted on it, subtracted by sixty feet or so, with additional yardage added to reach the little bullpen "bench" in an alcove with the blue awning hanging overhead. I had spent the majority of my Yankee game attendance in the gothic darkness of the tier boxes behind home plate, away from the retina-burning footcandle bake of the floodlights along either side of the stadium's crown. So being in left field was a new angle, but it did provide a vantage on the bullpens, which can come in handy if you are a pitching nerd.

Out there it was noticeable that just like any Bronx storefront business, Yankee Stadium has a large metal security gate door. It's well beyond the left field fence, leading onto River Avenue, the ambulance always parked there just like at any high school football game across the Midwest. I remember seeing the ambulance occasionally reached on a bounce by towering drives from Manny Ramirez or Jack Clark if you want to go back that far.

Someone, it might have been a neighboring threesome, was calling Orioles starter Doug Johns "Doug Toilets"—for high-altitude/low-brow denizens of the tier boxes this was an introduction to the classy version of Yankee fan humor apparently shared by the grounded gentry of the main boxes. The pitching matchup was a bit off in the Yankees favor, some could say.

There might have been a few more drinks than usual. After all, it was "David Wells Day" according to the mayor of the city. The previous game at Yankee Stadium was a perfect game tossed by the rotund Wells, who reduced the Minnesota Twins to a pile of rubble after most of the team had allegedly spent the better part of Saturday night and Sunday morning at the aforementioned Scores strip club. But who's counting? Certainly not Wells, "half drunk" or not.

After the Monday off-day, Boomer's drinking buddy Cone drew the start against the O's, whose fans still dutifully scream "O!" during the two occasions in "The Star Spangled Banner" when the word "Oh" is employed in the lyrics. I always thought that was kind of cool. When Orioles fans are on the road, it serves as a homing device to identify parts of the stadium that include people of their own ilk. I don't recall a large contingent of Baltimore supporters sounding off during the anthem, but we were probably still fumbling to find our chairs in the uncharted territory where Winfield's homers used to drop and the fans conversed with a pinstriped Rickey Henderson. In any case, later in the evening the Baltimore fans would be saying "Oh!" for an entirely different reason. Cone was down 4-1 by the end of the third, with geezer Harold Baines getting the best of him for RBI left and right, especially after Rafael Palmeiro ripped a double in the second inning. Of course, Cone hit Palmeiro in the third.

Looking on from the Orioles dugout was manager Ray Miller, an accomplished pitching coach who knew the risk/reward ratio of running a Doug Johns out against a David Cone. Miller, a man of many quirks and rituals, with several physics-based theories about lefthanders, had just seen his club swept in a four-game series at home by the nascent Tampa Bay Devil Rays, MLB's mistake-by-the-bay expansion franchise serving as one last paycheck for retiring ballplayers who desire proximity to their home links in Florida. In their inaugural season of '98, Tampa Bay's four-game sweep at Camden Yards marked the first road sweep in franchise history. So Miller's club was a frustrated one with borderline humiliation issues as they rolled into the Bronx.

Like he often did when he was in New York with Jim Leyland and the Pirates, Miller took the subway to the ballpark. He has professed to seeing a certain beauty in empty ballparks, he told a reporter for *The Annapolis Capital*. He got to the Bronx very early, and got to see George Steinbrenner on the field berating a stadium operations staffer about the conditions of some field box seats. There was still chatter of former-Oriole Wells' perfecto in the air. Miller met with Orioles brass and visited Monument Park beyond the left-center field fence.

In the visiting manager's office, Miller was pleasantly surprised by a token of welcome from Yankee skipper Joe Torre. This was no Dick Williams Padres/Braves quagmire of bad taste and beer tossing. This was the Bronx in the late 1990s—Torre at home as the toast of Gotham. Miller was greeted with three quality cigars courtesy of "Mr. Torre" as Derek Jeter preferred to call him.

The Orioles will always be known as the Earl Weaver concoction that sits back and waits for the three-run homer to get things done. Bunting, stealing, hit-and-run plays be damned. Even though there had been a half-dozen different managers at the helm since the Weaver era, somehow, like burnt toast, the odor of the Earl of Baltimore still lingered among the orange-and-black squad. And of course it would be a three-run homer that would kick-start the sequence of predictable events leading up to one of the game's nastiest blitzkrieg battles on one of the game's more hallowed diamonds.

Millennium Mike was checking out the bullpens again. He asked if I remembered the days of the bullpen carts, when relief pitchers used to get a somewhat embarrassing ride from the bullpen to the infield. Yes, I told him I remembered the golf carts outfitted with enormous caps of the home team, usually driven by the geeziest member of the grounds crew. When Bob Veale or Jeff Reardon climbed out of one of those, they automatically had the look of a kid being dropped off by dad at the school dance. *Please, leave me here along this dirt path, thanks, I'll walk the rest of the way.* It was also a long distance, I told Millennium Mike, if there was a fight on the field. There was a pause.

"Ever see a boxing match here?" I asked him.

"No, you?"

"No, but I was here for Gooden's no-hitter against Seattle."

Yanks Flushed by Johns

By this point in the game, a couple of doubles and a sac fly off Cone had the O's up 5-1 on the Yankees. Center fielder Brady Anderson gunned down Scott Brosius trying to score in the bottom of the fourth. So as the fifth inning arrived, the much-maligned Johns had given his manager a solid start, holding mighty New York to one run. Miller was looking like a genius—not in the Tony LaRussa self-proclaimed sense—but a smart guy who at least had a decent cigar waiting for him in his office.

Johns, a South Bend, Indiana, native, had met Cone before. It was during Johns's big league debut, starting for the A's on July 8, 1995. He faced Cone and the Toronto Blue Jays in Oakland. Cone had beaned Mark McGwire and the mild concussion had Big Mac sitting out a week of games. It was at least the third time in a seven-season span McGwire had been nailed on the batting helmet by a pitch. Rookie Johns responded dutifully by throwing behind Toronto's John Olerud in the next inning, earning an ejection and premature finish to his debut. It was the front end of a doubleheader that had more than one benchclearing incident after several hit batsmen.

If mistakes were made by Baltimore on May 19, 1998, it might have been Miller lifting Johns for Sidney Ponson in the bottom of the sixth. The native of Noord, Aruba, destined for a troubled career of off-field antics (see Chapter 16), cruised through the sixth inning. In the top of the seventh, Torre lifted Cone in favor of Darren Holmes, who opened the inning by plunking Anderson. No harm done, the Yankees got out of the inning and chipped away in their half of the seventh as Paul O'Neill and Tim Raines knocked in runs against Ponson, cutting the lead to 5-3.

After an uneventful top of the eighth for Baltimore, the stage was set for a Yankees comeback. Ponson got Brosius to pop out, then he walked Jorge Posada, who was batting for catcher Joe Girardi. Chuck Knoblauch showed the vaunted Yankee patience at the plate and also walked. Miller had seen enough of Ponson and yanked him for Alan Mills, who got Jeter to fly to right. Another trip to the mound for Miller (he always followed the same routine of adjusting his cap as he walked away from the mound, clapping once as he neared the foul line and then jogging the rest of the way to the dugout) brought in Norm Charlton to face O'Neill, who singled to score Posada. With Knoblauch at second and O'Neill at first, Miller came out for a third time in the inning, calling on his hard-throwing Dominican righthander Armando Benitez to face Bernie Williams.

Benitez was twenty-one when he made his debut with the Orioles in 1994, and by 1998, he was in his first $1 million season for the club. As Williams stepped in, Tino Martinez was taking his warm-up swings in the on-deck circle. Maybe he was thinking back to the 1995 season when he was with Seattle and Benitez nailed him in the shoulder. It was a nightmare eighth inning at Camden Yards. Kevin Brown entered the frame with the Orioles up on Seattle 2-0. By the time Brown, Benitez, and Mills were done with the inning, it was 9-2 Mariners. When manager Phil Regan brought in Benitez to replace Brown, Armando promptly walked Alex Diaz to load the bases. Designated hitter Edgar Martinez then stepped in and hit a grand slam. Tino was following Edgar to the plate. After the frustrated Benitez took it out on the Mariners first baseman, the benches emptied. Randy Johnson led the way for Seattle with a lot of finger-pointing, but few knuckles hit facial paydirt of any kind. After the skirmish, Regan lifted his angry fireballer for Mills. But the damage had been done and all the Bromo Seltzer in the world couldn't settle the collective stomachs of the O's and their angry fans.

Like the humiliation of surrendering a grand slam in the home ballpark, giving up a majestic towering drive that lands in the right field upper deck of Yankee Stadium is also an intense downer for any hurler. The tableau, as seen from, say, the visitor's dugout, depicts a broad sweeping wave of upper deck curling around the foul pole. To the left of the looming tier, the moon would often settle in the late innings above the

Grand Guignol grimace of the Utz potato chip girl, whose billboard titillates any bleacher creatures who dare turn their backs to the field. When Benitez tossed the unimaginative fastball, Williams' sweet swing, seen from any angle in the ballpark, seemed improbable to send the ball so high and so far. When they land in the tier seats in right, it's like they never come down—suspended in the heavens, the bank of faded blue seats the half shell to the Rawlings version of Venus. Home runs landing there suffer not the classless rattling around on the Diet Coke–soaked floor of the main boxes. When the destination is the upper deck, the ball jumps like a bean on the harsh vertigo angles of the "cheap" seat stairs and railings, ready at any second to plummet perilously straight down to the main boxes, bypassing of course the sheltered nancy boy loge.

Unless of course the stitched horsehide orb is embraced by a distant fan in nosebleed territory, a person who is definitely *not* entertaining clients of any kind, assuredly blue collar by his or her location and proximity to the upper reaches of the right field foul pole. Also enjoyable was the standard Williams home run anti-trot—his almost embarrassed head down duty-now-for-the-future circuit of the bases, certainly way too fast for a veteran of his years and experience, with his classical guitar street creds making him the Notorious B.I.G. of the Lincoln Center set.

Benitez looked like *Saturday Night Live*'s Tracy Morgan on steroids. His hat was too tight, his neck seemed double-jointed, his cheekbones a tad too high. His glove slapped at the new baseball from his exasperated batterymate Chris Hoiles. The crowd of 31,311 was giving it up for number fifty-one with a continuous roar as the Bombers took a 7-5 lead. The 6-foot-4, 180-pound reliever in the road grays paced the outskirts of the mound like so many before him.

One of those was Hall of Famer Robin Roberts, a visiting Baltimore pitcher who was in a fix against a Yankee slugger back on June 11, 1962. In his column in the *Bucks County Courier Times* from June 8, 1975, Roberts recalled his introduction to Yankee Stadium as he got acclimated to American League ball after fourteen years in the National League with the Phillies. The headline was "Umpires Usually Control Brawls" with a subhead: "Beanball Just Part of Game." Roberts' news peg was a Phillies-Padres fight involving Greg "The Bull" Luzinski charging Padres headhunter Bill Greif a few days earlier. As Roberts put it: "Luzinski . . . got tired of Greif throwing at him like he's a clown at the circus." Roberts then mentioned his second career start in the majors in 1948, when he was instructed by

Philly manager Ben Chapman to "loosen up" Reds batter Hank Sauer, who'd hit two taters against Philadelphia in the previous game.

Roberts next anecdote about beanballs took the reader to the hill on the steamy Monday night of June 11, 1962, when he was starting for the Orioles at Yankee Stadium. It was a contest involving not only the omnipotent pinstripers who would march all the way to the World Championship, but some interesting monikers. It was also an incident that showed the inaccuracy of the headline on Roberts' column as three New York City policemen were required to settle things down after the umpires could not.

Yankee starter Bud Daley, whose given name was Leavitt Leo Daley, hit brawny Baltimore rookie John Wesley "Boog" Powell in the head in the top of the fourth with the Orioles up 3-0. Powell had to be carried off the field and would spend the night in Lenox Hill Hospital. The woozy twenty-one-year-old outfielder was out of commission until June 19.

The first batter for the Yankees in the bottom of the fourth was slugger Roger Maris. Roberts blasted a laser pitch behind his head, which drew a death stare from the pensive lad from Fargo, North Dakota. With bat in hand, Maris started a slow walk toward Roberts to possibly exact his revenge. But before Maris got to the mound with his war club, he was tackled from behind by Orioles catcher Hobie Landrith, and the brawl was on in front of 12,046 customers in the Bronx. Maris insisted he was not "charging" the mound, and he cited Landrith as the cause for the ensuing violence.

The flannel tussle included both managers, who mixed it up quite suddenly as the incident appeared to be simmering down. Billy Hitchcock had been tending to Powell in the clubhouse when the Maris action began, and when he emerged on the field and deferred to home plate umpire Charlie Berry for information about what was going on, Yankee skipper Ralph Houk went nuts. The two were soon exchanging haymakers, though Hitchcock had a few Yankee players holding him back during the battle. When Orioles coach George Staller tried to help his skipper, Maris got him in a headlock. "That fight should have been on television," Roberts wrote of the manager tangle in his suburban Philadelphia column. Both skippers were ejected. Houk told the press he heard Hitchcock accusing Yankee pitchers of intentionally throwing at his players. Orioles coach Cal Ermer, given name Calvin Coolidge Ermer, was tossed by the umpires in the fifth inning for arguing a foul bunt call. During that same inning, Roberts was spiked in the foot by Tom Tresh on a play at first, but he had no hard feelings. "We won 5 to 3, that's it," Roberts told UPI after the game. "I'm not mad at no one." So the roll call for Roberts' game when he buzzed Maris included a Bud, Leavitt, John Wesley, Boog, Calvin Coolidge, and a Hobie. Rounding out the box score was a Hoyt, Cletis, Elston, Yogi, Moose, and Joe Pepitone for good measure.

Unlike Benitez and his crew in '98, Roberts and his Birds prevailed not only with a win, but they knocked the Yankees out of first place. The seven-time All-Star Roberts, known for his excellent control, was getting revenge on the team that bought him from Philly in October of 1961 only to release him in April of 1962. On May 21, 1962, Roberts signed with Baltimore. The brawl game in June was his first win as an Oriole. In August of 1962, he would beat the Yankees again for his ninth victory of the season. Roberts ended his column by citing baseball's unwritten rules. "If they do it, we'll do it. The beanball will always be in baseball, I guess. There are enough rules to control it and the umpires generally do a good job," Roberts concluded.

As Tino Martinez stepped in the batter's box following Bernie's home run that ruined everything orange-and-black, he already had an HBP by his name in the box score. Johns had plunked him during the sloppy first inning. With much of the crowd still standing and cheering Bernie, Benitez wound up and sailed a fastball high between the shoulder blades of Martinez. Hoiles stood up to make a moot effort to glove the pitch, and behind him umpire Drew Coble had some dramatic choreography he wanted to express. He stepped to his right and forward toward the mound and made a grand, operatic sweeping gesture with his right arm to indicate Benitez had been ejected from the game. Trouble was, in his gusto, Coble almost landed the first blow of the evening as he slightly grazed Tino's shoulder, causing the already pained first baseman to duck a little bit more. Tino's posture had him facing his own dugout, back arched and leaning forward with his legs straight and stiff. Once he avoided Coble, Martinez staggered forward a few steps while Hoiles and second baseman Mike Bordick instinctively walked toward Benitez, who appeared formless as he stared back at Coble and shrugged his right shoulder as if to reset it.

Australian Rules

According to David Wells' autobiography *Perfect I'm Not*, it was Darryl Strawberry who screamed an obscenity at Benitez and walked up the steps of the Yankees dugout with an unlikely deputy—Chad Curtis—in tow. Benitez eyed Strawberry, let his glove drop to the ground and with palms up gestured to the oncoming Straw, Curtis and the rest of the 28-9 Yankees with a "bring it" motion of his hands. Bordick and Hoiles suddenly became *West Side Story* understudies as the Orioles bench dutifully marched toward the mound. Neither squad was running—yet—it was a determined group gait to the hill. The running would come very soon, as the bullpen doors opened and the 6-foot-7 Yankee reliever Graeme Lloyd, a native of Australia, used his long strides to cover a lot of ground across that famous outfield.

As we rose up and would remain standing for the next twenty minutes like a soccer crowd in main box 342 in left field, Millennium Mike, who had just been telling me his weekend plans to take the wife to Atlantic City for "dinner and a show" shot me a look that said "now I know what you were talking about." The left field box seats wished the traveling Yankee bullpen a bon voyage as we had a decent angle on seeing the entire Yankee dugout empty for the march in our direction.

Ray Miller was doing his best to keep the peace around his ejected pitcher as the AL East rivals waltzed around the mound and infield grass. Running with Lloyd from the left center reliever depot was Jeff Nelson, an inch taller at 6-foot-8. Lloyd used his outback homing skills to trot directly at Benitez, swinging wildly and coming out from under his own warm-up jacket, as other Orioles grasped at the lanky hurler from Geelong, Victoria. Benitez backpedaled slightly as Lloyd's jacket further incumbered him. This allowed Benitez, who was throwing open-handed slap punches (an Earl Weaver legacy?), one of which landed as a pretty hard overhand right to Lloyd's head with Bordick watching the swirl of bodies directly behind Lloyd. The backward staggering continued as Lloyd, who would win a silver medal with the Aussie baseball team in the 2004 Summer Olympics in Athens, made one last lunge before toppling. Nelson then took a flying swipe at the moving Benitez and missed badly. The curling-stone momentum of the bullpen crew had set the phalanx of ballplayers in motion, and Benitez was naturally retreating toward his home shelter.

Tripping forward and right into the Benitez's open field parlor on the strip of grass between the dirt path in front of the dugout and the third base foul line was none other than Scott Brosius. Nineteen ninety-eight was to be his year, as he would make the All-Star team and win the

World Series MVP award after the Yankees demolished San Diego. But in the particulars caught on MSG Network videotape, Brosius came off looking rather like a chump. Or at least a guy not interested in tangling with the likes of Armando Benitez.

Brosius did kind of a half-skip in front of Benitez, who seemed to perk up a bit with some elbow room and the Yankee third baseman in front of him. Brosius looked off to his right, half-expecting another bullpen salvo or some type or reinforcements in the form of Curtis or even Chuck Knoblauch.

An eternity later, the idle Brosius was overcome with another surge of players and Benitez took cover on the top step of the Baltimore dugout. As he surveyed the scene to his right, a projectile sailed incoming from his left. It was Darryl Strawberry doing his Airborne Infantry impersonation, with Richard Wagner's "Ride of the Valkyries" playing in the background of his bald head. Strawberry landed a harsh left which carried both players into the *sanctum sanctorum* of the visitor's dugout. With Benitez tangled on the stairs, reeling from the blow, Strawberry stood alone on the floor of the dugout. Television cameras positioned at the end of the dugout captured winning pitcher Mike Stanton being corralled by Hoiles (still wearing his mask) and shoved into the lens. Stanton's elbow didn't quite enter viewers' living rooms as MSG cut to its other angle showing Alan Mills in his warm-up jacket doing an effective end-around the scrum on the stairs, using his right leg to push off the floor of the dugout upon landing, and lunging to deliver a devastating right cross to Strawberry's head all in one apparently rehearsed motion. The two tumbled backward at an awkward angle onto the dugout bench.

The Orioles dugout then became a Roach Motel of sorts. Everyone piled in, some on their backs. For a horrifying moment, it looked as if super-closer Mariano Rivera was going to be crushed against the dugout wall as he jumped in quickly after Mills decked the Straw. Rivera jumped up onto the dugout bench and was standing quite tall as a deluge of uniforms tumbled at him. Taking the high ground during this low-brow incident probably saved Rivera from harm.

David Wells, still restrained by Jimmy Key, was in the thick of the dugout pile yelling at Benitez who had been separated from Strawberry, who was being attended to by Joe Torre himself. Torre would walk Strawberry away from the melee as Darryl dabbed at the corner of his mouth, checking for blood. Apparently the vast array of dugout distractions (sports beverages, sunflower seeds, bat cork, steroid vials, copies of *Gallery* magazine) was enough to settle, or at least contain, those seeking to avenge Tino's suffering and those seeking to assuage Armando's inner fears. It was an odd case of the bench clearing, and then refilling, with a brawl still underway. A few seasons later, dugout railings were added at Yankee Stadium, so there would be no place for Mills, Strawberry, and Benitez to privately conduct their fisticuffs in the event of an identical, roving battle.

Yankees owner George Steinbrenner called it the "worst fight I've seen in twenty-five years," and this was coming from a man who lived in a Midtown hotel. He also called Benitez's hitting Martinez a "classless act." By the end of the night, Steinbrenner was joking with the press about fighting Orioles owner Peter Angelos to settle the differences, if it was the desire of the league office. Maybe his good mood could be attributed to Tim Raines coming in as the first batter after the fight and promptly depositing a Bobby Munoz pitch into the right field bleachers, of all places, giving the Yankees a salt-in-the-wound 9-5 cushion and adding another layer of misery to Miller's sad Birds?

Torre cited the Benitez trench warfare as a good example of the "downside of the DH," which makes certain types of pitchers very brave when it comes to nailing batters.

Most newspapers the next morning went with the photo of Lloyd's first blow to illustrate the colorful night in the Bronx. The *Daily News* had "Bronx Brawlers" on its back page, while the *Annapolis Capital* went with "Birds Brawl, Bow in Bronx" also with the Lloyd photo. The Aussie seemed to be levitating above the throng of military haircuts and shirt-grabbers, his straight arm further unifying an already unified unit still slightly hungover from a perfect game Sunday matinee. By the All-Star break, Torre's charges were toting an uncanny 61-20 record.

Among the usual uproar about sports violence, not enough penalties, etc., *Capital* columnist Joe Gross wrote this: "Armando Benitez, a youngster with an already brittle psyche, was victimized as much by the Orioles defeatist aura, as by the Yankees ballooning confidence."

The next night, Lloyd came in to relieve Hideki Irabu and got a rousing ovation from thirty-two thousand on hand at the stadium. Baltimore general manager Pat Gillick threw gas on his burning team when in the wake of the Benitez bash he made a few offhand remarks about how Latino players are more emotional and therefore more prone to fighting. Apologies on top of apologies were demanded. Benitez had already apologized but insisted he did not hit Tino on purpose; Miller had been remorseful and called Benitez "immature." Several Orioles players talked openly about the dangers of a high-90s pitcher intentionally throwing at anyone. Even with the tumbles down the dugout steps, there were no injuries except for Martinez's bruised back. He missed the next night's game and was listed as day-to-day with a deep bone bruise.

The fines and suspensions came swiftly. AL president Gene Budig said Benitez intentionally threw at Martinez and "the location of the pitch was extremely dangerous and could have seriously injured the other player." Benitez got an eight-game punishment and a $2,000 fine. Mills was ordered to sit for two games and fined $500. For the Yankees, Strawberry and Lloyd got three games each and $1,000 fines, while Nelson was docked $500 and suspended for a pair of games.

The saga of the modern-day free agent—or the highly tradeable headcase—dictates sooner or later public enemy number one will be wearing your team's jersey and be the latest Joe Hero. This is why Barry Bonds said he never shared his hitting secrets with teammates—because he'd probably be playing against them one day soon. In December of 1998, Baltimore traded Benitez to the Mets for Charles Johnson. From 1999 to 2003, Benitez became a target of Shea denizens with his fireballing dramatics as a closer. He was bridging the gap between John Franco's long-time service and the arrival of Braden Looper. More than once, Armando would walk the bases full as soon as he entered the game. In July of 2003, the Mets shipped Benitez to the Bronx for Jason Anderson and two minor leaguers.

Five years after he was the biggest target in Yankee Stadium on a cool May evening, he was donning the pinstripes as one of several set-up men for Mariano Rivera. Fans walking into the stadium and buying the August 2003 edition of the Yankees souvenir program—a $5 glossy called *Yankees Magazine*—got a double treat. On the cover was a sepia-toned shot of Jason Giambi in an old time Yankees uniform, part of the magazine's coverage of Old Timer's Day at Yankee Stadium. On the upper right ear of that same cover was the line "Inside: Benitez Poster." Tino Martinez was long gone to St. Louis, so it seemed safe to print the centerfold poster of Benitez in full pitching stride, his jersey slightly open at the top, hurling from the same mound he used to spark one of the nastiest pre-millennial brawls in a long time. His stay in pinstripes only lasted into August, when GM Brian Cashman dealt Benitez to Seattle for one of his May 19 attackers—and one of the best bullpen rat killers around—Mr. Jeff Nelson.

Inside a tavern called the Old Town in New York City is a photo on the wall behind the bar of Bronx-native John McSherry, the late MLB umpire, arguing face to face with Dodgers manager Tommy Lasorda. More accurately, they are standing stomach to stomach as McSherry—who was 6-foot-2 and tipped the scales at more than 330 pounds—tries his best to not get a close-up view of the nostrils of the slightly less rotund Lasorda.

When McSherry was interviewed following the brawl-marred August 12, 1984, game in Atlanta between the Braves and the Padres, he said: "It took baseball down fifty years, the worse thing I've ever seen in my life." That means something given the number of times McSherry had to go face to face with Lasorda and assorted other managerial gorgons throughout MLB. McSherry was manning first base in a game some refer to as the ugliest in baseball history. Nineteen ejections, three hit batsmen, fans in gym shorts and matching shirts carted off in handcuffs—all these factors might define "ugly" on a muggy afternoon in Ted Turner's city.

If McSherry's comment was taken literally, dialing the game back fifty years would plant it in 1934, when the seventh game of the World Series got out of hand in Detroit where Judge Landis himself had to pull Joe "Ducky" Medwick from the game so the series could conclude and to save Medwick from rabid fans throwing glassware and standard old-timey vegetable missiles. The unruly throng had their hats unblocked after Ducky slid in hard on the Detroit third baseman and fists began flying. It had been that type of World Series all along, typical Gas House Gang, Depression-era baseball.

The 1934 season saw dozens of fights in front of big holiday crowds carrying an air of menacing celebration, with plenty of airborne produce. McSherry must have done well in history at St. John's University.

The summer of 1984 had been a busy one for diamond brawlers. Maybe it was the George Orwell prophecy, the resignation of Vanessa Williams as Miss America, or the ugly political climate of the *Reagan vs. Mondale* presidential campaigns? The midsummer had seen a spate of fights, from Reggie Jackson and Bruce Hurst mixing it up in July to some Cards-Phillies nonsense and Braves-Reds mound charging (*C. Washington vs. Soto*) in June to the Mets-Cubs back-to-back malarkey dates in early August at Shea Stadium. The Dog Days were not about to get quiet.

In fact, the events at Fulton County Stadium would unleash the usual salvo of "black eye for the grand old game" columns from sportswriters wondering how a circus led by Pascual Perez gets booked into a respectable southern city on a Sunday in August. It could technically be known as *P. Perez vs. Lefferts*, but that late-inning HBP does not even tell a fragment of the whole tale.

It was, in the rarest of baseball phrases, the Padres year. They were ten and a half games in front of the second place Braves. Manager Joe Torre had Atlanta playing well and in pursuit of Dick Williams' club in NL West. And this weekend series had the Braves hoping for a sweep that would revive their chances at catching San Diego, the eventual NL champions in 1984 who were an enigmatic collection of souls. To name a few: Steve Garvey, the All-American Paternity Suit God; Eric Show, the jazz musician and John Birch Society member; Kevin McReynolds, the Arkansas recluse bound for stardom in New York City; Ed Whitson, the Tennessee native bound for a hellish stint in New York City; Dave Dravecky, who would later break his arm pitching and have it amputated in a battle against cancer; Goose Gossage, the Bronx Zoo survivor; future Padres skipper Bruce Bochy, who was born in France and has a large head; and Tony Gwynn, the hitting machine and future Hall of Famer.

The 1984 Braves, meanwhile, were another squad cobbled together by broadcast mogul Ted Turner, who kept around a core of Atlanta lifers such as Rick Camp, Bob Horner, and Rick Mahler.

Apparently on this particular Sunday in August, the Braves objected to Padres leadoff man Alan Wiggins getting some bunt singles and a stolen base during San Diego's 4-1 win on Saturday night. Friday night was a twi-night doubleheader the two teams split, so the pressure was on the Braves during Sunday's getaway to salvage half of the four-game set. Wiggins, who had evolved into a great leadoff hitter during the 1984 campaign, had stolen five bases in one game back in June. Once his bunts were down, it was nearly impossible to throw him out at first.

The tone for the contest was to be set with the opening pitch of the game from Pascual Perez. He nailed Wiggins in the middle of the back. The sub-narrative here is the duel involving this pair of drug-plagued ballplayers. Both Perez and Wiggins had well-documented problems with drugs, especially cocaine. Wiggins would pay with his life, dying of complications related to AIDS in a Los Angeles hospital in 1991.

Perez was arrested for cocaine possession in his native Dominican Republic in the offseason following his 1983 campaign. He wasn't able to join the 1984 Braves until May. Perez was well known for his quirks both on and off the field. In August of 1982, he got lost trying to find Fulton County Stadium and missed the game circling in his car on Interstate Highway 285, an Atlanta outerbelt. Five times he was absent without leave from the Braves in 1985, once because he said he forgot the departure time of the team's flight bound for San Francisco. When he was with the Yankees at the end of his career in 1991, he used to check the runner on first base by bending down and peering between his legs to the delight of the scant few in attendance at Yankee Stadium during Stump Merrill's unfortunate but courageous reign managing in pinstripes. Perez was a perpetual motion machine on the mound—all hand jive and leaping, his jerry-curl bouncing, his skinny legs propping the rest of him up at an odd angle, until he settled in to aim his zombie-like gaze at the batter.

August Sundays in Atlanta were known to make many citizens eschew their church clothes. But Braves fans, who would be lampooned for their passive ways during their team's hot (but unproductive) run through the 1990s, were not hesitant to turn up the heat and ride the opposition at Fulton County Stadium. In early September of 1981, with the Braves miles out of first place, a fan cracked Cesar Cedeno's emotional armor by riding him about his involvement in the shooting death of a woman in a Dominican Republic motel room in 1973. The Astros outfielder was so peeved he climbed into the stands to get the heckler to stop. He was fined $5,000 and initially suspended "indefinitely" by the league. But NL president Chub Feeney had him sit for two days before ending the punishment, declaring Cedeno had been subjected to "severe verbal and physical abuse" from the Atlanta fan.

The Braves-Padres affair of 1984 had onion layers of intrigue. As a cultural signpost, the problems in this game foreshadowed an East Coast/West Coast hip-hop rift that would develop by the end of the decade. Many of the participants in the extended brawl fulfilled premature appointments with the Grim Reaper. There was also a Yankees championship reunion of sorts, Dirty Kurt Bevacqua, various combat-ready fans resembling golfer Tom Watson, a Jeremiah Johnson lookalike named Bob Horner who made a trip from the broadcast booth to clubhouse to the field to get a piece of the action, shirtless ballplayers, Hitler references, and Vietnam vet Champ Summers. And it might also be noted there was a rookie home plate umpire on duty for all of this.

The saddest sight, though, had to be the young batboys for each club. Various TV camera angles caught them in the background sporting puzzled expressions. They looked as if they were at the scene of a car accident—perhaps one involving their own family. They were thrown clear, maybe out the opened rear window of the Country Squire station wagon, landing in a soft bed of timothy along the roadside. Groggy from the impact, the youngsters studied the actions of these high-paid adults, some of them wearing garish brown and yellow outfits, as they tried to hurt each other while spectators cheered and threw malt beverages.

An Edict from Dick

Reports indicate after the lead off HBP issued by Perez, San Diego skipper Dick Williams began shouting at the Atlanta pitcher and issued an edict to his mound corps to make Perez's plate appearances throughout the day an adventure in dodgeball. With the Braves up 2-0 in the second thanks to a Claudell Washington home run off Whitson, shortstop Rafael Ramirez led off with a single. Perez came to the plate with one out and Ramirez aboard. Whitson threw his first pitch behind Perez, which drew a warning from plate umpire Steve Rippley. The next Whitson offering came at Perez's feet and skipped past his catcher Terry Kennedy. He then struck out Perez, but Jerry Royster would come up with the clutch single to score Ramirez to put Atlanta up 3-0. There was speculation that had Whitson had better aim in his mission to plunk Perez, it would not have been such a messy day in Atlanta.

Whitson had his second go-round against Perez in the fourth inning. The benches half-emptied when his first pitch buzzed the lanky Perez's belt as the pitcher appeared to be squaring to bunt. Perez wielded his bat as San Diego catcher Terry Kennedy tried to get at him and Rippley pushed Perez away. Perez seemed to panic, hopping away from the home plate circle but still wielding his bat high and removing his own batting helmet. Atlanta first baseman Chris Chambliss intervened and quickly escorted Perez—bat still in hand—back toward the Braves dugout and away from any trouble. When Perez got back in the box, Whitson's second pitch came up and in, nearly striking Perez in the shoulder. Rippley had seen enough, and acting on his previous warning, he tossed Whitson and his manager Williams from the ballgame.

By the time substitute manager Ozzie Virgil had reliever Greg Booker throwing at Perez in the sixth, the Braves had a 5-0 lead. It was clear that either Perez was mastering the opposition, or the Padres were too focused on getting revenge against Pascual instead of scoring runs and winning a ballgame. After two tries at hitting Perez, including one pitch that sailed over Pascual's head, Booker and Virgil were ejected.

Graig Nettles homered off Perez in the top of the seventh for San Diego's first run of the game. In the eighth, Perez came to the plate for his fourth at-bat of the afternoon. The first pitch from Padres reliever Craig Lefferts nailed Perez in the forearm, even as Perez was stepping back in the batter's box and away from the plate, anticipating the arrival of the beanball. Finally, paydirt for a Padres hurler. The Braves poured onto the field *en masse* as Rippley tossed Lefferts, who began a sheepish walk off the mound toward the San Diego dugout, looking over his shoulder at the oncoming line of Braves players. The exhausted Rippley, seeing the charge led by point man Gerald Perry, paced forward pumping his pointed finger at the tide of Atlanta personnel, as if his stern warning or the force of his words could halt the march of cleats on sod. Lefferts' Padres teammates were a bit tardy in their arrival on the infield grass for this NL West reenactment of the Battle of Hastings. A lonely Steve Garvey dropped his first baseman's mitt and ran a diagonal interference pattern between the enemy and his retreating pitcher. Over his shoulder in futile pursuit— also trying some interference—was umpire McSherry. It was the eighth inning and many players might have thought this running clash to be the *coup de grace* of the long afternoon. As a pile formed on the mound, one player emerged with an intense focus. Enter: Champ Summers.

In an earlier chapter, Summers appeared as a participant in the 1976 *Matthews vs. Mitterwald* slobberknocker at Candlestick as a visiting Cub.

Summers made his name breaking into the majors at age twenty-eight after being discovered in a softball league after two stints of college and service with the U.S. Army in Vietnam. Summers was always described as "free-spirited" and the press, in an outdated nod to the titillation of the men's magazine, liked to point out his Playboy bunny tattoo under the skin of his shoulder. His father was a Navy prizefighter and railroad worker, and his mother was a cocktail waitress who also happened to be a pro bowler. He began his career with a cup of coffee on the 1974 Oakland A's, who dealt him in the offseason to the Cubs. He played a few seasons in Cincinnati and Detroit, where he seemed to catch on as a cultish fan favorite. He became known as a DH and was known for some adventurous play in the outfield. In 1982, he returned to the National League with the San Francisco Giants. In 1984, Summers was playing his final season in the bigs as a Padres reserve.

Summer's mission in the eighth inning was to get Perez. In the center of the melee at the mound, he noticed Perez was in the Atlanta dugout and was being restrained by Bob Watson of the Braves as he pointed at the pitcher. Finally, Summers broke loose. His run from the mound to the Atlanta dugout, hatless with his feathered hair bouncing and behaving, had an almost charming awkwardness to it.

Braves captain Bob Horner was on the disabled list and had been a guest in the broadcast booth as the trouble brewed in the early innings. In the sixth, he left the booth and went to the clubhouse to put on his Braves uniform. He was there, also hatless, waiting for Summers as San Diego's brawny number twenty-four arrived at the entrance to the Braves dugout. Both players resisted throwing punches, and Summers was still focused on Perez, whom he could see beyond Horner's shoulder. Holding the blue-padded dugout rail, Summers looked for another way past Horner, but a cadre of pursuing Braves arrived behind him.

But it was not an opposing player that brought down the man who faced enemy fire during the Tet offensive. It was a fan who had run on the field and grabbed Summers by the neck from behind. As the pair began to fall down, a spectator triangulation of fire seemed to form spontaneously. A blue-shirted fellow stepped up onto the roof of the dugout and pelted Summers with a cup of beer at very close range. As Summers continued to fall backwards with a fan hanging from his neck, a PGA reject—a front row dweller wearing lemon-yellow slacks, a JC Penney shirt and white shoes—inexplicably leaped from his perch over Horner and onto the falling pile. He regained his footing and seemed to just tug at the pile along with several Braves who were reaching down and trying to pry the fan off of the soaked Summers, who also had Horner and another hairy Atlanta player to deal with in close quarters.

The fight had moved up against the railing and police had to step in to restrain more fans from taking complete control of the dugout roof. Though the Tom Watson lookalike barely soiled his yellow slacks, he was led away in handcuffs by police. It took ten minutes to quell the disorder, and with their team up 5-1 and most of the excitement probably over, a surprising number of the 23,912 in attendance headed for the exits. Perhaps they wanted to get home to watch the closing ceremonies of the Summer Olympic Games being held in Los Angeles?

Ejections were announced after the eighth inning melee: Perry, Mahler, and Steve Bedrosian were tossed for Atlanta. For San Diego, it was another automatic for the acting manager, this time coach Jack Krol who had taken over for Virgil. Summers was also given the boot. Braves manager Joe Torre closed the cuckoo clock doors by lifting Perez for pinch-runner Brad Komminsk.

Reliever Donnie Moore would pitch the top of the ninth for Atlanta. Nettles was leading off and Moore hit him in the buttocks. Nettles spun around, hesitated one moment, sighed, dropped his bat, then charged Moore. Behind Nettles, Rippley made the now very familiar automatic ejection signal, which meant Torre and Moore were out of the game. But Moore had come down off the hill and was waiting for Nettles, greeting him with an uppercut from his gloved hand while dodging the charge at the same time. Nettles made the mistake of charging too fast, and his momentum carried him past Moore after the uppercut was delivered. Nettles spun wildly to try to change directions, but then the reunion of the World Champion 1978 Yankees was called to order. Braves first baseman Chambliss intercepted Nettles with a high bear hug while Atlanta catcher Bruce Benedict pulled a Three Stooges move and hit him low. This meant Nettles tumbled hard to the ground with Chambliss on top of him. Their old Bronx Zoo pal Goose Gossage completed the reunion as he again made his way in from the San Diego bullpen to mill around. Or so he thought. Watson grabbed Gossage for some world-class shirt-tugging and the two also went down. Above it all, "Dirty" Kurt Bevacqua of San Diego was wilding. He was throwing punches aimed . . . at nobody. Before his fists pounded the air madly, it appeared Bevacqua had struck one of his prone teammates with a blow in his haste to reach the Nettles-Moore tangle. Bevacqua seemed to have plenty of energy for the ninth inning of a brawl-filled game, and his tantrum brought some unintentional comedy to the tiresome spectacle.

Also squaring off for some confused peacemaking/shoving and flinging was Atlanta's Gene Garber and San Diego's Tim Flannery. Before the umpiring crew would order the benches and bullpens cleared for the final outs of the ninth inning, Flannery could be seen shirtless in the dugout, holding a bat and yelling at fans who had surged onto the roof of the San Diego dugout. After more drunken fans ran onto the field, umpire Mc-Sherry considered forfeiting the game to the Padres. Police were called in to line the perimeters and eventually play resumed. Ejected in the ninth along with Torre and Moore were Watson and San Diego's Gossage and Bobby Brown. Garber was called on to finish the game for Atlanta, and though the Padres put two more runs on the board via sacrifice flies, Dale Murphy made a fine diving catch of Garry Templeton's liner to center to end the game and give Atlanta a hard-fought 5-3 win.

Brown Shirts on Parade

The postmortem on the San Diego-Atlanta incident was indeed vast, as expected. When sixteen players/coaches are ejected and five fans arrested, heads turn and the headlines burn. Columnist Dick Young was outraged that Horner was not ejected or punished in any way after his trip from the broadcast booth to the brawl. San Diego manager Williams treated his ten-game suspension like a sequel to *Judgement at Nuremberg*. As the days wore on after the brawl and Williams dramatized his efforts to meet with NL brass, he started to resemble head of *Oberkommando de Wehrmacht* Wilhelm Keitel ever so slightly. (To add to the Rhinelander atmosphere, Lefferts—the San Diego pitcher who finally got the job done in hitting Perez—was born in Munich, while across the diamond, Atlanta's Glenn Hubbard was born at Hahn Air Force Base in West Germany.) Williams, a native of St. Louis, was known for his "my way or the highway" managerial approach. He's the only skipper to win pennants with three different teams, having taken Boston, Oakland, and San Diego to the promised land.

The league also handed out three-game suspensions for players who returned to the field for more action after being ejected earlier in the August 12 game. These included Summers for San Diego and Perry,

Bedrosian, and Mahler for Atlanta. Fines were dished out to Perez and Moore. Braves skipper Torre got a three-game suspension and fine. San Diego bullpen coach Harry Dunlop was also among the nonplayer personnel thrown out of the game.

San Diego limped home to face the Phillies, and Wiggins was again hit by a pitch, this time by Philadelphia hurler Jerry Koosman, who was quickly warned by home plate ump Jim Quick.

The day after their triumph over the boys in brown, the Braves left Atlanta to go to Cooperstown to play Detroit in the annual summer exhibition called the Hall of Fame Game. In the twenty-four hours following Beanball Sunday, Torre had called Williams an idiot and said his steadfast mission to harm Perez was a "Hitler-like" action. Claudell Washington told the *Syracuse Herald Journal* the fight and victory over San Diego could have been a spark Atlanta needed to catch the Padres. "If that doesn't boost morale," he said, "nothing will." Washington had previously tried to boost morale when he charged Montreal pitcher Scott Sanderson in May of 1983. When he was with Oakland in 1976, he also had a loud encounter with Mark "The Bird" Fidrych at Tiger Stadium. Regardless, Washington's Braves lost the 1984 Hall of Fame Game, and the Tigers went all the way to win the AL pennant.

The Padres prevailed in the NL in 1984 and faced Detroit in the Fall Classic, giving Champ Summers a curtain call of sorts at Tiger Stadium. But Williams didn't use the rebellious lummox as San Diego fell to Sparky Anderson's Tigers. Summers did, however, prevent rowdy Detroit fans from trashing the Padres team bus after Detroit won the championship.

In September of 1984, NL officials said president Chub Feeney had sent out bulletins to all the clubs in the wake of increased brawls to remind them they are "not in the fight business."

The obituary pages have been dotted with participants from this epic NL brawl. Umpire McSherry, who had to be hospitalized after working a few innings of Game 7 of the 1992 NLCS in Atlanta, died at age fifty-one after collapsing shortly after the first pitch of Opening Day in Cincinnati in 1996. McSherry was buried in the Gate of Heaven Cemetery in Hawthorne, New York, which also contains the final resting places of Babe Ruth and Billy Martin. Braves reliever Donnie Moore committed suicide in Anaheim in July of 1989 and was said to be despondent over surrendering a dramatic home run to Boston's Dave Henderson in Game 5 of the ALCS, when the Angels were one out away from a trip to the World

Series. In January of 1991, speedster Alan Wiggins died of complications from AIDS in a Los Angeles hospital. In March of 1994, Padres hurler Eric Show died in a California rehab center after taking a speedball. Rufino Linares, who started in left field for the Braves on August 12, 1984, died in a car accident in May of 1998 in his native Dominican Republic. In March of 2005, Braves pitcher Rick Mahler died of a heart attack in Jupiter, Florida, as he was preparing to work in the Mets organization.

As of this writing, both managers were alive and well. Torre's 1984 campaign with the Braves was his last in the Bigs before spending the next six seasons as a broadcaster for the Angels before taking over for Whitey Herzog in St. Louis in 1990. In 1996, he got a job with an obscure American League East club on the east coast and began collecting World Series rings. In November 2007 Torre signed on to manage the Dodgers. Williams lasted one more season with San Diego before heading off to Seattle for three frustrating years and then calling it quits. The Braves-Padres punch party still consistently makes Top Ten lists for sportswriters ranking the all-time best brawls, usually checking in around third or fourth in the order.

At age twenty-four in his official rookie year with Pittsburgh in 1981, Perez was involved in a bizarre bait-and-switch brawl that left 16,770 fans at Three Rivers Stadium uttering a collective "whaaa?" In the sixth, already down 5-1 to the Dodgers, Perez hit Bill Russell in the hand with a pitch to start the inning. Later in the inning, Perez hit Dusty Baker and was warned by umpire Dutch Rennert. All the while Reggie Smith, who was out with an injury, was yelling at Perez from the Dodgers dugout. Bucco third baseman Bill Madlock got involved, running verbal interference between the two. Reports indicate when Perez finally ended the inning by striking out Steve Garvey (with the Bucs then down 6-1 to the Dodgers) he yelled at Smith to meet him in the clubhouse tunnels. And that's just what proceeded to happen as both squads piled into the tunnels under the stands. Perez had reportedly raced through his own dugout but paused long enough to grab a bat. Photographers followed the players into the tunnel and reported no punches were thrown in the cramped quarters. The umpires followed the players into the hallways, and the mess took about five minutes to sort out. All the while, the fans were looking at a rather unattractive empty baseball diamond, wondering if the teams had heard of some oncoming natural disaster and perhaps fled in advance of the devastation. No punches were thrown, and no one was ejected.

The next day, newspapers ran an AP photo of what looks like an impromptu committee meeting in the hallway connecting the dugout to the clubhouse of Three Rivers Stadium, with dozens of Pirates standing with their backs to the camera. Just another Perez start, apparently.

After a horrendous 1-13 season for the 1985 Braves, Perez was released by the club on April 1, 1986—no foolin'. He sat out the entire year before signing with the Montreal Expos as a minor league free agent. He joined the big club in August of 1987 and went 7-0. In May of 1989, his final year with the Expos, he appeared as a reliever in Los Angeles and beaned Dodger catcher Mike Scioscia, who flipped his bat away and charged at Perez. Expos third baseman Tim Wallach intervened, cutting off Scioscia, and three other teammates had to guard the Dominican showboater from an angry Kirk Gibson. (Earlier in the game, Orel Hershiser threw behind Hubie Brooks, which had emptied the benches for a brief non-tussle thanks to good restraining work by home plate umpire Bill Hohn.)

Perez did two seasons with the Yankees, the last being 1991. In 1992 he was issued a one-year suspension for violating the MLB drug policy. Instead of serving the suspension, he retired with a career record of 67-68.

After the ugly win over the Padres, Perez would beat San Diego two more times in 1984 by almost identical linescores. Typically, he'd go eight-plus innings, hand it over to Garber and enjoy the victory. He beat them 5-2 in San Diego and then 4-3 back home in Atlanta in the final game of the season, putting the second-place Braves twelve games back. The finale was played without incident in front of a sparse crowd, and was completed in one hour and thirty-nine minutes, proving once again time flies when you're having fun.

Though it has been said baseball fights are predictably mild and lack the inherent danger of, say, trying to punch someone while skating on ice, things don't always go according to Hoyle during the doubleknit do-si-dos that occasionally sully a Major League diamond.

Like the time Cesar Cedeno of the Astros, homicide charges and all, went after the Mad Hungarian in St. Louis. The Astros center fielder was plunked by Al Hrabosky on May 6, 1977, but before Cedeno could knock the goulash out of the mustachioed reliever known for his feverish mound presence, Cards catcher Ted Simmons jumped on Cedeno's back and began his own beat-down. A brief AP report on this fight took an unusual measure of the emotional toll paid by the victims: "Numerous players suffered bruises and hurt feelings," the dispatch read. Among those with bruises were Houston pitcher Joaquin Andujar and Cards bench player Roger Freed, who were both ejected from the game.

Once again, Bob Watson, future MLB disciplinarian, weighed in with his share of gas to throw on the fire. "There should have been more punches thrown," Watson said. He was pissed off because Hrabosky was not thrown out of the game by umpire Bob Engle. Perhaps it was because Hrabosky wore a silver Gypsy Rose of Death ring to keep werewolves away? Hrabosky's intense pre-pitch routine, which he called "controlled hate," so incensed Bill Madlock that the two came to blows after a protracted at-bat.

The real damage from the Cedeno incident was absorbed by Houston coach Mel Wright. He had his glasses broken during the ten-minute melee. Is there an optometrist in the house?

Sometimes much more than a pair of eyeglasses is broken. The following are a sample of incidents involving suffering of a more serious nature.

FELIX MILLAN vs. ED OTT
(NEW YORK METS) (PITTSBURGH PIRATES)
August 12, 1977, Three Rivers Stadium, Pittsburgh, Pennsylvania

In their furious pursuit of the first-place Phillies, Chuck Tanner's 1977 Pirates squad was taking no prisoners as the dog days of summer arrived at the confluence of the two rivers that form the mighty Ohio. It seemed that since Bruce Kison's courageous July clash with Philadelphia slugger Mike Schmidt (and Greg Luzinski), the Buccos had been bashing foes and racking up suspensions left and right.

On August 5 in Cincinnati, the Pirates were blowing out the Reds 12-1 in the first game of a doubleheader sweep. Reds pitcher Joe Hoerner nailed Pirates shortstop Frank Taveras with two outs in the ninth inning, and Taveras responded by throwing his bat at Hoerner. In the ensuing fracas, the skinny Pittsburgh shortstop took a punch or two. The league office slapped him with a fine and a five-game suspension. Five days later, in the early innings of what turned out to be a five-hour, eighteen-inning marathon against the Cubs, Al Oliver went nuts on umpire Bruce Froemming after Oliver was called out for missing first base on a double. Before the start of the August 12 doubleheader against the Mets, the NL announced Oliver was being fined and suspended for four games. Oliver said later had he known his demonstrative verbiage was going to cost him so harshly, he would have gone ahead and punched Froemming.

Pirates catcher Ed Ott, the stocky former high school football and wrestling standout from Muncy, Pennsylvania, rescued Kison from the clutches of Luzinski back in July and also ended the Cubs marathon game with a pinch-hit sacrifice fly that gave the Pirates the 2-1 win. He sat out the first game of the August 12 doubleheader, which was a 3-2 Pittsburgh victory over the Mets.

In the nightcap, which would go twelve innings, Ott was intentionally walked in the sixth inning by Mets pitcher Bob Apodaca to set up a double play with Mario Mendoza coming to the plate. Mendoza seemingly obliged with a grounder to shortstop Doug Flynn. He flipped to Felix Millan, covering second. Millan had just come into the game in a double-switch, moving Flynn over to shortstop. Ott, at 5-foot-10, 198 pounds, came crashing in to second intent on breaking up the double play. He did, upending the 5-foot-11, 172-pound Millan. The native of Yabucoa, Puerto Rico, was not pleased with the situation. He stood up quickly and the pair exchanged heated words. With Ott making a rather large target near the base, the Mets infielder swung his fist with the baseball in it and clouted the Bucco catcher in the face. Millan, nicknamed "The Cat" was fighting a man known around his own ballpark as "Otter."

The ball-punch would be Millan's final gesture on a Major League baseball diamond. The Otter grabbed the cat, lifted him into the air and slammed him to the ground. He did not land on his feet. Millan's right clavicle—known as the collarbone and one of the lightest bones in the human skeleton given its size—broke on impact. He also suffered a separated shoulder. Millan squirmed in pain under the dark Pittsburgh sky and was taken off the field on a stretcher. Bobby Valentine (of *Valentine vs. C. Wright*) entered the game as Millan's replacement, taking over shortstop duties while Flynn was moved back to the keystone. Ott, who was ejected, was replaced by Duffy Dyer, who would single home the winning run in the twelfth inning, giving the Bucs a 6-5 victory and the sweep.

Had Millan let go of the ball and perhaps thrown it at Ott, he would have joined San Diego shortstop Enzo Hernandez in the creativity department for starting fights after broken double plays. After getting the force out at second base, Hernandez pelted Houston's Bob Watson (*let he who is without sin . . .*) in the middle of the back in July of 1976, sparking a brawl in the Astrodome.

Millan, who quickly became a Latino role model for city youth when he arrived in New York after being traded by the Braves in

November of 1972, had a pal in Pirates coach Jose Pagan, whom he talked to as he was being stretchered off the Three Rivers AstroTurf. Pagan tried mending some fences after the game. "Felix told me to tell Ott he was sorry, that it was his fault," Pagan said. "He said he lost his head. Those are Felix's words and I am his good friend. Ott also feels bad about this."

Bucco manager Tanner, feeling more like NL president Chub Feeney's whipping boy, also felt bad, but for different reasons. He lost his temper with reporters after the game. "Let me take a baseball and slam it into your face, then I'll say I'm sorry," Tanner told a UPI reporter. "Does that make it right? There's no room for being sorry in a situation like that. He knows what he did. I'm glad Ott did what he did." Tanner also let out some of his frustrations still simmering from the Taveras and Oliver suspensions.

Ott on many occasions proved to all comers that ex-footballers from Muncy, Pennsylvania, are not to be trifled with. He was rewarded for his hard work with a World Series ring in 1979 when Tanner platooned him behind the plate with Steve Nicosia. Ott's partner in catching crime also showed he could use his fists. During the frantic and brief celebration after Willie Stargell guided the Bucs through the Game 7 World Series win over the Orioles, Nicosia delivered a serious pounding to a Baltimore fan who was among many who ran onto the field as the Pirates tried to make it to their Memorial Stadium dugout and champagne-ready clubhouse.

Millan, a three-time All-Star who won two Gold Glove awards and was known for his small bat he choked up on, had surgery on his shoulder two days after his encounter with Ott. A doctor named James Parkes told a UPI reporter the thirty-four-year-old Millan, the accomplished sacrifice bunter who was almost impossible to strike out, would be shelved until the next spring. But the Mets had other plans. In December of 1977 the club purchased its old 1968 first round draft pick—infielder Tim Foli—from the San Francisco Giants. Foli and Flynn would man the middle infield for Joe Torre's sorry '78 Mets squad. Torre, who was a player/manager for a few months during the 1977 season, combined with Millan to set an interesting record in 1975. Millan had four straight singles in a game against Houston, and Torre grounded into four consecutive double plays. Millan's shoulder eventually healed properly and he played in Japan for three seasons and won a batting title there. He retired after the 1980 campaign. Millan told interviewer Dave Hollander in 2005 he never harbored any bad feelings toward Ott and that he too tried his hardest to break up double plays while running the bases. Especially with Torre hitting behind him.

JOE FERGUSON VS. BILL GREIF
(LOS ANGELES DODGERS)   (SAN DIEGO PADRES)
July 1, 1975, Dodger Stadium, Los Angeles, California

The invisible ink pen used to write baseball's unwritten rules would be a very valuable piece of memorabilia to possess. It would draw top dollars at the swankiest of auction houses. Trying a squeeze play in the eighth inning with a 10-1 lead usually means trouble for the team trying to get that eleventh run. Stealing bases in the eighth inning with a nine-run cushion is also forbidden, according to the unwritten bylaws.

For Dave Winfield, the 1975 season was his first with steady playing time for John McNamara's San Diego Padres. The twenty-three-year-old future Hall of Famer, standing 6-foot-6 and 220 pounds, started strong that season. In a June game against Montreal, he was struck in the wrist by a relay throw on an attempted double play by Tim Foli. Winfield sat out for a week. Another week passed, and he found himself batting at Dodger Stadium in the eighth inning on July 1, 1975. Johnny Grubb was on third with two outs. Winfield tried the squeeze play but fouled it off. Dodgers reliever Charlie Hough took note, and his next pitch clipped Winfield in his other wrist, the one spared by Foli's throw. The benches cleared, but no blows were struck as Dodgers catcher Joe Ferguson restrained Winfield from getting at Hough. Big Dave's wrist was hurting and he had to leave the game, but the Padres weren't done. Dick Sharon pinch-ran for Winfield and a double steal was attempted to get Grubb home. It failed, and Grubb was out at the plate he was so desperately trying to reach.

In the bottom of the eighth inning, Padres reliever Bill Greif, no stranger to the inside part of the plate, took over for starter Dan Spillner. He was ahead in the count against Willie Crawford, who was leading off the inning for Los Angeles. Greif was working Crawford extremely inside, and when his fifth pitch of the at-bat was a knockdown job a centimeter away from Crawford's ribs, Willie stormed the mound. He pummeled Greif, lifting him off his feet with several blows.

In the clubhouse, Winfield was having his wrist iced down. He heard the melee over the radio broadcast, and as he recalled in his autobiography *A Player's Life*, made it back onto the field just in time to see an ugly pile-up. Ferguson had hurled himself onto the top of the pile to get to Greif, and began a slow descent to the ground through a sea of arms and clenched fists. A Dodgers batboy, playing an Amalfitanoesque role, was off to the side trying to hold an angry Davey Lopes away from the fray. As tempers cooled off, the pile began to unravel. At the bottom was Ferguson, who, in his first season as the Dodgers regular catcher in 1973 set a Major League record by only making three errors in more than seven hundred chances. His jersey, Winfield recalled, was inside out and pulled over his head, covered in grass stains. "You could tell something was wrong," Winfield wrote. Ferguson finally stood up, then crumpled back to the ground. His right forearm was broken.

Ferguson was headed for surgery and done for the year, a fact that horrified Los Angeles manager Walter Alston, who thought the fight might otherwise motivate his troubled squad. The clubhouse mood had already been tested by a Steve Garvey flap in which a San Bernardino newspaper quoted teammates Ron Cey and Lopes as questioning the 1974 NL MVP's "All-American" image.

Greif stayed in the game and struck out Garvey to end it. Umpire Shag Crawford had ejected Crawford (no relation), Lopes, and yes, the seriously injured Ferguson, just for posterity.

The San Francisco native who had worked hard in the Dodgers minor league system was never the same after the broken arm. Such an anonymous injury, a bone lost in a pile with no real culprit, seemed unfitting for such an important player on the Dodgers. Steve Yeager was coming of age behind the plate for Los Angeles, and after a slow start in 1976, Ferguson was traded to St. Louis for Reggie Smith and Yeager would take over what could qualify as a jinxed position (Roy Campanella. Johnny Roseboro. Yeager's horrible throat injury in 1976). Ferguson bounced to Houston, came back to the Dodgers from late 1978 through 1981, then finished out his fourteen-year career with three seasons as a California Angel. Ferguson would enjoy coaching positions in the Dodgers organization and with Baltimore, and went on to hold several minor league coaching posts. In 2007, he was named manager of the Camden RiverSharks of the independent Atlantic League.

ANDRES GALARRAGA VS. DICKIE NOLES
(MONTREAL EXPOS)   (CHICAGO CUBS)
June 30, 1987, Le Stade Olympique, Montreal, Canada

The case of relief pitcher Dickie Noles can be approached from a host of interesting angles: extreme alcohol problems, a fight with a cop outside a Cincinnati bar, the knee injury from a fight that might have been a painful sequel to a bathroom mishap in Montreal. The year before his Cincinnati trouble, he landed on the disabled list for a couple of weeks after slipping on his bathroom floor in Montreal. Or there's his famous brushback pitch during the 1980 World Series, the one Mike Schmidt credits in his autobiography *Clearing the Bases* as "the greatest in World Series history." Schmidt called his teammate Noles a "gunslinger," which is another term for headhunter in many circles. It was during Game 4 of the Fall Classic that Noles buzzed Kansas City's George Brett. Royals manager Jim Frey was so incensed by the pitch he charged out of the dugout and had to be restrained. There was some milling around after Phillies third baseman Pete Rose intercepted Frey, but no real fighting. After Brett's buzzing, the Royals lost their mojo at the plate and the fightin' Phils went on to win the world championship.

Three seasons later, Noles was with the Cubs and had to leave the team to enter rehab. He was sentenced to sixteen days in jail for his scuffle with the Cincinnati constable. The hurt knee cost him ten miles per hour on his fastball and led to his eventual decline. But not before he did another stint with the Cubs during what was a very eventful 1987 for the lad from Charlotte with the NASCAR moniker.

On April 6, 1987, Noles had signed as a free agent with Chicago after a so-so turn with the Cleveland Indians in 1986. On June 30, the Cubs were in Montreal and were described by at least one Chicago sportswriter as "floundering." They had won only two of seven games on the road trip. The night before, however, the Cubs had prevailed, and Noles pitched almost two innings in relief, hitting Andres Galarraga with a pitch in the seventh. Noles and "The

Cat" exchanged a few words after the incident, but nothing escalated. Noles had also nailed Tim Wallach that same night. So when Noles hit Galarraga with a pitch for the second time in two nights in the eighth inning of the June 30 Cubs loss to the Expos, things got lively. Galarraga charged the mound and the punches flew. Cubs manager Gene Michael said he didn't mind Noles plunking Galarraga, because Dennis Martinez had hit Andre Dawson earlier in the game. Both Noles and Galarraga were ejected, but during the mess, Noles received a fracture to his forearm. He was out of action until August 21. Expos manager Buck Rodgers was rather blunt in his post-game comments after the Montreal win. "His [Noles] reputation as a headhunter precedes him and when he comes inside like that it gets a response," Rodgers said.

Almost one month later, Noles became a piece of baseball trivia thanks to some sleight of hand between Cubs general manager Dallas Green and Detroit GM Bill Lajoie. The Cubs sent Noles to Detroit for a player to be named later. That player would end up being Noles himself, as Lajoie opted to ship him back to the Cubs on October 23. He appeared in just four games for the first-place Tigers. In 2005, Noles, having been sober for quite a while, would take a job as a substance abuse counselor working in the Phillies organization.

The pudgy Venezuelan slugger Galarraga was no stranger to mound charges during his nineteen seasons. Later in his career, he'd storm Dennis Cook of the Marlins, and in August of 1998 he tore after Darren Dreifort of the Dodgers, who had hit him with pitches twice in a one week span. Dreifort ducked Galarraga's haymaker and grabbed his legs for a mound wrestling match. It was an unspectacular rhubarb, except for the fact Dreifort sustained cuts to his pitching elbow and had to leave the game. Galarraga was suspended by the league for three games. The five-time All-Star survived a battle with cancer, returning to play a few more inspirational seasons following his year off in 1999 for chemotherapy.

SEATTLE MARINERS BULLPEN
VS.
LOS ANGELES DODGERS
July 11, 1999, Dodger Stadium, Los Angeles, California

The last game of the season's first half is typically played in brisk fashion. Players are often caught up in anticipation of the three-day break interrupted only by the public relations spectacle and MLB office party called the All-Star game. On July 11, 1999, it was a typical sunny Sunday afternoon at Chavez Ravine, but nothing could brighten the mood of two West Coast teams playing their last game of their dismal first halves of the season. The Dodgers and Mariners—not exactly the natural rivalry interleague dreams are made of—were nonetheless fulfilling their interleague duties as mandated by MLB marketing wonks on Park Avenue in the distant city of Gotham. While most teams hungry for the grand getaway executed their games with predictable swiftness, the Dodgers-Mariners game lasted a brutal three hours and twenty-eight minutes, the longest of any played that day. Only two players from this game had to catch the flight east to appear in the All-Star game at Fenway Park—Gary Sheffield of the Dodgers and Ken Griffey, Jr., of the Mariners.

The trouble in Los Angeles started in the sixth inning. The Dodgers were up 12-3 when Frankie Rodriguez pitched way inside to Los Angeles' Mark Grudzielanek. The batter stepped out and had words; the pitcher pointed and returned the verbal fire. Grudzielanek told the AP after the game that Rodriguez was "saying some pretty vulgar things."

Seattle catcher Dan Wilson had things under control from the onset, craftily embracing Grudzielanek and keeping him from advancing on Rodriguez. Home plate umpire Rich Rieker was very hands off. It looked like the situation was contained. Then the Seattle bullpen arrived from their long jog. Hell did break loose thanks to three Dominican-born horsemen called Jose Mesa, Jose Paniagua and Damaso Marte. Piles of fights—like ravenous zombies from a George Romero film—seemed to surge from beneath the Dodger Stadium turf.

Peacemaker Wilson was quarantined by Eric Karros. Paniagua and Devon White tussled, and Mesa chose Dave Hansen as his dance partner. Marte, still on the run, reached over a gaggle of shoulders to punch Dodgers catcher Todd Hundley and the main fuse blew. Los Angeles bullpen coach Rick Dempsey, acting on advice of Lord Admiral Nelson, made a straight beeline for Marte and tore into him during the reliever's unimpressive St. Vitus dance. As they started to descend to Mother Earth, disabled Mariners outfielder Jay Buhner was shoved from behind and careened on top of the coach and reliever, along with Pedro Borbon of the Dodgers. While Marte and Dempsey were being crushed, Raul Mondesi and Seattle's David Segui were engaged in some Greco-Roman grappling, with Dodgers reserve catcher Angel Pena trying to assist or separate them, possibly both. Seattle's Butch Huskey took a special interest in Pena after a while, and Mondesi continued to get a face full of Segui's special blond hair dye as the pair untucked each other's jerseys, horns locked while staring off into the distance.

The television cameras captured rich details, especially of the bent-over Mondesi. His left back pocket contained a batting glove dangling out, while his right rear pocket was home to a circular can of smokeless tobacco product. Segui extended the dandy dispute to the fifteen-minute mark with a manly challenge to the entire Dodger dugout. Even the most somnambulant Dodger fans in their sun-splashed stupors responded with a hail of debris aimed at the playing field. Caught up in the Buhner rush to get Dempsey off his pitcher were Seattle outfielders Brian Hunter and utility man Charles Gipson, who were both injured. Gipson took the brunt of the pain, suffering a separated shoulder. The sixty-third-round draft pick, who was coming off a decent rookie season, would be out of action until Labor Day. Hunter would not return from the disabled list until July 27.

Mariners who were denied shore leave via game ejections included messrs. Marte, Mesa and Paniagua as well as "Bone" Buhner. For the Dodgers, Hundley was tossed along with Borbon and Dempsey.

The interleague nature of this contest made for an interesting dual announcement from presidents of both leagues a few days later as they dealt out the punishment with enhanced fury. Especially for Dempsey. He was fined $1,000 and slapped with a seventeen-game suspension. Jamie Arnold of the Dodgers, who was not ejected, was suspended for five games and fined $1,000. Hundley was docked three games and fined $2,500, with the NL office getting very specific about the reasons why: fighting, being out of control and using obscene gestures in view of fans and television cameras, according to language quoted in an AP story. Paniagua's punishment was equally well-documented. He got a five-game suspension and a $1,000 fine for what the AL office described as fighting, attempting to kick another player and using an obscene gesture. Buhner got three games and a $1,000 fine, Marte got three games and a $1,000 fine, and Segui was suspended one game and fined $2,000.

The frustrating year for Dodgers skipper Davey Johnson and Mariners manager Lou Piniella culminated in almost identical records for each club. Seattle went 79-83, while the Dodgers, who prevailed 14-3 in the game that put Gipson out of order, finished 77-85.

ERIC ANTHONY vs. PAUL QUANTRILL
(SEATTLE MARINERS)   (BOSTON RED SOX)
May 3, 1994, Fenway Park, Boston, Massachusetts

In a blasphemous display of in-game passion during the horrid strike year of 1994, the Mariners and Red Sox clashed on a bizarre night at Fenway when an intentional walk turned violent and two pitchers departed with injuries. Three months and seven days before the season would end with a labor dispute on August 11, Frank Viola was on the hill for Boston. He was one of two Red Sox pitchers who would not survive the third inning.

Down 3-1 to the Mariners, Viola opened the third inning by striking out Jay Buhner. Greg Pirkl and Mike Blowers followed with back-to-back singles, then Felix Fermin made the second out with a fly ball to Billy Hatcher in right. Viola then threw a wild pitch behind Seattle batter Eric Anthony. Viola, a New Yorker by trade who did time with the Mets, clutched at his elbow—the same one surgically repaired the previous September. He was done. Out of the game and into the hospital for more elbow surgery.

Viola was replaced by Paul Quantrill, who came in and promptly buzzed a high-and-tight heater under the chin of Anthony, knocking him to the ground. With first base open (Blowers and Pirkl moved up on the wild pitch) and Dan Wilson on deck for Seattle, Boston manager Butch Hobson reached into his shaving kit/bag of tricks and called for an intentional walk of Anthony after Quantrill had knocked him down. The rubber-armed reliever complied, issuing the intentional pass to the outfielder Houston traded to Seattle for Mike Felder and Mike Hampton the previous December. Halfway to first base, Anthony decided to ambush Quantrill. He rushed at him and put his shoulder down to tackle him. His head rammed the pitcher's midsection and the Fenway mound quickly became a messy sight. The combatants were evenly matched. Anthony stood 6-foot-2, 195 pounds; Quantrill, with the high ground advantage, used his 6-foot-1, 175-pound frame effectively. Until, that is, the scene became what English schoolchildren call a "bundle."

Anthony made sure Quantrill was at the bottom of the pile, and when the bodies were cleared, Quantrill's right hand was numb. It was as if he'd fallen into a snowbank in his birthplace of London, Ontario, and frostbite was setting in on his pitching hand. Quantrill followed Viola's path into the clubhouse, and Hobson trotted out his third pitcher of the inning in the form of a southern lad named Scott Bankhead. Anthony's intentional walk high jinks did not impress the umpiring crew, and the San Diego native was ejected.

Quantrill's stand, and his venting of a collective Fenway frustration centered on the loss of Viola, inspired the Red Sox to score five runs in the bottom of the third in what would become a meaningless 7-6 Boston win. The injury to Quantrill's hand turned out not to be serious. He was back on the mound May 6 against the Yankees in the Bronx. On May 31, Quantrill and Hatcher were dealt to Philadelphia for Wes Chamberlain and a minor leaguer.

Viola would attempt a comeback in July of 1995 with five starts for Cincinnati, and then six more the following year with Toronto. But that was it—after fifteen seasons, Viola put the creaky elbow in cold storage, and kicked back to watch the steady decline of the basketball program at his alma mater, St. John's University.

BOBBY VALENTINE vs. CLYDE WRIGHT
(CALIFORNIA ANGELS)   (MILWAUKEE BREWERS)
May 29, 1974, Anaheim Stadium, Anaheim, California

It was a Wednesday night in May in Anaheim. The visiting Brewers, perhaps lacking a certain glamour, were not helping to draw at the gate. Gene Autry's club was off to a frustrating start in a year they would finish last in the AL West. But the season was still young. How else to explain possibly the smallest crowd to ever witness a baseball fight? Only 6,787 filed into Anaheim Stadium on May 29, 1974. That was up from the 5,280 in the ballpark the night before. Maybe the fans were staying at home to read Alexander Solzhenitsyn's *The Gulag Archipelago* and pondering an Orange County future when the airport would be named after John Wayne? Nearby, Disneyland had just opened a new attraction called "America Sings" to replace the General Electric "Carousel of Progress," which was shipped off to Disney World in Orlando. The $6 million animatronic "America Sings" show featured an eagle with the voice of Burl Ives. Less than two weeks after this Angels-Brewers tilt, Disneyland would suffer its first "cast member" (Disneyspeak for "employee") fatality when an eighteen-year-old woman from Santa Ana was crushed between the walls of the "America Sings" rotating stages. It was also the year Bob Dylan took his family to the theme park.

Angels outfielder Bobby Valentine, a Connecticut-born product with an uber-Dodgers pedigree (Los Angeles' first-round pick in the 1968 draft, Tommy Lasorda's minor league superstar, married to Ralph Branca's daughter), stepped in against his old teammate Clyde Wright. The left-hander from Tennessee arrived in Milwaukee as part of a nine-player deal between the Angels and Brewers—a most unspectacular transaction. Valentine had arrived with the Angels as part of a similar multiplayer swap, but this one involved seven players and two heavyweights named Frank Robinson and Andy Messersmith.

First inning brawls usually reek of grudge, but there seemed to be no known history of ill-will between Wright and Valentine. Wright retired Mickey Rivers on a ground ball to first baseman George Scott, with Wright covering the bag. Dave Chalk then singled ahead of Valentine. Wright then threw a pitch that sailed over Valentine's head. Enraged, Valentine dropped his bat and marched toward the mound, taking three steps with both fists clenched. Wright came down off the hill to meet him. The pair yelled at each other, then Valentine threw two punches, landing one on Wright's eye and one on his jaw before they collapsed to the ground. The dugouts emptied, and the aforementioned Frank Robinson, in the middle year of a three-season West Coast residency ('72 with the Dodgers, '73 and '74 with the Angels) made the short trip from the on-deck circle to the fight and immediately took out Milwaukee catcher Charlie Moore, pounding him with both his fists as Moore lay on the ground.

Of course Valentine was going to get hurt during the melee. His history of injuries included a shattered leg the previous May when he ran full-speed into the Anaheim fence trying to track down a Dick Green home run. He'd also suffered broken facial bones from various beanings.

If anything, Valentine was a magnet for pain. When the smoke cleared, Valentine had a separated shoulder. Both he and Wright were ejected from the game, which the Brewers went on to win 7-5. Showing early signs of his soon to be famous propensity for never turning down an interview or mugging for cameras with his mini–George Hamilton act, Valentine spoke to the press while his shoulder was being iced on the trainer's table. The AP described his tone as "grim" when he told them "The pitch was right at my head. If I hadn't managed to get out of the way, it would have hit me right in the face." Having missed most of the previous season with the broken leg, there was a certain honesty to Valentine's assessment of the night's damage. "What the heck, it's only a dislocated shoulder," he said. Valentine was back in action on June 14 against the Red Sox.

The headliners of *Valentine vs. C. Wright* would both go on to make some noise in Japan. After the Brewers traded Wright to Texas in the 1974 offseason, he endured a pretty miserable year with Billy Martin's Rangers before heading for Japan. There, he threw a famous on-field fit after being removed from a game, and the Japanese fans quickly dubbed him "Crazy Righto." He was also involved in a fight with the East German hockey team while playing in Japan.

Valentine was traded to the Padres and then from San Diego to the Mets (for Dave Kingman) before playing his final season in 1979 with the Seattle Mariners. In 1985, he was named manager of the Texas Rangers and helmed that squad for the better part of eight seasons. In 1995, he became popular as manager of the Chiba Lotte Marines in Japan before returning to the states to manage the Mets for a turbulent stretch from 1996 to 2002. In 2004, he made a triumphant return to the Chiba team, a second stint that was going like gangbusters as of 2007.

Valentine is a baseball renaissance man. From his teenage years as an accomplished ballroom dancer, to his ownership of sports bars, and claiming on the Food Network he invented the wrap sandwich—the man never backed down from a camera or player. He had famous disputes with Rickey Henderson, grappled with Carl Everett, donned a disguise and returned to the Mets dugout after being tossed from a game, and worked as an ESPN baseball commentator after he was done with the Mets. He always fancied himself a rulebook stickler, but his in-game strategy and penchant for showmanship (the Lasorda Way of always upstaging the players) was subject to frequent questioning by skeptical Gotham baseball fans.

A glance at Valentine's blog in 2007 presented a personality mix of Joe Franklin, Denny Terio, Pops Racer, Hello Kitty, and Leo Buscaglia. One minute he was talking about Benny Agbayani's third kid being born, the next minute Valentine is off judging the Japanese Miss Universe pageant or a ballroom dance competition and attending every corporate event in Tokyo. One thing he did successfully was introduce a staple of New York City winterwear to the Japanese scene by constantly wearing a black leather peacoat. If he could only develop a hotel lounge singing act he might convince Scarlett Johansson and Bill Murray to do a remake of *The Fabulous Baker Boys*.

Doors, Laundry Carts, Clubhouse Walls

Frustration gets the best of starting pitchers on a regular basis. When that happens, they punch things. Often, in a moment of unwise decision-making, they use their pitching hands to deliver an angry blow to an inanimate object. Minnesota hurler Kyle Lohse did it to the door of Twins manager Ron Gardenhire's office in September of 2005. Lohse hurt the middle finger on his pitching hand after Gardenhire took him out of a game against Texas in the second inning. With the hand injured, he proceeded to continue beating the portal with a bat, and then went after the door to the Hubert H. Humphrey Metrodome worker's locker-room area.

Pirates hurler Oliver Perez knew better than to use his hand after a particularly bad outing in St. Louis in June of 2005. So he used his foot—he kicked a laundry cart and broke his left big toe. He missed two months of action and never really got back into the high-expectation groove he had occupied the previous season.

Kevin Brown has done his share of property damage through the years. He destroyed a toilet at the Dodgers quaint Spring Training home in Vero Beach, Florida, because a teammate had flushed while he was taking a shower and interrupted the hot water flow. In September of 2004, Brown had a bad game in the Bronx against the Orioles. He used his left hand to deliver hammer blows to a clubhouse wall. As it had done against generations of upset hurlers, the wall prevailed. The bones in Brown's hand did not.

The lowlight reel includes other memorable sights: Seattle's Tim Belcher versus a Yankee Stadium dugout telephone. Carlos Perez of the

Dodgers using a bat to reshape a Gatorade cooler at the end of the dugout. Toronto pitcher Mark Lemongello so enraged after a loss that he bit his own shoulder until it bled.

The list goes on and on and on, filled with the one-dimensional, prima donna rages symptomatic of a virulent strain of altitude sickness caused by the high elevation of the pitcher's mound.

A sizeable chunk of the smorgasbord of baseball violence exists
away from the playing field behind the closed doors of the clubhouse.
That is where the subspecies known as clubhouse gladiators ply their
trade. This chapter adds some violent yarns to complement the cases already examined, such as *Piniella vs. Dibble* and *R. Jackson vs. B. North.* The
latter was a brief but saucy battle conducted *sans* clothing and is naturally book-ended by the nude Goose Gossage battling teammate Cliff
Johnson in the clubhouse bathroom at Yankee Stadium in April of 1979.

What began as basic razzing escalated at the urinals when Johnson,
who'd had a bad day sulking on the bench against the Orioles, wanted to
know if the reliever could "back up" his words. Johnson, who was fully
clothed in his Yankee pinstripes, then shoved Gossage's head and the battle between two superheavyweights was on. As a few teammates separated
them, Gossage thought the fight was over and threw in one parting comment. He was then tackled into a shower stall by Johnson. Gossage put his
hand down to break his fall. In doing so, he tore his ulnar collateral liga-
ment in his right thumb, had surgery three days later and was out of action until mid-July. *C. Johnson vs. Gossage* served as a harbinger of strange
injuries and gothic angst that would plague the 1979 Yankees, a team that
lost Thurman Munson in a fiery plane crash in early August.

For clubhouse gladiators, the obvious venue is the locker room,
lounge, and even the shower stalls. Airplanes are equally awkward fight lo-
cations, as Texas Rangers Cesar Tovar and Joe Lovitto discovered when

they tried to duke it out in the aisle of their charter during a particularly rough losing stretch in the summer of '75. All they managed to accomplish was to send manager Billy Martin into a full-scale in-flight tantrum.

Yellow Press, White Teeth

Our first dispatch covers events three years after the Rangers high-altitude tiff. Here's a bit of Dodger discord within the drop-ceilinged bowels of Shea Stadium, circa August 1978. For the modern era media, the quintessential clubhouse tiff, post *Durocher vs. Ruth*, might have been Dodger teammates Steve Garvey and Don Sutton going at it in the visitor's clubhouse of Shea Stadium in New York. The overwhelming *whiteness* of this one struck a chord with the press, especially after it was learned the internal strife was caused by a newspaper article.

Thomas Boswell's piece in the *Washington Post*, in which he quoted Sutton as saying Reggie Smith was the real Dodgers MVP and that Garvey had succeeded in being the team publicity hound, was reproduced in the *Los Angeles Times* and therefore read by Garvey or one of his cronies. It was classic passive-aggressive ballplayerese among a team destined to win ninety-five games and represent the National League in the World Series. Saturday, August 19 had not been a great occasion for Sutton, who absorbed his tenth loss of the season in giving up seven runs (four unearned) in an 8-4 loss to the Mets. On Sunday, August 20, he was confronted at his locker at Shea by Garvey, who wanted to know why Sutton had said what he said to the dandyish baseball scribe from the *Washington Post*. The initial exchange was conducted in hushed tones, according to witnesses, and went on for two minutes. Then it quickly became heated as the right-handed pitcher known for his perm mentioned Garvey's wife Cyndy. Things escalated into the ugly Zip Code in a hurry as Garvey lunged at Sutton, grabbed him, and threw him against a row of lockers on the opposite wall. UPI reporter Milton Richman described the grapple as a bit of a catfight, with lots of scratching as the two Dodgers rolled on the floor attempting to land hamhanded blows. Watching the combat was Dodgers coach Preston Gomez, general manager and swimming expert Al Campanis, while teammates Reggie Smith, Davey Lopes, Rick Monday, and Bill Russell—four players not unaccustomed to baseball violence themselves—tried to pry Garvey and Sutton apart as they rolled on the cheaply carpeted floor. Suddenly the much-advertised Dodgers harmony was sullied, and Campanis scurried to try and contain this new scandal.

Dodgers pitcher Tommy John, who was autographing dozens of All-Star baseballs that were spilled from his locker during the fight, told sportswriter Phil Pepe *Garvey vs. Sutton* was "like two women fighting in the locker room over some guy."

When someone said "stop the fight, they'll kill each other," John said Joe Ferguson's reply was "good."

When they were finally separated, both players had scratched faces and Garvey was "groggy" according to Richman. "I don't think these things should come out like this in public," Garvey told the reporter. "If someone has something to say, they should say it to my face." By the end of Sunday's matinee at Shea, Garvey was sporting his scratched face and bloodshot eye on the field, while Sutton was in the dugout with a sizeable bruise on his cheek. Garvey's ninth inning single was part of a Los Angeles three-run comeback in the top of the ninth on the way to a 5-4 victory over the Mets.

Within a week, Sutton underwent some type of Christian New Age self-reflection that resulted in his apology to Garvey that sounded like he'd been drugged or was sipping some of the Reverend Jim Jones' Flav-Or-Aid. "The only possible reason I can find is that my life isn't being lived according to what I know, as a human being and a Christian, to be right," Sutton said in a prepared statement that he read while choked with emotion. "Because if it were, then there would not have been an article in a newspaper in which I would offend any of my teammates." Garvey, meanwhile, had apologized to the entire Dodgers roster for his Shea Stadium clubhouse explosion.

Meanwhile, in his column called "Tug's Locker" printed in the *Doylestown* (Pennsylvania) *Intelligencer,* Phillies reliever Tug McGraw wondered about the real estate ramifications of *Garvey vs. Sutton*. He pointed out the two were next door neighbors whose dispute would naturally be carried from the clubhouse to the neighborhood. "Be interesting to see who sells their house first," McGraw wrote in a blurb that described the incident as a "feud."

An Associated Press writer labeled *Garvey vs. Sutton* as a money battle based on envy. Sutton had been given the team's first long-term contract, a four-year million dollar deal, which was trumped by Garvey's six-year deal just a few months later.

Locker Stall Ordnance

Of course over in Orange County, the Angels were not to be outdone by Chavez Ravine denizens when it came to clubhouse gladiators. There was great mythology surrounding Angels bench player Chico Ruiz. He made his living as a reserve in Cincinnati and was doing the same with California in June of 1971. Phillies fans remember him as the man who stole home (with Frank Robinson at the plate) in the Reds 1-0 win that marked the beginning of Philadelphia's monumental collapse down the stretch in 1964.

The Cuban-born utility man was a jovial clubhouse presence who had a sense of humor about his "role" as a Major Leaguer. He toted a guitar and played corny songs to entertain his teammates. He kept everyone loose and pulled occasional pranks involving labor-intensive clothing alterations. As Reds teammate Pete Rose put it, Ruiz made an art of sitting on the bench.

Alex Johnson was more of an enigma. In an unusual case of excessive player movement at the time, Johnson was employed by eight different teams in a twelve-year span from 1964 to 1976. In 1970, Johnson and Ruiz were traded by Cincinnati to the California Angels in a deal that brought Pedro Borbon to the Reds. Johnson excelled with the Halos and earned a spot on the 1970 AL All-Star squad and the AL batting title with a .329 average. He had 202 hits and edged Boston's Carl Yastrzemski by mere percentage points on the final day of the season.

But with his offensive prowess came a price. He was fined dozens of times by manager Lefty Phillips for not hustling or running out ground balls. Johnson also gave sportswriters an earful of obscenities whenever they came near. His teammates were also his verbal targets on many occasions. There were high expectations for the 1971 Angels, but Johnson's moping in the dugout and repeated fines for not hustling set the tone for a fractured, tense clubhouse. A *Los Angeles Times* columnist reported several Angels players were armed with guns and knives in their lockers in case things turned violent. Off the field, Johnson was known as a sweetheart. As manager Phillips put it, when asked to compare Johnson to Dick Allen: "Once you get Richie Allen on the field, your problems are over. When Johnson gets on the field, your problems are just beginning."

The pressure cooker exploded in the clubhouse when Johnson and outfielder Ken Berry engaged in a lengthy fist fight. Johnson had already told his teammates he was ready to fight any one of them. Clyde Wright attempted to take him up on his offer by wielding a stool over his head, but was restrained by teammates as Johnson allegedly threw a bottle at the pitcher.

In an incident witnessed only by participants Ruiz and Johnson, legend has it Ruiz was sitting across from Johnson in the clubhouse and pulled out a handgun and pointed it at his truculent teammate. They'd both been used as pinch hitters in the game and were finished for the night. For the past year, Johnson had turned on Ruiz as a special target of abuse and torment. With gun in hand, Ruiz allegedly invoked the racial divisions plaguing the Angels that season. Johnson had bitterly contended his white teammates were insensitive to his plight as a black athlete. "I'm as black as you are, and I hate you," the Cuban-born Ruiz reportedly said. "I hate you so much, I could kill you!"

Ruiz denied the incident happened and said he didn't own a gun. Angels brass held a press conference the next day, backing up Ruiz's account. By late June, the Angels had suspended Johnson indefinitely. The player's union took up his cause, filing a grievance to overturn the suspension and fines on the grounds Johnson was emotionally disabled and needed treatment. An arbitrator found for Johnson, and he was treated by a pair of psychiatrists. Union head Marvin Miller, after extensive talks with Johnson, said the player was emotionally unbalanced and racial conflicts in the workplace were deeply affecting Johnson.

It later came out that Ruiz had, in fact, waved a gun at Johnson, but it was not loaded. Team officials at the time did not want to invoke immigration problems for their utility man, so a clubhouse coverup was in effect. In October of 1971, the Angels traded Johnson to Cleveland. He had stops in Texas, the Bronx, and Detroit before retiring.

Ruiz was killed in a car crash outside San Diego in February of 1972. Johnson was reportedly one of a few ballplayers to attend the Ruiz funeral.

Chavez Ravine Runway Ruckus

In yet another case of Southern California jock warfare, Mike Marshall, who spent his first nine seasons in the big leagues with Los Angeles, clashed with Phil Garner, who spent just over half an unspectacular season wearing a Dodgers uniform in 1987. Marshall, not to be confused with the resilient pitcher of the same name, was one of two Dodgers romantically linked with Belinda Carlisle of the 1980s new wave band The Go-Go's. The oft-injured Marshall stood 6-feet-5 inches tall, 218 pounds and had taken batting practice prior to a game at Dodger Stadium against the Phillies on September 2, 1987. Garner, 5-feet-8 inches and 177 pounds and thirty-eight-years old, went up to Marshall and told him (in a fore-shadowing of his managerial future) to go shag balls in the outfield. Marshall objected to this instruction from a fellow journeyman. The two argued and moved their dispute into the Dodgers dugout, and then into the runway leading to the clubhouse. In the confines of that hallway, the battle began when punches were thrown as the two descended to the floor. Official Dodgers fight disrupter Joey Amalfitano materialized to break it up, with the help of infielder Craig Shipley and a Chavez Ravine usher who gave the surface of the floor an abbreviated wipe with his rag and held out his hand for a tip.

Marshall had but a few abrasions, while Garner, he of "Scrap Iron" fame, sported a countenance with more scratches than a Go-Go's record on the floor of the punk club Whiskey A-Go-Go. He later said he was frustrated with his anemic hitting and his temper flared at Marshall's ex-pense. One Dodger player, upset with the freedoms allotted to Marshall by Dodger management, anonymously told the *Los Angeles Times:* "This thing has been brewing for a long time. I'm surprised it wasn't twenty-four guys against Marshall." Earlier in the season when the Dodgers were at Candlestick Park in April, Marshall provoked a venomous beer shower and mini-riot for his fist-pumping display after an extra-innings home run against the Giants. During his frequent stays on the disabled list, Marshall made no secret about leaving the ballpark early before games had concluded. These departures apparently did not sit well with Dodgers rank and file. The AP described the Dodgers hosting of *Garner vs. Marshall* as "the only sock they displayed all night" as the fightin' Phils won 6-2 to broom a three-game set.

Gunnery Sergeant Bonds, Private Kent

While dugout tiffs technically do not qualify as happening during "down time," it is the venue used by clubhouse gladiators who air dirty laundry in public. Many times television cameras outnumber players along any given MLB bench, so privacy has been reduced to an absolute minimum. Nose-picking hits the Jumbotron, snuff-dipping teaches the kids at home it is okay to go smokeless, and protective cup adjustments provide end-less titillation for certain types of home viewers. There have been many dugout tangos, most of them as exciting as junior high schoolers cutting the cafeteria line during lunch period.

A bilious confrontation of note occurred on June 25, 2002, in San Francisco. Giants second baseman Jeff Kent was bullying third baseman David Bell in the dugout. Barry Bonds decided to step in, telling Kent to back off. A shoving match ensued for all to see as Bonds sent Kent back a few steps with a strong push. Soon enough, manager Dusty Baker stepped in to settle down his house, but had to be restrained by trainer Stan Conte when he apparently threw his own brand of gas on the fire. Within a few years, both Conte and Kent would defect to the hated Dodgers to the south.

Baker ran interference for his grumpy players in the press, as Kent and Bonds were both quiet about the incident and Bell, as usual, was completely ignored. "Things like that happen all the time," Baker told the AP. "It usually doesn't happen in view of everybody on television. You saw the effect. The cause is our business." Baker then went on to make a rather awkward military analogy, which probably made Marines across the country bristle just a bit, perhaps cracking their "U.S.M.C." tattooed knuckles. "It's like on the last day of boot camp the sergeant asks if there's anyone who doesn't like someone and they fight it out," Baker said. "That way, you don't carry a grudge into battle." Kent? Bonds? Grudges? *Naaah.*

The Caged Mad Dog Sings

It would be tempting to just feature the time Bill Madlock lost his temper during batting practice when he was with the Pirates during Spring Training in 1980. Tossing a polite batting practice in Bradenton was Bucco farmhand Jeff Zaske, whose pro career spanned exactly eight days—from July 21 to July 28, 1984—when he made three appearances.

Madlock quickly grew annoyed with the meatballs Zaske was serving up from behind the pitching screen. "Throw harder!" Madlock reportedly yelled at the kid. Pirate wags around the cage, including Dave Parker, yelled at Zaske to "hit him!" Zaske's ill-advised next pitch grazed Mad Dog's left forearm and hit his ribs. He promptly walked out of the cage holding the offending baseball and headed directly for Zaske and punched him.

When Zaske was asked why he threw at the batting champion, he replied "They told me to." Madlock would later apologize for his Zaske zinger. Though Parker thought the whole thing was a joke, Madlock insisted it was not funny and was in fact scratched from that day's exhibition game. "I wouldn't have swung at him if he'd told me the ball slipped out of his hand," Madlock said.

Dick Gets Frank

Mad Dog's March madness paled in comparison to the regular season fireworks around the batting cage of Philadelphia's Connie Mack Stadium on July 3, 1965. The Phillies were taking batting practice before a game with the Reds. Dick Allen was getting ready to go in the cage and was being pestered by utility player Frank Thomas, who stood 6-foot-3, 205 pounds. It was an odd occasion, considering that the twenty-three-year-old Allen was coming off his Rookie of the Year season of 1964, was leading the NL in batting, and a few hours after the game was to be officially elected to appear in the All-Star game. So the 5-foot-11, 185-pound native of Wampum, Pennsylvania, proceeded to trade insults with the stubborn Thomas, when Thomas was next up in the cage. Teammate Johnny Callison, standing near Allen, teased Thomas about an ill-fated attempt to bunt the night before. At the time, Philly had seen race riots in the vicinity of Connie Mack Stadium, and tensions were still running high. Thomas was a fan favorite, but as Allen noted in his autobiography, the stubborn slugger had a penchant for picking on black players, especially Allen's team pal Wes Covington. And his supposedly innocent jokes were invariably plagued with horrible timing. Thomas was peeved and ignored the fact that the bunt taunt came from Callison. Instead he yelled at Allen "What are you, another Muhammad Clay, always trying to run your mouth off?" alluding to boxer Cassius Clay's recent transformation to Muhammad Ali.

Allen featured the Thomas incident as his opening chapter in his autobiography *Crash* written with Tim Whitaker. It was seen as an event that changed the way Allen was perceived in Philly, and like his tormented minor league days in Little Rock, altered Allen's career and approach to the game.

When Allen reported for his turn at batting practice, he noticed Thomas waiting for him, leaning his elbow on a bat. Allen walked right up to Thomas, a thirty-six-year-old Pittsburgh native, and punched him. Thomas responded by brandishing his bat and striking Allen on the shoulder. The incensed Allen then went berserk, relentlessly pounding Thomas as seven other Phillies tried to pry them apart. Allen got the best of Thomas, and also ended up punching Ruben Amaro as the fisticuffs unfolded. Allen's shoulder would swell up by the end of the game, when Allen considered the fight definitely over.

Thomas would pinch-hit in that night's game and hit a home run in the eighth inning. That night, the Phillies put Thomas on irrevocable waivers "for the best interests of the club" according to the front office. Manager Gene Mauch, no fan of Thomas's stubborn rabble rousing, tactfully explained to Thomas the decision was a no-brainer, given where both players were in their respective careers. Allen disagreed with the quick sending off of Thomas, who apologized to Allen, and was claimed by the Houston Astros on July 10. He retired after the 1966 season, which he spent with the Chicago Cubs.

Meanwhile, the Philly fans missed Thomas and were mad at Allen for the quick release of Thomas. Allen's next few seasons were stormy affairs in Philly. He was routinely booed after the Thomas incident and frequently battled the press and team management. When asked later by Whitaker if he would have done anything differently in *Allen vs. F. Thomas*, Allen responded: "I would have hit him harder. He never would have had a chance to hit me with a bat."

After the 1969 season, Allen was traded to St. Louis in the famous Curt Flood deal as the Cardinals outfielder challenged baseball's reserve clause. After a stint in Los Angeles, and a few seasons with the White Sox (during which he won the 1972 AL MVP Award), Allen was back with the Phillies in 1975, this time setting about to continue his borderline Hall of Fame career and his disobedience of manager Danny Ozark's Draconian regulations.

Dodgertown Bathroom Bash

God forbid someone use the toilet while Dodger pitching deity Kevin Brown is showering during Spring Training. In March of 1999, a teammate flushed while Brown was showering, causing the water temperature to soar. He got hot under his nonexistent collar, stormed out of the shower, into the toilet area, and destroyed the porcelain throne with a bat apparently kept in the tiled room for such a purpose.

Brown then put on his pants and stormed out of the quaint Vero Beach facility, the same one where he would tussle with Brian Jordan of the Braves a few seasons later. Maybe it was better plumbing that lured the Dodgers to Arizona for Spring Training?

Saying "Cheese" in Port St. Lucie

A much more colorful (and somehow less moist) Spring Training incident occurred at the New York Mets facility in Port St. Lucie, Florida, just down the highway from Vero Beach. It was March of 1989, and slugger Darryl Strawberry no longer considered first baseman Keith Hernandez his mentor. Not by a longshot. Hernandez was the Ed Koch of Mets clubhouse politics at the time.

The morning after tensions had boiled over between the two in a near brawl at a Port St. Lucie bar. It was official team photo time. According to the book *The Worst Team Money Could Buy*, by New York sportswriters Bob Klapisch and John Harper, the photographer was lining up the rows of players and had positioned Hernandez next to Strawberry. "I don't want to sit next to no backstabber," Strawberry reportedly said. To which Hernandez responded, apparently without a cigarette in his mouth, "I'm tired of your baby crap." With plenty of other cameras rolling nearby under the sun of Thomas J. White Stadium, Hernandez and Strawberry exchanged blows, screamed obscenities and had to be separated at least three times by teammates. Manager Davey Johnson suddenly had a situation on his hands. Hernandez was in his final season with the Mets after a glorious run. Toward the end of his stay in Queens, writers described his personality as "darkening." There were, of course, Strawberry *Esquire* interviews and player-written columns providing bulletin board material during the 1988 playoffs—neither of these clippings helped Keith's mood or demeanor among a team headed for some dark days as the 1990s beckoned. "Mex" missed all that. He cashed some more checks in Cleveland in 1990, hung up the spikes, did hair color commercials, *Seinfeld* appearances, and some TV broadcasting for the Mets.

Clubhouse Interview Disrupted

Rounding out this string of Spring Training malfeasance is a post-game interaction among San Francisco Giants players at their Casa Grande, Arizona, camp in March of 1978. Bill Madlock, no stranger to these pages, was harboring objections to some comments attributed to pitcher John "The Count" Montefusco about the quality of the Giants roster for the upcoming season. The Count was being interviewed when Madlock approached him and insisted he answer him right now and explain his comments about calling the Giants a "team of losers" or some similar insult.

Witnesses said Montefusco told Madlock to shut up or else be clouted with a bat. Madlock took that statement as his cue to start throwing punches, which he did.

Giants pitchers John Curtis and Randy Moffitt jumped on Madlock and The Count and broke up the dispute. Montefusco's left eye had a bruise above it, but he claimed it had been there before Madlock showed him his five-fingered press credential.

Shortly after the fight, Madlock and The Count were seen at adjoining dinner tables. They were not speaking, but they also were not punching.

Former Dodger Maury Wills was among the enemy in brown instructing the Giants on bunting and base running. "Things like this clear the air," he told the press, citing dozens of similar incidents when he played for the Dodgers. Madlock took a more deconstructionist route with his comments to the press: "We both have 'Giants' printed on our uniforms," he said. "We're here for one purpose—to get ready to win."

Like his stocky clubhouse nemesis, Montefusco, who won the NL Rookie of the Year award in 1975 and threw a no-hitter in Atlanta in 1976, had brushes with the law in his future. The product of the Jersey shore would move on to a brief stint with Atlanta, then San Diego, and finally the Yankees. In July of 1982, while he was with the Padres, *New York Times* writer Roy S. Johnson wrote a profile of The Count that had this line in it: "For now, Montefusco's problems appear to be behind him." 'Twere that it were.

His interest in horses saw him become a professional harness racing jockey in October of 1991 at Freehold Raceway. He trotted along without incident until 1997, when things got extremely ugly between The Count and his ex-wife, Doris. He was arrested and charged with aggravated sexual assault, terrorist threats, criminal mischief, and other misdeeds after allegedly going to her home in Marlboro, New Jersey, cutting the phone lines and holding her captive for almost two hours. Three weeks earlier, Montefusco allegedly threatened to kill Doris if she did not have sex with him. A week after he held her captive, he returned to the house and allegedly broke in and assaulted her again, violating a restraining order. He was arrested in Pennsylvania. Unable to raise his own bail money, Montefusco stayed in jail for two years before a jury acquitted him in November of 2000 of sexually assaulting Doris. He was sentenced to three years' probation for criminal trespass and simple assault. He spent a few seasons as a pitching coach for the independent Somerset Patriots of the

Atlantic League before stepping down because of arthritis discomfort. On Opening Day 2007, "The Count" appeared at AT&T Park with several other former Giants stars to commemorate San Francisco's hosting of the All-Star Game.

World Series Eve Woes

Any statements about internal player scuffles being part of dog-days inspired anti-boredom campaigns went out the window in October of 1974. The scene was Dodger Stadium the day before the start of the 1974 World Series between Oakland and Los Angeles. Typically, Charles O. Finley's team was in controlled chaos. Catfish Hunter was declaring himself a free agent quite suddenly, infielder Mike Andrews and his doctor were suing the team for his snubbing in the '73 Fall Classic, and "Blue Moon" Odom and Rollie Fingers were pounding each other in the clubhouse.

Unlike his botched and costly effort to separate Reggie Jackson and Bill North earlier in the season, Ray Fosse ran away from *Odom vs. Fingers*. A's trainer Joe Romo, perhaps jaded by the team's two consecutive World Championships, dragged out an evergreen brawl cliché when he told the AP "It was a friendly scuffle. It should break the monotony." Yes, how *boring* having the World Series on the next day's "to do" list, *again*.

The folks at nearby Lutheran Hospital might have questioned the friendliness of the pitcher-on-pitcher violence when the mustachioed future Hall of Famer Fingers checked in to have a gash closed with five stitches to his scalp. Witnesses said Fingers hit his head on a wooden post in the visitor's clubhouse. Details of the fight were sketchy, but it began with some shouting across the room just five minutes after the A's arrived at Dodger Stadium. One player said the dust-up began after Odom made a tawdry joke about Fingers' wife being left at the hotel—a standard gag from the pedestrian catalogue of sexually oriented ribbing common among ballplayers. A shopping cart was thrown and struck its human target, and there was blood and a gimpy leg or two. Sure enough, Fingers went out the next night and earned the victory in relief in Game 1. He would notch saves in Games 4 and 5 and take home the World Series MVP trophy. Yes, that was Odom next to him, arm-in-arm and soaked in champagne during the Swingin' A's third straight World Series clubhouse victory party, proving once again the green team from Oakland with the early '70s dynasty was the baseball version of *Finnegans Wake*.

Chapter 17:
DOWNTIME THROW-DOWNS

An examination of away-from-the-ballpark conflicts shows the settings are as varied as any television cop show. Barrooms, parking lots, street corners, bus rides, hotel lobbies, late-night diners—all are represented in a mix of milieus perhaps found in the dustbins of James Ellroy and Harry Crews. Baseball players pass lonely hours on the road, and sometimes tempting hours at home. What follows are accounts that escape the confines of box scores and gametime hours when uniforms are worn.

Sean Penn–style Pre-Game

Cameramen are often accustomed to inadvertent beatings during games. Players crash into the equipment pursuing foul balls, line drives ricochet off tripods, occasional obscene gestures are flipped their way. But 2005 was a year when television cameramen—especially the vulnerable species toting heavy equipment on their shoulders—were fair game for a moody pair of starters.

First it was Randy Johnson, freshly signed by the Yankees, pushing a cameraman's lens away from him while in full stride on a Manhattan sidewalk. His introduction to New Yorkers went like this: "Don't get in my face. Don't talk back to me, all right? Or you'll see what I'm like." It is no wonder, then, that Johnson's stay in the Bronx was a brief one. Then in late June, ex-Yankee Kenny Rogers made the Johnson incident look like a penny social. A week after he had injured his non-pitching hand punching water coolers in the Texas dugout, Rogers was trotting onto Ameriquest Field for a 4 p.m. pre-game warmup. When he spotted a cameraman from the local cable sports net, he said "I told you to get those cameras out of my face." He shoved the lens out of the way. When the cameras kept rolling, he calmly walked up to a second cameraman, grabbed his camera by the light fixture on the top, pulled it off, dropped it to the ground, and then kicked it. In the city where Abraham Zapruder heroically stood in Dealey Plaza on November 22, 1963 as a beacon of journalistic hope for all amateur lens-toters, here was a moody ballplayer threatening to do even more damage if the shutters kept clicking. The suddenly camera-less cameraman was injured by Rogers' invasive tactics and was stretchered away to a local hospital while "The Gambler" went ahead with his pre-game stretching. The lantern-jawed lefthander left an embarrassing public relations mess for Rangers brass to clean up over the next few days. General manager John Hart and owner Tom Hicks were apologetic and ashamed of Rogers' behavior, though manager Buck Showalter was strangely silent on the incident.

The forty-year-old Rogers, who had been boycotting the local media since Spring Training reports about his stalled contract negotiations, was charged with misdemeanor assault. His initial suspension by MLB was twenty games, with a fine of $50,000 as a side dish. The suspension was later reduced to thirteen games. Rogers apologized on July 6, 2005, and in March of 2006 he settled his case when he agreed to take anger management classes to reduce the class A misdemeanor assault charge to a class C misdemeanor, which did not include any jail time.

Though owner Hicks said "we'd like Kenny to retire as a Ranger," it did not come to pass. In 2006, the perpetual free agent signed with Detroit and keyed Jim Leyland's improbable run to the World Series. The Tigers dream ended with a Fall Classic loss to St. Louis. October in the Motor City did not pass without incident for Rogers. An autograph seeker had reportedly blocked the path of his vehicle on the way out of a parking lot. Police said the male fan beat on Rogers' car, which caused the Savannah, Georgia, native to spring from the driver's seat and yell at the man. He claimed Rogers grabbed him by the collar and had to be restrained, but several witnesses told police there was no contact.

Riverfront Welcome Wagon

So what if he wore white knit capes to his press conferences, curlers in his hair during pre-game warm-ups, threw his no-hitter while on LSD and liked to hit consecutive Reds batters in the first inning? Why couldn't Pirates pitcher Dock Ellis get a break?

Simply reporting for work with teammates Willie Stargell and Rennie Stennett on May 5, 1972, turned into a catastrophe of sorts, at least for Ellis' eyes. Though varying accounts of the incident have been published, the crux of the matter was that all three players were asked for identification as they showed up at Cincinnati's Riverfront Stadium player's entrance somewhat tardy and in a rush.

Ellis might or might not have had a woman with him, and it turns out the account claiming he was carrying a half-empty bottle of wine in a paper bag was a false observation by the rather overzealous security guard—just the type of person who sees half a bottle of wine as "half empty." The guard's name was David Hatter, and the Buccos saw him as quite mad on that day in May. With their clothing tight in the style of the '70s, the ballplayers were not keen on ruining their smooth lines with wallet bulges. The only ID they were toting were 1971 World Series rings with their names on them. Stargell also had a personal check on his person. After Pops and Stennett were granted entry, Hatter told Ellis his ring was not enough of an identity voucher. "I said 'Look, my clubhouse is over there and there's where I'm going,'" Ellis told the guard. Hatter then unholstered his pistol—one of three times he would do that during the incident—and ordered Ellis to put his hands against the wall. Ellis began cursing a blue streak, calling Hatter every name in the book. Seeing the gun, Stargell and Stennett ran for reinforcements from police, but returned quickly with half the Pirate roster running behind them, with manager Bill Virdon in the lead. Hatter had moved Ellis from the wall to the hood of a nearby car.

Seeing the cavalry on the way, the panicky Hatter unsheathed his can of mace and sprayed Ellis in the face with it. Hatter claimed he had kept his gun pointed to the ground and resorted to the mace because he saw Ellis clenching his fist as if preparing to throw a punch. The rebellious Ellis, who wrote in his autobiography that he had taken in a black female disc jockey the night before who had allegedly been beaten by white Cincinnati police officers, mocked his attacker, saying the macing was "beautiful" because it "makes me hate better." Hatter, who said he thought

Ellis was intoxicated, signed a complaint warrant against the twenty-seven-year-old pitcher. Ellis was charged with disorderly conduct.

Not since the 1970 winter ball season, when Boston's zany Bill Lee was jumped by a vengeful Ellie Rodriguez and two of his family members after getting off the team bus in Caguas, Puerto Rico, had a pitcher taken so much abuse on the doorstep of a ballpark. Lee had got the best of Rodriguez when Ellie, who had been a boxer on the side, charged the mound after being hit by a pitch in an earlier game.

When Pirates GM Joe Brown came out in full support of Ellis after the Friday night incident, the tables started to turn in Dock's favor. He contacted a lawyer about a possible counter suit, and a local television crew materialized as partial witnesses to the mace spraying as they were near the player's entrance when Dock got his special treatment. By Sunday, Ellis was back in Pittsburgh having his eyes examined. On July 10, a Cincinnati judge dismissed the charges after attorneys stated Hatter had settled the matter with Ellis out of court, asking the charge be dropped. Ellis said in his autobiography he later learned Hatter had died after suffering a blood clot from a broken arm caused by a motorcycle accident.

GM Brown, meanwhile, thought he could prevent future incidents by issuing official identification cards to the entire Pirates roster. Pittsburgh fans who knew Ellis, and many of the other rogues aboard the early '70s Bucco squads, knew better. Badges? *They don't need no steenking badges!!* A new World Series ring every year would have done the trick just fine, Joe.

Rock Star Rhubarb

Taking time out from his fight against Ticketmaster for ripping off fans attending his band's concerts, Eddie Vedder of Pearl Jam was getting loaded with White Sox pitcher Jack McDowell in a New Orleans punk rock/goth club called The Crystal. It was November of 1993, and "Black Jack" had just won the AL Cy Young Award. He was an acquaintance of Vedder because their wives were former roommates when Vedder was plying his trade in unknown musical acts in the classy city of San Diego way before Pearl Jam started selling millions of records.

The trouble was said to have started at the witching hour of 4:45 a.m. when, according to the AP reports, a guy walking past Vedder's "entourage" made a comment that offended Vedder. Who started it became the central question, as Vedder said it was this dude named James Gorman, and Gorman said Vedder was the attacker.

"He spit on me for no reason," Gorman said. "He grabbed me by my throat and started pushing me, and that's when things went wild." Witnesses noted Vedder was visibly intoxicated, and the singer had approached Gorman outside the club and verbally abused him. The argument escalated into pushing and shoving, and when bystanders tried to break them up, the spit started flying.

McDowell, who had an alt-rock band of his own, stepped in and grabbed Gorman from behind and the two fell down. McDowell suffered a gash on the back of his head and was taken to Charity Hospital for some early morning stitches to his scalp. Vedder, who has for years floated on the fringes of the game—hanging out at Wrigley Field, buying excessive amounts of memorabilia, jamming on stage with Red Sox GM Theo Epstein, etc.—was carted off to jail, charged with public intoxication (a New Orleans pastime) and fighting, both misdemeanors. Fellow Cubs fans would probably tack on extra charges for being caught hanging out with a Southside icon such as McDowell.

The last time McDowell got roughed up in such a fashion was when Blue Jays rookie Mark Whiten charged the mound against him at Comiskey Park in May of 1991. McDowell had just given up a home run to John Olerud, which gave Toronto the lead. The next batter was Whiten, and McDowell whipped a pitch behind the batter waist-high. Whiten came up the hill winding up a huge haymaker left that connected solidly with McDowell's face as benches and bullpens emptied onto the center of the infield. Umpire Joe Brinkman ejected both Black Jack and Whiten.

Super Joe/ Super Samaritan

Perhaps feeling a bit elevated after his first home run of the 1981 season, "Super" Joe Charboneau of the Cleveland Indians was part of a band of good Samaritans on the southside of Chicago. Hitting one of his four 1981 homers that night at Comiskey, Charboneau was probably feeling a bit invincible as he and his teammates were riding the bus back to their hotel, when they noticed a savage mugging going down on a sidewalk. They ordered the bus to stop and twenty-five Tribe players piled out onto the streets to break up the melee.

Charboneau, who was born on the outskirts of Chicago, was known for a variety of clubhouse eccentricities. The dyed hair was the most obvious, then moving down his 6-foot-2, 205-pound frame, the antics continued: he allegedly opened beer bottles with his eye socket and drank beer through his nose with a straw; did his own dental work with the help of whiskey and vise grips; ate cigarettes (on a $5 bet) and raw eggs still encased in their shells; removed his own tattoos with razors; and stitched his cuts on his forearms with fishing line. He was also stabbed in the ribs with a ballpoint pen by a fan at Spring Training, and hurt his back sliding head-first—also during Spring Training.

Oh yeah, he was the 1980 AL Rookie of the Year and the most fun thing to happen to Cleveland since lamprey eels were discovered in Lake Erie. He supposedly named his daughter "Dannon" because he liked that brand of yogurt. His son Tyson would grow up to hold a "senior piercer" position at a prominent Cleveland area piercing parlor. The family dog was named "Diarrhea." Charboneau had inspired a song "Go, Go Joe Charboneau!" that made some noise on local radio and had an infectious quality to it. So at least the sportswriters had the folklore copy flowing from the dreadful Indians franchise.

It was after a Monday night win over the White Sox on May 11, 1981, that the street mugging went down. It was three teens beating one victim with a club. "One of the guys said some things to Joe Charboneau and Joe decked him with one punch," a witness told the AP.

Super Joe might have saved the kid, but he couldn't save his Indians career come August. That's when he was demoted to AAA Charleston. The next season, 1982, would be his final one in the big leagues thanks to the bad back. His name would surface for "one-hit wonder" lists for years to come, and he did some minor league coaching and was a ballplayer extra in the movie *The Natural*.

All This Fightin' Makes Me Hungry

New York's true, unsung bouncers are the Greek waiters manning the twenty-four-hour diners throughout the city. After the clubs close, these men are assigned further babysitting of wasted patrons making ill-advised pit stops on their way home. It wasn't always club kids mixing it up in the booths among the insomniac limo drivers and other creatures of the New York night. Sometimes it was ballplayers as well—guys like David "Boomer" Wells.

Happy to return to the Yankees for the 2002 season after being traded to Toronto in the Roger Clemens deal in 1999, with a stop in Chicago added on for good measure, Wells was living on Manhattan's upper east side and enjoying the city's nightlife. Near his apartment was a classic twenty-four-hour New York diner called Gracie's Corner on 86th Street between First and Second Avenues.

On September 6, 2002, after twirling a complete-game five-hitter to beat Detroit at Yankee Stadium for his sixteenth win of the season, Wells was out partying with his personal trainer Scott Yeckenevich, who apparently was "off duty." They'd had dinner and went out to a few clubs, and Wells testified later he was not intoxicated (but had three or so tequilas along the way) when they entered Gracie's Corner around 5:30 a.m. It was the now-standard "I'll have an egg-white omelet" order for all those health-conscious workout fanatics who still find themselves visiting diners in the wee hours.

Police reports indicate twenty-seven-year-old Rocco Graziosa, a bartender from Yonkers, New York, entered the diner with a group of friends and started a conversation with Wells. In his autobiography *Perfect I'm Not*, Wells claimed the group made fun of his egg-white omelet order, telling him instead to order a cheeseburger "you big, fat fuck."

The 5-foot-6 Graziosa then went to a booth and sat down with his friends. Depending on whose side is believed as the truth, Graziosa claimed the 6-foot-4 Wells approached his booth and was upset that the group did not want to talk with him further. Wells claimed Graziosa had tried to join him and Yeckenevich in their booth, but was turned away. In any case, Graziosa sparked the incident by making a remark about Wells' deceased mother, whom he has memorialized in a tattoo on his chest. Wells approached Graziosa, who then wielded a butter knife as self defense. The pitcher claimed he was just walking past Graziosa's table when the bartender sucker punched him in the mouth and knocked him to the floor, with Wells striking his head on a table on the way down. Graziosa said Wells had leaned into their booth and was verbally menacing him as they exchanged insults about each other's mother. Yeckenevich rescued his client from escalating the argument into a full scale diner food fight, with extended fisticuffs and slaw throwing. He pushed Wells out of the diner and onto the sidewalk, where the bulky hurler called the police to have Graziosa arrested, especially after he saw the group high-fiving each other in celebratory fashion.

Transcripts of Wells' 911 calls got a few laughs, but what wasn't funny was Wells had two teeth seriously cracked by Graziosa. Wells insisted in his book that it was his sobriety at the late hour that kept him from returning fire and punishing Graziosa.

The next day at the stadium, Wells was excused from the team to have massive dental work done to fix his teeth. Graziosa, meanwhile, was charged with assault and menacing, and was convicted of misdemeanor assault in November. He also said he received many death threats from Yankee fans. Yankees brass was not happy with Wells being out on the town until 6:00 a.m., but no disciplinary action was deemed necessary. Wells went on to win the rest of his starts through September, despite razzing from his teammates about his very un-Wellsian encounter with the short guy in the diner. He finished with a 19-7 record and admitted in his book he must have been finally maturing by not punching back, breaking his hand, and getting suspended—things the old David Wells certainly would have done. In 2007, Wells, playing for his hometown San Diego Padres, was diagnosed with type II diabetes, forcing the rebellious pitcher to engage in a complete lifestyle overhaul.

Fistful of Troubles at the Pfister

If there was a baseball version of Stephen King's Overlook Hotel from his novel *The Shining*, then the Pfister Hotel in downtown Milwaukee would fit the bill. It opened in all its Victorian splendor in 1893, the dream of Milwaukee tanner Guido Pfister and his son Charles, in the east end of downtown Milwaukee. The lobby is a garish three-story affair with cherubs on the vaulted ceilings. For many years, the Pfister was the host hotel for MLB clubs in town to play the Brewers. So any patrons who were milling around the lobby in May of 1976 when the Baltimore Orioles arrived, got to see quite a sight. A midget was berating superstar Reggie Jackson about not wearing a tie when the team traveled. Closer inspection would have revealed it was in fact Orioles manager Earl Weaver getting in Jackson's face, jabbing his finger at him to go with his heated words. According to one of Reggie's many autobiographies, Reggie wanted to laugh but knew Earl was being serious in ripping his newly arrived outfielder in front of the whole team and those standing among the Richardsonian Romanesque opulence of the Pfister lobby. "I can't have you shitting in my face" was the Weaver quote that challenged Reggie's ability to keep a straight face. Several profanities later, the two grinned, shook hands, and the confrontation ended without physical violence.

Another newly arrived player had an interesting night at the Pfister in August of 1989. Outfielder Luis Polonia, who came over to the Yankees in the Rickey Henderson deal with Oakland the month before, was caught in an embarrassing situation in his room. A young female fan he'd brought back to the hotel from the ballpark turned out to be only fifteen years old. Her mother tracked her down via phone calls to her friends who were at the Yankees-Brewers game that night and saw the girl speaking to Polonia outside the team bus after the game at County Stadium.

When the mother called the hotel and could not track down her daughter, she called the police who were much more successful in finding her. The twenty-four-year-old Yankee was arrested on charges of second degree sexual assault, police said. He was freed on $5,000 bail. He told authorities he thought the girl was nineteen. Police said it was not clear if the girl had divulged her age to the Yankee outfielder. "According to people in the hotel, they say the girl looked like she was in her twenties, but her mother says fifteen," Yankees spokesman Arthur Richman told the AP in a bit of ham-fisted damage control. Stern disciplinarian Yankee manager Dallas Green was mildly aghast. "It's a shame to see that happen," Green said. "It's a personal thing. All you can do is warn people. You can't live their lives."

Polonia, who pleaded no contest to the charges, was found guilty in October and served sixty days in jail, during which he watched his previous team, the A's, play in the earthquake-stricken World Series against San Francisco. One report said Polonia kept his spirits up while behind bars knowing if the A's won the Series, he'd get a check for half a World Series share. During the 1990 season, the Yankees dealt Polonia to the Angels, but would see him back in non-prison pinstripes in the Bronx twice more before the Dominican speedster retired in 2001.

In September of 2000, a "Legends of County Stadium" news conference was held at the Pfister. Hall of Famer Warren Spahn, from the wayback glory days of the Milwaukee Braves, was asked for his take on why there are more fights in baseball these days than there were when he played in the 1950s. Spahn blamed it on the Latinos. The seventy-nine-year-old pitcher elaborated to stunned reporters: "When the Latins came to the game, they also brought their habits with them, so that now, we have people fighting with bats and charging the mound. The cultures are a lot different."

The event was part of a three-day celebration of the old Milwaukee ballpark that was in its final season of use before the opening of Miller Park. The Reds were in town for a three-game set, and there were a few Latino players who disagreed with Spahn. "The fights are about disrespect, whether the hitter disrespects the pitcher or vice versa," said Cincinnati shortstop Juan Castro of Mexico. "It doesn't matter if you're Latin or not." Reds catcher Benito Santiago said: "We don't need to be having comments made like that. It's something I don't agree with."

Among the players to duke it out at the Pfister were Rick Dempsey and Bill Sudakis of the 1974 New York Yankees. Though they fell short of catching the Orioles that season, the Yankees had closed out September with a 10-0 drubbing of the Tribe in Cleveland. The team flight to Milwaukee, usually just a few minutes in the air from Cleveland, was nightmarishly delayed, and by the time the Yankees arrived at the Pfister, it was well after midnight. Frustrations were running high, and many drinks had been consumed, observers said.

Sudakis, a utility player who did some DH duties for the '74 Yankees, was nicknamed "Suds" for reasons relating to his beer consumption. He also allegedly had threatened Lou Piniella with a hatchet during the 1974 campaign. Dempsey, serving as Munson's caddy, was a Tennessean from a theatrical family (who would later star in *Dempsey vs. Dykstra*). He was being needled by Suds as the exhausted players filed off the bus. By the time the two got to the revolving door at the Pfister entrance, they were trading blows. Some players already inside waiting for their room keys rushed out to break up the punchfest. Among those making a peacekeeping effort was Bobby Murcer, who quickly reached the bottom of the pile and had his finger stepped on and broken.

Manager Bill Virdon and Yankee GM Gabe Paul both offhandedly praised the incident as perhaps being good for the ball club. "Sometimes these things help you," Virdon told the AP. Paul's comments were a bit more embellished, invoking the spirit of the Gashouse Gang of 1930s St. Louis, a comparison perhaps a tad grandiose for Virdon's AL East charges. Especially when, without Murcer in the lineup, they lost to the Brewers the next day in extra innings, and the Orioles clinched the division.

Not to be outdone by a utility man and a backup catcher, two ham-and-eggers from the Pittsburgh Pirates bullpen squared off in the bar at the Pfister in May of 1998. When two Ohio boys get to drinking, often times the fists start flying and the whole thing turns into a shirtless scene from the movie *Gummo*. Such was the case for Pirates reliever Marc Wilkins, sporting the artsy "c" in his first name despite his Mansfield, Ohio, roots, and Jeff Tabaka of Barberton, Ohio. Perhaps they got in a dispute about which is the best bar in Athens, Ohio (The Union), or the quickest way to get to Bowling Green (don't go), or maybe their card game had indeed gone awry. In the end, their argument escalated to the point where Wilkins decked Tabaka, breaking his jaw and landing the former Expo on the disabled list. "We were both at fault. We were both arguing," Wilkins told the *Pittsburgh Post-Gazette*. "I'm sure if we hadn't been drinking, he wouldn't have come at me and I wouldn't have hit him."

Finally, no hotel saga is complete without a jewelry heist. In July 2004, Cubs pitcher Matt Clement and his family had $15,000 worth of jewelry pilfered from their room at the Pfister. That is a lot of bling for a white guy from Butler, Pennsylvania, to be toting, yes, but still—can't a Cubbie get some Cream City respect? Milwaukee police investigated and soon arrested a Pfister employee who was brought up on felony burglary charges by the Milwaukee County district attorney, who, like the sheriff and other law enforcement types, was kept quite busy by ballplayers through the years.

Chapter 18: ANGER MANAGEMENT

Occasionally some nitpicking dimwit sitting on a barstool will harp on the fact that pro baseball managers also wear the team uniform. No matter how old, overweight, gray, groggy, gout-ridden, or senile—the old dudes running the show suit up with the rest of the team. It is good camouflage for hiding from sign-stealers. It builds camaraderie if you are a reader of *Ranger Rick* magazine. They set the rules, make out the all-important line-up card, travel at the front of the bus and plane and are allowed (and encouraged) to resemble Wilfred Brimley on occasion.

Sometimes the managers get in the way. Insubordination ensues, causing, as Jessica Hahn used to say in her infomercial "headlines, scandal and controversy." Other times these role models, school principals, chaperones, and authority figures lose their own marbles and temper, and clash with each other, umpires, front office brass, fans, and opposing players. The locales of these disputes range from the limelight of the pitcher's mound conference, the cramped aisle of the team plane, the managerial office space in the bowels of the stadium, under the fluorescents of the clubhouse, or in the hotel bar or lobby. Often the explosion occurs in foul territory, or in a dugout runway, or a disjointed post-game press conference. As it says on the popular office coffee mug: "You don't have to be crazy to work here, but it helps."

The bottom line: When baseball managers sit on a dugout bench and cross their legs, sigh, rub their jaws and lift their caps to scratch their heads, they are miles above the status of suit-wearing brethren who stand behind a row of guys on skates, or crouch uncomfortably on a shiny hardwood floor amid uncomfortable folding chairs, or whatever it is those aliens with headsets and windbreakers are doing on the overcrowded sidelines of an NFL game. What follows is a Petri dish of managerial upheaval. Most incidents involve mutinous ballplayers attacking skippers, others involve manager-on-manager violence, or manager versus umpire, or skipper against fan. The vast number of Billy Martin incidents are covered in his own chapter.

There was one tasty General Manager vs. Player clash worth noting. It was July of 1978 in Montreal. Expos GM Charlie Fox was no stranger to diamond dukes. He was coaching third for the Giants when Marichal clubbed Roseboro back in '65 and—as Giants skipper—also fought Angels reserve catcher Jack Hiatt during '73 Spring Training. Fox stormed into the 'Spos clubhouse at Le Stade Olympique before a game against the Braves and started reading Montreal's Chris Speier the riot act because of his batting slump. He was especially peeved after seeing Speier take a called third strike with two men on base in a 3-1 loss to the Braves the night before.

Staff ace Steve Rogers, who was the Expos player rep and one of about eight players circulating near the Fox-Speiers discussion, stepped in on behalf of his infielder. "That's just the kind of thing we don't need in this clubhouse," Rogers reportedly told the fifty-six-year-old Fox. The pitcher then told the GM to vacate the premises. Fox did not obey, and instead went face-to-face with Rogers in a shouting match that included several verbal challenges on both sides. Rogers gave Fox a solid shove, and the fiesty GM hauled off and landed a solid left to the jaw of the twenty-eight-year-old Expos hurler and then left the room. That night against the Braves, Speier hit for the cycle. "There was a motivating factor tonight that I don't want to talk about," Speier said after the game as all parties clammed up about *C. Fox vs. S. Rogers*.

The next fight to be examined takes a violent page from the rite of Spring Training. No, this is not Jim Leyland and Barry Bonds barking in each other's faces during the Bucs Florida warmup to the 1991 campaign. This one went well beyond pre-game lip service to become one of the more notorious player-manager tiffs to go down around the Ides of March.

LENNY RANDLE vs. FRANK LUCCHESI
(TEXAS RANGERS)   (TEXAS RANGERS MANAGER)
March 28, 1977, Tinker Field, Minnesota Twins
Spring Training Facility, Orlando, Florida

Their names are forever linked, and even at first glance Lenny Randle and Frank Lucchesi are an extreme study in contrasts. Randle's street cred would impress Snoop Dogg. Leonard Shenoff Randle was born in Long Beach, California, in 1949, raised in Compton and starred in football and baseball at Arizona State University. He picked baseball when the Washington Senators took him in the first round of the draft. The 5-foot-10, 169-pound switch hitter learned how to bunt from Ted Williams, who was running the '71 Senators, a team that became the Texas Rangers in 1972. That made Randle "an original Ranger." He played seven different positions over five seasons with Texas. His trade to the New York Mets on April 26, 1977 had two major causes: his intense interest in starting as the Rangers second baseman, and his objection to an adjective his fifty-year-old manager Frank Lucchesi used to describe him in the press. Randle bounced around after doing well with the hapless Mets, and became famous for a stunt in Seattle where, as the Mariners third baseman inside the Kingdome, he got on his hands and knees and blew a slow-rolling ball hit by Kansas City's Amos Otis from fair territory into foul. A teammate on that same 1981 Seattle team was Rick Auerbach, the player the Mets sent to the Rangers in the 1977 trade. Randle is also in the history books as being at the plate at Shea Stadium on July 17, 1977 as the Mets entertained the Cubs. It was 9:34 p.m., and the lights went out—all over New York City—a night that became the famous "Summer of Sam" blackout. In 1978, he tripled off Tug McGraw in Philadelphia on the famous 4-2 count as everyone—including Randle, the umpire, his teammates—had a momentary memory lapse regarding ball four. McGraw said he knew it was ball four, but threw the next pitch anyway, quickly wishing he hadn't. At age forty-six, Randle, a yoga practitioner with some martial arts training, fluent in Italian and Spanish, had a four-day stint as a replacement player during the MLB lockout in March of 1995. He was cut because his defensive skills were said to be lacking.

Randle found success winning a batting title in the Italian baseball league after retiring from MLB service in 1982. He played four seasons in

Italy and bought a home near Bologna. He also tried his hand at stand-up comedy during his retirement. As of this writing, Randle was running baseball instruction schools on the west coast.

Frank Joseph Lucchesi was born in San Francisco in 1927 and by age twenty-three was managing in the minor leagues. He would spend nineteen seasons at the helm of various backwater franchises, a hod carrier riding the famed buses and amassing more than one thousand six hundred wins. In 1954, while at the helm of the Pine Bluff Judges in Pine Bluff, Arkansas, Lucchesi had to have surgery to relieve a blood clot in his brain. His appearance was that of any extra from any given movie about Italian-American organized crime.

In 1970, the Phillies gave Lucchesi his first Big League managerial post. He managed three seasons there before yielding to general manager Paul Owens a few weeks into the 1972 season. Lucchesi managed Texas from halfway through the 1975 season through the beginning of the 1977 campaign. At age sixty, Lucchesi would take his last MLB managerial post when he served as an interim skipper for the Chicago Cubs after Gene Michael was fired. Lucchesi began the 1975 season as Billy Martin's third base coach with the Rangers. When Martin repeatedly clashed with the front office, suspecting Lucchesi was talking to the brass behind his back, Billy was fired and Lucchesi was handed the job and maintained a 35-32 record with the team. Randle, who was on the '75 Rangers roster, was a big fan of Martin's leadership. Randle would later refer to Martin as his "godfather." When Lucchesi took over, Randle's problems with his manager began to simmer, and would continue to do so throughout the 1976 season, when Lucchesi's Rangers ended up tied for fourth in the AL West with Randle batting .224 as the starting second baseman.

When Randle showed up for Spring Training in 1977, he was told he would be competing for the starting second base job with Bump Wills. Lucchesi then proceeded to spend early March giving Wills the majority of the starts at second base, perpetuating a Spring Training myth annually foisted on players when they are told there will be "competition" for jobs. Most of the time, the club has already decided who is starting where, so the "competition" is often farcical and therefore psychologically taxing on the odd man out.

On March 24, reports indicated Randle was fed up with the situation. Lucchesi had praised him for his hard work in camp, but then announced Wills had won the second base job. Randle ran into the Texas clubhouse to pack two duffle bags with every intention of leaving the Rangers. Teammates Mike Hargrove and Gaylord Perry reportedly intercepted Randle and talked him out of quitting. Reports also indicated Lucchesi expressed disappointment in Hargrove and Perry's actions, wanting instead for Randle to quit. That's when Lucchesi told reporters (in a quote that has several dozen interpretations floating around): "I'm tired of these punks saying play me or trade me. Anyone who makes $80,000 a year and gripes and moans all spring is not going to get a tear out of me."

On March 28, the Rangers were in Orlando to play the Twins. Pregame activities were in full swing at Tinker Field, a baseball diamond sitting in the shadow of the Citrus Bowl football stadium in central Orlando. Lucchesi and the twenty-eight-year-old Randle met behind the batting cage and Randle reportedly requested he and his manager talk about Lucchesi's comments. Minutes later, Randle took a step back and struck the 5-foot-8, 180-pound Lucchesi in the face with his fist, hitting his manager several more times as he fell to the ground. A Rangers spokesperson said Lucchesi didn't "remember a thing after he was hit the first time." Randle reportedly continued the beating of his manager while he was on the ground. Horrified teammates, led by Bert Campaneris and Jim Fregosi, rushed to get Randle off of Lucchesi. The manager was bleeding from a lacerated lip and suffered a broken cheekbone in three places, two broken ribs, a concussion and back injuries. He was hospitalized for five days and his cheekbone required surgery. Lucchesi had said he was ambushed with his hands in his pockets. Randle, whom after the beating jogged to the outfield to run wind sprints as if nothing had happened, denied the claim. Randle reportedly wanted to apologize in the days after the assault, but Lucchesi was not receptive to the idea. "It's one of the worst things I've ever witnessed," Rangers outfielder Ken Henderson told the press. "No way I'm going to play on the same field with him again."

Rangers general manager Dan O'Brien suspended Randle thirty days without pay, which would be roughly $13,000 in salary. In addition, Randle was fined $1,000 on a battery conviction and $10,000 by the team.

Texas sportswriters were especially vigilant about Lucchesi's use of language when he called Randle a "punk." Though "punk" was a musical genre coming to the fore in England and New York City at the time, the southern writers emphasized it was a derogatory prison term especially offensive to blacks. Lucchesi had not apologized to Randle up to that point, and Randle reportedly had joked with teammates about being called a "punk." There was also a report he discussed the attack before-hand, asking the advice of teammate Bert Blyleven.

On April 27, just a few days before his thirty-day suspension was to end, Randle was traded to the Mets for Auerbach. Lucchesi would be fired at mid-season and the Rangers went through an infamous managerial merry-go-round. Eddie Stanky was hired but quit after one game in Minnesota. Connie Ryan took over as interim manager, but did not want to step up as full-time skipper. Harmon Killebrew reportedly turned down the offer, and on June 27, Billy Hunter stepped in to guide the Rangers to a second place AL West finish at 94-68, eight games back of the juggernaut Royals.

In his relatively brief managerial career, Lucchesi did rack up a few suspensions. In 1976, his vehement disagreement with umpire Rich Garcia over balls and strikes led to a three-game punishment toward the end of that season. In his abbreviated stint with the Cubs, Lucchesi was suspended two games for bumping umpire "Cowboy" Joe West in St. Louis after a strike call on Andre Dawson.

While serving as Texas third base coach in August of 1974, Lucchesi sparked a near brawl when he menaced the Milwaukee dugout at Arlington Stadium. Apparently he didn't like the commentary from the bench while trainers were tending to a Milwaukee player injured by a sliding Mike Hargrove. Lucchesi ended up in a shoving match with Brewers outfielder Ken Berry.

Lucchesi filed a civil suit seeking damages for his injuries and continued pain from the Randle beat-down. In December of 1978, Randle and Lucchesi settled out of court in Orlando, with the ballplayer reportedly surrendering $25,000 to the manager.

Both parties were emotional at a press conference after the settlement. "I hope never again does something like this happen in baseball," Lucchesi told the AP. "I hope he has ten years of good luck in the big leagues." Randle insisted on a public handshake, saying "Shake, and let's both have our tears."

During testimony the day before, Lucchesi said he did not intend to apply the offensive and possibly racist term "punk" to Randle. The next morning, before court reconvened, the "amicable" settlement was announced but not fully disclosed. Billy Martin was among the parties waiting to testify, showing up in support of Randle and professing that Lucchesi had taken the Texas managerial job from him. Other reports, including one Martin biography, listed the Reverend Jesse Jackson, Hank

Aaron, and Curt Flood as among the other parties who were slated to testify on Randle's behalf.

In March of 2006, Randle was the subject of a feature story in a Dallas newspaper. He told the reporter he had no comment on the beating he administered to Lucchesi back in '77. Randle and his former manager/punching bag appeared at a 1993 Texas Rangers reunion game, but Lucchesi was reluctant to completely mend fences with Randle.

LOU PINIELLA vs. ROB DIBBLE
(CINCINNATI REDS MANAGER) (CINCINNATI REDS)
Sept. 17, 1992, Riverfront Stadium, Cincinnati, Ohio

The blurry locker-room footage tells the tale of two raven-haired Reds using manly skills to bridge the communication gap between manager and closer. Throw into this mix an alert press corps, and an otherwise dull milieu is suddenly spiced up by the unfolding of a *Rashomon*-style internal feud. The Reds were not going to catch the Braves in the old NL West. The magic of 1990 was long gone, and by early October, Piniella would hand in his resignation as manager of the Cincinnati ball club.

In March of 1991 at the Astros Spring Training site in Kissimmee, Florida, I remember seeing Reds prospect Reggie Jefferson jogging slowly past a batting cage. Inside, the sound of baseballs being crushed by Louisville Slugger wood echoed especially loud. The volume was high enough that he stopped in his tracks and rushed to the side of the cage to see who was hitting. Curious myself, I followed him. Was it Chris Sabo? Eric Davis? Hal Morris? When we leaned against the mesh siding of the cage to get a glimpse, we saw manager Lou Piniella swinging a bat like he was twenty-five years old and ready to take on Pudge Fisk. He was wearing a dimestore nylon mesh Reds cap with an adjustable strap, but that didn't matter. The man was hitting frozen ropes against a pitching machine that looked to be cranked up to the high nineties. He began to sweat through his windbreaker as rain fell outside the cage, surely delaying the afternoon exhibition. That only made him hit more, and hit harder. By the time he was finished, there was applause from several Reds minor leaguers who had gathered with slack jaws as Sweet Lou swung away. It was an inspiring sight. He had been alone, and after his fifteen-minute session, he had a crowd and had certainly communicated a message of sorts. *I can still do this. I mastered this game, you youngsters have yet to do so.* Heed my word. Observe. Learn it. Or, as Leo Durocher put it in the closing pages of his autobiography: "By my rules, the manager is the boss, and you respect him and you play like hell for him." So it was hard not to root for Piniella when he ran from his office in Riverfront Stadium into the locker room and tackled Rob Dibble and the two wrestled around awkwardly in their underclothes.

During the dog days of the 1991 campaign, Piniella was the key peace-maker in a Reds dugout tiff between pitcher Jose Rijo and third baseman Sabo, who had just committed a costly error that helped Cincinnati lose yet another game. It was during a dismal 10-25 streak that dropped the de-fending World Champions five games under .500. "Go fight the other team, don't fight among yourselves," Piniella told his players.

The fuse for *Piniella vs. Dibble* was lit the night before, when Piniella thought Dibble had trouble getting loose in the bullpen. Somehow, the communications model between closer and manager broke down. Piniella thought, via information from his staff, that Dibble's shoulder was bothering him. So with a one-run lead in the ninth inning, Sweet Lou called on Steve Foster to close the game for his first Major League save. This did not sit well with Dibble. Reporters dutifully found him in the clubhouse after the game, and Rob was quick to denounce his manager, referring to him with an obscenity and reiterating he did not have any shoulder problems.

The pack of writers, led by Hal McCoy of the *Dayton Daily News*, then shuffled to Piniella's office and informed him of Dibble's barbed comments. Preferring a face-to-face, Piniella arose and marched past the writers and headed straight for Dibble at his locker. The rest was a beefy blur. Dibble called Piniella a liar. Piniella then uttered the mysterious line that could have come from John Goodman's Mad Man Mundt character in the film *Barton Fink*: "You don't want to be treated like a man!" This was followed by the pair storyboarding their own wrestling picture right there on the clubhouse floor for a half-minute or so before nearby team-mates separated them.

The reporters were then booted from the clubhouse while the Reds minded their dirty laundry. When the doors reopened, "no comment" hors d'oeuvres were being served. The real story wasn't Piniella losing his temper again, it was Piniella's tantrum not involving the umpires, whom he was growing estranged from with each passing ballgame he managed. His reputation as an umpire-baiter dates to his present day managerial duties. Just a year before, he riled the umpires' union to the point where Gary Darling filed a $5 million suit after Piniella made claims Darling was biased against the Reds. His hat-kicking and plate dusting days in Seattle were still ahead. His days of being tossed to the ground by umpire Durwood Merrill were way behind. As expected, as the Reds pursued the Braves down the stretch in '92, their frustrations meant Sweet Lou did a fair amount of damage to Marge Schott's dugout water coolers.

The clubhouse combat left no lingering malaise as Dibble was back as closer the next night against San Diego, notching his twenty-first save. He'd finish with twenty-five on the season. An AP report summing up the flamethrowing reliever's lengthy rap sheet pointed out rather banefully: "It was Dibble's first altercation with someone on his own team."

Piniella vs. Dibble was certainly not as violent as *Randle vs. Lucchesi*, but it did mark a rare instance when the manager starts the action. Going back to 1942, shortstop Arky Vaughan threw his Dodgers uniform at his manager Durocher, and the two decided to square off under the Ebbets Field stands. As Brooklyn's skipper, Durocher also brawled with the Giants Carl Furillo in September of 1953 and as player/manager for the Dodgers tangled with Mickey Owen of the Cardinals. Of course, as a player with St. Louis, he famously fought Brooklyn manager Casey Stengel at Ebbets Field in May of 1936. (There was no more bizarre Durocher moment than the time in July of 1970 as manager of the Cubs when he got into a shouting match at the plate with Pirates pitcher Dock Ellis, who just one month earlier had pitched a no-hitter on LSD against San Diego. Both dugouts emptied and players surrounded the twenty-five-year-old streetwise, take-no-prisoners pitcher and the sixty-four-year-old tough guy who used to hang with George Raft. To add to the generation gap theme, the pitching matchup that Sunday afternoon at Wrigley Field was Ellis against Chicago's Ferguson Jenkins, who ten years later with the Texas Rangers would be arrested at the Toronto airport for possession of cocaine, marijuana, *and* hashish.)

Piniella knew he was a lame duck under Marge Schott's ownership situation in 1992. Sweet Lou was bound for a solid ten-year run managing the Seattle Mariners. Schott demanded apologies from Piniella and Dibble after their September scuffle, but there were no St. Bernard dogs,

Nazi armbands, vodka, cigarettes, or gas-guzzling automobiles involved in the matter. And someone said Cincinnati was a dull place? Read on.

PETE ROSE vs. DAVE PALLONE
(CINCINNATI REDS MANAGER)   (MLB UMPIRE)
April 30, 1988, Riverfront Stadium, Cincinnati, Ohio

Somewhere in the Queen City, perhaps in the Clifton section (or in a hotel lounge near the airport—which is in Kentucky, don't ask), there's probably a stand-up comedian asking his audience: "Didja hear the one about the redneck gambler with the most hits of all time and the gay umpire?"Any physical contact between umpires and other uniformed MLB players is treated like a fight, according to the rulebook caste system. The protected men in blue are also immune to public disclosure of any punishments for their misdeeds, according to league officials.

Spring fever was setting in on a Saturday night in Cincinnati. The Reds and Mets—the two franchises that gave the game *Rose vs. Harrelson* and *E. Davis vs. Knight*—were locked in a close game. Many of the 33,463 on hand along the Ohio River were large groups of local students being rewarded for their high GPAs with a spot in the cheap seats at Riverfront.

In the seventh inning, frustrated Reds starter Tom Browning was called for a balk by home plate umpire Eric Gregg. This allowed Mookie Wilson, who had just tripled, to score. Browning, who had hit Gary Carter with a pitch in the sixth, then proceeded to plunk batter Tim Teufel. Words were exchanged and Darryl Strawberry charged from the Mets dugout to mete justice upon the curly head of Browning. The Reds pitcher and Mets outfielder were both ejected.

The crowd then enjoyed the thrill of a Reds three-run rally to tie the game 5-5. In the ninth inning, the Mets were threatening. Howard Johnson was on second base with two outs. Wilson was batting against Reds closer John Franco (a future Mets captain). He hit a grounder to shortstop Barry Larkin who made an unsteady throw over to Nick Esasky at first base, pulling him slightly off the bag. With Johnson rounding third base and the Reds waiting to see if they had the third out, umpire Dave

Pallone hesitated in making his call before finally ruling Wilson safe at first. Johnson scampered home with the go-ahead run as hell broke loose in Hamilton County. Reds manager Pete Rose stormed out of the dugout to confront Pallone. Wild gesturing ensued. Pallone, a non-union umpire who was a replacement umpire during a union work stoppage in 1979, had a history of feuding with former Reds shortstop Dave Concepcion. He admitted to purposely blocking the shortstop's view of the plate while in the field, and calling him out on strikes, then ejecting Concepcion on a pitch he later admitted he "missed." Instead of walking away from the livid Rose, Pallone made some gestures of his own to demonstrate how Larkin's throw pulled Esasky off the bag. In the process, his finger accidentally poked Rose just beneath his eye. The incensed Charlie Hustle blew his top and shoved Pallone twice. Rose was of course heaved from the game and the two were separated. Meanwhile, the Riverfront crowd used the field as a collective Dumpster for their rage. Everything was thrown onto the green carpet—cups, cigarette lighters, portable radios. In the Reds broadcasting booth, announcers Joe Nuxhall and Marty Brennaman denounced Pallone and his call on the air, barely audible over the roar of the bloodthirsty crowd. One Reds blogger later described the student sections as being in a "geek frenzy" during the sit-down riot. It took the grounds crew fifteen minutes to clean up the joint. When play resumed, Pallone was greeted with a fresh hail of debris. Crew chief John Kibler, at least feigning a slight fear for his scab colleague's safety, sent Pallone to the umpire's clubhouse for the final four outs of the game.

The punishment handed down from commissioner A. Bartlett Giamatti was harsh. Times had changed since August of 1981 when Phillies manager Dallas Green bumped umpire Steve Fields, knocked his cap off, then kicked the headwear as part of his disagreement over a force play at second base. Green was suspended five games and fined $1,000 by NL president Chub Feeney, a punishment accompanied by standard hemming and hawing from the oversized skipper whose cap never quite fit his head.

Rose got thirty days and $10,000, a sentence that would spark a lasting ill will between baseball's all-time hits leader and the brainy MLB commissioner.

Both participants in *Rose vs. Pallone* would meet rather humiliating, public demises. Pallone would go first. At age thirty-six, he resigned "under pressure of being fired" in September of 1988. The commissioner's office called it a leave of absence. Pallone's name had been linked with a

1987 sex scandal involving young boys in Saratoga Springs, New York, though Pallone was never charged after the case was investigated. He had reportedly run up gambling debts after losing wagers made on sports other than baseball. He had been found innocent on a 1983 drunk driving charge, and in 1985 MLB security honchos were concerned about reports of Pallone picking up men at a gay bar in St. Louis. Five years after that probe, his book came out, and so did he. In 1990, Pallone authored *Behind the Mask: My Double Life in Baseball*, which outlined his struggles as a homosexual entrenched in the national pastime and how he was ostracized for being a replacement umpire in 1979. As of 2007, Pallone was working as a motivational speaker and was using videotape of his rough encounter with Rose as part of his presentation.

In August of 1989, Giamatti permanently banned Rose from baseball for his involvement with gambling. Tell-all books, All-Star game appearances, ambush TV interviews, and vitriolic debates about Rose's reinstatement and Hall of Fame worthiness would become standard media content throughout the next decade. When Pallone announced his resignation, Rose played the role of one gambler supporting another. He told the AP "I have nothing to say against Dave Pallone. He made a bad call, but to be honest, I do not think he's a bad umpire." Rose was also convinced their heated meeting at Riverfront Stadium in April of 1988 had little to do with Pallone's forced dismissal.

EARL WEAVER vs. TERRY COONEY
(BALTIMORE ORIOLES MANAGER)   (MLB UMPIRE)
July 17, 1982, Memorial Stadium, Baltimore, Maryland

If Baltimore's legendary schlock filmmaker John Waters ever decides to do a baseball movie, he need only look as far as his backyard to find a prototypical local character to cast as the irascible, hot-tempered short guy manager. Earl Weaver could easily have given Edie the Egg Lady or Divine a run for their money when it came to distasteful tantrums and public rants. Given the right pair of cha-cha heels, Weaver could have been an underground cinema star in addition to a Hall of Fame manager. Weaver began his managing career in the mid-1950s in the Orioles system. In seventeen seasons running the big club, he won one World Series (1970) and was ejected from games ninety-eight times, including one banishment during the 1969 World Series. Weaver elevated arguing with the umpires to mythical levels. His animated affronts often upstaged his players and were a source of endless enjoyment for Baltimore fans. Listed generously in media guides as 5-foot-7, 175 pounds, Weaver often had to be creative to get into the faces of taller umpires to make his point—the bill of his seemingly oversized Orioles cap was many times considered a lethal weapon.

On Saturday, July 17, 1982, the Orioles were hosting the Seattle Mariners for an evening contest at Memorial Stadium. There were 21,082 souls on hand to witness some Weaver pyrotechnics in the bottom of the fourth. With his team up 4-3, Eddie Murray grounded into the always-interesting 3-6-1 double play, which is a grounder to the first baseman who throws to short for the out at second, with the shortstop relaying the throw back to first, where the pitcher is covering the bag. First base umpire Terry Cooney rung up Murray as part of the twin-killing. Weaver disagreed with the call and ran onto the field to argue his case.

The night before, Cooney ejected Weaver from the game when he took the glove and ball from his pitcher Dennis Martinez to demonstrate on the mound what a balk looks like. This time around, Weaver was gesticulating his way around Cooney's face when his right hand touched the umpire's face in what many writers described as a "slap-punch." Weaver was ejected, along with Orioles leftfielder Gary Roenicke, who had been objecting to the call loudly from the bench, as was coach Ralph Rowe.

Weaver said his hand striking Cooney was accidental, of course, and American League president Lee MacPhail noted there was no malicious intent. But an umpire had in fact been hit in the face, so the guilty party named Earl Weaver was suspended seven games and fined $2,000. It was the fifth suspension of Weaver's career.

Weaver was creative in the postmortem of the incident. He released a statement that was a spoof of his own "Manager's Corner" pre-game radio show and referred to his suspension as a vacation. Cooney and Weaver met to discuss the incident and both came away with a mutual respect for each other. Most of Weaver's beef was with MacPhail, as usual. Cooney, who had been umpiring since 1975, noted how he'd never had a problem with Weaver until the series with Seattle when the arbiter tossed the manager from the game on consecutive evenings. In fact, the Cooney incident was Weaver's third ejection in five games. Having announced earlier in the year he was stepping down from his managerial post after the 1982 campaign, Weaver's lame-duck tenure was getting wackier as the months dragged on.

JIM RICE vs. JOE MORGAN
(BOSTON RED SOX) (BOSTON RED SOX MANAGER)
July 20, 1988, Fenway Park, Boston, Massachusetts

Known more for its symbolism than actual fisticuffs, this dispute involved a fading superstar, an interim manager, pinch hitter Spike Owen, and, given the media frenzy surrounding the franchise, years of debate about Boston's inability to embrace black athletes.

Joe Morgan was just slightly more than a week into his assignment as interim manager of the Red Sox. He had replaced John McNamara, who couldn't seem to inspire the Red Sox since their 1986 World Series loss to the Mets. Morgan was a snowplow-driving New Englander and therefore a fan favorite at Fenway. As he turned the 1988 Red Sox around, their winning ways became known as "Morgan Magic." But Jim Rice, used mostly as a DH in his penultimate year in a Boston uniform, considered Morgan anything but a magician. On the night of July 20, 1988, with Boston up 5-4 on the Twins, the Red Sox put a runner aboard in the eighth inning with Rice on deck. As he was stepping into the batter's box, Rice was called back to the dugout and Spike Owen, a light-hitting reserve infielder, was sent up to pinch-hit in what Morgan saw as a sacrifice bunt situation.

Rice, who wore only a Boston uniform in his nineteen-year Big League career during which he put up Hall of Fame–type numbers, expressed his displeasure when he stepped down into the cramped Fenway dugout. An unwritten rule had been violated, the one that says managers should not embarrass veterans by pulling them for pinch hitters while they are at or near the plate, or yank them from the field for defensive replacements.

The 1978 AL MVP yelled at Morgan and tried to get him to come into the dugout runway. When the fifty-seven-year-old manager did not budge, Rice jumped on him, grabbed him by the shoulders and dragged him down the stairs into the tunnel for a shoving match. Teammates intervened before real punches were thrown, Marty Barrett told the AP. Television cameras did catch most of the tussle, as well as the highly quotable old school line Morgan issued to Rice: "I'm the manager of this nine!" Meanwhile, Owen successfully sacrificed the runner to second in a game the Red Sox would win in ten innings.

By the time the Red Sox issued punishment to the thirty-five-year-old Rice, Morgan's "interim" label had been dropped, and general manager Lou Gorman told the skipper he would guide the Red Sox the rest of the way. There was speculation *Rice vs. Morgan* was the result of a communication breakdown—many in the dugout said they knew Owen was going to pinch-hit for Rice—Morgan said he had told Rice beforehand. The manager was supported by the front office and most of his players, so he had no hard feelings. "I'm not a guy who holds grudges," Morgan told the press. "I don't expect an apology because I don't believe in apologies."

Rice was suspended by the club for three days, costing him $30,000 in salary. He stormed out of a meeting with Gorman when the news of the suspension was delivered.

"I have great respect for Jim Rice, but you can't have anybody physically intimidate or question a manager's authority," Gorman said.

Boston sports columnists had a field day with the latest Rice incident, calling for harsher punishments. Rice was not known for an amicable relationship with Boston's press, and the star's rather unceremonious dismissal from the club at the end of the following season spoke volumes to the antagonism that existed between Rice, the club and Boston's press corps. Others saw *Rice vs. Morgan* as another chapter in the tense race relations within the team's culture. Not surprisingly, not long before "Cowboy Up" and "The Idiots," the icy Boston clubhouse for many decades was described as "Nine players, nine cabs."

TERRY BEVINGTON vs. PHIL GARNER
(CHICAGO WHITE SOX MANAGER) (MILWAUKEE BREWERS MANAGER)
July 22, 1995, Comiskey Park, Chicago, Illinois

As manager-on-manager clashes go, this one was more involved than the Tony LaRussa-Buck Showalter pre-game shoving match at Yankee Stadium, and a little more rich and colorful than the 1967 Dave Bristol-Billy Hitchcock post-game duke-out in Cincinnati. Though Hitchcock's taking on tough Ralph Houk during a larger Orioles-Yankees donnybrook in 1962 is certainly worth noting (see Chapter 13), *Bevington vs. Garner* had a certain sideshow quality to it as backyard brawl adrenaline overtook Midwestern stoicism in a rather forced regional rivalry.

In Terry Bevington's two and a half seasons (1995–97) managing the White Sox, the Akron, Ohio, native won very few popularity contests. His management style bristled with ballplayers and sportswriters, and he was made famous by the time he made a trip to the mound and called for a reliever from the bullpen—a routine gesture—except no one had been warming up in the bullpen.

We last encountered Bevington as one of the first mates in trying to help a hapless Robin Ventura after his foolish charge of Nolan Ryan's mound in 1993 (see Chapter 2).

Phil Garner, a Tennessee native with the nickname "Scrap Iron" from his playing days in the late 1970s, had a brewery-sized chip on his shoulder when it came to Chicago. The Milwaukee skipper felt there was no justification for the White Sox to look down on their Wisconsin neighbors. He seemed especially determined to stoke the competitive fires when the Brewers played the White Sox. Garner went so far as to challenge White Sox broadcasters Hawk Harrelson and Tom Paciorek to a fight. In 1994, Garner was accused of harboring a similar regional hatred for the Cubs, because Willie Wilson had sparked a Spring Training brawl in Arizona. He and Milwaukee pitcher Ricky Bones bickered back and forth over a previous exhibition game HBP, a subsequent Wilson triple, and the aging speedster releasing his bat toward Bones after swinging at a pitch. After the sun-baked benches cleared in Chandler, Arizona, Wilson told the *Chicago Daily Herald*: "Ever since Garner became the manager there, they've become the dirtiest team in baseball. This shit has got to stop."

Down the road, Garner was at the helm of the Detroit Tigers during the massive *Palmer vs. Parque* assault (see Chapter 3) and while helming the Houston Astros in 2005, managed against Ozzie Guillen and the White Sox in the World Series. It was Guillen who helped to spark the incident of July 22, 1995, on a Saturday night on the Southside of Chicago. Just a month earlier, these teams had clashed when White Sox reliever Rob Dibble went headhunting against the Brewers.

Guillen got things going in the seventh inning. The White Sox were up 3-2. Guillen stole third base, and when third baseman Jeff Cirillo took the throw, he fell backwards onto the runner. Guillen pushed him off and of course the two exchanged unpleasantries. Garner and a few of his players left the dugout and walked toward third base where they were soon greeted by Bevington. Milwaukee first baseman Kevin Seitzer and Garner reportedly unleashed some strong profanities toward Bevington, and as Garner got closer to him, Bevington—perhaps recalling his eyewitness role in *Ventura vs. Ryan*—embraced the Brewers skipper and put him in a headlock. It was a preventative move, he said later. At 6-foot-2, 190, Bevington held sway over the scrappy Garner (5-foot-10, 177) and they danced around and wrestled a bit, until Chicago's dugout finally emptied and the players were able to keep their managers from exchanging any actual blows. "I could have hit him, but I wasn't out there to fight," Bevington told the *Chicago Daily Herald*. "But I wasn't going to get beat up."

The league office issued a statement calling the altercation a "painful setback to baseball." AL president Gene Budig suspended both managers four games each. Garner began serving his immediately, saying he didn't want an appeal hanging over his club and that he "respected" the authority of the league office. Garner, a three-time All-Star in sixteen big league seasons who hit .500 in the 1979 World Series win for Pittsburgh, was determined to move on from the Bevington battle. Perhaps he wanted to get back to scheming new ways to jack up the Milwaukee-Chicago rivalry. Bevington, whose playing career consisted of seven lackluster minor league seasons in the Yankees' and Brewers' organizations, saw Garner's lack of appeal as an admission of guilt. Bevington also stuck to his own guns, claiming innocence via self-defense and was insistent on appealing the suspension.

Almost two weeks later, with Budig ready to hear his appeal, Bevington withdrew it and began serving his four-game sentence. He said he backed down after "talking to a couple of people I respect," who told him Budig would not back down from the four-game suspension. Among those respected people was White Sox GM Ron Schueler, who would fire Bevington two days after the 1997 season and put an end to another painful public relations era on the Southside.

TRACY JONES vs. BOB SEBRA
(SEATTLE MARINERS)   (MILWAUKEE BREWERS)
June 30, 1990, Kingdome, Seattle, Washington

The protagonists were two unknowns, and rightly so because this half-hour brawl is better known as the night Brewers manager Tom Treble-horn blew his stack. The last day of June in 1990 also marked the final Major League appearance for Milwaukee reliever Bob Sebra. He was sent down to Denver after this game with a five-game suspension he would never serve. The Ridgewood, New Jersey, native ended his big league career with a 15-29 record, including his 6-15 season with the 1987 Expos. His middle name was "Bush"—not the best name to be floating around on the birth certificate of a professional ballplayer.

Sebra was mopping up a tough game against Seattle—the Mariners had taken a 4-0 lead before the Brewers could record one out. Jeffrey Leonard hit two homers and gainfully employed his "one flap down" home run trot, further incensing Milwaukee. His second homer came leading off the eighth against Sebra. Edgar Martinez, hit by a Teddy Higuera pitch back in the first, boomed a double off the center field wall. Seattle's firebrand Tracy Jones was the next batter, and Sebra hit him under the elbow. Jones, a 6-foot-3, 220-pound wannabe journey-man who came up with the Reds in 1986, bolted for the mound and was met halfway by Sebra as the benches spilled onto the faded lime green Kingdome turf. Jones thrashed around trying to get to Sebra, and before long Treblehorn was being pursued with furious intent by Seattle reserve infielder Jeff Schaefer. They tore at each other viciously, whirling through several side battles and a dancing Edgar Martinez, who seemed to stay on the fringe of the human tornadoes. (Edgar would make up for it with his furious mound charge against Anaheim's Lou Pote in 2001.)

Schaefer was seen kicking at Treblehorn, who blended in with the swirl of active players thanks to his unmanager-like skinny physique. Mil-waukee catcher B. J. Surhoff seemed determined to free his manager from the clutches of the demon-infested Schaefer. Eventually, Seattle coach Bill Plummer got between Treblehorn and Schaefer, but the disturbed Mariner kept wailing away at his own man. Mariners reserve catcher Matt

Sinatro then offered his services to help halt Schaefer's friendly fire, but he was cut off at the pass by Milwaukee's Dale Sveum, who was attacking Schaefer from behind as Sinatro was conveniently absorbed into another tugging pile.

When the chaos finally died down under the hideous indoor lighting, Treblehorn was escorted back to the Milwaukee dugout by a young Gary Sheffield sporting an M.C. Hammer era flattop haircut. Sheffield looked fine, despite having tangled with half the Seattle bullpen. Treblehorn looked like he'd been in a bus accident or caught in some type of local coffee stampede. His jersey was torn completely open, as was his undershirt, and the long-sleeve jacket he was inexplicably wearing beneath his road grays. He had a contusion on his right temple and was dabbing his mouth to check for blood. Schaefer had, at one point, body slammed the Milwaukee manager. Apparently, that was not enough. In an astounding oversight, Schaefer was not ejected until later in the inning. After play had resumed, he was in the on-deck circle and was mouthing off to the umpires, who had heard enough and tossed him as he stood among the lead donuts and pine tar rags. Strange, frontier justice in the Pacific Northwest.

Seattle manager Jim Lefevbre, who looked downright lazy in comparison to Treblehorn, said the Milwaukee skipper was guilty of instigating and then prolonging the carnage under the domed roof.

Treblehorn, a former high school social sciences teacher, was in his next to last year managing the Brewers. He'd taken over in 1986 and made a few strides with the organization. He would serve as a more-than-adequate link from the George Bamberger era to the Phil Garner regime. He was known for his youthful exuberance, penchant for study, emphasis on psychology, and for being a very fast talker. Treblehorn could not, however, talk his way out of some hefty punishment.

The raft of suspensions brought sportswriters to the research morgue to dig up MLB's Madame DeFarge list from that San Diego-Atlanta doozy back in 1984 (see Chapter 14). Four players from each team, plus Treblehorn, were suspended by AL president Bobby Brown. Milwaukee saw its manager get five games, in addition to the Denver-bound Sebra getting five games. Gary Sheffield, Mike Felder, and B. J. Surhoff got three games each and $300 fines. For Seattle, Jones, Gene Harris, Randy Johnson, and Schaefer were given three-game suspensions.

Many players said they were shocked by the severity of Brown's decisions. When Treblehorn started serving his suspension, he told the AP it was causing "irreparable harm to my psyche," and making him feel like an outcast on his own team. Earlier in the week, Treblehorn reacted to Lefebvre's charges: "I chose not to talk long and loud and cry about things. Maybe it was to my own disservice that I didn't." He then went on to call the fight "adolescent and immature."

Mid-April is a good time to visit Billy Martin's grave. The history of these early spring days is one drenched in violence.

The bloody laundry list includes the Virginia Tech massacre, the Oklahoma City bombing, the Waco siege, the Columbine High School shootings—all orbiting around the federal income tax return filing deadline and Hitler's birthday. Of course the mist of gravitas that trails behind these tragedies throws Martin and his baseball antics into a cartoonish haze of escapism, his folly employed one tantrum at a time as a back-page soother of savage beasts. He was an anti-glamorous power broker ultimately doomed to a genius pawn's existence. Martin followed his mother's advice from his early days in Berkeley: "Take shit from no one." And he died his own violent death in the ratty cab of a pickup truck crashed into a cold drainage ditch in Broome County, New York, on Christmas Day, 1989.

The Gate of Heaven Cemetery is a sharp turn off the Taconic Parkway in Hawthorne, Westchester County, roughly 25 miles north of Yankee Stadium. The final resting place of Babe Ruth, the guy who built the joint on River Avenue, and his wife Claire, is approximately a third-to-first base throw from Martin's grave plot in section 25. Martin's grave has more of a modern take on baseball fame than Ruth's traditional headstone with its depiction of Jesus holding the hand of a small child, flanked by a motivational platitude from Cardinal Spellman. But The Sultan of Swat's plot carries a rather staid, Harry Truman-to-Dwight

Eisenhower sobriety about it—no crowns or Yankee "logos" or baseball imagery of any kind.

Martin's grave has his Yankee uniform number "1" cut out of the red marble on either side of the sprawling stone. On a mid-April visit, only a few poker chips left behind on the marker were any indication that Billy's cult following had followed him to the hilly graveyard that also has the grave of umpire John McSherry and the plot of Wellington Mara—the icon of a New York family that specialized in an inflatable ball sport played in cumbersome protective padding. Some visitors had left pennies atop Martin's tombstone, which bears his full name Albert Manuel Martin.

In preparation for visiting Martin's grave, it was time to call columnist Dave Anderson, who writes for what Jimmy Breslin always referred to as "the *New York Times* newspaper." Like Dick Schaap and other New York City sportswriting legends of their era, they all seem to answer the phone on the first ring. No taped machinery or screening of calls. No Blackberry.

The Pulitzer Prize winner was, like many sportswriters, at home with the family on Christmas Day 1989 and learned the news of Martin's boozy death from a television report.

"You knew somehow that he would end up in that kind of death," Anderson said. "He could never escape problems. You felt sorry for him because he never really conquered that, but if had, he might not have been the same guy we knew."

Anderson sees Leo Durocher whenever he is asked his thoughts about Billy Martin. "Martin was an infielder, like Durocher, pugnacious, loud, noisy and often profane," Anderson said. He defers to the beat writers who spent time in the trenches as the true chroniclers of Martin's flying fists.

"I was never a witness to his actual fights," Anderson said. "But Billy was fun to be around because you never knew what he was going to say, but it would always be something that was a story. If you were a newsman, you enjoyed him as a subject but didn't necessarily like him as a person. Nobody wanted to take him home to dinner."

As a player and manager, Martin could not back down from fighting authority. He had plenty of fight in him, even on his most hungover day.

"Nowadays, nobody is quite that wild, but you have to remember, for all his problems and fights, he was a *drinker*. And that's how a lot of these things started," Anderson said. Martin was, as stated in *Wild, High and Tight:*

The Life and Death of Billy Martin, by Peter Golenbock, "an alcoholic who drank and fought publically" as well as a "baseball genius" who "may never join the hallowed hall where he should rightfully be placed next to his mentor, Casey Stengel."

Numerous Knuckle Acquaintances

Wilt Chamberlain had his mythically extensive quantification of women he'd bedded. Talk show legend Joe Franklin has the uncanny ability to recite the exact number of times a certain celebrity appeared on his television program. Trying to compile the number of jaws, eye sockets, noses, lips, cheekbones, ears, ribs, and abdomens that have been on the opposite end of a Billy Martin punch is indeed impossible data to process. It would take exhaustive confirmation via bartenders, bouncers, hotel concierges, flight attendants, bathroom attendants, clubhouse workers, and night watchmen to come up with that number.

In 1952, Charles Dexter of *Baseball Digest* was already hip to the fact that Martin was a brawler. Billy had only been with the Yankees since 1950, and Dexter had chronicled his sandlot battles in West Berkeley and a survival of the fittest youth proving ground at a Catholic Church charity camp. He also covered Martin's landmark confrontation with notorious baseball nutter Jimmy Piersall in 1952 at Fenway Park. Piersall was a rookie, and seemed to take offense at Martin's coziness with Yankees manager Casey Stengel, who discovered Martin and encouraged the Yankees to buy him from the Oakland Oaks in October of 1949. In Billy's first season of riding the bench behind Yankees second baseman Jerry Coleman, he had done plenty of bench jockeying against the opposition, enough to earn the nickname "Arcaro" after the famous horse jockey.

Piersall was picking on Martin before the game in Boston, making fun of his large nose, calling him "Pinocchio" and "Schnozz" and finally a "busher." That was the last straw. Piersall had dared him to a fight, and Martin quickly accepted as both players went to their dugouts and into the runways under the Fenway stands. Yankee coach Bill Dickey caught wind and was running after Martin with hopes of preventing bloodshed. No such luck. Martin and Piersall met in the hallway and Billy nailed him with two quick rights to the face and Piersall fell to his knees, bloodied. Dickey and Boston pitcher Ellis Kinder broke up the fight. Soon, Piersall was hospitalized for his mental problems as a diagnosed schizophrenic.

When Martin learned of Piersall's condition, he said, "I was ready for the guys with white coats myself." Martin later told his pal Mickey Mantle of the Piersall fight that he'd "knocked that guy crazy."

Later that season, Martin punished St. Louis Browns meanie Clint Courtney, who slid spikes up into him at second base. Martin responded by tagging Courtney right between the eyes with his glove. It was the third out, and as Martin walked back toward the Yankees dugout, Courtney followed right on his heels. Martin stopped in his tracks, turned quickly and threw two quick rights to the stunned Courtney's jaw. The frenzied fracas that followed saw Martin toss around a few umpires, which earned him a fine from the league. Courtney was tossed from the game, but Martin remained. The two would meet again the next season, when Courtney made an ill-fated run at Yankees shortstop Phil Rizzuto as the St. Louis catcher tried to stretch a double, seeking revenge for being bowled over at the plate by Gil McDougald the inning before. After Courtney's spikes cut Rizzuto in two places on his leg, the Yankees infield descended on Courtney and administered a beating. Allie Reynolds had subdued Courtney's arms, and Martin connected, knocking off his glasses and cutting his face. Bobby Cerv promptly came stomping in from center field and crushed Courtney's glasses that had fallen off during the dispute. It turned out Martin had been waiting to get at Courtney since an incident in their days in the minor leagues, when Courtney spiked an old buddy of Martin's who was later killed in the Korean War.

Stengel was encouraging Martin's brawling personality, noting it was good for the team to have someone to confront bullies from the opposing dugout. Soon enough, Martin was appearing at baseball old-timer's banquets and telling none other than Ty Cobb that the Georgia Peach would have lost some teeth had he come into his second base with spikes flying.

After Coleman was called to serve in the Marines during the Korean War in 1952, Martin would excel at second base for the Yankees for most of the decade. His roommate during this time was Mantle. Stengel encouraged their drinking and carousing, along with Hank Bauer, Whitey Ford, and Joe Collins. During this decade, Martin developed his quote about never having started a fight in his life. In 1953 during the offseason at a Nevada bar, Martin got in a fight with a fellow tippler who said he could beat him at golf. Bars were his coveted territory, where he had a right to drink, he would say. At a celebration of Martin's birthday in 1957 at Manhattan's Copacabana nightclub, Martin and several other Yankees brawled with some delicatessen workers after they hurled racial insults at Sammy Davis, Jr. This incident gave Yankees general manager George Weiss the excuse he needed to trade Martin in 1957.

In addition to the Copa mess, Martin's clash with White Sox outfielder Larry Doby, after Doby had told Yankee pitcher Art Ditmar he'd stab him with a knife after a brushback pitch, helped seal Martin's fate with Weiss. The Yankee brawler was traded to the Kansas City Athletics the next day in a deal involving a dozen or so players.

Martin's next big fight as a player came in 1960 when he was with Cincinnati. He'd made a stop in Detroit and Cleveland after his Kansas City exile. While with Cleveland, Martin had his face smashed by a beanball from Washington Senators hurler Tex Clevenger. Martin had a rough recovery in the hospital during which both eyes were swollen shut, a sight that caused a visiting Clevenger to weep, according to Golenbock's second book on Martin.

Playing under another brash manager in Freddie Hutchinson of the Reds, Martin again became a sparkplug for the whole team. Martin's legs were telling him he was at the end of his playing career, and his throwing beer-fueled punches at a sad-sack daytime customer in a Tampa bar during Spring Training didn't help him any.

In May of 1960 at Crosley Field, Martin took on 6-foot-9 Phillies pitcher Gene Conley during a twelve-minute brawl sparked by Reds hurler Raul Sanchez's hitting three of four Philadelphia batters. Philly manager Gene Mauch had charged the mound to get at Sanchez, and the entire infield turned into a western saloon brawl, with Martin squaring off against the beanpole Conley, who was the last batter plunked by Sanchez.

When Cubs rookie pitcher Jim Brewer threw behind Martin's head in August of 1960, Martin let his bat fly toward the pitcher on his next swing. He missed badly up the first base line, so he went to pick it up. Words were exchanged on the way. Martin nailed him with a classic sucker punch as he bent down to pick up his bat. With Brewer down, Martin's teammate Cal McLish did further damage to Brewer's face with repeated blows to his cheek. Brewer would end up suing, and Martin stayed mum on who actually did most of the damage to the pitcher's face. Nine years later and several court proceedings down the road, Brewer ended up winning $22,000 in damages in a battle that turned out to be a legal one-upmanship between Cubs owner Phil Wrigley and Reds owner Bill DeWitt.

All's Well That's Boswell

In 1961, Martin had played with the Milwaukee Braves and the Minnesota Twins, and chose to retire while with the latter club. He stayed with the Twins organization as a scout and later a third base coach.

In 1969, Martin had his first managerial post at age 41. That's when he clashed with Twins pitcher Dave Boswell, who landed in the hospital after absorbing repeated blows to the face in a Detroit bar fracas that also involved outfielder Bobby Allison. With the Twins in the thick of a pennant race, team ownership—upset Martin was out drinking in a bar with his own players—could not yet bring itself to fire Billy. Martin had instilled confidence in the Twins that led them to the division crown well ahead of the Oakland A's. But Baltimore swept Minnesota in the playoffs. A week later, Twins owner Calvin Griffith, having survived the public relations nightmares of the Boswell incident and a 1966 incident in which then third base coach Martin clouted Twins traveling secretary Howard Fox over a dispute regarding a hotel room key, dismissed "Wild Bill," even after he delivered the team to the playoffs in his first year at the helm.

Martin left Minnesota and moved due east just a few miles to hang his managerial hat in Detroit in 1971. Martin would repeat his pattern of taking over a team and bringing it to the promised land as his 1972 Tigers won the AL East. They were a band of tough guys and headhunters. Martin grew more cantankerous and skinny and had a dugout confrontation with Willie Horton (Billy was wisely restrained from making physical contact with Horton, who was opting out of the lineup because of an eye injury). It was in Detroit through his pal and perpetual pitching coach Art Fowler that Martin met bar owner Bill Reedy, the man who would be riding with him in the doomed pickup truck on Christmas Day, 1989.

After three winning seasons in Detroit, Billy headed south to lead the sorry franchise known as the Texas Rangers. Martin had gone from being the "Little Dago" to "Bronco Billy," commanding a cast of outlaws and renegades. They would survive "Ten-Cent Beer Night" in Cleveland (see Chapter 6), having Jimmy Piersall hired as a public relations assistant, and Martin's inevitable slow path to alcohol-induced self-destruction was underway. On the team plane in 1974, Martin punched out Rangers traveling secretary Burt Hawkins after he suggested the club organize the player's wives into an official "auxiliary." The sixty-five year-old Hawkins, who had a heart condition, was merely forwarding the idea proposed by his wife. In 1975, Martin attempted to fight Elliot Maddox of the Yankees during a Spring Training brawl set off by Texas pitchers unloading bean balls. Halfway through the 1975 campaign, Martin was fired from his Texas gig. The Yankees were next, and Billy picked up the reins of the Bronx ballclub from the understated leadership of Bill Virdon. Martin was introduced at the Old-Timer's game, played at Shea Stadium in Queens—the temporary digs for the '75 pinstripers as they awaited the completion of a Yankee Stadium renovation. Martin said being the Yankee skipper was "the only job I ever wanted." With owner George Steinbrenner calling the shots, the manager/owner dynamic in the Bronx would make for very good theater and sports page fodder over the next decade or so. The Bronx Zoo was indeed open for business.

By 1977, things came together in grand fashion for Billy's squad. Reggie Jackson's arrival in New York set several fires under Martin as he juggled massive egos and superstar personalities throughout the clubhouse. Martin and Jackson had their famous televised dugout scuffle in Boston when Reggie was benched in the middle of an inning for not hustling in the outfield.

After being fired for the first of four times by Steinbrenner 94 games into the turbulent 1978 season, Martin had an offseason fight with a reporter in Nevada who refused to show his notes to a friend of Billy's as the three of them sat in a cocktail lounge. The reporter was nailed twice in the face by Martin's fist, and charged his attacker with assault. They settled out of court for a reported sum of $8,000 and Martin publicly apologized for hammering the writer.

Someone Has to Sell Marshmallows

Martin was with that same friend from the Nevada fight—Howard Wong—when one of his most famous fights occurred. They were stuck in Bloomington, Minnesota, after a hunting trip in October of 1979. Martin was supposed to catch a plane to Dallas to visit Mantle, but missed the flight. Martin and Wong went for drinks at the hotel where Martin was to stay overnight to catch another flight the next morning. A man at the bar recognized Martin and started a baseball conversation with him. Billy and Howard had already had a half-dozen scotches when the man, Joseph N.

Cooper, a marshmallow salesman, made the grave error of praising Dick Williams and Earl Weaver as fine managers. An incensed Martin called Cooper an asshole for making the Williams/Weaver comment. This led to Martin punching Cooper in the mouth, dropping him to the ground. His lip was cut and needed 20 stitches.

Steinbrenner had already warned Martin about hanging around in bars, where his anger was often transformed into physical violence after Martin started drinking. Billy was fired again. Laughably, Martin told college students he was lecturing in December that he'd never put on a Yankee uniform as long as Steinbrenner was team owner.

Martin returned to his home soil to manage the Oakland A's in 1980. In 1981, he got in a scrape with umpire Terry Cooney and bumped him while kicking dirt on him. Cooney charged him with assault, and Martin was suspended and fined $1,000. "Billy Ball" was in effect in the Bay area, and sure enough Martin had the A's playoff bound by 1981. With Steinbrenner dangling a return to New York in front of him, Martin figured out a way to get fired in Oakland so he could return yet again to the Yankee fold. In 1983, Martin was again in pinstripes and was again fighting in a hotel bar. This time it was the Anaheim Hyatt, where the fifty-five-year-old Martin encountered a real estate investor who offered to buy Billy a drink. Martin called him a name, and the man responded by throwing a matchbook at the Yankee manager. The real estate guy then attempted to apologize, but when he tapped Martin on the shoulder, Billy turned quickly, grabbed him by the shirt and delivered a solid blow to his jaw.

A month later, feuding with Steinbrenner again, Martin exploded when the Yankee boss fired his ever-present drinking pal and pitching coach Art Fowler. The team was in Cleveland, and when the Tribe went up 6-0 on the Yankees in the first inning, Martin took a chair and shattered a clubhouse urinal to bits.

Tinku Star Reincarnate?

In February of 2007, the *New York Times* ran a feature in its international section under the headline "Sacaca Journal: Indian Ritual Fades Into Blur of Drinking and Fighting." The story told of a ritual called Tinku, conducted for many centuries by the Indians of Bolivia's high plains regions. It has Andean roots and predates the arrival of the conquistadors. Every February, subsistence farmers from the various Indian villages in the region trek to larger towns for Tinku, which involves dancing, drinking of a rye-based fermented beverage called *chichi*, followed by ritualized yet untethered street fighting. Many times the combatants are from rival villages, and the flowing blood of the battles is meant to settle landholding disputes, embolden fertility or bring good luck at harvest time, anthropologists said. Getting the communal violence out of the way during an annual festival also helps reduce conflicts during the rest of the year, the report said.

A larger Tinku is held in the town of Macha each May, when local police often have to use tear gas to disperse massive crowds going toe-to-toe with bare fists. Foreign tourists are charged admission to see some of the street bouts and enjoy the music and dancing.

"Tinku is like a psychologist that helps us overcome our traumas," a Sacaca cultural official told the *Times*. "We have a lot to learn about the world, but the world also has a lot to learn from us."

If there has been reincarnation on the baseball diamond, a betting man might favor the odds that Billy Martin was a Tinku participant in a previous life.

Former Yankees pitcher and New York media whipping boy Ed Whitson might agree. The Cross Keys Inn in Baltimore was the site of one of the game's most extended off-the-field rumbles in September of 1985. Martin had already had a tussle with a pair of honeymooners in the hotel bar after the husband thought Billy insulted his wife regarding her "pot belly." The shoving match was quickly broken up by Yankee pitcher Rich Bordi, with help from Rickey Henderson and Dave Righetti.

The next night, Martin had arranged to meet Dale Berra and his wife for cocktails in the hotel bar. Whitson, whom Martin had scratched from his scheduled start because he thought his arm was tender, was also in the bar and had a few drinks in him. As he talked to a Yankee fan from Binghamton who had traveled to Baltimore to support his team, Whitson quickly got belligerent when Martin entered the bar.

As an argument escalated with the fan, Martin was alerted to the situation and went over to try to calm his pitcher and keep him from scrapping with the fan. Whitson, who was no fan of Martin's handling of the pitching staff, started swearing at his manager. Martin threw the first punch and cut Whitson's lip. Ron Hassey got between them, and Whitson was hustled out into the lobby. Martin charged out after him, and while Whitson was still being held back, he charged at the pitcher. With his arms being held, Whitson unleashed a mean karate kick to Martin's groin area. Martin went down, screaming "I'm going to kill you!" Whitson was then dragged to the parking lot where he punched Dale Berra after tearing his sweater. Martin was not finished. He got up and went outside. Whitson went berserk and broke free of his handlers and charged his manager like a bull, tackling him to the concrete. Martin was bleeding from the nose.

A hotel security guard who then helped separate them in the parking lot told the AP the Whitson-Martin tilt was "one of the most brutal fights I've ever seen." Whitson, at 6-foot-3, 195 pounds, had a distinct advantage over the 5-foot-11, 165-pound Martin.

Martin spent much of the night trying to get at Whitson, who'd gone to his hotel room and was being watched by coaches Lou Piniella and Willie Horton. Martin suffered a broken forearm and two cracked ribs courtesy of Whitson. "I tried to fight, but I can't fight feet," Martin told the AP. Whitson was sent home by Yankees brass for the remainder of the road trip. When he returned to the team, Martin acted as if nothing had happened.

In 1988, Martin was sixty years old and had just married his fourth wife, Jill, who was thirty-one. He was back managing the Yankees for a fifth time, with pitching coach Fowler back in his company as well. Martin was drinking more than ever, and in May, after getting thrown out of a game the Yankees would eventually lose to Texas in Arlington, Martin turned yet another bar into a gladiatorial arena. This time it was a strip club called Lace. Martin had gone there with Mantle, who had some words with some local guys who were apparently dating some of the strippers. Mantle soon went home, leaving Martin behind at the bar. He'd thought the locals were just joking with Mickey. When Martin went to the men's room, three guys were waiting for him and battered him around the room, then dragged him toward the back door staircase and threw him down the stucco-walled corridor. His ear was bleeding severely after scraping along the wall. Bouncers from Lace apparently picked up the heap of a man bleeding in their parking lot and put him in a cab directed back to the Yankees hotel.

When the cab arrived around 3 a.m., every guest in the hotel, including the Yankees and Steinbrenner, were milling about the lobby waiting out a fire alarm. Yankee trainer Gene Monahan saw how bad Martin was when he got out of the cab and took him directly to a hospital for treatment, perhaps saving him from bleeding to death in his hotel room.

"I feel kind of embarrassed because usually when I get in a fight I get my punches right in," Martin told the AP. His fighting days were, apparently, over at last. Don Mattingly was quoted in the papers: "Who would hit a sixty-year-old man? That's like beating up your grandfather."

By the end of 1989, Martin would be dead. His funeral was at St. Patrick's Cathedral in Manhattan, attended famously by Mantle, President Richard Nixon, and Steinbrenner (who were pictured together in a widely publicized photo). One day after his death, the Internal Revenue Service filed three liens against Martin's estate, seeking recovery of $86,137 in back taxes.

There are four inscriptions on Martin's grave marker in Gate of Heaven Cemetery. Two short ones: "Forever #1" and "Until we meet again." The larger ones read: "I may not have been the greatest Yankee to put on the uniform but I was the proudest." The other simply reads "St. Jude pray for us" with a carved image of the patron saint of seemingly impossible or difficult causes. He is always depicted carrying some type of Topps medallion of Jesus Christ and is known as a true friend and beacon of hope to those feeling helpless and alone. St. Jude died after he was beaten with a club, then beheaded. This certainly did not transpire in a Texas strip club.

Martin's grave plot is a pleasantly comfortable spot in the sprawling Westchester bone yard. A few feet in front of his stone, slightly elevated on the hill, is a marble bench. It is nice to sit on, but when visitors remember it is Billy Martin lying in front of them, there's a natural urge to remain standing, as he always did in the dugout. Put hands in back pockets, let the team-issued satin warm-up jacket bulge out above the elastic waistband, maybe ride the other team's dugout a little and keep your players alert and in the game. Do things like notice the excessive pine tar on an opponent's bat. Know which pitchers are easily rattled. Have faith in an outfielder doing time in a Michigan prison and turn him into a fine major leaguer. Throw dirt on an umpire? Maybe. Maybe not.

The only guys throwing dirt at the Gate of Heaven are the numerous cemetery workers. They wear green uniforms and circulate in carts full of planters and landscaping tools, and they throw that dirt with a certain nonchalant finality.

They also keep the Martin grave bench clear, which is how it should be.

INDEX

pitchers, 13–28, 235

Pittsburgh Pirates, 34–36, 104, 163, 164, 222–25, 251

Podsednik, Scott, 116

Polonia, Luis, 33, 257

Posada, Jorge, 109

Proly, Mike, 126–28

Pulliam, Josh, 95, 97

Quantrill, Paul
  vs. Eric Anthony, 231–32

Ramirez, Aramis
  vs. Ben Sheets, 34–36
  vs. Javier Vazquez, 34–36

Randle, Lenny, 74
  vs. Frank Lucchesi, 263–67

Reilly, Mike, 80–81

RFK Stadium, 78

Rice, Jim
  vs. Joe Morgan, 274–75

Ripken, Cal, Jr., 172

Riverfront Stadium, 54, 85, 178, 251, 267, 270

Rivers, Mickey, 89–90, 150

Robinson, Frank, 233

Rodriguez, Alex, 152–54

Rodriguez, Ivan "Pudge," 17–18

Rogers, Kenny, 141–42, 249–50

Rogers, Steve, 262

Rose, Pete, 30
  vs. Dave Pallone, 270–72
  vs. Derrel "Bud" Harrelson, 44–48

Roseboro, Johnny, 143–44, 165
  vs. Juan Marichal, 63–67

Royals Stadium, 52

Ruiz, Chico, 240–41

Ruth, Babe, 9, 10

Ryan, Nolan, 62
  vs. Robin Ventura, 15–21

San Diego Padres, 149, 210–19, 225–27

San Francisco Giants, 24–28, 59–60, 63–67, 85–86, 143–45, 246–47

Sanders, Reggie, 134

Schaefer, Jeff, 278–79

Schmidt, Mike, 124–25

Seattle Mariners, 105–7, 146, 231–32, 278–80

Seattle Mariners bullpen
  vs. Los Angeles Dodgers, 228–31

Sebra, Bob
  vs. Tracy Jones, 278–80

Segui, David, 171, 230

Shea Stadium, 44–48, 86, 112–14, 134, 140, 159, 178, 238

Sheets, Ben
  vs. Aramis Ramirez, 34–36

Shelby, John, 131

Siebert, Sonny, 183–84

Silva, Carlos, 173–74

Simmons, Ted, 221

Simon, Randall, 163–64

Slaught, Don, 164

Slaughter, Enos "Country," 10

Smith, Bobby, 109

Smith, Dave, 86

Smith, Hal, 104

Smith, Reggie, 86–87, 98, 150, 218

Smoltz, John, 159–61

Soto, Mario, 56–57, 60–61

Spahn, Warren, 257–58

Spiers, Bill, 99–101

Sprague, Ed, 106

Stearns, John
  vs. Gary Carter, 112–14

Stewart, Bob, 80

Stone, George, 49

Strawberry, Darryl, 55, 141, 193, 204–5, 206, 208, 246

Sturtze, Tanyon, 33, 153

Sudakis, Bill, 258

Summers, Champ, 213–15

Sutton, Don, 238–39